HISTORY OF MANKIND
CULTURAL AND SCIENTIFIC DEVELOPMENT

VOLUME II
THE ANCIENT WORLD
1200 BC TO AD 500
PART TWO
FROM ABOUT 500 BC TO THE CHRISTIAN ERA

PUBLISHED FOR THE

INTERNATIONAL COMMISSION FOR A HISTORY OF THE
SCIENTIFIC AND CULTURAL DEVELOPMENT
OF MANKIND

BY

GEORGE ALLEN AND UNWIN LIMITED
LONDON

HISTORY OF MANKIND

CULTURAL AND SCIENTIFIC DEVELOPMENT

VOLUME II

By LUIGI PARETI

Assisted By

PAOLO BREZZI and LUCIANO PETECH

THE ANCIENT WORLD

FROM ABOUT 500 BC TO THE CHRISTIAN ERA

PART TWO

Translated from the Italian

By Guy E. F. Chilver and Sylvia Chilver

FIRST PUBLISHED IN 1965

930
P21a

*Prepared under the auspices and
with Financial Assistance of the
United Nations Educational, Scientific and
Cultural Organization*

Consultants for
Volume II

Dr Guy E. F. Chilver
(Queen's College, Oxford)

Professor J. Filliozat
(Collège de France)

50,417
July 1965

PRINTED IN GREAT BRITAIN
in 11-pt. *Plantin* type
BY UNWIN BROTHERS LIMITED
WOKING AND LONDON

*Text paper supplied by Walter Makin & Co. and made by Watson's of Bullionfield
Bound by Key & Whiting, London*

CONTENTS

PART TWO: FROM 500 BC TO THE CHRISTIAN ERA

ILLUSTRATIONS

PART TWO

FIGURES

All line drawings were executed especially for this work by Stella Robinson in collaboration with R. G. Hadlow.

MAPS

The maps of Volume II were prepared by Hallwag, A.G., Berne, on the basis of original material supplied by Professor Luigi Pareti and his associates.

PART TWO

MANKIND FROM ABOUT 500 BC TO THE CHRISTIAN ERA

CHAPTER VII

WORLD HISTORY:
500 BC TO THE CHRISTIAN ERA

I. THE FAR EAST

a. *China*

THE states which formed the political constellation of China were now no longer feudal, and the struggle between them took on substantially different features during the period traditionally called the 'Warring States' (*ch'an-kuo*, 481–221 BC). (Map VI.) Such will to federalism as survived grew gradually weaker, and it finally vanished with the failure and eventual disappearance of the office of hegemon (*pa*). The tendency now was not to federate with one's neighbour but to obliterate him, a tendency towards conquest pure and simple. In these struggles the old tribal aristocracy bled to death. The new methods of warfare had removed its pre-eminence in the art of war; the appearance of iron, the development of irrigation and agriculture, the flourishing of crafts and the spreading of brisk trade had sapped its economic basis. In its place a new, different type of landed nobility arose, and at the same time there was a growing trend toward consolidation of the central power within the single states. Among the various philosophical and political schools increasing importance in public affairs was assumed by the 'Legalists' (*fa-chia*), whose ideas were harsh and militarist, favouring a centralized and almost totalitarian constitution. They provided the theoretical background for a unified state; and in the principality of Ch'in they provided both the pattern for the later bureaucratic empire and the nucleus round which it was formed.

The beginning of this period is marked by the last efforts at federal organization. Two of the three states which had dominated the scene in the preceding period, Ch'in in the upper and middle valley of the Wei and Ch'u on the middle Yangtze-kiang, still maintained their position, though somewhat weakened. But the third, Chin in the middle valley of the Huang-ho, disappeared in the course of the fifth century; it gradually splintered into three successor states, Wei, Han, and Chao. For a moment a new factor came on the scene, the state of Wu in the lower valley of the Yangtze, a state whose racial basis was only partly Chinese. In 482 it attempted to obtain recognition as the leading power; but its fall was as meteoric as its rise, and in 473 it was destroyed. Most of its lands were annexed by another southern state, this time almost wholly non-Sinic in language and race, Yüeh in the coastal provinces south of the Yangtze. Kouchien of Yüeh tried to wield the position of *pa* after 473, but his inept successors could not maintain themselves at the level of their founder; and in 333 the state was destroyed by Ch'u.

Meanwhile in the far north the Chinese peasantry, who were the backbone chiefly of the principalities of Wei and Chao, spread their advanced form of agriculture as far as natural conditions allowed, that is to say as far as irrigation was possible. Some of the backward populations of the frontier strip were assimilated; others were driven towards the steppe and the desert,

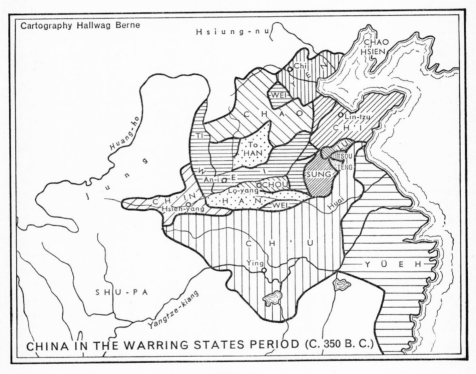

CHINA IN THE WARRING STATES PERIOD (C. 350 B.C.)

MAP VI

where they developed a new form of life completely antithetic to sedentary agriculture, namely pastoral nomadism. Chao in particular added to its power during this process of expansion, both by increasing its population and economic potential, and also by building a formidable army on the new model which gradually came into being when cavalry took the place of war chariots.

Ch'in remained in obscurity during the fifth century, but after 419 it began to exert a strong pressure towards the east and south. Duke Hsiao (361–338), aided by his great minister Shang Yang, reorganized the state on 'Legalistic' principles, constructed a new capital, Hsien-yang (near the present Sian-fu), and in 343 secured election by the chiefs to the office of *pa*: this election was confirmed by the fainéant Chou king. But the dignity had lost all significance: the original conception behind it was played out, now that in these years every prince, one after the other, had assumed the royal title. The final success of Ch'in was assured by the conquest of Ho-hsi (on the banks of the middle Huang-ho) in 330, and by the annexation and settlement of the rich region of Shu and Pa (the modern Szechwan) in 316. Against the constant pressure from Ch'in and Ch'u (and to some extent Ch'i) the other states tried to defend themselves by allying both among themselves and with one or another of the larger states in a regular system of alternance, called by historians the 'vertical and transverse' alliances (tsung-hêng).

In its broad outline the political problem was now more simple. The feudal system had broken down, and the fiefs had merged into three major units together with a few minor ones. Now that all attempt at confederation was at an end, these units had become real independent states; and the one political factor they had in common was a complicated game of alliances and wars. From the ethnic standpoint they included a number of non-Sinic elements, though these were gradually being Sinized.

The interminable struggle reached its end in the years following 256. The Chou dynasty was formally deposed. King Chêng of Ch'in (reigning from 247), with the aid of his chief minister Li Ssǔ, ended the work with the conquest of the remaining states, including Ch'u in 223 and Ch'i in 221.

Chêng ruled over a state of which the essential constituents were the basins of the Huang-ho and the Yangtze-kiang. The long war had completely wiped out Chou feudalism in this huge area, and Chêng and Li Ssǔ applied to it the centralizing and authoritarian principles of the Legalistic School, which had represented the moving spirit and the strength of the Ch'in state. The country was divided into thirty-six provinces under governors sent out by the central power. This constructive work amounted to the creation of a new order: to give it outward significance, Chêng in 221 took the title of emperor (huang-ti), and posterity therefore knew him as Ch'in Shih-huang-ti. With him begins the history of the Chinese empire which lasted until 1912. The first emperor reigned for only eleven years; but the work accomplished in that time—largely due to Li Ssǔ—was immense, and it left an indelible mark on the country. A powerful effort towards uniformity, excessive in its rigidity but a natural reaction to centuries of turmoil, seized in its grip the whole Chinese people. Writing was standardized, and local variations eliminated; weights, measures, and also coinage, were unified. An attempt was even made to impose uniformity of thought. Every memory of the past was attacked. In order to obliterate all material which might be used for hostile propaganda the government proceeded to confiscate and destroy most of the existing literature, particularly the Confucian writings. The adherents of Confucianism, who had increased continuously in numbers and influence during the preceding century, were persecuted. A further policy was the promotion of conquest and colonization in the far south, which till this time was practically unknown territory. The occupation of modern Kuangtung opened the way for Chinese colonization of the south, though its political integration was only made definitive a century later, and its Sinization was a slow process; in the south-west it is not fully accomplished even today. A corollary of this very slow development was that the far south was regarded as colonial or half-colonial territory, almost to the end of the period covered by this volume.

The founder of the empire and his minister carried their work to its conclusion. But their iron harshness imposed such sufferings on the people that rebellions broke out. They were partly led by the remnants of the old aristocracy, but for another part they represented a spontaneous rising of the farmers, the first hint of those peasant revolutions that were a recurring feature of Chinese history during periods of decay. The dynasty fell only three years after Shih-huang-ti's death in 210; Ch'in with the policy it stood for became anathema in historical writing. There followed five years of civil war, till Liu Chi, a rebel chief of peasant origin, defeated all his rivals and founded the Han dynasty (202). He built a new capital, Ch'ang-an (Figs 3 & 4), at some distance from the Ch'in capital of Hsien-yang in the Wei valley, which had been sacked and destroyed.

During the civil war feudalism had revived, and the founder of the Han dynasty had to take account of the change.[1] At first in the new Chinese state, provinces and fiefs co-existed side by side. But then the fiefs lost all political and administrative significance, and became simply titles granted to great lords who were government pensioners. The structure of government and the administrative system of the Ch'in rulers, the work of the Legalistic School, were preserved in substance, but there were important modifications and concessions. Above all the spiritual outlook was completely altered when Confucianism was accepted as the political philosophy and theoretical foundation of the state, as it gradually came to be in the course of the second century BC. There now came into existence a characteristic figure, who more or less dominated public life in China down to the early twentieth century. This was the gentleman-official, highly educated, well versed in Confucian writings, and generally the owner of fairly wide landed estates. In theory he was chosen for his post among the best men in China, by methods which later developed into a regular system of state examinations. But in practice the combination of bureaucrats, literati, and landowners, with their monopoly of the difficult system of writing and the refined administrative technique, became eventually a semi-closed caste.

Till now China had concentrated on its own problems, but under Wu-ti (141–87) it turned outwards and began its first phase of imperial expansion. The far south of China, northern Vietnam, and parts of Korea, were formally annexed, all of them territories which after centuries of integration with China absorbed a full measure of Chinese thought and civilization. The struggle with the first great empire of the Steppes, the Hsiung-nu in modern Mongolia, began about 200 BC and was carried to a conclusion with bravery and incredible tenacity. From that moment the problem of the northern frontier, which means the problem of the nomads, became one of the basic factors in Chinese history; and it remained so for nineteen centuries. It was in the context of this struggle that Chang Ch'ien carried out his adventurous mission into central Asia between 138 and 125: this opened up for China the caravan routes across the Tarim basin, and put it into direct contact with the western countries, i.e., with the eastern outposts of the Iranic world. Not only were the foundations of geographical knowledge immensely enlarged, but a variety of artistic and religious concepts reached China by these routes and contributed in some measure to shaping Chinese culture.

Wu-ti's successors reaped the harvest of his breadth of vision and his tenacity. By the middle of the first century BC the Hsiung-nu could be considered subdued; and at the same time the whole Tarim basin passed under Chinese domination and was given a special administration of colonial type. But by now the dynasty was in decline. The political position of the emperor had been weakened to the advantage of the Confucian literati, but still more to that of influences working through the female side of the court, i.e. brothers, cousins, and other relatives of the various empresses. By the end of the first century all effective power was in the hands of the Wang family; and its head Wang Mang took the final step when he deposed the Han dynasty and proclaimed himself emperor.

b. *Central and North Asia*

The darkness of prehistory begins to lift over central and northern Asia in this period, but for the earlier part of it we are entirely dependent on archaeology for evidence. It tells us of the metalworking centre of Minusinsk on the upper Yenisei, the products of which between the fifth and first centuries belong to the Tagar II culture and are characterized by the use of iron. The Scytho-Sarmatian element was still dominant at the beginning of the period, but from the beginning of the third century the Indo-Europeans yielded their position to the Altaic peoples. Before that happened, however, this great civilization of the Steppe flowered for the last time in the magnificent culture of Pazyryk in the Altai mountains. The Kurgans (funeral mounds) of Upper Altai, frozen deep in the ground, have preserved under particularly favourable conditions the remains of a fine art and of the luxurious life enjoyed by these great nomad princes. The influence of Achaemenid Persia was strongly felt, even after the fall of that empire; it was the decisive element in the civilization of these regions, and provides the first example of that posthumous expansion of Iranic culture which will often meet us again. There were many occasions on which Iranic light flashed eastward after it had been extinguished in the country which originally kindled it.

On the frontiers of China meanwhile the Chinese peasantry were pressing relentlessly northwards in search of new lands. No name is associated with this resolute advance, but it pushed the less civilized peoples of the border country, the Ti and the Jung, back towards the steppe and the desert. Its limit was reached only when the Chinese could no longer find conditions permitting the artificial irrigation required by their intensive form of agriculture. On the other side the amorphous populations which retired northwards were compelled to change their mixed economy for one based on nomadism and pasturage. The non-differentiated frontier belt was now replaced by a sharply marked border-line, even though its position fluctuated from time to time; it was the frontier between agriculture and cattle-raising between sedentary people and the nomads, between two opposite and irreconcilable worlds. We have seen already how the problem of the nomads became one of the basic factors in China's history. But later a similar process began outside the northern frontiers, largely as a reaction and as a legitimate defence against Chinese aggression, when China became organized and unified into a centralized empire at the end of the third century. This was the origin of the first empire of the Steppes, the empire of the people whom the Chinese called Hsiung-nu and who are certainly identical in name, and perhaps also to some extent in race, with the Huns who appear in the history of Europe. The founder of the new state was T'ou-man (the names of these rulers are known only through their Chinese transcriptions): he died in 210/209, and is thus a contemporary of Shih-huang-ti, the founder of the Chinese empire. The Hsiung-nu empire reached its zenith with Mao-tun (209–174). China, several times invaded, made great efforts to defend itself by arms and by diplomacy; but its heavy and slow-moving armies could not prevent continuous devastation of the frontier districts at the hands of the horsemen from the steppes.

The most important result of Hsiung-nu expansion was a large movement of populations with consequences felt over all Asia. Practically the whole effort of T'ou-man and Mao-tun was concentrated on the people called Yüeh-chih, originally settled in the modern Chinese province of Kansu. Lao-shang (174–161) completed the work of his father Mao-tun when he defeated and killed the enemy king, made his skull into a drinking cup, and drove out the Yüeh-chih. The latter, deprived of their ancestral lands, migrated westwards. Their attempt to settle in the Ili valley was frustrated by the Wu-sun, a red-bearded people with blue eyes, who were perhaps Indo-Europeans. The Yüeh-chih then moved into territory which is today included in the Soviet Republic of the Kirghiz; and there they found a temporary home by turning out the previous inhabitants, the Sacae, in about 150 BC. In their turn the Sacae launched themselves on the Greek kingdom of Bactria, which collapsed under their attacks, and then passed on into Iran, and beyond it into India. Shortly after this (perhaps about 125) the Yüeh-chih resumed their advance and settled in Bactria: a century later the Kuṣāṇa organized them into a powerful state, which extended across the Hindu Kush into India.

South of the steppe belt extended a desert region, sprinkled with oases of

varying size. Where these oases were relatively large a state based on agricultural economy would come into being, like Sogdiana and Khwarezm
(Fig. 3) at the end of the sixth century: Soviet excavations, particularly those
by Tolstov, have brought to light in that region a rich and manifold culture.
In small oases city-states grew up (Pl. 21a), *poleis* whose economy was partly
agricultural but even more commercial. The oases on the northern and
southern fringes of the arid desert of Takla-Makan were of this type: their

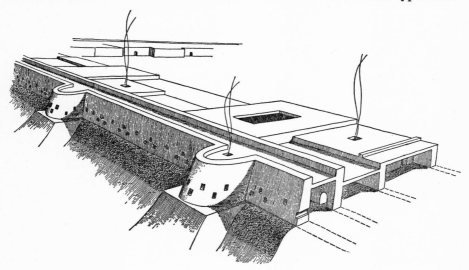

Fig. 3. Reconstruction of the wall of an early Khwarezmian citadel
(after S. P. Tolstov).

position determined the direction of the two caravan routes between West
and East, called by the Chinese *pei-lu* and *nan-lu* (the northern and the southern route). The wealth of these states combined with their political and
military weakness and with their commercial and strategic importance, to
make them for many years a coveted prey for their neighbours, the nomads on
one side, the Chinese on the other. Between 135 and 127 Chang Ch'ien was
sent as Chinese ambassador to propose to the Yüeh-chih that they resume war
against the Hsiung-nu. His diplomatic mission failed, for the Yüeh-chih
refused; but a result of the mission was that the Chinese gained knowledge
of the roads to central Asia and the countries of the West. A gateway was
thus opened, which was never closed again. Through it was passed throughout the centuries a traffic as fruitful in ideas and culture as any that history
has seen. Central Asia became the meeting ground of the movements started
by all the great civilizations of the time, Iranic, Hellenistic Greek, Indian,
and Chinese. In turn they inspired one another, but it was not only the countries on the border of Asia to which this trade brought new ideas and

M*

invigorating force; in the end a new civilization, highly original in its eclectic outlook, was created in the heart of central Asia itself.

In the political field the struggle between Hsiung-nu and Chinese influence continued for several decades, until China eventually prevailed. The decisive war had been begun by the emperor Wu-ti. He attacked the Hsiung-nu in the heart of the Gobi desert, and for this purpose he sought as far as Ferghana the large and robust horses of central Asia, the only breed which could make his technically inferior cavalry capable of holding their own against the mounted archers of the steppes. About 119 the former homeland of the Yüeh-chih in Kansu was occupied and colonized by the Chinese. Their patient work of penetration into central Asia reached its climax when the Tarim basin was organized as a protectorate in 60 BC. The Hsiung-nu were now enfeebled by the struggle and soon fell a prey to internal dissensions, successfully exploited by the skilful Chinese diplomacy. Their state split into two, and the eastern section recognized Chinese overlordship in 51.

The western Hsiung-nu migrated westward on to the steppes of Kazakhstan, but were pursued and dispersed by a daring Chinese expedition in 36. They fled north-westwards and vanished from the Chinese field of vision; but it was probably they, or others who took their name, who, after four centuries of wholly obscure existence reappeared in the orbit of the western world as Attila's Huns.

At the end of the first century BC the issue between nomads and sedentary peoples seemed, thanks to centuries of immense effort by the Chinese people, to have been settled in favour of the latter. But it was only a temporary victory.

c. Japan

The scene of the last phases of neolithic 'Jōmon' culture was mainly northern and eastern Japan. Its features are pottery which, though technically backward, was of serious artistic merit, with manufactured goods of a high order though entirely made of stone. Metals were still completely unknown. Later the predominance of Jōmon began to be challenged by the 'Yayoi' culture, attested in the first century BC in Kyushu and datable from Chinese bronzes found in the same tombs; its name derives from a ward of Tokyo where its earliest remains were found. Nevertheless Jōmon still maintained its position in the north in prehistoric and historical times. Meanwhile the Japanese took shape as the people which we know today. The first bearers of the Jōmon culture were the Ainu, a Caucasian people, but they were later pushed back to the north of the main island (and later into Hokkaido) and gave place to a people of mixed proto-Malayan and Mongoloid elements. The latter seem to have acquired their leading features rather early; for the Yayoi culture presents remarkable homogeneity and uniformity.

2. INDIA

About 500 BC a centre of some importance began to exert political influence in northern India, namely the Magadha kingdom in what is today southern Bihar. Under Bimbisāra and Ajātaśatru, both contemporaries and patrons of Buddha, Magadha influence extended over neighbouring districts, especially after the opposition of the Vaiśālī kingdom had been broken. For the first time a centripetal and unifying force disturbed the equilibrium of the north. It will meet us again at irregular intervals in the course of history, though it finds resistance in the difficulties of communication over these enormous distances and in the political looseness inherent in Indian society.[2] The latter factor may seem paradoxical, but is in fact a logical result of the subdivision of society into castes which despite apparent social harmony have no political consistence. The history of the Indian sub-continent throughout the Hindu period is that of the alternating expansion and contraction of a great power in the Ganges basin. The greatest period of expansion, under the Mauryas in the fourth and third centuries BC actually embraced all India. Later empires were on an ever-decreasing scale, until after the seventh century AD the process ceased entirely and gave place to a system of zonal equilibrium. This, though precarious, was destined to endure: in fact it lasted till the Muslim conquest in the twelfth–fourteenth centuries.

The Bimbisāra dynasty was succeeded in Magadha by the Nanda (c. 370–320) who had their capital at Pāṭaliputra (modern Patna), the principal city of northern India for about a millennium. At the same time Persian rule survived in the Punjab, being exercised through the two satraps of India and Gandhāra. Iranic influence grew weaker during the fourth century and to all appearance it was eliminated by the bold expedition of Alexander the Great. But Alexander in fact was a restorer: he conceived and carried out his expedition to recover the Indian boundaries of the Achaemenid empire, of which he felt himself to be the legitimate successor. Hence the mutiny of the armies of Macedonia and the Greek League at the Hyphasis: they had reached the theoretical limits of the empire they had set out to conquer.

Alexander organized the Indus valley as something between a province and a protectorate, but the system crumbled as soon as he was dead. His passage into India had been an event of very little importance, to judge from the complete absence of his name in Indian tradition.[3]

In the anarchy which followed Alexander's death an adventurer of genius named Chandragupta came to the fore. He became known during the struggle against the Macedonian officers, and with the prestige he had acquired he made his way into Magadha. There with the aid of his minister, a great statesman named Cāṇakya or Kauṭilya, he dethroned the Nandas and founded the new dynasty of the Mauryas (c. 320–187), quickly extending his rule to cover all northern India, including the districts which had been Macedonian. (Map VII.) Seleucus' expedition to the borders of India in 305–4 ended with a

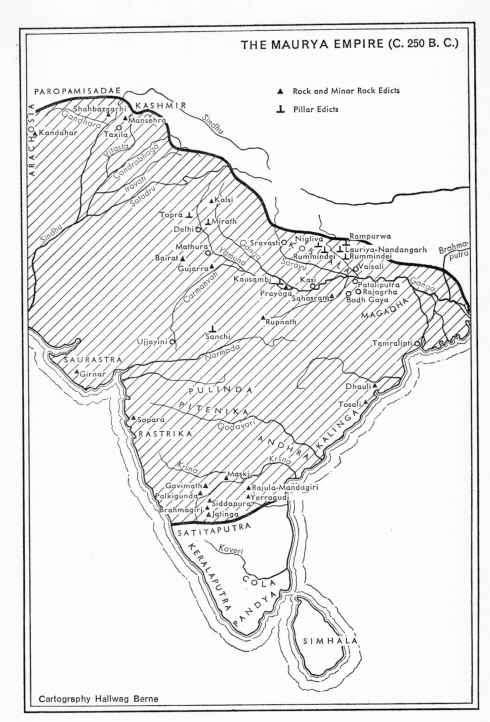

THE MAURYA EMPIRE (C. 250 B. C.)

▲ Rock and Minor Rock Edicts

⊥ Pillar Edicts

PAROPAMISADAE

KASHMIR

ARACHOSIA

Shahbazgarhi
▲Mansehra
▲Kandahar
Gandhara
Taxila
Vitasta
Candrabhaga
Iravati
Satadru
Sindhu

▲Kalsi
Topra⊥
Delhi⊙ ⊥Mirath
Sravasti
Nigliva
Rampurwa
⊥Lauriya-Nandangarh
Mathura⊙ Rummindei ⊥Rummindei
Bairat▲ Yamuna KOSALA ⊥Vaisali
Gujarra▲ Ganda Sarayu
Carmanvati Kausambi Kasi⊙ ⊙Pataliputra
Prayaga Sahasram ⊙Rajagrha
Bodh Gaya
MAGADHA
Brahma-putra
Ganga

▲Rupnath

Ujjayini⊙
⊥Sanchi
Narmada
Tamralipti⊙

SAURASTRA
▲Girnar

PULINDA
PITENIKA
Dhauli▲
Tosali▲
KALINGA

▲Sopara
RASTRIKA
Godavari
ANDHRA
Krsna
Krsna

Maski▲
Govimath▲ ▲Rajula-Mandagiri
Palkigunda▲ ▲Yerragudi
▲Siddapura
Brahmagiri▲ ▲Jatinga

SATIYAPUTRA
Kaveri
KERALAPUTRA
COLA
PANDYA

SIMHALA

Cartography Hallwag Berne

MAP VII

treaty recognizing Chandragupta as ruler not only of India but of Aria, Arachosia, and the Paropamisadae. Normal diplomatic relations were started, and we have fragments of a valuable description of the country given by Megasthenes, the ambassador of Seleucus to Pāṭaliputra.

Chandragupta and his son Bindusāra extended the Maurya empire over the whole of India, with the exception of the southern tip. Bindusāra's successor Aśoka (c.273–236) is a figure of the first rank in Indian history. Indian epigraphy really starts with him; and he was responsible for the active propagation of Buddhism within India and outside it. With Aśoka Buddhism ceased to be a small local sect of Magadha, and became an all-Indian religion, looking forward to becoming an all-Asian religion. Aśoka's inscriptions reveal his pacifist convictions, the care he showed for his subjects, and his burning zeal for *dharma* (the moral law). From a strictly political standpoint, however, this period saw a standstill to imperial expansion, followed immediately afterwards by a precipitous decline. Meanwhile the international contacts of the Maurya rulers extended to Ceylon, to the Iranic peoples on the border, and to the contemporary Hellenistic kings: the last included Aṃtiyoka (Antiochus I), Turamāya (Ptolemy II), Aṃtekina (Antigonus Gonatas), Māga (ruler of Cyrene), and Alikasudara (Alexander of Epirus).

The end of the 3rd century saw the rapid decline of the Mauryas, and also the futile expedition to the borders of India launched in 206 by Antiochus III. About 187 the Mauryas, now rulers of little more than Magadha itself, were deposed by Puṣyamitra, the representative of a reaction in favour of the old religion. His dynasty, the Śūṅga (c.187–75), was purely brahmanic, but (as is so often the way in India) this entailed no kind of persecution of Buddhism. The Śūṅgas successfully resisted Greek invasion; but their resistance was purely passive, and counter-attack was out of the question. Under their successors, the fainéant dynasty called Kāṇva (c.75–30), Magadha had for the time being come to the end of its position as a unifying force; and for several centuries it disappears again into obscurity.

The North-West (modern West Pakistan), with its Iranic associations, had secured independence of the Mauryas even before the arrival of Antiochus III. Some decades later it again saw a Greek army on its own soil. One of the Greek kings of Bactria (Demetrius according to some, Menander according to others) invaded India and pushed as far as Pāṭaliputra, to which he laid siege. The venture failed,[4] but at least the Punjab and parts of Sind remained in Greek hands. About 130 BC the Bactrian kingdom collapsed under the attacks of the Yüeh-chih, and the last Greek rulers took refuge in Afghanistan. About 100 BC the Greek territories in India were divided among various kings, who are known only from their coins. Of these rulers the most important was Menander (second century BC): he clearly symbolizes the cultural union of Indians and Greeks, and is the chief figure in the Buddhist dialogue called *Milindapañha* (Menander's Questions). Nevertheless one must emphasize the strangeness of the phenomenon by which Hellenism apparently began to exert cultural and artistic influence in India only after the Graeco-Indian kingdoms had come to an end.

The Sacae meanwhile, after occupying Bactria, had penetrated into Iran, where they failed to break the Parthian barrier, but settled in the country which from them took its name of Śakastan (the modern Seistan). From there they made their way through the deserts of Gedrosia and poured into India, crossed the Indus, and took the Indian Greeks in the rear, driving a wedge into their territory by the occupation of Taxila. The Greek kingdom of eastern Punjab was overcome and soon disappeared from existence; the western kingdom kept up a feeble resistance in the mountain fastness of the Kabul valley. The Śaka introduced into the Indus valley a somewhat loose feudalism, under which the various *ksatrapa* (satraps) recognized the overlordship of the Śaka king of Drangiana, and later had their own 'King of Kings' in the Indus valley; but this central authority was always very weak. Amid the feudal anarchy of the Śaka, the last effort at Greek resistance, and the eclipse of Magadha, north India at the beginning of our era was shattered into very small fragments.

The history of the peninsula south of the Vindhya mountains is almost unknown. In Orissa a great ruler appeared for a moment in Khāravela (first century BC); but he is an isolated figure, and Orissa never again played a significant part in Indian history. Further west the Sātavāhana kingdom was created by Śimuka in the second half of the first century, and had a great future in the period which follows.

When the curtain of history rises on the Dravidian south, it is found divided into three solid and lasting political formations, which contrast with the alternance of empires and fragmentation of petty states in northern India. The three states are the Cola on the Coromandel coast, the Pāṇdya at the tip of the peninsula, and Cera, or Kerala, on the south-west coast. All three kingdoms are political creations of the Tamil people (and also of the Malayalam, whose language branched off from Tamil relatively late).

The island of Ceylon was colonized by Aryans, at a date not precisely determined but probably as late as the fifth or fourth century BC. From the outset the invaders were organized into a kingdom, and in the second half of the third century they were converted to Buddhism by Aśoka's brother Mahinda. From that time Ceylon remained a strong outpost of Buddhism in the south.

3. THE PERSIAN KINGDOM

In 512 the Persian king Darius had made an expedition to the Danube and beyond it, against the Thracians, Getae, and Scythians.[5] When he returned to Sardis he left officers in the Balkans, Megabazus and his successor Otanes, who established a bridgehead in Europe, taking possession of Perinthus, Byzantium, part of the Thracian Chersonese, and the islands of Lemnos and Imbros. These extensions of the Persian empire were followed by treaties designed to win over the king of Macedon and then by an attack on Naxos; at the same time commercial privileges were granted to Egypt and Phoenicia. The result was a violent revolt of the Ionian colonies, who remembered the flourishing trade they had once enjoyed and saw it damaged by their new masters. The insurgents were quickly joined by Aristagoras, tyrant of Miletus,[6] and by the dynasts of Caria and Cyprus; moreover an appeal was made to the Greeks of the homeland, who were also threatened by the Persian advance. Sparta, however, made no move, and several states preferred to make sure of friendship with Persia; Athens and Eretria gave help, but the few ships they sent were withdrawn after the rebels failed to take the acropolis of Sardis in 498. Meanwhile Persian punitive measures were beginning. Cyprus, Caria, and the Hellespont were occupied, and the Ionian navy was defeated at Lade; finally in 494 Miletus was subdued with great slaughter, and much of its population was transplanted.

Darius now decided to resume his European conquests. In 492 he extended his occupation of Thrace and Macedonia; and in 490, after destroying Samos and receiving the submission of the Cyclades, the Persian forces burned Eretria and landed in the Bay of Marathon, north of Athens. His objective was to punish Athens and restore its tyrant Hippias, who had taken refuge at his court. The Spartan allies of Athens sent no help, but the Athenians succeeded in defeating the Persians and subsequently prevented the fleet from landing off Athens itself.

In 486 Egypt revolted against excessive tribute and Darius was unable to launch a quick counter-attack against the Greeks. He was succeeded in 486 by his son Xerxes, who put down the revolt in Egypt and another in Babylonia, and then completed his father's preparations in the west. The new Persian expedition consisted of enormous forces on both land and sea. It started in the spring of 480, was victorious at Thermopylae, and invaded Attica. But it then suffered three defeats, first on sea at Salamis, then on land at Plataea in 479, and thirdly in another sea battle at Mycale on the Asiatic coast. Ten years or so later the Persian squadrons were again beaten at the mouth of the Eurymedon in Pamphylia.

Shortly afterwards Xerxes and his eldest son were assassinated, and the throne passed to his second son Artaxerxes I. This king was immediately occupied in putting down a Bactrian revolt supported by his brother; and he then had to contend with Inaros of Egypt, who attempted, with Athenian aid, to liberate his country from Persian domination. The war lasted six years and ended with the reconquest of Egypt by Persia and the conclusion of a treaty with Athens. The latter fixed the harbour of Phaselis as the limit for operations by the Greek and Persian fleets, on the west and east respectively.

Yet the decline of Persian power was continually manifested by court tragedies and by the rebellions and political quarrels of the satraps. On the death of Artaxerxes in 424, for example, his son Darius II had to get rid of two of his brothers before he secured the throne; and his reign (423–404) saw repeated revolts by satraps, the most serious being that of Pissuthnes in Lydia in 414. The king wanted the two Greek coalitions, headed by Athens and Sparta, to wear one another out, but his satraps favoured first one city then the other; and he finally replaced one of them by his own son Cyrus the Younger. Meanwhile Egypt regained its liberty and kept it for sixty years.

These difficulties were repeated under the new king Artaxerxes II (404–358). He started with open rivalry with his brother Cyrus the Younger, who fell at Cunaxa in 401 after waging war on the king; and he had to put down his wife and three of his sons who were aspiring to the succession. He was then engaged in war with Sparta in Asia Minor from 401 to 394. In this war, it is true, the Spartan navy was destroyed at Cnidus: and in the 'Corinthian' war which followed a Greek coalition was organized against Sparta, permitting the revival of Athens under the leadership of Conon. But this did not prevent the Spartans from achieving a revised political settlement, under which they recognized Persian domination over the Greek cities of Asia but secured Persian support for the Spartan hegemony in Greece (386).

The next king, Artaxerxes III (358–338), rid himself of all possible contenders for the throne, and ruthlessly suppressed rebellions in the empire with the aid of Greek mercenaries. But his harsh treatment of the Asiatic Greeks began to attract the attention of Philip II of Macedonia, whose expedition in 336 was designed to help them. The expedition ended in the same year, when Philip was assassinated; but a few months later Artaxerxes too was murdered, and after a brief reign by his younger son Arses (who was quickly eliminated) the throne passed to Darius III (335–330). This king, however, was defeated by Alexander the Great at Issus and Gaugamela; after the fall of Persepolis he fled to the eastern satrapies, where in 330 he was put to death by Bessus, satrap of Bactria. His murderer usurped the Persian throne under the name of Artaxerxes IV, but he was brought to book by Alexander, who entered Bactria after his occupation of Hyrcania and Drangiana. The conqueror then took Sogdiana on his way to India (327). By now all the Persian possessions had passed to the Macedonian; he took over the rights of sovereignty and used the seals of the kings he had put down.

4. THE HEBREWS AND THE DIASPORA

The Hebrews who had been transplanted into Babylonia fairly quickly learned how to adapt themselves to their new situation. Many of them achieved so satisfactory a position in life that they refused to return to their country when the time came. Yet longing for the lost home country remained keen, partly because the prophets and priests kept it alive. The years of waiting were ended by a rapid and unexpected solution, when the various victories won by the Persian king Cyrus brought about the fall of the Chaldean kingdom in the middle of the sixth century. Since he had shown tolerance to other conquered peoples who had been subdued by his enemies, the Hebrews too sought to return home; and permission was immediately granted, conforming as it did with Cyrus' political principles. The decree appears in *Ezra* I. 2–4, but may be only a résumé of the original. It was for these reasons that Cyrus figured in later Jewish tradition as the 'Anointed', chosen by God to give freedom to his Chosen People.

Those who decided to leave moved in the spring of 537. Lists of their old homes had already been prepared, and they proceeded to take them over on arrival: but they met with many difficulties. The miscellaneous people who had remained behind under the government of Babylonian officials viewed the newcomers with a jealous eye; and the hostility of their Samaritan neighbours was supported by the Persian governors of the district. We know very little about Cambyses' reign; he undoubtedly passed through Palestine on his way to Egypt, but there is no evidence of dealings with the inhabitants. Under Darius an important event occurred. When the prophet Haggai persuaded the Hebrews to start rebuilding the Temple they incurred suspicion from the local satrap, who inspected the work and reported to the king. But Darius, who discovered Cyrus' edict in the central archives, not only gave his consent but bestowed a number of favours. So between 520 and 515 the Temple was set up.

For the ensuing period we are unfortunately without evidence. It appears that the Samaritans offered new opposition to the attempt to rebuild the walls of Jerusalem and prevailed on Artaxerxes to have the work stopped: perhaps even what had been erected had to be pulled down. But Artaxerxes II in 398 started a new series of generous concessions by the Persian kings to the Hebrews. Meanwhile the relations between the small Jewish state and its powerful neighbours became less important than internal Jewish politics, and this remained true till Alexander's conquest.

The period of Alexander, who took possession of Palestine in 332, passed off fairly quietly for the Hebrews. Their troubles came during the struggle between the Diadochi, since both the Seleucids and the Ptolemies coveted southern Syria and it only finally became a possession of the former in 195. Another cause of grave disturbances lay in the plan of Antiochus IV to Hellenize Palestine by prohibiting the practice of Hebrew religion and turning the Temple into a heathen shrine. In the subsequent rebellion, supported by Rome, Judas Maccabaeus reoccupied Jerusalem in 165, and together with his brothers asserted the independence of the country. This was recognized in 142 when the Hasmonaean princes were given the official title of 'High Priests and Princes of the Jews'. They vigorously defended this independence against the Syrian kings, and in the period of Syrian dissolution they extended the area of their state, especially under John Hyrcanus. Soon after this, however, the internal peace of the country was disturbed by the quarrels of the two factions, Pharisees and Sadducees, which became marked in the reign of Alexander Jannaeus; and affairs were made worse by the rivalry between his sons Aristobulus and Hyrcanus II. The latter was supported by Pompey, who besieged and took Jerusalem in 63. Hyrcanus was left in charge with the title 'ethnarch', but had to pay tribute to Rome.

Aristobulus' son Alexander attempted rebellion, but the proconsul Gabinius (57) replied by dividing Judaea into five districts, each under separate administration. Hyrcanus II remained pro-Roman throughout and continued as High Priest, later supporting Caesar in the Civil War and giving him assistance in his Egyptian campaign. He was rewarded by receiving his principality and title of ethnarch once more; and his power was extended to cover the Jews of the Diaspora.

When Cassius was in charge of the East after Caesar's death he imposed a heavy war-tax on the Jews and sold part of the population as slaves. This weakened the power of Hyrcanus at a time when he was also being challenged by the pro-Parthian faction: Judaea lost many of its territories and several leading men were murdered during the struggles of the court. After the battle of Philippi (42) Antonius confirmed the position of Hyrcanus, but conditions remained so bad that various embassies invited Antonius to abolish the principality and annex Judaea to the province of Syria.

The Parthian invasion of Syria (40) saw Hyrcanus deposed and the pro-Parthian Antigonus put in his place; but the latter was beheaded when Herod recovered Jerusalem with Roman assistance. Earlier, as a refugee in Rome, Herod had been made king, and at his death his possessions were divided between his three sons; in AD 6, however, Judaea was once more directly taken over by Rome and became a province.

The Hebrews of Palestine remained markedly hostile to the ideas and practices which had grown up among other peoples. Their resistance to the introduction of Gentile rites and customs into Jerusalem was the background of many famous scenes in their rebellion. Meanwhile all their writings in the last centuries of the Old Testament period emphasize their firm resolve to defend their traditions jealously and to keep their people apart from the world around them.

For a long time, however, the phenomenon known as the 'Diaspora' had been in progress, and Jews were scattered in the principal centres of the Mediterranean basin, sometimes even in cities farther afield. Not only had there been numerous forced deportations, but there was no room in the small mother country for all its sons; and the more enterprising among them planned to gain a better position by settling in commercial and business centres. We have a wealth of evidence about these Hebrew colonies, but much of it has reached us by pure chance, such as that relating to the important post of Elephantine on the southern frontier of Egypt: very probably there were many other colonies of which we know nothing. The various local rulers generally tolerated or even encouraged these Jewish groups, on condition that they did not disturb public order and that they respected the fundamental laws of the state they were in. A decree of the Roman senate in 138 shows concern for the Hebrews scattered from Egypt to Cappadocia, and from Pergamum to the Greek islands. The foundation of Alexandria in Egypt made a strong appeal to the Jews. They had ancient links with the country; and Alexander, who was anxious to populate his new city, made their conditions of residence attractive. They had a quarter of their own, and in time the Hebrew population of Alexandria exceeded that of Jerusalem; it has been estimated at 100,000 in the middle of the first century BC, and in Philo's day there were a million Jews in Egypt as a whole. Similar development can be seen at Antioch in Syria. The Jewish communities of the Diaspora kept up close relations with one another, and exchanged letters. At the head of each was a college of magistrates for administrative and judicial affairs: there were various officials, and the archisynagogus presided over religious meetings. Although they had close relations with the Gentiles among whom they lived, and often spoke their languages, even the Jews of the Diaspora undoubtedly kept themselves substantially apart from the world around them. They remained faithful to God's Law, and retained that national religious outlook which is the main feature of Hebrew history throughout antiquity. Yet it was in these foreign surroundings—at Alexandria above all—that an event took place which had vast importance for the cultural and spiritual history of a large part of mankind. This was the translation of the Bible into Greek, involving the adaptation by one mentality of the expressions and ideas framed by a mentality which was very different. This development was not regarded favourably by strict Jews, even in later times. But for the Jews of the Diaspora it was a necessity, for they no longer understood their original language and yet were unwilling to give up their sacred texts. The work was started at the beginning of the third century, and by the middle of the second all the ancient books had been translated. The legend was invented of the Seventy translators (72 to be precise) who finished the work with great speed; but in fact there were many and occasionally competing authors at various dates and of varying merit. For a long time the 'Septuagint' was given exclusive official recognition, but later other translations appeared; and beside them a complete literature was written by the Hellenistic Jews to defend the tenets of Hebrew religion among non-believers (as time went on proselytism among the Gentiles was by no means rare). Some books which entered the Old Testament were written in Greek from the start, *Maccabees* and *Wisdom*, for example: the latter book, with six others, is not in the Hebrew Bible, but Catholics regard it as 'deutero-canonical'. But these too show the same sharp divergence from Hellenistic thought, being severe in their condemnation of all idolatry and in their rejection of syncretistic views. None the less a process of dilution inevitably set in as well, leaving marked traces and valuable results.

5. THE DEVELOPMENT OF GREECE

a. *Local Hegemonies*

In the years immediately following the Greek victories over Persia the Spartan Pausanias, victor of Plataea, tried to retain command of the confederate Greek fleet. He began the liberation of the Hellenic colonies on the Asiatic coast; but he lost the support both of his government and of his crews, and in 478 he gave up his command. Leadership of the island states, and of the seaboard cities on the far side of the Aegean, now passed to Athens, whose statesmen were at first united in the policy of forming an alliance against Persia: in this matter Themistocles, the democratic victor of Salamis, was at one with his old rival Aristides, the actual creator of the 'Delio-Attic' League which was formed in 478 to pursue the war of liberation. Each participant city made a contribution, some in ships and crews, others in money. But the Athenian politicians soon split: the conservatives wanted, while fighting Persia, to retain Spartan friendship, but the democrats were anxious for the dissolution of Sparta's Peloponnesian League. The influence of the former, led by Cimon, made possible a resounding naval victory over the Persians at the Eurymedon (c.469), while Sparta was reinforcing her league. But then came a lull in the war with Persia; the allies grew discontented, and reluctant to pay tribute; and the rivalry between Athens and Sparta grew more marked. In 464 Sparta's Helots revolted, and Cimon led an Athenian army to Sparta's aid; but Sparta suspected the anti-oligarchic sentiments of the Athenian troops, and curtly dismissed them. Power at Athens consequently passed to the democrats, above all to Pericles, whose programme was Athenian hege-mony, to be obtained by all possible means. War with Persia was carried on by aiding an Egyptian revolt (c.460–455); an attempt was made to break Sparta's confederacy (460–446); and Athens tried to become leader of a unified Western Greece against the Sabellian invasions of Magna Graecia and against the predominance of Syracuse in Sicily. But this ambitious programme was too much for Athenian strength; it came to grief in all three fields. Cimon momentarily returned to power, but after his death in Cyprus Athens made peace with Persia in 449. A peace with Sparta, intended to last thirty years, followed in 445.

When he returned to power Pericles attempted a more restricted programme. Action against Persia was stopped; and the allies were reduced to subjects, since their tribute was no longer needed for the Persian war but went to make Athens a splendid metropolis and build its economic strength. The 'mirage' of the West was still in view: the Athenians founded Thurii in Magna Graecia and gave help to the Elymians and Chalcidians in Sicily. But the chief aim was to resume action against Sparta and Corinth. This new programme evoked opposition to Pericles within Athens itself, and several of his friends were put on trial. But in 434 Athens allied itself with Corinth's colony Corcyra, the second naval power in Greece; and the provocation offered to Corinth eventually led to an ultimatum being delivered to Athens from the Peloponnesian League, and so to the long struggle known as the Peloponnesian War, which began in 431. Pericles saw only its beginning, for he died of the plague in 429; after his death the struggle between democrats and con-servative pacifists still went on at Athens. The first phase of the war (431–421) brought no concrete results: Athens, powerful at sea, attacked the Peloponnesian coasts and captured Pylos in Messenia; Sparta with its land power ravaged Attica, destroyed Plataea, and occupied Heraclea in Trachis and Amphipolis in the 'Thraceward' area. Athenian action in the West was once more unsuccessful. Yet in the peace of 421 Athens was able to retain maritime hegemony.

Soon, however, the war parties at both Athens and Sparta gained the upper hand, and the war was renewed, made wider and more complex when a third coalition headed by Argos came into being and played the other two off against each other. But now Athens suffered a series of disasters. The Spartans permanently occupied Decelea and prevented all cultivation in Attica; a powerful expedition to Sicily came to unrelieved failure in 413; the Athenian exile Alcibiades crossed over to the enemy, and enabled the Spartans to build a fleet by obtaining for them Persian gold; and a large number of subject allies revolted.

These reversals of fortune brought about an oligarchic revolution at Athens in 411. Later, it is true, democracy was restored, Alcibiades was recalled from exile, and the war at sea improved; there was even hope of economic aid from Persia. This was not to be. Shortly afterwards Alcibiades was exiled again, and Sparta formed an alliance with Persia; despite several heroic actions in the war the Athenian position became desperate. Finally they were defeated at Aegospotami, deserted by their allies, and blockaded by Spartan forces. They were compelled to recognize the political supremacy of their enemy, to pull down their walls, and to adopt an oligarchic constitution once more (404).

The domination of the Greek world by Sparta in the next generation meant domination by the 2,000 full citizens who alone composed the narrow oligarchy in that city. The acquisition of hegemony made the 'Lycurgan' constitution out of date; but the struggles between the royal houses and the Ephorate were still a hampering factor, and Sparta's army and navy had not shared in the technical progress attained by other Greeks. Moreover Sparta was doing nothing to retain the sympathy of the allies it had won from its rival. They began to realize that they had only changed masters, compelled as they were to adopt oligarchies, pay tribute, and maintain Spartan garrisons; often they were at the mercy of terrorist governments formed by returned exiles thirsting for revenge. Revolts and revolutions followed, put down with equal violence; the case of Athens, which is best known to us, is typical. For some time they were forced to adopt an oligarchic régime. Political rights were confined to 3,000 persons with 30 delegates at their head; and the whole was supervised by 700 Spartan soldiers and by the board of police known as the Eleven. From this Athens was liberated by a group of exiles, and the democratic government which they restored took on the hard task of rebuilding their city after its disasters. But the restoration was intransigent, and the philosopher Socrates, the greatest citizen whom Athens could boast in the moral and spiritual fields, fell a victim to its narrow outlook (399).

In 401 Sparta incurred the anger of Artaxerxes II for having sent help to his defeated brother Cyrus. The charge that Sparta had received foreign gold to maintain its position was admitted to be groundless, but it became involved in a war in Asia Minor against the Persian satrap Pharnabazus. In his turn the king distributed money among Sparta's enemies, and built up a coalition against it which began the so-called Corinthian War. In Greece the Spartans were victorious, but they were defeated at sea near Cnidus by a fleet under command of the Athenian Conon (394): this enabled him, still with the help of Persian gold, to rebuild the walls of Athens, which took part in the last phase of the Corinthian War and still had dreams of maritime hegemony. Sparta was saved by the peace of 386. It recognized that the Greek cities of Asia Minor, together with Clazomenae and Cyprus, belonged to the Great King; and he in his turn put the Spartans in a position to make all the cities of Greece autonomous, and thus to dissolve the political league to which they belonged and to impose oligarchies and tribute upon them. The immediate cause of the end of Spartan hegemony and the beginning of the Theban came when a Spartan garrison seized by force the citadel of Thebes. A party of Theban democrats under Epaminondas and Pelopidas replied by expelling the Spartan garrison and overturning the Theban oligarchy. Thebes recovered its hegemony in Boeotia (379) and made an alliance with Athens. The Athenians in 377 once more became the centre of a maritime league of seventy cities; the Thebans pressed on with their war against Sparta until they defeated it decisively at Leuctra in 371.

The new hegemony met with resistance as soon as it began: a coalition was made between Athens, Sparta, the Isthmiac states, and Thessaly. Epaminondas replied by invoking diplomatic help from Persia and by military action. Pelopidas fell in a victorious action in Thessaly, and the war was carried into the Peloponnese where Epaminondas was also killed in a victory at Mantinea (362). With the death of the two great Thebans the democratically based hegemony of Boeotia fell rapidly apart. It had been no more careful than its predecessors of the legitimate aspirations of its allies; and it was incapable of holding its own against Macedon, which had a more powerful army than its own.

Macedon, a large and populous area with important agricultural and mineral wealth, had found in its Argead dynasty a force which gave it a marked measure of Hellenization. King Philip II, who came to the throne in 359, was an excellent strategist with admirable lieutenants. After strengthening and reorganizing the army, he used war and his family connections to extend his dominions, both in the Balkan hinterland and on the Aegean coast, where he occupied the gold mines of Mount Pangaeus.

Thebes now tried to deprive the Phocians of their seat on the Amphictiony. When the Phocians, supported by Athens, Pherae, and Sparta, offered resistance, Philip intervened in favour of the Thessalians, who became his subjects and elected him their chief magistrate. He next occupied and destroyed Olynthus, to which Athens sent help too late (348). Returning to central Greece, he took and garrisoned Delphi, where he assumed the presidency of the Pythian Games (346); then he besieged Byzantium, but that city appealed to Athens and he was unsuccessful in forestalling Athenian reinforcements (340). A new coalition of Greek cities was now formed to counter him, but he moved quickly and routed their forces at Chaeroneia (338). Soon after this representatives of all the Greek states except Sparta met at Corinth and created a federation of free cities in alliance with Philip; the king assumed command of the League army and navy, to resume the war against Persia.

b. *The Conquests of Philip II and of Alexander*

The political progamme of Greek union against Persia, proclaimed since the first twenty years of the fourth century by Gorgias, Lysias, and Isocrates, was finally put into action by the influence of Philip II of Macedon. The Graeco-Macedonian League furnished troops and ships in adequate numbers to free the Greeks of Asia from overlords whose weakness had long ago been shown in face of the 10,000 Greek mercenaries at Cunaxa in 401, and who could only count on Greek and Phoenician mercenaries to man their fleet. War was declared when the Persians intervened in Europe on behalf of Perinthus, contrary to the peace of 386; and in 336 a first corps of 10,000 Macedonians crossed into Asia Minor. But the assassination of Philip and the succession of his twenty-year-old son Alexander put off the actual operations for two years. During this time the new king, who had been proclaimed general of the Panhellenic League, carried out a series of operations in the Balkan peninsula, on the Danube, in Illyria, and in Greece itself (where he besieged and destroyed his enemy Thebes). He thus removed opposition and danger from his rear before becoming engaged in the East.

The first objective of the great enterprise was to take from the Great King all Asia Minor, Syria, and Phoenicia, with the naval bases on the Mediterranean. This was achieved by the victory at the Granicus, the capitulation of Sardis, and the taking of Miletus, in 334, by the battle of Issus in the following year, and by the fall of Tyre in 332. After this Alexander occupied Egypt, which acclaimed him as liberator and 'Pharaoh', and to which he gave its new capital of Alexandria. (Map VIII.)

In the spring of 331 he returned to Asia, crossed the Euphrates and Tigris, and defeated Darius at Gaugamela. Darius took refuge in Media, and his conqueror occupied, one by one, the places he had used as capitals, Susa, Persepolis, and Ecbatana. Receiving news that Bessus, satrap of Bactria, had captured and executed Darius and usurped his throne, Alexander occupied Hyrcania, Drangiana, and Bactria, and had Bessus condemned to death. He then took possession of Sogdiana, and finally penetrated into India as far as the Hyphasis (326). At this point he had to meet the longing of his soldiers for an end to their labours; and he needed to put the conquered lands

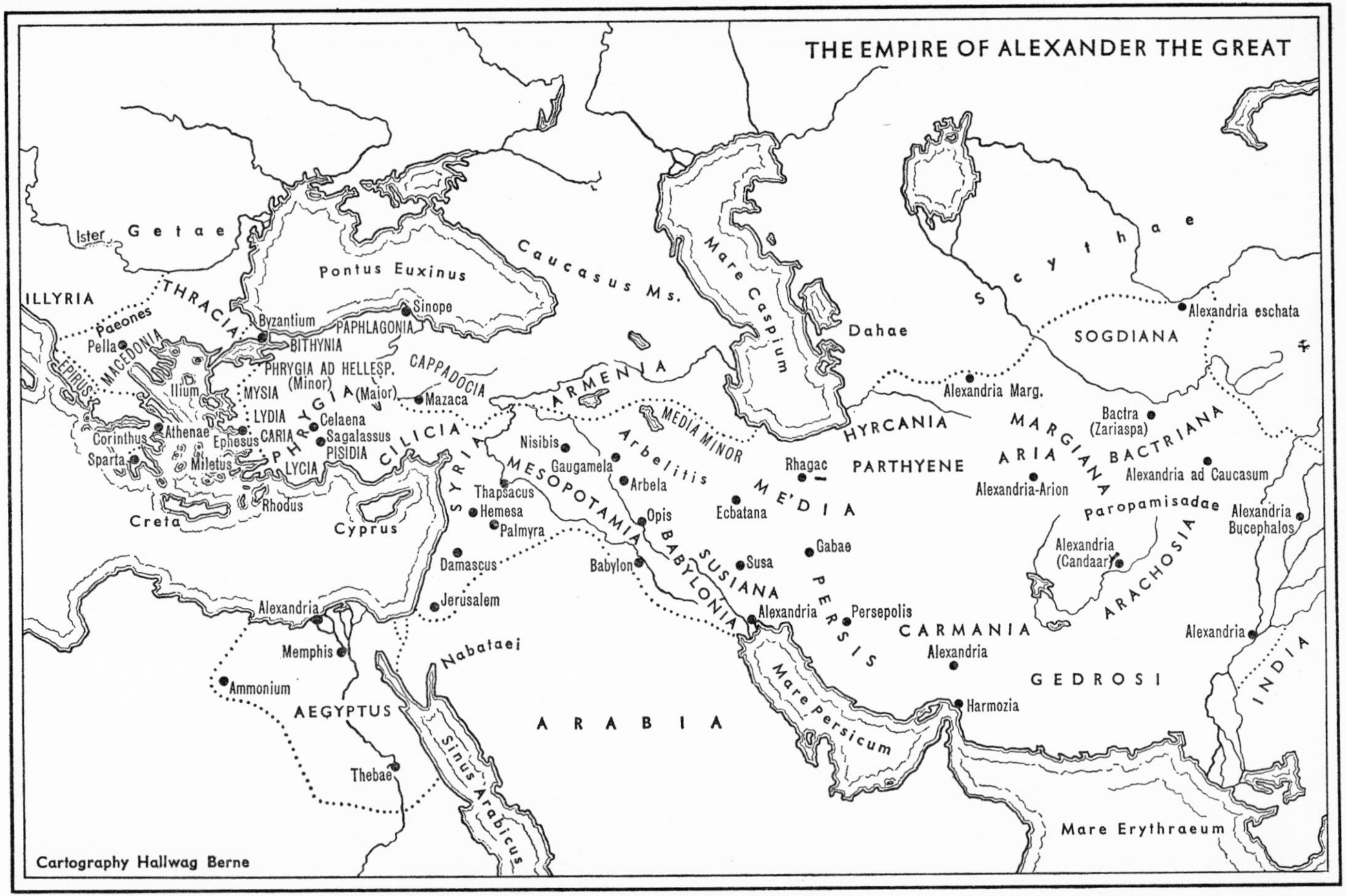
THE EMPIRE OF ALEXANDER THE GREAT
Ister
Getae
ILLYRIA
THRACIA
Paeones
Pella
MACEDONIA
EPIRUS
Ilium
Athenae
Corinthus
Sparta
Ephesus
Miletus
Creta
Rhodus
Pontus Euxinus
Byzantium
Sinope
PAPHLAGONIA
BITHYNIA
PHRYGIA AD HELLESP. (Minor)
MYSIA
LYDIA
CARIA
LYCIA
PHRYGIA (Maior)
Celaena
Sagalassus
PISIDIA
CAPPADOCIA
Mazaca
CILICIA
Cyprus
Caucasus Ms.
ARMENIA
MEDIA MINOR
Arbelitis
Nisibis
Gaugamela
Arbela
MESOPOTAMIA
SYRIA
Thapsacus
Hemesa
Palmyra
Damascus
Jerusalem
Opis
Babylon
BABYLONIA
SUSIANA
Susa
Ecbatana
MEDIA
Gabae
Rhagac
PERSIS
Persepolis
Alexandria
Mare Caspium
Dahae
HYRCANIA
PARTHYENE
Alexandria Marg.
MARGIANA
ARIA
Alexandria-Arion
Scythae
SOGDIANA
Alexandria eschata
Bactra (Zariaspa)
BACTRIANA
Alexandria ad Caucasum
Paropamisadae
Alexandria Bucephalos
Alexandria (Candaar)
ARACHOSIA
Alexandria
INDIA
CARMANIA
Alexandria
GEDROSI
Harmozia
Mare Persicum
Mare Erythraeum
ARABIA
Nabataei
Sinus Arabicus
Alexandria
Memphis
Ammonium
AEGYPTUS
Thebae
Cartography Hallwag Berne

MAP VIII

in order. He therefore returned to Susa, where he was recognized not only as king of the Macedonians and general of the Greek League, but as king of Asia, Pharaoh of Egypt, and King of Kings of the Persian lands. He put the conquered Persians on a level with the Macedonians, and employed them together in the army and in the administrative services, as well as permitting fusion of religions and mixed marriages. He founded a number of cities in the Persian districts, settling both veterans and immigrants from Macedonia and Greece; and he developed trade between the different regions of the new vast empire, in which he made Babylon the capital but Greek the official language. At the moment of his death he was preparing and even equipping new expeditions of conquest and exploration, designed to make him master of a still larger empire, a world empire embracing the Caucasus regions, Arabia, and the central and western Mediterranean. But in 323, at the age of 33, he died.

c. *The Hellenistic Empires*

The main obstacles to the preservation of Alexander's work and schemes were the separatism existing in several satrapies, the desire of the Greeks to regain their autonomy, and the hostility between the Macedonian conquerors and the Persians whom Alexander had raised to their level.[7] For a brief time the political unity of the vast new empire was maintained because the troops were loyal, and because Perdiccas, aided by Craterus, was supreme among the 'Diadochi' or surviving generals. At this stage the worst difficulties were encountered by Antipater, who had to meet a Greek rebellion, instigated mainly by Demosthenes (d. 322).

Meanwhile the Diadochi were gradually turning the areas they governed into personal domains, and forming coalitions to carry on their feuds. At each temporary peace a new distribution of territory was made. One such settlement was made at Triparadeisus in 321, another in 311 when five clearly demarcated states were distinguished, each under its separate king. The settlement after the battle of Ipsus in 301 recognized four major states and two minor ones, as follows: (1) Macedonia and Greece, (2) Thrace and Western Anatolia, (3) Syria and Mesopotamia, (4) Egypt and Libya, (5) Cyprus, (6) Caria and Cilicia. After a complicated sequence of events Antigonus Gonatas succeeded in imposing his rule on Thrace as well as on Macedonia and Greece; and thus for about a century following 276 the empire was divided into three main parts, with three 'Hellenistic' dynasties descended from Alexander's generals. The Antigonids had Macedonia and the other Balkan regions: the Seleucids in Syria and Asia were regarded as successors of the Achaemenid kings of Persia; the Ptolemaic dynasty in Egypt was successor to the Pharaohs. (Map IX.)

Of these three the richest and most populous was the Seleucid kingdom, more extensive on the east than the Persian empire, though smaller on the

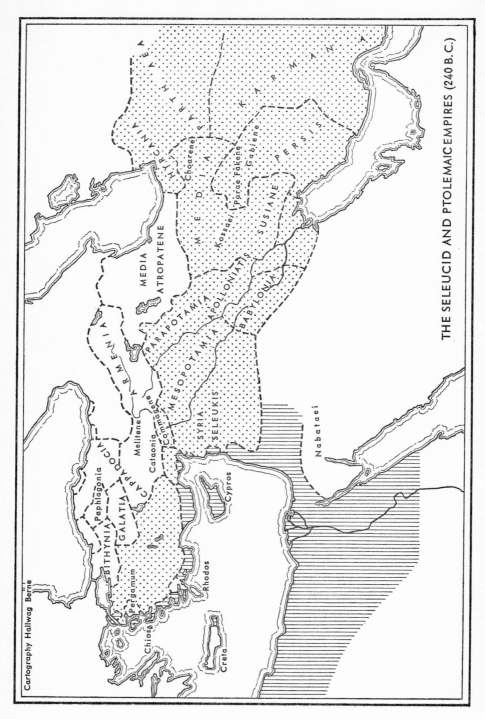

Cartography Hallwag Berne

BITHYNIA
Paphlagonia
GALATIA
Pergamum
Chios
CAPPADOCIA
Rhodos
Creta
Cypros
Catfonia
Melitene
Commagene
ARMENIA
MEDIA
ATROPATENE
PARAPATAMIA
MESOPOTAMIA
APOLLONIATIS
SYRIA
SELEUKIS
Nabataei
BABYLONIA
SUSIANE
Kossaei
Parae Fakene
Gabiene
PERSIS
KARMANIA
MEDIA
Choarene
HYRCANIA
PARTHAEA
ARIA

THE SELEUCID AND PTOLEMAIC EMPIRES (240 B.C.)

MAP IX

west because Egypt was excluded. Yet its many races were too various, and were often separated from one another by deserts; centrifugal tendencies appeared in the peripheral districts. Moreover the barbarian Celtic tribes called Galatae drove a wedge between the Iranic culture of eastern Asia Minor and the Greek culture of the western zone. But the worst disadvantage from which this political formation suffered was that commodities carried from eastern districts to the Syrian coast and Egypt depended on Egyptian vessels to find their markets. For long periods Egypt dominated the two areas of sea, for it controlled Cyprus and very often the Aegean islands, and at some periods the Cilician, Lycian, and Carian coasts as well.

The Ptolemaic kingdom was the smallest of the three. But being compact and thickly populated it was always ready to expand its power, especially as it had an effective fleet in Mediterranean waters.

The least populous and the poorest of the three was the kingdom of Macedon, and its history was the most troubled. It had to contend not only with the Balkan tribes and the Celtic invaders, but with the difficulties caused by dissensions and disorders among the Greeks. All Greeks wanted freedom, but each city in turn would aspire to exercise a hegemony of its own.

Within the Seleucid sphere a growing number of states were gradually attaining independence, not only in the East but also such kingdoms as Pergamum, Bithynia, Pontus, Cappadocia, Galatia, and Pisidia, in the western areas. But the main rival of the Seleucid kingdom was always the Ptolemaic empire, which in a series of wars (as was mentioned above) tried repeatedly to establish at least temporary occupation of the coasts of Syria and Asia Minor and of the adjacent islands. The main problem of the Macedonian kingdom, on the other hand, was its continuous struggle with the Greeks, who were longing for independence. This is the theme of the Chremonidean War, which began against Antigonus Gonatas in 267 and in which Ptolemy II gave Athens and Sparta support in an unsuccessful attack on Macedon; and also of the wars of Aratus of Sicyon, the moving spirit of the Achaean League, against Gonatas and his successors Demetrius II and Antigonus Doson. In 226, however, the Achaean League was defeated at Megalopolis by Sparta, which had come into prominence after the social reforms of Agis IV and Cleomenes III. To hold their own the league sought support from their recent enemy, Antigonus Doson, and the Spartans in their turn were defeated at Sellasia in 222. Antigonus now succeeded in uniting all Greece (except Athens, Elis, Messenia, and the Aetolian League) in a more stable alliance with Macedon. But an anti-Macedonian coalition was formed against his successor Philip V, with Athens and the Aetolian League at its head, and the war was only ended in 217 by the Peace of Naupactus, which Philip concluded to free his hands for measures of protection against the danger of Roman penetration into the Adriatic.

d. *The Struggle for Hegemony in Western Greece*

While the Greeks of the East, in the first decades of the fifth century, were menaced by Persia, their compatriots in the West had to face the threat of Etruria and Carthage combined. The Etruscans still maintained some control in Campania and were hostile to Cumae. The Carthaginians with their foothold in Sicily prevented any fresh Greek foundation in the western part of the island; and they gathered to their side some of the native population, together with those Greek colonies which were opposed to Syracuse and Acragas, the dominant powers. For some time the Etruscans and Carthaginians had been in actual alliance to control the Tyrrhenian Sea and frustrate the Greeks.

But in 480–479 the two great tyrants, Gelon of Syracuse (who started as tyrant of Gela) and Theron of Acragas, routed the Carthaginians at Himera and removed any hope of a counter-attack for three-quarters of a century. The Etruscans were equally crushed. They moved to attack Cumae on the death of its tyrant Aristodemus, but were decisively defeated at sea before the city by the intervention of Hieron, the new tyrant of Syracuse, who put an end to their empire in Campania (473). For some time Greek civilization in the West seemed secure; and under the Deinomenidae (Gelon and Hieron) and under Theron of Acragas, Sicily enjoyed a period of great power and cultural splendour.

In time the two cities lost their hold on their respective confederacies; and the resulting wars between the towns which had been subject to them, and between parties of mercenaries who had lost their employment, allowed the native Sicels and Elymians to throw off the yoke of their Greek overlords for a time. These events encouraged the Athenians to think that they too might gain a foothold in Sicily; and on two occasions, about 454 and in the years following 433–432, they showed what they had in mind. At the same time they entertained the possibility of establishing their hegemony in Magna Graecia, but this too came to nothing. At this time Magna Graecia, after its liberation from the Etruscans, was being menaced by the expansion of the Iapygians, from modern Puglie, and by the gradual descent of the Sabellian immigrants into Samnium, Campania, Lucania, and Bruttium. The dissensions among the Greek colonies made it easier for these tribes to defeat them one by one and gradually to reduce them to subjection.

The first check to Athenian dreams of Western hegemony came in Magna Graecia, where the new colony of Thurii, founded in 446, quickly passed from their control. The Siceliotes too gave them an awakening in 424 by holding a peace congress and showing the Athenians the door. In 416 new struggles broke out, between Segesta and Selinus and between the Chalcidian cities and Syracuse. The Athenians sent very powerful fleets and armies to Sicily to support their friends, but their expedition ended disastrously under the walls of Syracuse, which was reinforced by the Spartan Gylippus after a fruitless siege (415–413).

Neither the Chalcidians nor the Elymians had been able to achieve their freedom through Athenian intervention; but a few years later the Elymians sought aid from Carthage. So, after seventy years of inactivity in the island, the Carthaginians came back to enlarge their base and to take revenge on Syracuse and Acragas. Selinus and Himera were taken and destroyed by their army in 409, and Acragas in 406. In 405 Dionysius I failed to rescue Gela, though shortly afterwards he became master of Syracuse; and at the peace which followed Carthage emerged mistress of three-fifths of Sicily. Dionysius however turned to large-scale military preparations on his own account. After reinforcing the defence of his capital and making an alliance with Sparta, he reunited eastern Sicily under his rule. This empire, though small, had a splendid cultural history, and Dionysius increased his power in three directions. Between 397 and 368 he four times resumed war with the Carthaginians and pushed them back beyond 'Platani' (southern Himera). Secondly, in alliance with Rhegium and the Lucanians, he took the field against the Italiote League and occupied modern Calabria as far as the isthmus of Catanzaro. Finally he broke with the Lucanians and defeated them in battle; and he then proceeded to plundering raids, followed by colonial enterprises, in the upper Tyrrhenian Sea and northern Adriatic.

But the empire of Dionysius I was already beginning to dissolve under his successor Dionysius II, who acceded in 367. His reign was disturbed by the continual attempts to supplant him made, with varying success, by his maternal uncle Dion, the philosophizing friend of Plato. Later, when Dionysius II returned to power in 347, Syracuse's mother city Corinth sent Timoleon against him. This statesman, who died in 336, exiled the tyrant, established a moderate oligarchy at Syracuse, and freed it from Carthaginian pressure. He put an end to the petty tyrants who had established themselves in the various cities and to the raiding hoards of mercenaries who were roaming round their territories.

About twenty years later Agathocles (317–289) became master of Syracuse. His programme was twofold. He first formed a league of Siceliote Greeks to turn the Carthaginians out of the island, and he even ventured on an expedition to Africa to fight them there (310–306). Then he tried to reunite Magna Graecia as well under his hegemony; after the death of Dionysius I this country, deprived of protection from the Siceliotes, was gradually subjected to Sabellian and Iapygian pressure, and one after another the Greek cities were losing their independence. Tarentum had received help from Sparta under King Archidamus (342–338), from Epirus under King Alexander 'the Molossian' (336-331), and again from Sparta under Cleonymus (beginning in 303); but these rescue operations had had little effect, and the dangers were growing all the time. At last Agathocles began the task of establishing a hegemony from outside in Magna Graecia, and he took his conquests farther: he occupied not only Croton but Corcyra. But his death in 289 broke his empire, which split up into a number of tiny states under tyrants or mercenary armies (Messana for example); and the Sabellians on the one side resumed their advance in Italy, the Carthaginians on the other their occupation of Sicily. In 285 Thurii, and in 282 Locri and Rhegium, appealed to Rome for help against the Sabellians: Rome put a garrison in these cities, and made an alliance with Croton. But in 280 a quarrel between Tarentum and Rome occasioned the last intervention in Magna Graecia and Sicily by a Greek adventurer who tried to create an empire for himself by assuming the protection of the Western Greek world; this was Pyrrhus, king of Epirus. But Pyrrhus was unsuccessful in both fields of operation. In Italy Rome defeated him, and in Sicily the independent spirit of the Greek colonies and of the natives was too strong.

6. ITALY AND ROMAN DEVELOPMENT

At this point we must say something about events in the rest of Italy and of the rising hegemony of Rome. At the turn of the sixth to fifth centuries the aristocracy of the 'gentes', which had overcome the foreign rule of the Etruscans and set up the republic, established its ascendancy at Rome. The ruling Etruscan power, however, had been responsible for Rome's hegemony over Latium; with their fall the hegemony collapsed, and had to be rebuilt step by step. At the same time Rome had to face an economic and social upset, which was caused by the fall of the Etruscan kings and made more severe by the patricians' monopoly of power. When the plebeians aspired to improvement of their social and political conditions, the resulting struggles between them and the patricians led gradually to a more even balance of power, the main steps being the Laws of the Twelve Tables (451–450), the Leges Valeriae Horatiae, and the Leges Canuleiae. Meanwhile the Latins had attempted to separate from Rome; but they were defeated at Lake Regillus, and in 493 Rome contracted an alliance with them on equal terms, into which the Hernici were later admitted. The Romans were thus enabled to confront the Volsci and the Aequi in the south, in wars which lasted over a century between 497 and 393. At the same time they were engaged against the Sabines and the southern cities of Etruria on their northern front; they became masters of the territories of Fidenae, Veii (taken in 396), and Capena (in the following year). Eventually they secured the fortresses of Sutrium and Nepete, and made an alliance with Caere.

Once again, however, the hegemony of Rome was overtaken by catastrophe. From the end of the sixth century[8] the movement of the Celts from Gaul to the Danube valley had been accompanied by a penetration of these peoples into northern Italy, where they wiped out part of the Ligurian and Etruscan tribes and accelerated the southward progress of the Oscans and Umbrians. At the beginning of the fourth century, the Celts began a series of raiding expeditions with horse-shoed cavalry into central Italy; and one of these (the chroniclers synchronize it with Greek events in 386) pushed down as far as Latium, defeated Roman resistance on the river Allia, and entered the city of Rome, putting it to fire and sword. These disasters had serious consequences: the Latins and Hernici left the Roman alliance, the colonies of Velitrae, Satricum, and Circeii revolted, and the Etruscans, Volsci, and Aequi resumed hostilities. The collapse was almost complete, but Rome reacted energetically. After strengthening its walls and reinforcing its treaties with the few cities which had remained loyal, it engaged for a generation in wars of reconquest against the Latins, Hernici, Volsci, Aequi, and Etruscans. In the outcome Rome's hegemony, by the middle of the fourth century, again extended to Circeii and Terracina on the south, and to Caere, Sutrium, and Nepete on the north. The new hegemony was recognized in 348 when a fresh maritime treaty between Rome and Carthage was signed; and its internal strength seemed guaranteed by the new method of treating the conquered states, whereby each was given a distinct status varying with the services or hostility it had shown to Rome. To the most loyal among them Rome was ready to bestow its own citizenship. Meanwhile a greater measure of social equality was established at home. Generous concessions were made to the *plebs*, the constitution was reorganized, and a further set of reforms strengthened the Roman army and made it more compact.9

It was now clearly necessary to attend to the movements of the Sabellian tribes. These were showing a tendency to expand from the mountain country and to dominate the plains below; indeed part of the plain country was already occupied by tribes of like race, who had acquired civilization through contact with Greeks and Etruscans. The first skirmishes were concerned with possession of the Liris valley. For a time Rome and the Samnites were allies, but the alliance was broken when in 343 the Campanians asked Rome for aid against Samnium. This first war (343–341) was short and of little consequence; the Samnites were engaged against Tarentum, to the help of which had come Archidamus of Sparta and later Alexander of Epirus; and the Romans were held up by a concerted revolt of the Latins, Volsci, Aurunci, Sidicini, and Campanians, which occupied them until 334. But the war which broke out in 327–326 between Rome and Neapolis, the Roman advance towards the Adriatic and Apulia (Arpi became an ally and Luceria a Latin colony in 325), and its attempted alliance with Lucania, all gave the Samnites the impression that they were being encircled. So began the Second Samnite War (c. 324–305), fought at first with varying fortunes in Samnium, Apulia, and Campania, and even at the southern gateway to Latium; later Rome faced a revolt among the Apennine peoples, and the Etruscans entered the war against it. Finally however it obtained victory on all fronts. In the north its system of alliances was extended to new districts of Etruria and Umbria; in the south it cleared the route to the Adriatic, put down the revolts, and reoccupied part of Apulia. The Samnites were thus decisively beaten, and the new status of the Roman League was recognized by a third treaty between Rome and Carthage in 306.

But a few years later, about 300, a new and still larger coalition came into being against Rome. It eventually comprised the Samnites, certain Apennine tribes, some of the Sabines, Umbrians, and Etruscans, and also the Gallic tribe of the Senones. Its formation was reported to Rome by the people of Picenum and Lucania, and so began the Third Samnite War (299-290). The hardest-fought battle was at Sentinum (295). This split the coalition apart, and Rome was able to subdue each member in isolation from the rest, by campaigns in Umbria, Etruria, Apulia, Samnium, and the central Apennines. In the next decade the Senones were defeated; and the Gallic tribe of the Boii, who had intervened in Etruria, were crushed at Lake Vadimon. The conquest of Etruria was now complete. At the same time Rome rescued the Greek city of Thurii from attacks by the Lucanians, Bruttians, and certain Samnites; garrisons were also planted at Rhegium, Locri, and other Italiote cities. All the harbours of Italy, from Pisa to Thurii and from Apulia to Ariminum, were now in Roman hands.

Yet an ancient treaty with Tarentum, made when conditions were very different, prevented Roman ships from sailing north of the Lacinian promontory. Believing that this was a dead letter, Rome sent a small fleet to cruise in the direction of its Adriatic possessions (282); and this led to war with Tarentum. After trying to embroil Rome with the Samnites, Lucanians, Apulians, and Bruttians, the Tarentines appealed for help to Pyrrhus, king of Epirus (280). In the early operations Pyrrhus succeeded in gaining control of southern Italy, from the country of the Hirpini to the straits; but he could not break through Rome's defence along the line Venusia-Beneventum-Neapolis. When he resumed his action after an unsuccessful expedition to Sicily, Pyrrhus was defeated at Beneventum and retired to Epirus (275). Tarentum was left to its fate, and soon fell into Roman hands.

It was in these same years that Rome brought the conquest of northern Etruria and the maremme to its conclusion, while in the south it recovered what it had lost in Magna Graecia and completed its conquest of that area. At the same time it entered into friendly relations not only with tribes across the Adriatic but with the distant Ptolemaic kingdom of Egypt.[10] It helped to put an end to Seleucid dreams of obtaining mastery both in Egypt and in the areas occupied by Ptolemaic forces in the Syrian and Aegean Seas.

a. *The Romanization of the Peninsula*

About 264, therefore, of the whole peninsula from Pisa and Rimini to the Straits of Messina, one quarter was covered by the Roman state, one tenth by the Latins and Latin colonies, and the remainder by the organism known as the *socii*, the allies of Rome. The size of this residue clearly marks a slowing-down, almost to a complete halt, of the 'ladder' system whereby the allies received Roman citizenship and were admitted into new 'rustic' tribes. There were doubtless selfish motives for this change in policy, but it was also in part justified by the entry into the Roman League of new races, whose assimilation

21

(a) *Aerial view of Dzanbas-kala,*
     on the right bank of the Amu
     Darya, Uzbekistan. The area
     covered is 200 ms. × 170 ms.

(b) *Ordos, bronze finial, two ibexes*
     with turquoise in layin the
     nostrils, height 0·12 ms.

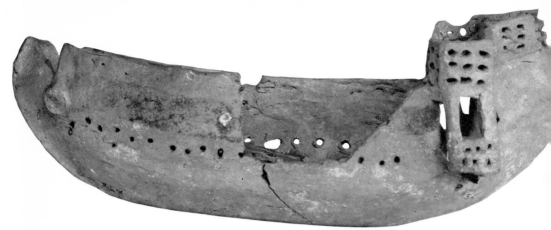

22   NAVIGATION, II

    (a) *Terra-cotta model of a boat from Amathus*, c. 500 BC

    (b) *Model of a Greek galley, fourth century BC, broadside*

came slowly and with difficulty, and whose desire for autonomy, together with their distance from Rome, made them less conscious of the benefit of Roman citizenship. For the time being, then, they were not very anxious for the grant; and Rome thought it better, while orientating the different peoples of Italy upon itself as their leader and co-ordinator, to strike various types of alliance with them, some favourable, some less so. These treaties broke up the pre-existing political ties and, as previously, graded separate sections of the conquered populations at different levels.

In this way the slow process of cultural and administrative unification went on. It had already been attempted in some parts of the peninsula by other imperialist powers; but though some of the geographical, racial, and historical factors were favourable, others were certainly not. Rome was the only power which successfully completed the process. From the outset a feature of its civilization was its power to take everything capable of assimilation which was offered by the races with which it came into contact or alliance, especially the Etruscans, Greeks and Italians—whether their contribution was indigenous or imported—and then to weld the result into a coherent whole. It lay in the midst of many peoples whose evolution was in its critical stage, at the centre of various streams of trade and culture; the racial amalgam of its population, though complex, had solidity; and it was thus able to absorb the civilization of its neighbours and to blend it with its own. The result was a new Italo-Roman culture, capable of being transmitted to other peoples: we find it in language and customs, in cults and ritual, in art and techniques, and in the genres and sentiments of Latin literature. In this way the more the city accepted new citizens from various parts, and the farther it travelled from the restricted Latin basis of its foundation, the more firmly it established itself as a union of racial and cultural elements from every region of the peninsula.

Yet while Rome became Italianized, Italy was also being Romanized. There were Romans and Latins in the colonies, in the rural tribes, on land distributed to individuals, and in garrisons abroad. Citizens and allies served together in the armies; and the process was also aided by the development of trunk roads for trade and communication. Moreover Romanization never involved suppressing or doing violence to the natural features of particular regions. The old political leagues were dissolved; but once this had been done the indigenous population of each region continued to be in a majority, and retained its old dialects and literary languages, its own municipal administration, its special usages and customs, and the legal traditions peculiar to the area. Sometimes it might eventually forget such things of its own accord in face of Roman importations, but more often the indigenous and imported would mix. We have already seen how these developments can be traced not only in linguistic phenomena but in the history of society, law, religion, literature, and art.[11]

b. *Conflict with Carthage*

Although the treaty between Rome and Carthage had been renewed in 278, Carthage during the war with Pyrrhus had shown a clear desire to assert its position in Italy, and on the other side Rome in 270 entered on relations with Hieron II, tyrant of Syracuse. Together with the Carthaginian eparchy and the Mamertine state at Messana, Hieron was master of one of the three main political formations in Sicily; and it was through his doing that the Mamertine state in these years had gradually lost power, until it had to seek help from both Rome and Carthage. The Carthaginians put a garrison in Messana, but their strategic position there was too grave a threat to Italy. Rome was driven to assist the Mamertines, while Hieron veered towards Carthage. In the First Punic War (264–241) Hieron quickly withdrew from the struggle. The Romans in the early stages were supported by the natives in the island, and became involved in increasingly severe actions on land and sea, including a disastrous expedition to Africa. In the end they defeated the Carthaginians decisively at the Aegates Insulae (241).

Three-quarters of Sicily remained in the hands of the Romans and they were now allied with Hieron as well as Messana, who between them occupied the other quarter. But the island only became a 'province' in 227, when Rome imposed the same status on Sardinia and Corsica, both of which had been permanently occupied between 238 and 230.

In the years following the First Punic War Rome led an expedition to defend the northern Etruscan cities and also Massilia against the Ligurians, whose territory was now in part occupied. Two further campaigns were designed to exact retaliation from the Adriatic pirates and to give support to the Greek colonies against the Illyrians: the result was the annexation of Histria. Rome then strengthened the alliance with the Ptolemies and made contact with the Seleucids, and also with several Greek cities, particularly Athens. It had once again to take action against the Gallic advances into central Italy: the Gauls were defeated at Telamon (225); and Rome followed this with victories in the Gallic lands of the Po valley, and founded the colonies of Placentia and Cremona. Finally they secured themselves against the progress of the Carthaginians, who had occupied all southern Spain and were giving assistance to the anti-Roman activity of the Gauls. They imposed a *diktat* that the Carthaginians should not cross the Ebro, and they made an alliance with the powerful Iberian city of Saguntum.

The Carthaginian general Hannibal replied by besieging and taking Saguntum, which led to a rupture between Rome and Carthage, and to the outbreak of the Second Punic War (218–202). Hannibal invaded Italy, and in the early part of the struggle won a series of victories, which led to revolts by several Roman allies over southern Italy. The next phase was a war of attrition in this part of Italy, combined with the revolt of Syracuse from Rome (213) and an alliance between Hannibal and Philip V of Macedon (215). Rome then counter-attacked. In the First Macedonian War a number of Greek powers gave it support; and the successful sieges of Syracuse and Acragas brought it to complete occupation of Sicily. It conquered practically the whole of Punic Spain; and the last stage was the expedition to Africa of Publius Scipio, later called Africanus the Elder. Hannibal followed him, but he was decisively defeated at Zama in 202. The possessions of Carthage in Africa were then overcome, the Numidians receiving independence; and the Roman possessions in Italy were reorganized. The revolted peoples were punished, and colonies were settled in their territories; the Ligurian and Gallic territories to the north of Pisa and Ariminum were conquered once again, with the foundation of strong colonies on both sides of the Po. Sardinia and Corsica were pacified; and Rome's allies the Veneti were freed on their eastern border from attacks by the Carni and Histri, the Latin colony of Aquileia being founded as an advanced watch post.

Meanwhile the equilibrium in the eastern Mediterranean between the Hellenistic powers, and also between the Greek states, was being upset. In 203 Philip V of Macedon and Antiochus III made a compact to extend their respective empires, the former in Greece and Asia Minor, the latter at the expense of the Ptolemies in Phoenicia and Judaea. When the Greek states which were harmed by this compact appealed to Rome, its first act was to request that the Hellenes be respected; when Philip attacked Athens and the Greek cities in Thrace, Rome fought the Second Macedonian War (200–196), in which the factions in the Greek cities took part, some on Philip's side, some on Rome's. Philip was decisively beaten at Cynoscephalae in 197; and next year the Roman senate, under the influence of Scipio Africanus, the great statesman who had willed the preservation of defeated Carthage, compelled Philip to evacuate Greece. The Greek cities were made allies of Rome and were solemnly declared by Titus Flamininus to be free. But Philip was left independent; and he too was made an ally. Rome found him of use as a defender of the Mediterranean countries against the barbarian peoples in the north of the Balkan peninsula.

All this time Antiochus III was asserting his power at the expense of the Greek cities and other states of Asia Minor, especially Pergamum and Rhodes; he was threatening the Ptolemaic possessions, and also aimed to occupy the Thracian Chersonese. He was urged on by his guest, the exiled Hannibal, who proposed an invasion of Italy from the Balkans, and he was supported by the anti-Roman cities in Greece. But when the Seleucid forces began action with a landing in Greece, they were defeated at Thermopylae by Manius Acilius Glabrio in 191 and had to give up all further operations outside Asia. In 190 the war was resumed in Asia. In a short time Antiochus was irrevocably defeated at Magnesia on the Hermus by L. Cornelius Scipio, who during the campaign (but not at the final battle) was aided by his brother the great Africanus. Peace followed at Apamea in 188. Antiochus lost his possessions north of the Taurus chain, but he remained independent and kept everything south of that line. Most of the Greek cities of Asia Minor were made free, and the states of Pergamum and Rhodes increased their territories. So the network of Roman alliances was extended. Rome still adhered to the policy of Africanus: it wanted no direct possessions in the East, but simply the enlargement of its system of alliances to preserve the balance of power.

But Africanus and the section of the governing class which shared his views had their opponents, not only over foreign policy, but over their domestic programme of eliminating class conflict, improving the lot of the poor, and gradually conceding citizenship to the conquered peoples. By degrees the opposing policy gained ground. Its chief supporter was M. Porcius Cato; and since it identified the interests of the state with those of the 'nobilitas' its principles included the enslavement of conquered peoples, a check to all concessions to the lower orders, no extension of citizenship, and keeping the provincial areas in a subject status.[12]

These new policies were disagreeable to the Greek world, which was already torn apart, almost to the point of anarchy, by the struggle for hegemony. They were also disagreeable to Macedon, both to Philip V who had always wanted to rebuild his power, and to his son Perseus who succeeded him on the throne in 179. The latter tried to organize against Rome a movement of the popular classes in Greece; the result was the Third Macedonian War, which completely overturned the earlier settlement made by Rome in Greece, in the Balkans, and in Asia Minor. After the victory of L. Aemilius Paullus at Pydna (168) the Roman senate adopted the line of naked imperialism.[13] Macedonia was divided into four republics which were subjected to tribute; Greek cities which had revolted were punished and made to give hostages; and in Asia Minor the republic of Rhodes and the kingdom of Pergamum lost both territory and importance, on the ostensible ground that their attitude to the war had been ambiguous, though their main crime in fact was that they had grown too strong.

At this point the war mentality and imperialist outlook of Rome found their chief exponent in Cornelius Scipio Aemilianus. The stage was set for a series of conflicts; for on their side Rome's allies, both in the East and in Africa, were dissatisfied with their kings and with their pro-Roman governing classes, while the provincial territories were disturbed by rebellious movements. The result was the ruthless destruction of cities such as Corinth, Carthage, and Numantia, and the creation of new provincial areas, in place of allied states, in Greece, Africa, and Spain.

For a decade (164–155) the Roman government had tried to involve itself as little as possible in Greek local quarrels and in the dynastic struggles of Asia and Egypt. But it then took the side of Ptolemy Euergetes of Egypt against his brother Philometor; and in Syria Rome supported Alexander Balas against Demetrius I, being not opposed to the gradual collapse of Seleucid power in its eastern territories. Meanwhile it had to take up arms against a certain Andriscus, who was attempting to restore the Macedonian monarchy after its destruction in the partition of 168. In 148–147 Macedonia, including the Illyrian and Epirote districts, was reduced to the status of a province. But at the same time the ambitions of the Achaean League had created a condition of perpetual disorder in Greece, especially in the Peloponnese, so the Roman government decided to reduce the league to its original proportions. L. Mummius defeated the Achaeans at Leucopetra; and in 146 he destroyed Corinth, enslaved its population, and made its territory into *ager publicus*. The revolted Greek cities were annexed to the province of Macedonia; the remaining cities, including Athens, were left as allies of Rome.

At the same moment in Africa the peaceful coexistence of Carthage and the Numidian kingdom of Masinissa broke down. Masinissa was anxious to extend his territory, and Carthage, receiving no help from arbitration by Rome, was forced to take up arms in its defence. It was defeated, but Cato maintained that its recent revival constituted a danger which must be destroyed. Under his continual prompting Rome mobilized, demanding that Carthage should be pulled down and its population transplanted ten Roman miles from the sea. When the Carthaginians offered resistance, their city was besieged, taken, and destroyed (146). The destruction of lesser Punic cities followed, and the Carthaginian territory was made into a province with the name of Africa.

Part of the Iberian peninsula had already been made into two provinces, called Hispania Citerior and Ulterior. Here too Rome, whose military forces were thin, was slow to enlarge its conquests, and even had to deal with a series of revolts and native attacks, especially from the Celtiberians and Lusitanians. The cautious policy of Ti. Sempronius Gracchus secured peace for a quarter of a century (179–154); but then disorder started again when independently of one another the Lusitanians and Celtiberians revolted. The conciliatory action of M. Claudius Marcellus seemed to have restored the situation, but Rome then despatched to the front new generals, whose policy was imperialistic and whose methods were those of terrorism—L. Licinius Lucullus, his legate Scipio Aemilianus, and the praetor Servius Sulpicius Galba. Their behaviour prompted a new outbreak of the Lusitanian revolt under the leadership of Viriathus between 147 and 139; and between 143 and 133 the Celtiberians also rebelled again, formed strongholds around Termantia and Numantia, and inflicted repeated losses on the Roman commanders. Finally in 134 Scipio Aemilianus laid siege to Numantia, and next year he succeeded in taking and destroying it, selling the survivors into slavery. The violent methods of imperialism shown in the destruction of these three cities, Corinth, Carthage, and Numantia, brought new strength to Rome's empire. But they had reactions in Rome as well as in its dominions, and were in part responsible for the series of crises which characterized the last days of the Republic.

c. *Political and Social History from the Gracchan Age to Caesar*

The great conquests had transformed the economic picture of Italy. It was once based on smallholdings, but the way was now open for the creation of *latifundia* for pasturage and arboriculture; slave labour was generally adopted; and the small proprietors and free workmen were ruined. Some enlightened men, who were trying to halt the excessive power of the *optimates*, saw and denounced the danger, but conditions became continually more serious. Some evidence is given by the slave revolts, often supported by the country proletariats. They were at first sporadic throughout Italy (139–132) and then came to a head in the First Servile War (136–131), which was accompanied by similar movements in Greece and Asia Minor.

It was against this background that the two brothers, Tiberius and Gaius Sempronius Gracchus, made their largely unsuccessful attempts to find a remedy for the social and political evils. Tiberius tried to rebuild the peasant class by reviving an old law which set a limit on the amount of *ager publicus*[14] allowed for tenure by a single family; he could then redistribute what was over. He also attempted to break down the political power usurped by the senate and restore it to the people, which in his view had the right to dispose of the property and lands of Attalus III, king of Pergamum, since the king had left the Roman people as his heir. One result was a revolt by a pretender to the Pergamene throne named Aristonicus, who was supported by the lower orders and the slaves of the country; but the Pergamene kingdom was made into the province of Asia. Gaius Gracchus continued the agrarian policy of his brother, but also sought support from the knights against the *optimates*; he promoted the foundation of colonies outside as well as inside Italy, and the relief of the allies by granting Roman citizenship.[15] The reaction to the Gracchan programme strengthened the imperialist policies of the nobles, who were now led by the Metelli and had reached an understanding with the knights. One concrete result of this was the creation of new provinces in Asia (mentioned above) and in Narbonese Gaul. But the knights broke with the senate and once more allied with the popular party; and the responsibility for this lay with a former colleague of Metellus named Gaius Marius.

Marius had the good fortune to have deserved the credit for two great victories. He overcame Jugurtha, grandson of Masinissa, who had occupied all Numidia and murdered his cousin the Roman nominee Adherbal; the long and eventful Jugurthine War (111–106) ended with the partition of these territories into two kingdoms allied with Rome. Then in Narbonese Gaul and in the Po valley Marius defeated the Cimbri and Teutones (104–101), the advanced guard of a German migration, who had penetrated into Roman territory and defeated the legions several times. On top of the military effort needed to achieve these successes came the Second Servile War in Sicily (104–101), and M. Antonius' action against the pirates in 102, which led to the formation of the provinces of Cilicia and Pamphylia. But meanwhile Mithradates VI Eupator, king of Pontus, was organizing a large anti-Roman coalition in the East. He overran the Crimea, partitioned Paphlagonia and Galatia with Nicomedes II of Bithynia (104–103), and engineered a scheme to win Cappadocia. When it became known that Marius was meditating a war of reprisal the coalition remained inactive, and the danger had been averted for the present. Yet Marius had now been discredited in the eyes of every party. After allying himself in 103 with the democratic leaders Saturninus and Glaucia, during his consulship in 100 he allowed them to be murdered, so the nobles gained the upper hand again, and Marius withdrew from politics. M. Livius Drusus made a disinterested but utopian effort to reconcile the parties and to reach agreement on the various issues of the day by securing concessions from each side. But the scheme failed, and the way was open for the armed conflict (90–88) between Rome and the Italians. The Roman government would not grant the citizenship the Italians sought: instead they fought and won, and then felt bound to grant it after all.

Meanwhile the fortune of politics was passing to L. Cornelius Sulla, formerly legate to Marius and the actual conqueror of Jugurtha. In 88 war broke out with the anti-Roman coalition organized round the king of Pontus; and for this, the victorious First Mithradatic War, Sulla obtained the command over the heads of the Marians. Marius was driven into exile, but he later returned with force at his back,[16] and became master of Rome in alliance with Cinna. But after indulging in the most ruthless massacre of his opponents he died a few days after entering on his seventh consulship; and the brief and bloody dictatorship of the popular leaders Cinna and Carbo (86–83) was no more fortunate. Sulla returned in triumph from the East, routed the Marians with C. Marius' son of the same name at their head, and entered Rome. There he assumed a dictatorship for any period he might think necessary to prepare a new constitution. The senate remained the chief organ of government, but it was a senate greatly diluted by the introduction of large numbers of knights. The aim was a balance between classes and a levelling of living standards. Large distributions of land were made to veterans. The magistracies were reorganized, the civil power of the urban magistracies being separated from the power of the pro-magistrates—the generals and provincial governors. At the beginning of 79, when Sulla judged his task complete, he resigned the dictatorship and retired into private life until his death in 78.

After the death of Sulla the struggle between *optimates* and democrats (or Marians) broke out afresh.[17] Two of the latter, Sertorius and Perperna, crossed to Spain and tried to make it a base for the war against the nobles by organizing the native population. But the feature of the period was the rise of the military glory of Cn. Pompeius and then his attainment of political power. He conquered Sertorius and settled Spain (77–72); then he came in at the death to destroy the last bands of rebel slaves under Spartacus,[18] who had already been decisively defeated by Licinius Crassus (73–71); he became consul with Crassus in 70; in 67 he defeated and exterminated the pirates who were infesting the Mediterranean. In that year he succeeded L. Licinius Lucullus, who had conducted the second war against Mithradates and Tigranes between 74 and 67. Tigranes was compelled to surrender, after pressure had been put on his father-in-law Phraates III of Parthia, and Mithradates was pursued by Pompey into the Caucasus. Pompey created three new provinces, Pontus-Bithynia, Crete with Cyrenaica, and Syria; and he organized a number of vassal states, including Jerusalem, which was left in the hands of the Hasmonaeans after its siege and capture in 63. He then returned to Rome in the winter of 63/2. But while these events were occurring in Pompey's orbit, the star of C. Iulius Caesar was rising at Rome. An unsuccessful attempt was made to involve him in Catiline's conspiracy on behalf of the proletariat against the oligarchic government in 63. In the next year he was praetor, and in 61 he was pro-praetor in Spain. From there he returned to obtain the consulate for 59. But first he had made a secret pact with Pompey and Crassus, known as the First Triumvirate, which was renewed at a conference at Luca in 56.

In 58 Caesar, with extraordinary powers for five years, took up his command in Cisalpine Gaul, in Transalpine Gaul (Narbonensis), and in Illyricum. His first action in Gaul was to check migration by the Helvetii; he then threw back the German Ariovistus and crushed the power of the Germanized tribes of Belgica; then he took action to stop fresh intervention by Germans from beyond the Rhine, and by Britons from their island. His plan was to create friendly federations in Gaul, centred on the tribes which for some time past had favoured Rome. But just when his project was nearing completion, the bases for understanding between the triumvirs began to crumble. Julia, daughter to Caesar and wife to Pompey, died; and Crassus was killed, in an expedition undertaken against the Parthians in 54 and 53. Pompey, who ought to have taken over the proconsulate of Spain for five years in 54, stayed in Rome as the real arbiter of the state. News of the decline in Caesar's political position reached the Gauls, and was the part cause of a general revolt under Vercingetorix in 53 and 52, the embers of which were still smouldering in 51 and 50. The revolt was crushed; but it compelled Caesar to change his plan, and to give the conquered country a much less liberal settlement in the shape of a province.

Although Caesar made many efforts to reach a settlement with Pompey and the senate, their schemes to take away his command before the date that had been fixed brought on the Civil War. This saw the Roman world divided between the two triumvirs, and the soldiers supporting each were locked in armed conflict.

The war began in Italy, but later passed over to the Balkans. In 48 Pompey was crushed at Pharsalus, and was then put to death on the Egyptian coast by the guardians of Ptolemy XIV. In consequence Caesar as victor occupied Egypt, and settled it as a vassal kingdom, after which he crossed to Asia

Minor and defeated Mithradates' son Pharnaces at Zela. He then made himself master of Africa, which had been in the hands of the younger Cato; and Spain was won from other Pompeian survivors by his victory at Munda in 45.

He now returned to Rome; and in the last months of 45 and in early 44 he reformed the state to make it the imperial power he desired. The faction fights were to be ended: Caesar (and his successors after him) was to be dictator and ruler of the state for life; and the members of the state were to be increased by grants of citizenship to provincials. The provinces, now governed by responsible officers, were gradually to rise to the level of Italy; and Rome would have become the metropolis of a bilingual world, creating a harmony between the Greek and Latin civilizations. But in March 44 Caesar had decided to launch a last great military expedition, to conquer the Parthians who had killed Crassus and then to return to Rome with a vast demonstration of power through the Caucasus, Scythia, the Danubian and Rhine areas, and Gaul. Before this colossal expedition could set out Caesar was murdered by a group of senators on 15 March, 44 BC.[19]

d. *From Triumvirate to Empire*

Power was successfully taken over by the consul Marcus Antonius, who had been a loyal collaborator with Caesar and was supported by the people and by the veterans. For a brief moment he was ready to negotiate with Caesar's murderers, but only to give him time to rouse the mass of the people against them; and the two leaders of the conspiracy, M. Iunius Brutus and C. Cassius, left Rome and crossed to the East. But Antonius' leadership of the Caesarians was now challenged by the young C. Octavius, known as C. Caesar Octavianus because he had been adopted by Caesar. After some delay he arrived from Epirus, collected forces of his own, secured support from a group of senators, and made an alliance with another of Caesar's murderers, Decimus Brutus. He attacked and defeated Antonius' army, and claimed the consulate; then in November, 43, he reached agreement with Antonius and Lepidus, and formed a triumvirate which the senate were compelled to recognize. The triumviral programme was to avenge Caesar and to preserve the principles of his imperial ideas. After removing their opponents by bloody proscriptions they moved to attack Brutus and Cassius, who had made themselves masters of the East. These two were defeated in two battles at Philippi (42) and forced to suicide. The triumvirs now made a division of the areas they were to rule, though they were hampered by the continued existence of anti-Caesarian forces in the pirate fleet commanded by Sextus Pompeius, son of Pompey the Great. Antonius in the East planned a war on the Parthians and Armenians: against the latter he was successful, but against the Parthians he failed. He combined with Cleopatra, queen of Egypt, to found an empire of the Hellenistic and Oriental type. Octavian meanwhile removed Sextus Pompeius and Lepidus (36), and thus became sole master of the Western world. The struggle between

N*

the two surviving triumvirs grew progressively more acute and finally developed into war. This was ended by the battle of Actium, after which Octavian in 30 took possession of Egypt, and Antonius with Cleopatra committed suicide.

Octavian remained sole ruler. He refused the dictatorship, but retained his supreme command of all armed forces and his complete control of finance. He made the senate his ally: it was now convinced that one man must rule, and it gradually conferred all power on him by spontaneous and official grants, embraced generally by the title Augustus which was accorded in 27. For one period of ten years after another Augustus was made proconsul of his provinces; he had sanctity through the full tribunician power conferred in 23; and in 12 BC he became Pontifex Maximus.

The senate was radically overhauled, the chief change being that it was now bound to ratify the conclusions of a 'consilium principis' composed of persons in Augustus' confidence. A new bureaucracy drawn from among the knights was entrusted with the government of certain imperial provinces and with the discharge of a number of other tasks. The provinces were divided into senatorial and imperial, the former being the pacified areas, the latter those where units of the army were needed. A slowing-up is noticeable in the process of transforming the provinces by grants of citizenship; but meanwhile colonies were founded, and large public works were carried out in Rome, Italy, and the provinces. Apart from the troops needed to protect the emperor's person and to garrison Rome and Italy, the armies came to be stationed on the frontiers of the empire, their total size (excluding contributions from allied states) being reduced to about 300,000 men. Attention was given to the regular financial arrangements, and an imperial treasury was created as well. The conquest of Syria was completed; in the Alps Rome's territories were expanded; the defence systems on the Euphrates and the Danube were improved; and an attempt was made, but later abandoned, to occupy Germany as far as the Elbe. If we add the care taken to secure a trained successor with many years of tutelage behind him, we now have the main features of the Augustan empire, whose principles included the maintenance of Italy's superiority over the provinces, though the government ensured that the Italians should show themselves worthy of this preferential treatment.

7. THE TRANSFORMATION OF THE GREEK EAST

During the empire of Alexander and the Diadochi, and under the Seleucids after 301, there was a process of close fusion between Greek and Oriental civilizations in the parts of the East which the Macedonians had conquered. Even in the Far-Eastern provinces, especially Bactria, this reached very high levels, being largely responsible for the cultural exchange between the Hellenized world and foreign parts. It was precisely in Bactria, however, that we also find the first moves towards independence among the Seleucid provinces;

and this led gradually to the formation of the Parthian power under the Arsacid kings. In the middle of the third century, with the help of the local Greek cities, the satrap Diodotus of Bactria created an independent state under Greek rulers. After a few successors of Diodotus' line Euthydemus of Magnesia usurped the throne, but the Greeks governed the country for a century, down to 140 BC. They extended their territory to take in Arachosia and the areas of the Punjab and Sind, and accomplished a considerable task in promoting exchanges between the cultures of the Greek and Indian worlds. The middle of the third century, which saw the rise of the Bactrian kingdom, was also the period in which the Scythian Arsaces murdered the Seleucid satrap of Parthia and became master of his territory. He declared its independence and founded what became the nucleus of the Arsacid empire, an amalgam between Scyths and Iranian Parthians. Arsaces was succeeded in 248/247 (the Parthian era begins on 14th April 247) by his brother Tiridates, who used Bactrian aid to annex Hyrcania and Comisene; his successor Artabanus I (214–196) added Coarene. The renewal of Seleucid expansion under Antiochus III meant a setback for the Parthian empire. But after the discomfiture of Antiochus by the Romans at Magnesia (189) a revival occurred under Phraates I, who occupied the country as far as the 'Caspian Gates' and thus opened the way to Media and Persis, both of which countries were soon afterwards annexed by his successor Mithradates I (c. 171–138). This king also took over Elimias (Susiana), Babylonia, Adiabene, and Seleucia (141–140), and adopted the seal of the Achaemenids together with their ancient title, 'King of Kings'. He was ruler from the Caspian to the Persian Gulf, and the Seleucid Demitrius II, who tried in vain to check his progress, was defeated and taken prisoner. Arsacid history in fact consists of an unceasing struggle to defend their western frontiers against the Seleucids and later the Romans, and their north-eastern frontiers against nomad invasions. As early as 155 the Sacae had occupied Śakastan (modern Seistan), which bears their name.

The next king, Phraates II, lost certain territory to Antiochus Sidetes, but recovered it when he defeated and killed the Seleucid king. He in his turn fell fighting against the Sacae, who under pressure from the Yüeh-chih had destroyed the Bactrian kingdom and become masters of Sogdiana, Hyrcania, Comisene, and finally Adiabene. His successor, Artabanus II, thrust the Sacae back, but he too was killed in battle in 124.

The first act of Mithradates II (c. 124–88) was the recovery of Babylonia and Caracene, which had become independent in 126. Then in the east he seized western Bactria from the Sacae as far as the plain of Merv, and in the north-west took possession of certain Armenian territories. By taking advantage of the new caravan routes to China he was able to expand the trade of his subjects in both directions, thus establishing Parthia's first political contact with the Roman world in an embassy sent to Sulla when he was praetor in Cilicia in 92. But the last years of his reign, and the twenty years which followed, saw another setback, caused by endless internal disturbances, as a result of which the territories lately won from Armenia were lost and in 77 Sanatruces, a king imposed by the Sacae, secured the Parthian throne.

The power, however, passed to Phraates III (*c.* 69–*c.* 57). This king refused an alliance against Armenia offered by the Roman commander Lucullus, who promised the disputed territories as his reward. An alliance on the same terms with Pompey was accepted; but after Phraates had taken a lukewarm part in the war his hopes were frustrated, and after lengthy negotiations he had to be content with the cession of Adiabene.

Phraates III was murdered by his two sons, Orodes II who secured the throne in 57, and Mithradates III who was engaged in continuous war with his brother until he himself was removed in 54. Meanwhile the Roman triumvir Crassus was starting the campaign against Parthia which ended with his disastrous defeat at Carrhae in the following year. The result of this was that Orodes not only reconquered Mesopotamia but was able to cast his eye on the Syrian and Anatolian lands, although in 50 a counter-attack by Cassius Longinus pushed the frontier back to the Euphrates. It was crossed by both powers in the years which followed. After the death of Cassius at Philippi the Parthians invaded, but Orodes in person was defeated by the legions at Gindarus in 38, and his successor Phraates IV (37–2 BC) had to meet a severe threat from the triumvir Antonius, who prepared an expedition as the avenger of Crassus. But the Roman invasion passed off without inflicting harm, and indeed caused a breach between the Romans and Artavasdes I of Armenia. During the civil war between Octavian and Antonius, Phraates IV tried to pursue his policy of expansion by securing Armenia, but his dreams were ended when Augustus united the Roman power. In 20 BC he had to agree to restore the standards and prisoners taken at Carrhae to the emperor's stepson Tiberius, and to accept a policy of friendship with Rome, to which he sent four of his sons as pupils. At the beginning of our era he was succeeded by Phraates or Phraataces (2 BC–AD 4), his son by an Italian woman named Musa.

8. ARMENIA

Armenia was inhabited by people of the old Urartic stock who had mixed with 'Armenoid' and Indo-European immigrants. As a semi-independent satrapy under the Persians, it had been loyal to their kings but had been governed by two dynasties of its own, in Armenia Maior and Armenia Minor. It was then occupied by Alexander the Great, but on his death the satrap Orontes declared the country's independence, which was maintained, despite the threat offered by Eumenes of Cardia, in face of all the successors. It was only much later that Antiochus III succeeded in obtaining suzerainty over this large area, still divided into the two satrapies of Greater and Lesser Armenia, one east and the other west of the Euphrates. But the country regained its independence after Antiochus' defeat at Magnesia in 189, with Artaxias ruling in Greater Armenia and Zariadres in Lesser. The decades that followed were marked by the rise to power of the Parthians, whom the Armenian kingdom had to recognize as overlords; but in the subsequent period of Parthian weakness Tigranes II, the new and active ruler of Armenia Maior, was able to put an end to this state of affairs. The king now annexed Armenia Minor, extended his territory on the south at the expense of the Parthians in Upper Mesopotamia, and took Cappadocia from its king Ariobarzanes. When the latter fled to Rome in 93, Tigranes made an alliance with King Mithradates Eupator of Pontus and invaded Cilicia and Syria, sealing his new power by taking the title 'King of Kings' and by founding a fresh capital at Tigranocerta. But by these means he had provoked the opposition of Rome. As its enemy in the Mithradatic Wars he first lost Cappadocia, given back to Ariobarzanes by Sulla; and in 69 the campaign of Lucullus deprived him of all his Western conquests, though by a desperate resistance in 68 and 66 he halted his enemy in Lesser Armenia.

When Pompey succeeded Lucullus, however, the Romans entered Artaxata, and Tigranes was forced to give up Syria and Armenia Minor, and to recognize Roman suzerainty. The victory of the Parthians over the legions of Crassus in 53 brought Armenia, under its new king Artavasdes, into the Parthian system, but it was recovered for Rome by Antonius. Though Artavasdes once more tried to escape from dependence on Rome, he was held responsible by Antonius for the failure of his Parthian expedition and severely punished: Artaxata was taken, Artavasdes made prisoner, and Armenia made a fief for Alexander the son of Antonius and Cleopatra. During the civil war between Octavian and Antonius the legions were withdrawn, and under its new king Artaxes Armenia reverted to Parthia; but on the king's death in 20 BC, Augustus now being master of the empire, Tiberius his stepson put on the Armenian throne a new king, Tigranes III, who accepted Roman suzerainty. After later rebellions Rome found other kings, the Median Ariobarzanes (imposed by Gaius Caesar in 1 BC), Artavasdes II, and finally Tigranes IV.

NOTES TO CHAPTER VII

1. The view that there was feudalism during the Han is supported by many Marxist historians, and in particular by the overwhelming majority of contemporary Chinese historians.

However, they see the existence of this feudalism not only and not primarily in the fact that Liu Pang revived the institution of land grants to the aristocracy, but in the fact that the entire system of social and economic (and in particular agrarian) relations during the Han was based on principles characteristic of the feudal mode of production (see, e.g., L. I. Duman, 'O sotsialnoekonomicheskom stroye Kitaya v 3 v. do n. e.—1 v. n. e.' [On the Social and Economic Structure of China from the third century BC to the first century AD], *Voprosy istorii*, 1957, no. 2).

The institutions introduced by the Ch'in, which the authors think limited 'feudalism', in fact did not stand in the slightest contradiction to the feudal mode of production, but were merely a characteristic, specific feature of it. (L. S. Vasilyev.)

2. The history of India that we are reconstructing is summary and condensed: it enumerates successive invasions and struggles which are brought together in the account, but which in reality were spread over a very long period in time and across a vast area. Peaceful periods and regions were not lacking but historians ordinarily abandon the study of their products, which prove their existence, to philologists and archaeologists. The frequency of conflicts is in reality no greater in India than in other countries of the world. Even the political anarchy of the eighteenth century, which led to the British conquest of India and contributed to a belief in the congenital propensity of India to anarchy, had as its counterpart the European wars which had repercussions in India and helped to unsettle it.

One does not see why the division of society into classes should have necessarily removed political stability from the time when it represented the normal structure and not an occasional situation. At any rate a demonstration of the assertion would be useful. Struggles took place between classes but mainly between peoples through invasions or rivalry among princes. The classes took part in the struggles as a group but not always in a direction leading to anarchy; it was the Brahmans who most fiercely opposed Alexander's invasion, so Arrian tells us (*Anabasis, VI*, 2). The classes who took political action were not always those in the *varṇa* social scale. The Buddhists supported invaders on several occasions, although they themselves recruited from all classes without distinction.

In any case the multiple dynastic changes (frequently separated by long periods in time) did not always introduce many modifications into a society which was culturally unaffected by these changes.

3. Except, as Professor J. Filliozat notes, that Alexander's invasion had lessened Persian power without substituting a comparable Greek power. So the Oriental empire could regain the satrapies conquered by the Persians in the sixth century B C.

4. The failure was largely due to Seleucid interference.

5. In this expedition Darius first secured the submission of the tribes of Thrace, then crossed the Danube and led his army through the regions which are now Moldavia and Bessarabia, the natives retiring before him. The Transdanuvian campaign was fruitless, and its motives are obscure: possibly Darius was concerned to obtain further information about the tribes Persia had encountered on its Caspian frontier.

6. Aristagoras, if not the architect of this revolt, was at least an early convert, and lost his life fighting for the Thracian mines coveted by Miletus. If commercial pressures were all-important in causing the rising (and the question is most obscure), it seems likely that Milesian interests were prominent: there may have been distress resulting from the loss of their main source of raw wool when Sybaris in Italy was destroyed *c.* 510. But a further cause must have been the rise of 'democratic' elements (i.e. of a citizen class jealous of the families which, often with Persian support, had been dominant hitherto): this factor was recognized by the Persians after the revolt, when they established 'democracies' instead of tyrannies in the cities. The revolt cannot therefore be explained wholly on commercial or nationalist lines.

7. Professor C. Danov considers that more weight should have been given to the ethnic and economic forces, as distinct from the political and military events, which led to the dissolution of Alexander's empire. Some of the economic factors are treated in Chapter IX.

8. For the chronology see above, p. 78 with note 29.

9. The Roman *plebs* obtained equal rights with the patricians not as a result of 'generosity' on the part of the latter, but as a result of a bitter and protracted struggle. (E. M. Shtaerman.)

10. Professor Ch. Th. Saricakis maintains that such relations are most improbable in the early third century B C. But though the treaty with Egypt, dated by Livy to 273, may not have had any serious significance, by the later part of the century Rome was undoubtedly a power which no Mediterranean monarchy could fail to recognize as a competitor for hegemony. On this whole subject the views of M. Holleaux, *Rome, la Grèce et les monarchies hellénistiques* (Paris, 1921) have found wide acceptance: on the Egyptian treaty see his pp. 46 ff.

11. Professor C. Danov considers this account of Roman imperialism to be far too favourable. To him the fundamental policy of Rome was expressed in their maxim 'divide et impera', and he regards it as misleading to speak of the conquest of the peninsula as bringing about the Romanization of Italy and the Italianization of Rome. Professor Pareti's view, however, is reinforced, not only by the story of Italian loyalty during the Second Punic War, but by the development of Romano-Italian religion, literature, and art (see Chapters XI and XII).

12. Although these were doubtless the views of certain second-century senators, it is questionable whether Cato held them. Though brutal in his attitude to slaves, Cato is not known to have favoured harshness to the Roman *plebs* or to the provincials (apart from his hostility to Carthage): the salient feature of his foreign policy was his anti-Hellenism, which led him actually to oppose any annexations in Greek lands, while at home he advocated reconstruction and reform on traditionalist lines and was active in promoting public works. For a brief sketch see A. H. McDonald in *Oxford Classical Dictionary* (1946), s.v. 'Cato'. Another reason for the differences between second-century Roman statesmen over foreign policy was the division of the senate into groups, each with political and economic interests in particular areas; this phenomenon has been attractively analysed by E. Badian, *Foreign Clientelae* (Oxford, 1958).

13. Professor C. Danov insists that Rome aimed at outright conquest as early as the First Punic War. Far-sighted Greeks certainly feared the 'cloud in the West' long before the battle of Pydna, cf. Polybius, V. 104, 10. Yet the motives of Rome's foreign policy in the late third and early second centuries are highly controversial: M. Holleaux, *Rome, La Grèce et les monarchies hellénistiques* (Paris, 1921) argued for self-defence; G. de Sanctis, *Storia dei Romani*, IV (Turin, 1923) for aggressive militarism; E. Badian, *op. cit.*, pp. 62 ff., for fear combined with desire for revenge.

14. This was land to which the Romans acquired title after a conquest, but which they had allowed squatters to occupy. See below, p. 488.

15. The grievances of the allies, which C. Gracchus sought to remove by grants of citizenship, had been fanned by the Gracchi themselves; for the 'public land' which Tiberius' law redistributed was often in the hands of allied proprietors.

16. It was actually Sulla in 88 who was the first to march on Rome with armed force.

17 For fuller analysis of the political and constitutional struggles of this period see Chapter X. After the land confiscations which Sulla effected in 81 the social discontent in the Italian countryside was severe. Catiline's conspiracy (see below) was based on genuine distress, whether or not the motives of its leader were sincere.

18. For this rebellion, the most terrible of all the Servile Wars, see below p. 487 and p. 497

19. For the features in Caesar's rule which led to his murder see below, p. 502.

CHAPTER VIII

THE DEVELOPMENT OF LANGUAGE
AND WRITING TO THE CHRISTIAN ERA

I. LANGUAGE

a. *Chinese and Its Diffusion*

IN the history of Chinese it is essential, though difficult, to distinguish the factors affecting speech from those affecting writing. In regard to the former, the chronological picture is very hazy, and the grammatical development of classical Chinese is scarcely perceptible. Thanks, however, to Karlgren's work, the phonetic development, at least in the great northern capitals, is better known, though we know very little about other Chinese dialects.

In 213 BC occurred the great reform of the script imposed by Li Ssǔ, which we shall discuss later on. An official list of standard characters was set up and promulgated; and this helped to settle the form of the written language. But the most decisive factor was the conscious and unconscious imitation of ancient authors by the writers of the Han Dynasty. The Chinese literary language was then fixed in the form which it preserved down to the twentieth century. Meanwhile its use spread gradually as the result of colonization and cultural assimilation during the period of the Warring States.

The language of the Li Ssǔ period (the end of the third century BC) was approximately what modern sinologues (Karlgren, Simon, Forrest) call Archaic Chinese, which began about 500 BC. The Proto-Chinese of the *Shih-ching*, described in Part I, underwent in this period its most rapid and profound changes. Above all, the majority of the 'Phonetic Compounds' were fixed at this time. Some of the final occlusives of Proto-Chinese now vanished: the consonantal clusters at the beginning of words, which were one of the salient features of the previous phonetic period, were simplified. These phonetic changes seem connected with the fact that, with the breakdown of feudalism and the coming of the unifying central government of the Ch'in, supremacy was won by linguistic forms belonging not only to other areas but to social levels different from those of the nearly extinct aristocracy.

From the point of view of vocabulary the Chinese language continued to develop almost without resorting to borrowings from other languages; it found in itself sufficient resources to indicate new ideas and new material objects as soon as the need presented itself. The autochthonous character and independent vocabulary of Chinese is one of its fundamental features at all times. Chinese is, and has always been, one of the few languages which have not applied to foreign tongues for the creation of technical and philosophic neologisms.

b. *Languages in India*

In this period the linguistic geography of India shows a progressive, though very slow, spread of Aryan speech southward, as far as the present-day confines of the Dravidic languages.

Classical Sanskrit ceases to be a spoken language and becomes finally fixed, in all its richness and complexity, in Pāṇini's great grammatical work.

The Prakrit dialects continued their development and became in this period the official languages of administration in the great Indian states. The earliest Indian inscriptions are those of Aśoka (third century BC) and they are all in Prakrit, slightly differentiated in four dialects according to the regions in which they were inscribed. This Aśokan Prakrit is particularly interesting as it is presumably very close, though not identical, to the spoken language of the north Indian ruling classes of that time. Even after Aśoka too it was used officially and it was employed in all the rare inscriptions of this period.

There is no direct evidence for literary Prakrit in this period. It is reasonable to assume that the oral teaching of the new religions, Buddhism and Jainism, used some Prakrit dialect; but it was only fixed as a written form in the following period.

c. *Iranic*

The official language of the Achaemenid conquerors, Old Persian, never succeeded in becoming either the common language or the language of administration (which used Aramaic). It was rarely used and rapidly declined, and this is proved by Artaxerxes' documents. Parts of the epigraphic monuments of Darius and of Xerxes were written in this language in our period.

Alexander's conquest removed it from circulation except as a dialect, and it was used as such in Persis, in south-western Iran, its birthplace, during the centuries which followed. Although there is no literary evidence, the eastern Iranic dialects survived into the Hellenistic period and the succeeding centuries and were never eclipsed by the use of Greek. This is particularly true of Sogdian, which did not develop until relatively late.

Naturally as soon as the eastern satrapies detached themselves from the Seleucid empire, Greek, which had been adopted there, slowly gave ground to a revival of the earlier languages, and to the growth of Aramaic as a common cultural language.

We shall complete the story of Middle Iranic in its two groups in Part III, although their first phases of development must certainly have occurred before the Christian era.

d. *Semitic*

The Semitic languages, and particularly those of the north-west, have several general features. They continued to be used in the Asiatic and Egyptian areas, but their use was less common, since they were supplanted in the East by Aramaic, which was also a Semitic language, and in the western Mediterranean by Punic, which was derived from Phoenician. We shall return to Punic later.

From the fifth to the third century we have a great many, though usually short and uniform, Phoenician inscriptions, but by the first century Phoenician had been supplanted by Aramaic. Similarly Hebrew, which had been used in the fifth–fourth centuries for writing the ancient religious and legal texts, was gradually infiltrated by Aramaic. By Alexander's time Aramaic had been substituted for common use even though scholars and nationalists continued to write in pure Hebrew until about 100.

In Egypt however the Hebrews became accustomed to Greek. This led to the Septuagint translation of the Bible, and to the preference for Greek shown by oriental Christendom.

During this period Aramaic had spread over a very wide area and replaced the old tongues such as Accadian, Phoenician, and Hebrew. We have tablets, written in Aramaic in Babylonia during the Persian domination in the fifth century and parchments which are specimens of the Aramaic of the Achaemenid empire administration. Later evidence of it is found in Cappadocia, in the Caucasus, and in India. It reached its greatest extension from about 300 BC onwards, with many autonomous regional developments. A Palestinian Aramaic can be distinguished, and also a form of Biblical Aramaic with continually increasing Aramaic features used for the transmission of certain biblical texts: for example in the books of *Ezra* and of *Daniel*, which spread as far as the Jewish colony of Elephantine in Egypt, founded in the fifth century. The Nabataeans, given their racial background, produced an Aramaic with Arabian overtones, but in Palmyra, although it was dominated for a long time by Arabian elements, from 43 BC onwards we find documents in a language similar to the Palestinian Aramaic of the next century.

In Babylonia Aramaic appears from the seventh century onwards, and from the Persian period there are the sixth- and fifth-century tablets mentioned above. From other easterly areas there are some 'Syriac' inscriptions of Edessa.

Phoenician, as we have said, had its own colonial development, with few regional differences, in Punic. The documents which have come down to us are mainly from the fourth century BC onwards, and have been found not only in Africa, but in Spain, Sardinia, and Sicily. At the end of the third century BC Plautus in his *Poenulus* has given us ten Punic verses in a Latinized form of vocalization, and the manuscripts also contain a version in Libyan Punic. A mutilated form of Punic, called Neo-Punic, is attested in inscriptions from the time the Punic zone came under Roman domination, and some of these are bilingual, in Neo-Punic and Latin. Punic spread through the neighbouring peoples and was used as a commercial language by the Berbers and Numidians of northern Africa.

The southern Semitic languages, those of an Arabian type, can be divided into three zones. One lay more to the north, to which we can assign the people stationed along the great caravan routes from Syria towards the Persian Gulf and the Yemen. On the first of these routes states had centred round the oases of el Giof and Taimā; on the second, round the oases of Lilyān near Dedan, and Tamūd, near the Gulf of Aqaba. The written texts can be dated from the second century BC to the sixth century AD.

The central Arabian district was inhabited by nomads, and has left no written documents before the Christian era. However in the southern region —in the Yemen and in the oases north of Hedjaz—the agricultural and sedentary life favoured the growth of an early civilization and state system. In our period these peoples, speaking a number of kindred dialects, were dominated from about the third century onwards by the Sabaei who had gradually assumed control of the area. From about 500 the southern Arabian dialects crossed over to Ethiopia on the African continent to the region later known as Abyssinia. There the natives added Cushite features to them. When a unified state arose in the first century BC the dialects assumed a more homogeneous form.

e. *Greek Dialects and Idioms*

The Greek dialects imported into the colonies suffered for various reasons. The colonists themselves were mixed in race, for a number of different stocks would take part in these foundations, and later foreigners would be brought in. Moreover over the centuries the colonists lived in increasing intimacy with the natives, who became Hellenized, but in their turn influenced the Hellenes. This is clearly shown in Sicily where there were mixed Ionic-Doric colonies, such as Himera; at Syracuse too there was heavy Aeolic penetration into the Doric tongue, and the Syracusan poets Epicharmus and Theocritus constantly use terms which are Siculan in origin. It can be seen too in the diverse peoples with whom they came into contact in the colonies, where, especially in popular speech, new sub-species of Greek dialects were formed: for example, in the colonies of Italy, and in such areas as Provence, Catalonia, the Adriatic, the Pontus, Cyrenaica, etc.

This development certainly had its effect upon literary Greek. But here there was a tendency in authors to copy the use of other dialects than their own—either because the dialect in question had been used successfully in the literary genre being attempted, or because the people who spoke it were politically or culturally dominant. As a result three different literary languages were in use from the end of the sixth century and the beginning of the fifth.

The first one was basically Ionic, and was used, for example, by the first prose writers up to Herodotus; the other two were fundamentally Doric—one used in Greece (cf. Pindar and Bacchylides), the other in the West (cf. the two Stesichori, Epicharmus, and later Archimedes). It must be understood, however, that each of these authors altered, modified, or mutilated the adopted model to suit his own tastes.

At the end of the fifth century, however, Attic became the common language partly because of Athenian cultural supremacy and also because the Sophistic movement was creating a uniform intellectual atmosphere. Gorgias, a Sicilian Greek, was one of the earliest to write in Attic. A new prose was shaped at Athens: one that no longer shifted from form to form, but, free from poetic conventions, was dominated by logic and rationalism. It loved to talk of mankind, the city and concrete reality, and, therefore, of history, science, morals, and politics. It took varied forms with different authors, but in all of them it was sober, precise, measured, as subtle as could be, capable of expressing irony, and of making a point understood by barely alluding to it.

Alexander's conquests had a decisive influence on the use of Greek as the official language of the Macedonian empire: not only in areas such as Aegean Asia where it had been spoken for centuries by the Greek colonists, and, side by side with Aramaic which had spread with the Persian empire, by the indigenous people. It was used also in the predominantly Iranic areas such as Pontus and Cappadocia; in Syrian and Mesopotamian zones where the Semitic languages, especially Aramaic, were dominant; in Egypt; and as far distant as India. It is true that after a few decades the following three countries broke away politically: India in 316 and again near 100, Bactria about 246 and again in 188, and Parthia (with the Arsacids) in 247 and 188. But in less distant parts of these areas Greek lasted as the language of the upper classes, of the well-educated, and of the people in the Greek cities, against the earlier languages and dialects used by the commoners and country people.

This Greek, the Attic *koiné*, was used everywhere in the Hellenistic world. It penetrated into Macedonia and was taken by the Macedonian conquerors throughout their vast empire through court channels and by the Graeco-Macedonian colonies. It was an Attic different enough from the genuine one spoken at Athens; while it had lost some of its own peculiarities it had been influenced by the other Greek dialects, especially Ionic, and by the acceptance of some barbarian neologisms. A common language of this kind is quite well known to us through Egyptian papyri and the translation of the Bible by the 'Seventy'. All the other dialects spoken in the Aegean Greek world gave way before its slow advance.

Much the same thing happened later to the Doric literary languages, and especially to those of the Peloponnese which were mainly Corinthian in origin, but had also spread in the Graeco-Italian world through the dominance of Syracuse and were current in north-western Greece. Even if the dialects persisted in popular usage, they were no longer employed in literature, except in a few areas such as Laconia. A tidy version of the vulgate tongue, with its Attic base, came to be used by the non-Athenian Hellenistic prose writers: they all expressed themselves clearly but their manner tended to be heavy, abstract, monotonous, and without elegance. The poets continued to use the traditional dialects for particular genres but their work is mostly an erudite and painstaking mosaic.

It is worth our reviewing briefly the various qualities and types of Greek civilization which succeeded in imposing themselves on the Hellenistic world. In the parts of Asia Minor nearest the Aegean, where for centuries Greek colonies had clustered on the shores and their language had penetrated the interior, many new Greek cities had been founded by the Diadochi, the Seleucids, and the lords of Pergamum, Bithynia, and Pontus. At least fifty of these cities formed a sort of ethnic girdle behind the coastal zone. As inscriptions show, the spread of Greek language and culture was massive although, especially in the east and centre, the indigenous languages were not completely obliterated; they were confined to country areas. The most famous Greek centres for literary production were Cos, Samos, Ephesus, Rhodes, Lampsacus, Byzantium, Chalcedon, Pergamum, Perge, and Nicomedia.

In Cilicia there already existed old Greek colonies such as Soloi and Mallus, and the Diadochi and the Seleucids had formed others by settling Macedonian veterans and Greek colonists. Here Greek penetration went fairly deep. The court of the Seleucids gathered together writers and philosophers from all over Greece, and they set up their schools there. The Hellenization of southern Syria was less strong, but always marked: they had already had phil-hellene dynasts, such as Strato of Sidon about 370; the Diadochi founded a Graeco-Macedonian 'dodecapolis' in Transjordan; and the Seleucids, later followed by Pompey, stationed a number of new Greek colonies there. But the political discontent and persistence of indigenous cultures, especially that of the Hebrews, worked against Hellenization.

In heavily populated Mesopotamia, the seat of a thousand-year-old civilization, the few Greek cities founded by Alexander, the Diadochi, and the Seleucids were more centres for absorbing Oriental culture than for the diffusion of Greek values. However they did not lack indigenous writers who used Greek, such as Berosus, Diogenes, and Seleucus of Seleucia.

The Greek sites founded by Alexander and the Seleucids farther to the east were quickly paralysed when the areas in which they lay broke away politically, even when their new dynasts wanted to adopt Greek ways.

Finally in Egypt where Alexander had added Alexandria to the old trading stations at Naucratis, and the Ptolemies had founded Ptolemais and several outposts on the Red Sea, the Greeks spread as colonists even in the country districts; and for long periods Mediterranean regions with ancient Greek civilizations, such as the Cyclades and Cyrenaica, depended politically on Egypt.

These Egyptian Greeks preserved their own language and succeeded in converting to its use the educated portion of the Semitic element in the country, namely the Jews, who, especially in Alexandria, constituted one of the fundamental elements of the population. But though many of these Greeks became the dominant cultural element at the court and in the country, so much so that Egypt became one of the great Greek literary centres—they never succeeded in eclipsing the indigenous language and culture of Egypt although they won over some of the better-educated people such as Manetho.

In any case the establishment of the Hellenistic *koiné* was not entirely uniform, even in language. The accurate observer will notice perceptible differences in the Greek manifestations in different areas: each one reveals its own tendencies in taste, customs, and literary production.

When Rome gradually extended its dominion in the Asiatic and most of the Oriental world, it did not attempt the impossible task of substituting Latin for Greek as the cultivated language. Aware of the revival that was taking place, except in a few areas, of earlier languages and civilizations with Iranic, Semitic, Syrian, and Egyptian roots, Rome was content to protect the Greek culture of the upper classes. This was achieved by supporting Greek teachers of Grammar, and by the creation of more Greek colonies especially in the more inland Anatolian areas and also in Syria, even though sometimes there were competing Latin elements in these colonies. Even though the Arsacids of Parthia, and other dynasts outside the confines of the empire, indulged in the knowledge and diffusion of Greek language and culture, Rome was not able to stop the reappearance of Aramaic and Arabian speech in Syria and Mesopotamia, nor of the Iranic languages in Pontus and Cappadocia.

f. *Italic Languages*

In the last centuries of the ancient world the production of inscriptions by the various peoples of diverse races who had inhabited Italy before and after the Roman conquest slowed down. The greater part of the Etruscan inscriptions, from Etruria proper, and those from the short-lived Tyrrhenian empire—to the south, east, north-west, and in part of the Po valley to the north—come from the fifth to the third centuries, which period must have seen the *floruit* of Etruscan literature. The Po valley has revealed a variety of inscriptions. There are several groups attributable to the North Etruscans, and conceivably a few texts founded on Ligurian: later on we shall have something to say about the Celtic texts. But there are also about 200 Venetic inscriptions of Illyrian type, comparable to some extent with the 200 or so Messapian inscriptions of the fourth century and later from Puglie. At many places on the coasts of Magna Graecia and Sicily Greek dialects continued to be spoken and written. In inland Sicily the Siculans and Sicanians cut inscriptions of a 'First Italic' type; and from the extreme west of the island we have coin legends inscribed by the Elymians, and some texts from the Punic colonists. Similar Punic inscriptions are found also in Sardinia, though there they were still using primitive pre-Indo-European dialects.

We have yet to speak of the 'Italic' languages of the continent. The areas where 'First Italic' dialects were spoken got modified because of the movements of the Oscan and Umbrian 'Second Italic' speaking peoples; both dialect groups were also affected by Latinization. Of the three most important linguistic events in Italy in the second half of the first millennium BC we shall discuss later the consequences of the Celtic migration. The others were the Sabellic migration and the Roman conquest with the Latinization it brought about.

Between the sixth and fourth centuries the Oscan and Umbrian peoples were on the move, and to some extent became superimposed on each other. The consequence was a linguistic change over much of the Italian peninsula, from the central districts to the extreme south. This affected the peoples of European speech, the First Italici, and also the Iapygians and Greek colonists: it also affected the survivors of pre-Indo-European speakers on the coasts of the Adriatic and Etruria. The displacement of these people carried a southward movement by Umbrians, Oscans, and the Volsci—a mixture of the two; this wedged itself between the Latins and the Ausones and Aurunci as far as Antium.

The southward migration of these Oscan bands had various results. Their first movement founded the Picentes, Praetuttii, Vestini, Paeligni, Marrucini, Marsi, and Frentani. The second founded the Samnites (Hirpini, Penti, Caudini, and Carecini), who submerged the Ausones and Opici but also created the Campanians. The third created the Lucanians, from whom the Bruttii were a later offshoot; and this time the Oenotrian Italici were submerged, and the very existence of the Greek colonies in southern Italy was imperilled. Naturally, the differences between the various Oscan dialects are largely due to fusions with earlier peoples. The inscriptions show evidence of hybrid language, for example the mixture of Etruscan and Campanian which followed the expansion of Etruscan power.

The advance of Oscan speech was not halted even at the Straits of Messina, because the Siculans employed strong bands of Oscan mercenaries, especially Campanians and Samnites, in the fifth and fourth centuries. The Oscan penetration, either as new citizens or as conquerors, in both Greek and non-Greek cities, had the effect of introducing a marked Oscan element into the island. This was denounced as a grave danger in the letters attributed to Plato, and is borne out on inscriptions and coins.

Romanization of Italy. Generally speaking, Romanization did not make the ancient pre-Roman languages of Italy disappear. But it gradually substi-

tuted Latin for literary and administrative use and in the exchanges
between educated people. At the same time vulgar usage in the cities, and
even more in the country, declined into dialects heavily larded with Latin.
Just as in modern Italy there are both a literary language and a number
of dialects, so in ancient times too there was a form of bilingualism
between Latin and local dialects.

The penetration of Latin as the educated language had various and diverse
phases. At the beginning it was spread by the Roman and Latin colonists
planted in territories of foreign speech; individual Latins were enrolled in
rustic tribes; and the Roman armies were temporarily stationed in the
various regions. Trade, too, was made easier by new methods of communication. Later on, in every part occupied by Rome, in the Marsic country and
in Umbria, in Apulia and Picenum, hybrid blends of Roman and indigenous
peoples were formed, as we see from inscriptions.

With the system inaugurated at the beginning of the fourth century, of
granting Roman citizenship which they could exercise in Rome, to the
inhabitants of allied cities, Latin spreadi n the *municipia*; but at the same time
some of the new citizens migrated to Rome and brought their foreign speech
to the city. But from then on educated people in the cities became systematically and spontaneously bilingual, speaking Latin and a local dialect at the
same time. This explains, for example, the request from the Cumaeans in
180 to Rome for permission to use Latin in their forum (Livy, XI, 42). It
explains too why, from the beginning of the second half of the third century,
so many of the most famous writers of Latin did not come from Latium.
Naevius came from Campania; Livius Andronicus from Tarentum; Pacuvius
from Brundisium; Ennius from the country of the Sallentini; Plautus from
Umbria; Accius from Picenum. The temporary flood of imported slaves of widely
different origins no more than mildly upset the balance of this development.

Let us repeat that it was only gradually that the various Italic languages
ceased to be written. They were preserved in everyday speech and were the
distant base of the modern dialects, the mixture of Latin and native languages
spoken in every part of Italy. This is why Oscan was still written in the first
century of the empire at Pompeii; why, at the time of Strabo, a few kilometres from Rome the Falisci spoke a different language from the Latins;
why Dionysius of Halicarnassus says in the time of Augustus that Etruscan
still existed. According to Arrian, Rhaetian and Celtic were still spoken in
Hadrian's time: about AD 175 Oscan, Greek, Etruscan, and Celtic were
spoken, according to Aulus Gellius. Apuleius says that the Sicilians were
trilingual: they spoke Siculan, Latin, and Greek.

The persistence of the ancient pre-Roman languages existing in a Latinized
form side by side with the Latin of the educated classes, and the influence
they had on each other, explain the regional quality of the Latin used even
by great writers if born outside Latium (cf. Livy's *Patavinitas*). This is all
the more true of the Latin used by educated people in particular areas

(according to Cicero, *Brutus*, 171, in the Celticized zones). It also explains hybrid constructions of names of persons and places.

We can also understand in this way the persistence in modern Italian dialects, and through them in literary Italian, of ancient word-formations and of phonetic phenomena derived from Ligurian, Sardinian, Corsican, Greek, Etruscan, Celtic, Oscan, Umbrian, or Venetic. We can see the reason for the differences and the frontiers between the dialects: they conform in general with those of the ancient pre-Roman languages. Compare, for example, the area of Celtic dialects in modern Italy with the part of the Po valley occupied in ancient times by the Celts. Compare also the neighbouring dialects, Ligurian, Venetic, and Middle-Italic, with the old areas of the Ligurians, Veneti and Italici.

Romanization of the Provinces. What we have said about the Romanization of Italy was repeated on a much larger scale in the western and northern Roman world. In general the rest of the world was left to its Greek culture, except in the east where Greek lost ground in the revival of native languages. We shall return to this argument in Part III, and shall only consider it briefly here. At the end of the third century and in the first decades of the second century BC power and policies pivoted round Scipio Africanus the Elder, and his belief was that the conquered countries, Carthage, Macedonia, and the Seleucid territories, having become allies, should, in collaboration with Rome, undertake the task of civilizing the neighbouring barbarian world. In the Mediterranean world there should be three areas: one Latinized, one Greek, and the third Punicized: this triple division lasted for some time. But the allied states became subjects towards the middle of the second century, and one of the three areas, the Punic, gradually lost its function. It lay between the Latin and Greek areas and was encroached upon, and so reduced in size, by both of them. At first Punic literary works were translated into Greek (Hanno, Himilco and Mago); then Greek was used by Carthaginian writers, such as Hannibal, for his books on strategy, and later by the Numidian king Juba II. Finally Punic scholars migrated to Greek countries—Hasdrubal, known as Clitomachus, is an example; he was an academic teacher in Athens from 127 to 110.

At the same time Numidian scholars stopped writing in Punic and began to write in Latin. There are many examples: Hiempsal II, cited by Sallust; the comic writer Terence; and the naturalist, Turanius Gracilis. Meanwhile the classic works of Punic culture, like those of Mago, were translated into Latin as well as Greek.

From then on the Mediterranean world, and in general the Roman-dominated world, split into two dominant linguistic zones, Greek and Latin. There were a few temporary interruptions. Greek entered the Western world through Sicily and the area round Massilia; and Latin entered the East in parts of Asia Minor and Syria where Roman colonies were wedged between

Greek and Aramaic and other native spheres of influence. This led to a
Syriac literature written in Latin, of which Publilius Syrus the writer of
mimes is a prototype as early as the first century B C.[1]

Rome had no illusions that it could supplant Greek culture in the Hellenic
and Hellenistic countries. On the contrary it supported it against the revival
of pre-Alexandrian Oriental languages. It created two concepts, which were
vigorously asserted and realized by Caesar. As educated people knew the
two languages, all scholarly works produced throughout the empire could
remain bilingual in Greek and Latin; in the metropolis, Rome, this bilingualism was almost universal. The second concept was that Latinization should
be the only process in the western, non-Hellenized section of the empire:
in the former Carthaginian Africa, Spain, Gaul and its adjacent areas in
Italy, and in the central Balkans north of the Hellenized regions.

In all these areas Romanization was much slower than it had been in Italy;
this was partly because of the different ethnic background, and also because
of the slow rate of colonization and of grants of Roman citizenship. As a
result the linguistic assimilation, and the more far-reaching mergers and
hybridization, were hindered. In each of these provincial zones the original
language flourished in everyday speech; the indigenous Iberian and Celtic
languages while continuing to be universally used in ordinary life were slowly
transformed into a local Latin 'patois', which served as the base for the later
languages.[2] See for example the surviving Celto-Iberian inscriptions from the
second century A D. By the first century B C we find Latin writers of Spanish
origin, such as the two Hygini; and from Narbonese Gaul came the grammarian M. Antonius Gnipho, the two poets Cornelius Gallus and Terentius
Varro Atacinus, and slightly later the historian Pompeius Trogus.

In the Hellenized East, Rome had been unable to stop the ethnic regional
differences from having a profound influence on both spoken language and
literature. This phenomenon became even more noticeable in the area which
got slowly Latinized. In these there not only developed several distinct, and
distinguishable, kinds of vulgar Latin, but also several forms of the literary
language, each giving a fairly clear stamp to the literature of a particular region.

Evolution of Roman Speech. All this was important in the development of
the spoken language in the city of Rome. Its ethnic structure was being
completely transformed by the influx of *cives Romani* who came from widely
different subject countries, and also by the complex origin of the slaves
and freedmen who congregated there. This state of affairs was to be more
marked during the Imperial period, but could already be seen in the early
days of grants of citizenship, which started with Camillus in the fourth
century B C. Numerous neologisms, with grammatical and phonetic features
of a non-Latin type, thus could enter Rome from the Oscan, Umbrian,
Etruscan, and Greek countries. At the same time various forms of literature
gradually made their way to the capital. From the Oscan country came the

Fabulae Atellanae, masked plays, both in the original and in translation. From Caere, where the fourth-century Romans sent their sons to school (Livy, IX, 36), and from other deeply Hellenized Etruscan towns, came writings on history, religion, and augury, together with didactic and poetical works, the products of those Tyrrhenians who had once been masters of Rome. Some of these were in translation, such as Tarquitius Priscus' works. Falerii introduced the Fescennine verses: and from the Hellenic country, where the Sibylline Books had come in the sixth century from Cumae, Rome received the translation of the *Odyssey* by Livius Andronicus. Meanwhile the Messapian Ennius translated the 'Sacred History' of Euhemerus into Latin; and the first Roman historians, before Cato's day, were writing their annals in Greek.

g. *Celtic Languages*

According to Caesar there were special ties between the Goidelic-speaking Belgae who entered Gaul in the Hallstatt period in the first Celtic migration, and the Armoricans, maritime people who lived between the mouths of the Seine and Loire; and it is certainly the case that the two peoples acted together during Caesar's campaigns. From archaeological evidence one may believe that the split occurred about the fifth century. At the same time Caesar himself, and he is confirmed in this by Pliny and Ptolemy, asserts that the Celts in Britain derived from the Belgae and Armoricans; and he cites as evidence their linguistic affinities and the racial names they have in common, as well as the co-operation they gave to the people across the channel. Archaeological evidence confirms that up to the fifth century BC Britain was occupied by pre-Celtic, and, consequently pre-Indo-European, peoples, who slowly accepted Celtic civilization from the coast of Gaul opposite;[3] this continued when these territories were invaded by the second wave of Celts, commonly called 'Cymric'.

Tradition recognizes Celtiberi in the Iberian peninsula, and history tells of the struggle Rome had with a people of this name in the third century. The presence of Celtic elements, mixed in various ways with the pre-Celtic population, is attested by inscriptions, coin-legends, and place-names; between these and the Goidelic dialects there are fairly certain affinities,[4] but with the Cymric dialects affinities are less common. This may be the result of the number of superimposed invasions, and of forms of hybridism which were certainly different, and possibly more complete, than those found in Gaul.

From the sixth century onwards we find a third area of Celtic civilization in the Danube valley, and this view is confirmed by tradition. It was due to conquest by the Celts of Gaul, or rather to their partial return to countries where they had lived in earlier times,[5] and where they had closely intermingled with Illyrian elements.

The fourth Celtic invasion, that into the valley of the Po, is better known from tradition, written texts, and archaeology. Here the Celts entered the western and central zones before they moved into the south-east. And where they merged with the Ligurians and North Etruscans they created a linguistic and ethnic mixture. Tradition recognized this hybridism and was uncertain whether certain peoples should be called Ligurians or Celts; it is supported by the language found on the so-called Lepontine inscriptions which are written in a mixture of Celtic and Ligurian. On the other hand the inscriptions of the so-called North Etruscans in the eastern area are a mixture between Celtic and Etruscan. It is only in the Apennine mountain regions that the Ligurian element remains pure as we see in the inscribed *menhir* of Luna.

The fifth and farthest Celtic expansion was towards the east, and is proved by the ethnic wedge of 'Galatic' people who settled in the middle of Anatolia during the third century. They divided the Hellenized western area from the eastern zone in which Iranic culture revived. The Galatians gradually contaminated their Celtic dialect, as is shown by their personal and place-names, with predominantly Greek admixtures, which led to the Romans describing them as the Gallo-Graeci; their dialect also acquired Phrygian features from the population they had supplanted.

The other Celtic languages were Latinized in varying degrees: a phenomenon which in our period was well advanced in the Po valley, Narbonensis, and Celtiberia. The block grants of Latin and later of Roman citizenship given by Pompey and by Caesar, first to the Cispadani and then to the Transpadani, made a great contribution to Latinization in the Po valley. The most obvious result of this rapid Romanization, which did not kill the Celtic dialects but transformed them into a Celtic-Latin patois, is provided by the Latin literature written by men born in the Celtic part of the Po valley. As early as the first half of the second century BC the Insubrian Caecilius Statius was writing his plays; in later periods we have Valerius Cato, Cinna of Brixia, Bibaculus from Cremona, and also Cornelius Nepos, Catius and Albucius Silo. They prove that the Celtic zone was not slower in Romanization than either the Venetic, where Catullus, Aemilius Macer, Vitruvius, and Livy had their homes, or the Etruscan area north of the Apennines, which produced Virgil of Mantua.

We have already mentioned Narbonensis. In Spain the Latin inscriptions allow us to put the fusion of Latin and Celtic in the Celtiberian region back to a period earlier than the Christian era. In general the languages of southern Spain seem to have disappeared earlier than those of Celtiberia and of the north and west.

h. *German Languages*

The first expansions of Germanic populations outside present-day north-western Germany, which had been their temporary home, were probably those beyond the Rhine into Belgica. At the same time, or possibly earlier, the Celtic Belgae may have reached this region. In any case it is probable that it was the expansion of the Germans towards the south and the west that caused the Celts to move into the homes they occupied in historical times. The Helvetians, for example, still remembered having once occupied the region between the Hercynian forest, the Rhine, and the Main (Tacitus, *Germ.*, 28).

In Caesar's time[6] the majority of the inhabitants of Belgica, that is to say all those outside 'Belgium' (which was the term he used to describe the purely Celtic area), were mixed with Germans from beyond the Rhine. These Germans formed the greater part of the population even though they had quickly adopted Celtic language and customs because of the higher level of civilization among the Belgae. How this came about is clear: it was not only that the Germans wanted conquest but also that the Celts, who needed help in their own internal struggles, invited them in. Groups of Germans and Germanized Belgae then crossed over from Belgica to Britain at the end of the previous period and at the beginning of our own. In Britain we find Menapic and Caledonian Germans (Tacitus, *Agricola*, 11) and Tacitus himself asserts linguistic similarities between some of the Britons and the German Oestii.

The first mention of German soldiers penetrating into Italy in an expedition against the Romans is given in the *Fasti Triumphales*, under 222 BC, which include a triumph over the Germans. These Germans were 'Gaesates', that is mercenaries of the Celts armed with the *gaesum*.

A century later we hear of the great expedition of Cimbrians and Teutons, which first succeeded and then came to grief with great slaughter. They roamed round the Roman provinces and the non-Roman areas of south-western Europe in their search for land in which to settle. Because of their constant movements and the disastrous result they could not modify language in any perceptible way. The first real contact between Rome and the German world occurred with Caesar, whose campaign in Gaul had three main aims: to save Helvetia from the Germans; to prevent the hordes under Ariovistus, whom he chased out, establishing themselves permanently in Gaul and bringing in other Germans from beyond the Rhine; and thirdly so to weaken the Germanized tribes of the Belgae that he discouraged Germans from crossing the Rhine to reinforce them. Augustus later was to carry the same policy east of the Rhine, but with impermanent results. The work of Romanization in this region falls in the period following the one we are now describing.

2. WRITING

a. *Chinese*

In the field of Chinese writing the important event of this period is the reform, better described as a codification or standardization, carried out in

213 BC by Li Ssŭ, the great minister of the first emperor of China. It was in the main a unifying measure, which resulted in a list of about 3,300 characters being compiled. For this purpose Li Ssŭ made use of a system which had already existed for some time, the system of 'radicals'; this he codified, and gave it official sanction. Most Chinese characters belong in fact to the class in which a radical and a phonetic are compounded, the sixth (*hsing-shêng*) of the classes mentioned in Part I. The importance of this act was immense: it assured the uniformity of the written language, in whatever spoken dialect a written passage might be read aloud. From this time on there were no changes in the internal structure of the Chinese characters. All that happened was an enormous increase in their number during the course of centuries, partly to answer new needs, but partly also because they got invented arbitrarily without any real necessity for them. The form of the characters was initially still the Seal form: in the earliest period, that of the Warring States, the Great Seal script was used (*ta-ch'uan*), but later the Little Seal script (*hsiao-ch'uan*). In the official script (*li-shu*) adopted by the Ch'in chancery, and inherited later by the Han, a step had already been taken in the direction of more cursive forms. From that script was derived the formal style of writing (*ch'iai-shu*) used under the Han dynasty, and this corresponds in almost every respect to the modern form. The adoption of the writing brush, mentioned below, meant that a finer and more artistic *ductus*, with elegant curves, came into fashion, a flowing and continuous script instead of the angular scribbling produced by the old reed pen. The Chinese ideogram in this way could become a work of art; and in fact calligraphy reached the level of one of the great arts in China, often being appreciated as highly as painting.

Writing material was revolutionized by the invention of the brush pen, ascribed by tradition to Meng T'ien, a Ch'in general, about 215 BC. But we have already seen in Part I that the brush pen was in existence almost a thousand years earlier: it seems that Meng T'ien's service consisted mainly in perfecting its construction and popularizing its use.

For a long time writing was still on tablets of wood and bamboo: but in addition silk came into increasing use, especially after the brush had completely ousted the reed pen.

b. *Indian*

The first records of the new Indian scripts are the inscriptions of Aśoka in the third century BC. These presuppose a considerable previous history, but at present we cannot determine what that history was.

Common to all Indian writings are their syllabic nature and their very strict and precise adherence to the facts of the language. The unit in writing is the *akṣara*, which indicates a simple or compound syllabic sound, which always ends in a vowel. Short a is always inherent in the consonant, while the other vowels and diphthongs are indicated by special signs placed above, below, or alongside the *akṣara*.

The alphabets used on Aśokan inscriptions are two in number, Brahmī and Kharoṣṭhī. The former, which spread all over the sub-continent and is the parent of all modern Indian scripts, is *par excellence* the alphabet of India. It has thirty-nine simple (i.e. uncompounded) letters and is written from left to right. In Part I we have already discussed its possible origin. A southern variety of Brahmī seemingly isolated is the script of the stūpu of Bhattiprolu.

The history of Kharoṣṭhī writing, on the other hand, is very clear. This is a script written from right to left, confined to the extreme north-west in India, but employed also in the Indian trading colonies of central Asia. It is evidently an adaptation of the Aramaic script to meet the needs of a Prakrit dialect. Aramaic was the official alphabet of the Achaemenid government, and had consequently been known for centuries in the old Persian satrapy of India when this area, which now forms part of Afghanistan and of Pakistan, passed under Maurya domination about 300 BC (we have inscriptions of Aśoka in Aramaic). To produce Kharoṣṭhī, the Aramaic script was probably recast with the Brahmī script as a model. This we may suppose not only from the form of several letters but from the fact that the governing phonetic principle is the same in the two scripts, which are both of syllabic type and adhere closely to the actual sounds. Kharoṣṭhī writing, though always confined to a very narrow area, remained in use until the end of our next period; then it became extinct. It left no survivals either in India or elsewhere, and must therefore be regarded as a phenomenon which was isolated in time and space and had no consequences for the history of writing.

c. *Aramaic and its Derivatives*

From the moment in the sixth century when Aramaic suddenly attained a wide expansion and was taken up as the language of trade and administration between the various parts of the Persian empire to the west of the Tigris, there was a practically corresponding growth in the use of the Aramaic alphabet even where earlier systems survived.

The Hebrew zone is an instance. From the time of the Maccabean kingdom (second century BC) to its final subjection by Hadrian (second century AD) coins prove the persistence of a revised form of Old Hebrew in nationalistic circles. At the same time, by a fusion between Aramaic and Old Hebrew writing, a new form, the 'Square Hebrew Alphabet', became established: its earliest known document is dated 176 BC. This new system later became common, but for the first centuries of its use we have only sparse evidence on ossuaries, sepulchral inscriptions, and papyri (the earliest is from the beginning of the second century AD); only much later is it found used for biblical texts.

The Palmyra script is fairly close to Square Hebrew, and its earliest documents go back to the last decades of the first century BC, but it is attested with several hundred texts up to the fall of Palmyra in AD 274, from Palmyra itself and in different parts of the ancient world where Palmyrenes happened to be living. It is found in two forms, monumental and cursive (sometimes vertical) with a few ligatures between letters.

Aramaic alphabets that penetrated farther south underwent more rapid diversification, with a predominance of cursive forms. Nabataean was one of these, attested from the third century BC, and from it neo-Sinaitic was derived; but for the latter we have evidence only from the Christian era (see Part III).

Farther east Aramaic spread on a very wide scale, to some extent in the period with which we are dealing. This was true of the Iranic zone: in the north-east of Iran they used the so-called Arsacid Pehlevīk script, and in the south-west Sassanid Pehlevīk or *pārsīk*, both of them derived from Aramaic towards the end of the third or in the second century BC. Only the cursive forms have come down to us, most of them rather late, but we have a Pehlevīk document on parchment from the first century found in Persian Kurdistan.

For southern Arabian alphabets, see Part III, Chapter XIV.

d. *Ethiopian*

The Ethiopian zone, and Nubia in general, officially used the Egyptian language and script for a long time, even after the country had made itself independent of Egypt. But about 200 BC the local language gained supremacy; and a new system of writing was created for it, of which the oldest documents date from the second and first centuries BC. They are in two forms. The first one was hieroglyphic but with twenty-three signs (including vowels), almost all of them alphabetic. They differed from Egyptian in phonetic value, form, and direction. The second was cursive and it is subject to argument whether its characters were a simplification of Egyptian demotic, or a derivation from the southern Arabian alphabets. The evidence is discussed in Part III.

e. *Punic Scripts*

In the Carthaginian area the Punic script was converted from the second century onwards into the neo-Punic. This had both a lapidary and a cursive form. It carried frequent ligatures, had a number of local variations, and showed clearly the influence of Latin writing. It lasted for half a millennium, and was also used in Sardinia, where neo-Punic inscriptions are found from about 200 BC.

A derivative of Punic script, with some modifications and the addition of some old characters peculiar to the region, is the Libyo-Berber writing, which in its older form is sometimes called Numidian. Some of the evidence for it comes from bilingual inscriptions, in Libyan and Punic, Libyan and neo-Punic, or Libyan and Latin. There must also be a relationship between

(a) *Silver denarius: oath of the Italian Allies during the Social Wars*

(b) *Coin of the 'gens hostilia' with presumed head of Vercingetorix*

(c) *80 drachms, copper coin with head of Cleopatra, 45–30 BC*

(a)　　　　　　　　　　　　　　　　　[M.C.

(b)　　　　　　　　　　　　　　　　　[M.C.

(c)　　　　　　　　　　　　　　　　　[Berlin

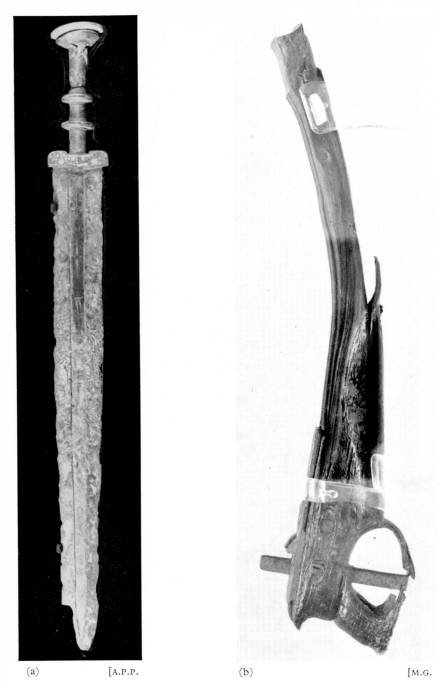

(a)   [A.P.P.   (b)   [M.G.

24 (a) *Bronze sword from Li-yu'in Shansi, Warring States period*
      (b) *Crossbow of the Han dynasty*

the Punic and Iberian scripts, of which there were three main types, Turdeta-nian (or Andaluso-Turdetanian), the writing of southern Hispania Citerior, and the writing of northern Citerior. The evidence for these Iberian systems consists of coin-legends and short inscriptions on a variety of objects, going back to the fourth or third century BC and forward into the Roman imperial period. All of them probably possess the same Punic substratum, but local differences have been increased by the addition of certain characters and the modification of others. Various causes brought about these modifications. There was intrusion by old pre-Punic characters, peculiar to the districts in question and sometimes perhaps akin to Berber signs; new elements were drawn from the scripts of newer civilized peoples, Greeks and later Romans, with whom the Iberians came into contact; and Celtic features entered Spain when the Celtiberian people took shape.

f. *Greek Alphabets*

In the period after 500 BC the Greek alphabets continued to spread from the Hellenic colonial areas to the neighbouring countries of foreign speech. But sometimes alphabets of different colonies converged on the same spot; and in other Greek districts hybrid systems of writing resulted from the action of an imperial power within the region, or from the mixture of races in a single colony. The Etruscan alphabet, which derived from Cumae, is an example. At first we find two distinct types, one in Southern Etruria the other in Northern, but during the sixth and fifth centuries these became a single alphabet, with some letters modified from the originals, others abandoned, and one or two more invented (like the sign 8 used for f.). On the other hand when the Etruscans appeared as conquerors in Campania, and Etrusco-Campanian inscriptions began to be cut, we notice a new influence, coming directly from the Chalcidian Greek alphabets. Similarly when the Etruscans also extended their empire to certain parts of the Po valley they took their own alphabet with them, an alphabet distinct from the one of North Etruscan type which the country had previously used.

But meanwhile the Greek alphabets continued to have their effect, direct or indirect, on all the systems of writing which existed in the Mediterranean lands. They entered the Iberian peninsula through the Phocaean settlements, and came to the Sicans and Sicels of Sicily by way of various colonies, of which the chief were Selinus, Gela, Syracuse, Zancle, and Himera. In the Italian peninsula the Umbrians and Oscans got their Greek type of writing through the intermediary of the Etruscans, modifying and adding to it to suit their own idioms; but there are also Oscan inscriptions written in a straightforward Greek alphabet.

In Greece itself in 403 BC the Athenians decided to adopt the Ionic alphabet officially, though it did not come into general use for many years after this date. Within a few decades this had become the alphabet used generally by all Greeks, and the various systems of the previous centuries were forgotten. Meanwhile both the uncial and cursive scripts grew up by the side of the lapidary form and were used for manuscripts. From the time of Alexander the Great onwards changes in Greek cursive writing can be used to date Greek documents to a generation, if not a decade. Other alterations in the signs were made for calligraphic reasons, such as the addition of apices and other forms of ornamentation, and the use of ligatures, 'sigle', and other abbreviations. Accents and other phonetical signs were invented about 200 BC.

g. *Latin*

Our present period is that into which, with a few early exceptions, all the archaic monuments of Latin script fall, and even they are rare before the end of the third century. The script originally had twenty letters, but it had no aspirated sounds and therefore no letters to correspond with them. In the third century Z was dropped and G was added; in the first century Z was adopted again, and Y was added in the transcriptions of Greek words.

The progressive penetration of the Latin language into the Western countries conquered by Rome brought with it the spread of the Latin alphabet. It reached its farthest extension in the imperial period.

Latin inscriptions use ligatures to join two or three letters, especially at the ends of lines. Characteristic features are the standard systems evolved for abbreviations, and the way in which a point, or a number of points above one another, were used to separate words.

NOTES TO CHAPTER VIII

1. Professor A. Lesky points out, however, that Publilius (though probably born at Antioch) was educated in Rome.
2. Professor A. Tovar notes that although Strabo (III, p. 151), drawing on Artemidorus, implies that the Romanization of much of southern Spain was accomplished in the second century BC, yet there are Celto-Iberic inscriptions from this area three centuries later.
3. For the strongly held view, supported by Professor P. Bosch-Gimpera, that Celts crossed to Britain long before 500 BC, see above, Part I, p. 106, note 28.
4. Professor A. Tovar expresses confidence that the Celto-Iberic dialect is closer to Goidelic than to any other form of Celtic spoken in Gaul or Britain.
5. Dr P. Oliva calls attention to the mingling of these Danuvian Celts with peoples of Illyrian stock, exemplified by the Eravisci who lived near Aquincum (Buda) in Roman imperial days.
6. Professor F. M. Heichelheim notes that we have only Caesar's own word for this view— though there is no good reason for rejecting it.

CHAPTER IX

THE DEVELOPMENT OF TECHNIQUES, TRADE, AND SCIENTIFIC LIFE

I. CONTACTS BETWEEN THE GREEK AND MIDDLE EASTERN WORLDS

THE period from 500 BC to the beginning of our era saw a gradual extension of contacts and cultural exchanges between the Greek colonies dotted round the Mediterranean on the one hand and the Eastern countries on the other. Moreover wider and more distant areas were becoming involved in both directions. The initial cultural relations of the previous period had been limited to the Aegean world, western Anatolia, Syria, and Egypt; and there had been alternating phases of intensity. Relations were highly developed in the Minoan and Mycenaean Ages, declined in the Geometric period which followed, then recovered again in the seventh and sixth centuries, and were finally weakened again after the conquests which made the Persians masters of south-west Asia and Egypt.

At the beginning of our period the Greek world had come near to destruction at the hands of the Persians and of the other barbarians who assailed it simultaneously in the West.[1] The victories of 480 and 479 put an end to their enemies' hopes. In the eastern Mediterranean there followed a period of sporadic warfare and armed vigilance, until half-way through the fifth century the Greeks made peace with the Persians, to free their own hands for their fruitless domestic struggles for hegemony in Hellas. This gave Persia the chance of greater intervention in Greek affairs in the period when Sparta was succeeding Athens, and Thebes Sparta, as the leading state in Greece. The Persians contributed money to help in extending these conflicts, since through them alone could the Great King exercise control of the Greek states amid the shifting balance of power. The culmination of this phase of history was reached with the Peace of Antalcidas in 387–386. Persia's *de facto* supremacy in the last decade of the fifth century and at various periods of the fourth was of decisive importance in intensifying cultural relations between Greece and the East, though it is very difficult, if not impossible, to be clear whether Greece had greater influence on the Middle East in these years or the Middle East on Greece. All the countries which had been Persian, and others beyond them, were then conquered in the war begun by Philip of Macedon and completed by Alexander. But so far from interrupting the complicated pattern of give-and-take the conquest actually promoted it, though in some areas the Greek element came clearly to the fore. It emerged as the predominant force in the large cities, both old and new, in which the

Greek population was concentrated; and this was especially true of the
great *metropoleis*, where cultural foundations pursued scientific work
according to the canons laid down by Aristotle and his school.

The resulting synthesis of Greek and Oriental cultures was a far-reaching
phenomenon which lasted for many centuries, although the areas affected
and their political masters were often changing. The first to get detached
from the Hellenistic kingdoms were the areas farthest east, where Hellenic
ways survived up to a point, but were gradually reinforced by native forms;
of these the Parthian kingdom is an example. Then one by one the Hellenistic
powers gave place to Rome. But instead of attempting to Romanize its
eastern possessions, Rome encouraged the growth of Greek culture, or
rather of the combined Hellenic and Oriental culture which was already
dominant in the East. This had marked influence on every other part of its
great Mediterranean empire. At the same moment new routes and new
trade relations were taking shape between that empire and the Far East,
carrying western commerce as far as China.

The advent of the Roman empire entailed therefore a vast increase in the
cultural relations between East and West. Every country felt the effect,
from India and China to Spain and Gaul. The next stage is to examine the
process under various heads—production, manufacturing methods, commercial techniques, and scientific advance—whether single peoples were responsible for them, or a number of people combining or borrowing from one
another as a result of the unity of their cultures. We may start with agriculture.

2. MAJOR TECHNIQUES

a. *Agricultural Advances*

Conditions in the Far East. Water control in China was mostly a concern of
the central government. It was indeed one of its major duties and responsi-
bilities in a country where intensive agriculture (which meant its whole
economic life) depended so much on flood-control and artificial irrigation:
a strong, authoritarian central government was best qualified for com-
mandeering and co-ordinating the huge mass of labourers required. This
function of the government is much more important in China than in the
West, and it has been regarded as the main characteristic of Oriental despot-
ism (theory of K. A. Wittfogel); an extreme view which does not seem to be
supported by the historical facts.

It is in any case true that the power of Ch'in in the third century BC (and
the ensuing foundation of the Chinese empire) was based to a large extent
on great irrigation works in the Wei valley and on the possibility of sending
grain supplies to the fighting troops.

From the point of view of the state, canals served a double purpose: first
for the transport of taxes, i.e. for navigation; secondly for irrigation and

flood-control. The same applied to the great rivers, though with them the second purpose was more important. The problem of the Yellow river, of the enormous quantity of silt it carries and of its ruinous floods, is the central one in the history of Chinese hydraulic engineering.

Canal building began when the rise of private land ownership, and the simplification and consolidation of Chou feudalism into a few large-size regional states, made available both the manpower and the managerial organization necessary for the purpose. It coincided also more or less with the recognition of the fertilizing qualities of the loess slime carried by the western rivers. The first canal was perhaps the Hung-kou, which joined the Huang-ho, near K'ai-feng, with the Pien-ho (afterwards integrated in the Grand Canal); it was probably dug at the beginning of the fifth century BC. The great wars of the period saw several large enterprises inspired by military purposes, such as the digging of the Hai-kou, connecting the Huai with the Yangtze-kiang. It was ordered by Fu Ch'ai, ruler of Wu, in order to ensure supplies for his troops. Shao Hsin-ch'u (381–334) dug the Ch'ien-lu Pei in southern Honan, by a barrage on a northern tributary of the Han river.

Ch'in rule is marked by three great enterprises. They are: (1) The canal built by the engineer Chêng Kuo for the princes of Ch'in and Han. It diverted the Ching river along the foot of the northern hills, discharging it into the Lo river. The result was an irrigation canal of more than 100 miles, which was finished in 246 BC. It was repaired and renewed several times, and remains today one of the greatest hydraulic works of China.

(2) The Kuan-hsien canal in Szechwan. The governor Li Ping started it after 250 BC, and it was finished after his death about 230. The Min river is divided by a stone jutting into two channels. The eastern one is an irrigation canal and is led through a cutting about 100 feet high. Both are then sub-divided in lateral (526) and sublateral (c. 22,000) canals, all of which discharge into the Yangtze-kiang below Chiating. The maximum level is reached in June–July, the minimum in December–March. For more than two thousand years the local people have followed the advice of Li Ping, 'to clear out the beds and to keep the dykes low'; this is done by large annual works of dredging and repairs.

(3) In contrast the Ling-ch'u canal is intended for transportation. It joins two rivers in Kuang-hsi, i.e. between the Tung-t'ing lake and Canton. It seems to be the work of the first emperor Shih-huang-ti, built for supplying the army which was sent to the conquest of Yüeh (south China) in 219 BC. It involves a diversion of part of the Hsiang waters by means of a stone nose into an artificial canal on the hill slopes; and the canal goes to join the Kuei river.

Sluice gates appear at the end of the first century BC; but the greatest step towards a regulated internal navigation, i.e. the invention of lock-gates (double sluices), was not to come before the T'ang period.

Agriculture in China was the basis of economic life, and thus of paramount importance. This is reflected in an old ritual, the ceremonial hand-ploughing of a furrow in the precincts of the Temple of Heaven; it was done personally by the emperor on New Year's day, i.e. in the first half of February, and indicated the beginning of the agricultural year. It was one of the most sacred and cherished imperial privileges.

Agricultural technique varied according to the regions, but in the core of the Chinese lands (the lower Huang-ho) tilling was intensive and the procedure was very careful, almost equivalent to horticulture. The tools of this period are known only from the form of ideographs, from the shape of coins, and from scanty literary references. Foremost among agricultural implements was the *lei*, a digging fork, originating from the old Shang territory; and the *ssŭ*, a sort of hoe either of wood or of metal, probably originating from the Western territories. The plough was a late comer. Oxen were at first only employed for drawing carts. Some scholars maintain that ox-ploughing came into use between the fifth and the third centuries BC; but it appears that there is no literary evidence for it earlier than a passage of the *Han-shu* referring to *c.*90 BC. Of course, with the coming of the plough the *lei* and the *ssŭ* became mere supplementary tools; they did not, however, disappear; it was simply that their form underwent evolution.

What we know about Indian agriculture in this period derives only from stray references in Buddhist texts and from the somewhat schematized body of rules and prescriptions given in the *Arthaśāstra*; the latter, however, concerns more the administrative and fiscal aspects of farming. Agriculture centred round the village (*grāma*), surrounded by its arable lands (*grāma-kṣetra*). Smallholding was the rule, and cultivation was done directly by the owner. Landless labourers were despised and occupied a low place in society. Large estates were rare but did exist, usually in the hands of Brahmans. Village cattle were entrusted to a common herdsman (*gopālaka*); cattle-breeding was still important, although the gradual increase in cultivated land was reducing the amount of pasture. Cattle-lifting was a common evil and is mentioned fairly frequently in the epics. Village lands ended in wild jungle of which the products were exploited to a small extent in order to supplement agriculture. Of the technical side of farming we know next to nothing.[2]

In the Mediterranean Zone. With the growth of population in the Greek homeland it became increasingly necessary to increase cereal imports. This could be done partly by direct increase in home production, and partly through action by the Greek colonies scattered along the shores of the Mediterranean.[3] Grain, often in the form of tribute, was acquired from the native populations, who would accept in return Greek manufactured goods, both common ware and works of artistic merit. But at the same time Greece itself was making use of intensive methods of cultivation, fostered by the propaganda of didactic writers on the subject, such as Charmantides of Paros, Apollodorus of Lemnos, and Androtion of Athens. In this connection certain pages of Xenophon's *Oeconomicus* are of interest, as are also parts of the Theophrastus' *Historia Plantarum*. The rotation of crops was improved, the two-field system of grain alternating with fallow giving place to a three-field rotation of winter grain, summer grain, and fallow; and for the fallow year there was usually substituted a sowing of vegetables or fodder, the latter including lucerne, the 'Median' herb introduced from Persia. Many areas too had vineyards, oliveyards, and orchards of figs between the arable fields, and in some areas cereals actually gave way before these other products.

Except in places like Athens, where Solon's laws favoured the smallholders, and Sparta, where egalitarian methods prevailed, the land both of Greece and of the colonial world was at the beginning of our period still mainly in the hands of large owners or *gāmoroi*. But in many cities, such as Syracuse and Megara Hyblaea, the progress of democratic ideas led to revolution and the distribution of land among the lower classes, while in other places the liquid capital that was accumulating found an investment in land and promoted the formation of agricultural properties of medium size. In the next centuries the indebtedness of smallholders and the abundance of slave labour were factors favouring large estates, but there was a continual counter-movement in the direction of smaller properties; and these ups and downs were linked throughout with the struggle between farmers and capitalists for political power. The condition of the smallholders was later made worse by the use of slave labour. They were dispossessed of their lands and reduced to the status of a starving country proletariat, and all the while with the development of agricultural methods pasturage and arboriculture gained at the expense of cereal cultivation.

Before the Romans became masters of Italy Etruscan agriculture had reached a high level of prosperity. During their imperialist period they made known advanced methods of land reclamation and drainage, enabling the cultivation of areas which had earlier been fenland or ruined by floods. Their vast underground canals or tunnels in Latium are a memorable example. Conditions in the colonies of Magna Graecia were also flourishing until the region was seriously affected by the spread of malaria. Sicily made considerable strides towards becoming a granary for the export of cereals; but with the continuous growth of large fortunes there the *latifundia* based on pasturage and arboriculture made their appearance again, and the island turned instead to the export of wine, oil, and livestock products, such as hides and cheese.

When Etruscan rule in Latium ended, the large estates of the previous lords were divided into small plots for the native population, but these plots could not be exploited to provide all the food required. This was mainly on account of the deforestation carried out to enlarge the arable area, which increased the amount of flooding and made the abnormally shallow humus more easily washed away. While the older lands were turned to pasture it was continually necessary to find new ones, and this was one of the main

reasons for the spread of Roman conquests. It also meant that after conquests
had been won part of the population of Latium would be settled as members
of the rural tribes in colonies, moving farther afield as time went on; and it
was also responsible for the practice of regarding one third of conquered
territory as *ager publicus* at the disposal of Rome. The converse process is
also noticeable: many of the wars in central Italy resulted from the need felt
by various hill peoples to move their flocks down in winter and consequently
to contend with peoples already in occupation for possession of the plain
country below.

In the third and second centuries BC individual assignations of land and
colonial foundations continued. The social policy of Scipio Africanus the
Elder tended also to favour smallholdings, and then came the Gracchan
distributions, plots being taken from *latifundia* which had been created by
arbitrary squatting on public land. With the smallholdings resulting from
these and other factors came a revival of Italian grain production. But
factors working in the opposite direction made this revival precarious. War
devastations, and the ruin of smallholders who were conscripted for military
service and lost their land through debt and mortgages, were accompanied
by the intolerable competition which slave working presented to the older,
patriarchal, types of agriculture. Moreover the owners of *latifundia*, who
possessed the means needed for converting the soil, gave preference to
cattle-breeding or the growing of vines and olives, while Italian corn was
subjected to ruinous competition from provincial imports, either obtained
as tribute or purchased at cut prices.

Yet the defects inherent in large estates run by slave labour were quickly
apparent both in Italy and in the provinces, especially in Sicily. Although
slave labour required a larger working force, it perpetuated primitive techniques in such processes as cutting, threshing, and sifting. Moreover the
cultivation of cereals tended to be abandoned entirely, being given sixth
place by Cato among the profitable operations of the country, after wine-
growing, horticulture, willow plantations, olive-growing, and pasture. The
spread of *latifundia* in the provinces not only led, in Sicily above all, to the
frightful Servile Wars, with the country populations giving help to the
slaves, but they made it harder for Rome to get the grain imports it needed
for the *frumentatio*, the corn it distributed to the *plebs* in the city. So by a
slow but perceptible process the Roman government began to break up the
big Sicilian estates and increase cereal cultivation in the island, generally
by means of tenants who each worked a small plot.

Meanwhile in Italy too the *latifundia* were continually reviving, and we
find the free labourers joining the slave revolt of Spartacus. When to this
were added new wars and the depredations of the pirates in the Mediterranean, it became clear that Italy must at all costs be made self-supporting
in agricultural production. To this programme the settlement of veterans by
the triumvirs and others made some contribution; but under pressure of the

new danger revealed when the younger Pompeius occupied Sicily, and the grain ships failed to arrive, Augustus made the revival of agriculture one of the fixed points in his policies. He secured the co-operation of poets and agricultural writers to put out his propaganda.

Whereas therefore Cato's agricultural work in the second century, like Mago's book translated from the Carthaginian, gives us a picture of large and medium-sized Italian farms worked by slaves, in Varro, Hyginus, and Virgil we return to the patriarchal ideal of moderate or even small undertakings, run by a family with the help of free labourers.[4]

b. *Mining and Metallurgy*

Theophrastus tells us that in 415 BC the Athenian Callias acquired a fortune by working Spanish cinnabar (from Almaden). In later times the Spanish mines passed into Roman hands and were heavily exploited, the raw material, according to Pliny, being carried to Rome. The method of producing mercury from cinnabar is described by Theophrastus, and later by Dioscorides and Pliny.

Scientific working of the gold-bearing deposits of Mt Pangaeus in eastern Macedonia was of great importance to Greek economy. Legend ascribed their discovery to Cadmus, but they were known to the native Thracians (the Edonians) at least as early as the seventh century. These natives, who exploited them in a rough and ready way, later resisted attempts made first by Darius and then, after the Persian Wars, by the Athenians, to take possession of them. The proximity of these mines explains the foundation of the Athenian colony of Amphipolis in 437, the capture of the city by Spartan Brasidas in 424, and the occupation of the place by Philip II in 358. Philip, who set great store by these mines, founded the city of Philippi to the north of Pangaeus to keep watch over them, and at the same time exploited the other veins of gold in Chalcidice near by.

Pliny in later times speaks of two additions made to the old washing technique for the recovery of gold from the sands of river beds, and probably both were invented in our period. One, practised in Spain, was the use of hydraulic pressure to break up the lumps containing gold; the other involved reconstituting the gold-dust by means of mercury, which was later removed by filtering and distillation.

c. *Textiles and Silk*

Silk was the most important textile of China, one of the main products of its economy and its chief item of export; it is also the only one of which remnants from this period have been preserved. It was produced in China from the very earliest times; cocoons have appeared among remains of the Yang-shao period, and actual fragments of silk were found encrusted on the patina of a bronze axe of the Shang period. Silk fabric was recovered from the

o*

Ch'ang-sha mounds (fourth–third centuries BC). Woven silk was discovered in the Korean tombs at Lo-lang (c. 825 BC–AD 100) in watch towers along the Chinese *limes* on the Etsingol river (100 BC–AD 100), and at Pazyryk in the Altai (some centuries BC). Han green taffeta was found as far west as Palmyra. We know also from the classical authors that Han silks (*Sericae vestes*) freely reached the Roman empire in the first centuries of our era and created a considerable effect there; they were often re-woven in other patterns. As is pointed out elsewhere, silk played such an outstanding role in the economy that in the period 200–600 it served as currency for larger transactions.

In the Greek and Italian worlds wool was still the fabric chiefly used. For some centuries linen cloth was still imported from the East, especially from Egypt, and was used for luxury goods. Later on flax was grown in the Aegean at Amorgus, in the Po valley near the Ticino confluence, in Spain, and in other districts, all of which were thus able to manufacture all kinds of linen, from the finest (*byssus*) to the cheapest varieties.

The first Greek mention of cotton is found in Assyrian cuneiform texts, and later in Herodotus and Ctesias; its use spread after Alexander's expedition to India. We are told that his Macedonian soldiers used it mainly to cover pillows and saddles. The earliest factories grew up at Antinopolis, Tralles, and Damascus, where light, delicate muslins or cambrics were made, and also coloured materials. Later on imitation fabrics came into use, manufactured from fibres grown locally, for instance in Cappadocia, Cilicia, Judaea, and Elis, though they were always regarded as a form of linen.

Aristotle tells us that silk from cocoons of larvae was invented at Cos by a woman named Pamphile. Other silken materials were used at Amorgus and Tarentum in the manufacture of sails: and at the latter town they spun the *pinna*, a secretion of the mollusc.

Later on, from the first century BC, Chinese silk became known. But the stuffs imported from China were exceedingly expensive and were also thought to be too stiff and heavy, so they were often unpicked and then woven again with an admixture of woollen, linen, or cotton threads. This probably took place in industrial cities, on the Sinai peninsula and at Cos.

There is evidence of sporadic employment of certain other fibres, such as hemp, mallow, or amianthus.

d. *Pottery*

Chinese ceramic in this period is more uniform than that of Shang or early Chou. Production, however, was still highly decentralized. The main centres were Chin-ts'un (near Lo-yang), Hai-an, and Hui-hsien in northern Honan. Chou pottery may be classified as follows: (1) Grey ware (the overwhelming bulk); (2) red ware; (3) black ware (found at Hui-hsien only). The last-named is highly refined and represents the non plus ultra of Chou ceramics. The forms were mostly *li* tripods and round-bottom jars, for the greater part inspired by contemporary bronzes. A new technique of ornament, that of painting, was gaining acceptance by the side of the older ones.

During the Warring States and Early Han periods the main producing sites were Shou-chou in An-hwei (the capital of the state of Ch'u where the earliest examples of Chinese stoneware have been found) and Shao-hsing in Chekiang (the capital of Yüeh). Slightly later are the centres of Hsi-an and of Ch'ang-sha, the latter with some peculiar pieces covered with a tin sheet in imitation of bronze. Hellenistic influence, such as decoration with 'Cupids' and vine-leaves, is noticeable in Chinese pottery of the Han period.

Japanese pottery of this time belongs to the late Jōmon period (neolithic). It is characterized by a decoration impressed on the surface of vessels by means of tressed cords, called Jōmon. The forms were varied, but mostly utilitarian. Decoration, although on a high level of aesthetic refinement, was based on simple geometric patterns, without any tendency toward animal forms or the imitation of nature. The potter's wheel was still unknown.

Indian pottery was always intended for daily use rather than for ornament; and thus it remained always a village industry and hardly ever reached a real artistic level.

The Painted Grey ware was followed in northern and also in central India by the Northern Black Polished ware (fifth to second centuries BC), which is characteristic of the Iron Age in India; it was the pottery in common use in the Mauryan period, being found at Pāṭaliputra, Sarnath, Rajghat and above all at Ahicchatrā. It is wheel-made and thin, with a highly lustrous surface; the colour is usually grey, sometimes ranging to black, and has a steel-like appearance (Fig. 4). On the whole its technical level is very high. In the south of India a Black and Red ware is fairly common throughout the first millennium BC.

In the fifth and fourth centuries BC Greek pottery reached its highest level of perfection from every standpoint—purity of the impasto, lightness combined with durability, faultless firing, delicate shapes, artistic decoration, and transparent though brilliant varnish. These requirements were constant, but they were attained with such wealth of variety and individuality of inspiration that pottery, even in fragments, is often enough to determine precisely the date and particular provenance of the objects found in an excavation, and also of their setting.

The finest of the Greek pottery traditions was to be found in the workshops of Attica. Their products were at first decorated with black silhouettes on the red ground of the vase; but later the figures were drawn in outline on the red clay and the ground between them was covered in black. Both styles were liberally imitated outside Attica, and sometimes the figures were enlivened by painting some features in other colours. (Pls 11 and 12.)

Other techniques used locally include (a) encaustic decoration on a whitened ground, found for example at Canusium in Apulia and Centuripae in Sicily; (b) the use of red varnish to brighten the surface of the vase, found at Samos, Arretium, and other places; and (c) the *bucchero* style of Etruria. (Pl. 46.)

Decoration in relief was another novelty of this period. It was achieved by moulding fresh, unfired clay with a tool, or impressing it with a stamp (which was sometimes a coin or medal); and very often metal vases were

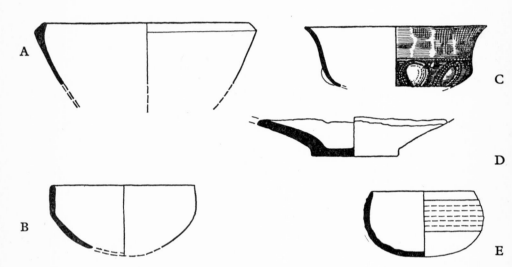

FIG. 4. Northern Black Polished Ware. A, B.: from Rupar; C: from Taxila; D: from Hastināpura; E: from Ahicchatrā; (after M. Wheeler).

taken as a model. The subjects were very varied, including not only architectural design but the representation of flowers, animals, and human beings. Another technique was the *barbotine*, in which the vase was covered with a clay slip which was then modelled and either varnished or painted.

The large number of different shapes included large jars, amphorae, pitchers (*hydriae*), oil-flasks (*lekythoi*), mixing-bowls (*craters*), saucer-shaped cups (*phialai*), drinking-vessels, lamps and so on. They had different purposes, but also corresponded to variations in local and personal tastes.

e. *Glass, goldsmith's work, and scent*

A number of relatively simple processes for glass manufacture were evolved during this period. Plain cast glass, sometimes moulded, was employed instead of metal or pottery for objects in common use, like jars, bottles, plates, amphorae, and cups. Ptolemaic Egypt had complicated techniques for blowing, turning, and spinning glass, and for painting it in many colours; sometimes coloured pins of glass were worked into a mosaic. An example of painted glass from the second century BC, probably from the school of Tarentum, has been found at Varafodio in Calabria. In the *vicus vitrarius* at Rome many kinds of glass were made—not only window-panes, urns, and scent-containers, but also ornamentation for buildings, of which a well-known example is the theatre of Scaurus.

The goldsmith's art in China is first known in the gold and silver inlays on Shang and Chou bronzes; inlay grows still more abundant in the Huai period and remains for centuries the most important branch of this art. Its technique was probably imported from the West, but perfected in China. Objects cast in pure gold are known from the Huai period; among the earliest are the Hsin-chêng gold sheets (*c.*575 BC), with geometrical designs and a pattern of interlaced serpent-dragons. Later we have chiefly sword-mountings, dress ornaments, dress hooks mounted with jade, and jewellery. They were rare at first, but became more common when contact with the West grew closer, in the fourth–second centuries. The general forms however remained the same; the technique also, both in casting and for inlay, did not essentially change. The gold plaques from the Ordos region, like the same region's bronzes, show strong influence from the animal style of Steppe art. Cast silver cups and toilet boxes also appear in this period.

Han gold work is marked by the appearance of granulation, shown for example on dragons from the Lo-lang tombs in northern Korea. This technique is doubtless influenced by Indo-Persian art. Jewellery proper is, however, rare and consists only of hair ornaments, finger rings, and bracelets.

Indian jewellery has a very ancient tradition, as is shown by the finds at Mohenjo-daro and Harappā. The craft is also repeatedly mentioned in Buddhist texts. But actual specimens of this period are very rare. The remains found at Pātaliputra are an example, and help us in reconstructing the technique of this art by providing the tools used, finished and unfinished products, and evidence concerning every stage of the process. But in the main we are still limited to reproductions of jewels and ornaments on terra-cotta figurines (e.g. Ahicchatrā) and stone reliefs (e.g. Bharhut and Sanchi). The only exception is beads, made of shell, gold, bronze, copper, and chiefly of glass, which are abundant at Taxila in the north and at Brahmagiri in the south, as they were at Harappā and Mohenjo-daro.

Some of the peculiarities of the jewellery made in Mediterranean lands are worth attention. The most delicate jewels are those made in various countries in imitation of Greek models: extremely heavy and clumsy work was produced when Greek influence faded or disappeared. This is markedly the case with Etruscan work from the fifth century onwards, when cultural contact between Etruria and Greece became isolated and tenuous. Some types of jewellery spread widely, such as the 'set' pearls, which were probably made first in Syria but are later found in Egypt and Etruria, and also in China.

There was a considerable advance in the working of semi-precious stones in the Hellenistic period,[5] both in Greek countries and in those which borrowed their technique. The process reached a high level of artistic achievement, and we know the names of famous masters, such as Pyrgoteles in Alexander's time and Satyreios in the reign of Ptolemy I. The same period saw the first appearance of genuine cameos, made especially for princes at Antioch and Alexandria. They were used in many ways, sometimes worked into vases or musical instruments, sometimes sewn onto fabrics, strung on necklaces, or set in rings; and they frequently depicted the features of some high personage. They were regarded as jewels of exquisite merit, and were sought after by every potentate as far as the Crimea.

Precious stones were also much in use at Hellenistic courts, in jewellery and in other objects of value, such as diadems, cups, and goblets.

People of elegance in Greece were using scent and cosmetics freely well before the Hellenistic age began. Most of them were of Eastern origin. The scents used by Aspasia and by Crito were actually made the subject of treatises; and in the fourth century the comic poet Antiphanes gave a detailed analysis of the scent used by a courtesan. In his *Historia Plantarum* (Book IX) Theophrastus describes the substances which went to make scents, cosmetics, and hair-dyes. That Greeks in the second century BC commonly painted their faces we know from Plautus' *Mostellaria*, which was based on a Greek original.

f. *The Development of Small-Scale Industry*

Information on industrial organization in India is scanty and wholly limited to literary sources. The *Jātaka* refer to a standard number of eighteen handicrafts (wood-workers, smiths, leather-workers, painters, ivory-carvers, weavers, jewellers, etc.). On a lower level there were the debased crafts, which inflicted the stigma of social inferiority on those who practised them; for example the hunters, fishermen, butchers, tanners, snake-charmers, dancers, musicians.

Localization of crafts and industries appears at a very early stage. This localization could be by street, by quarter and even by village, each unit consisting wholly or mainly of craftsmen of the same trade. Industry was free and the state did not control prices, except for its own purchases through official valuers.

From the very beginning craftsmen are found organized in strongly built and closely knit guilds (*śreṇī*) which even cut across the boundaries of caste. The *Jātaka* again give the number of eighteen for them; but this of course is wholly conventional. Membership was mostly hereditary, as indeed was the occupation itself. The guild was governed by a headman called (in Pali) *jeṭṭhaka* or *pamukha*. Within the guild apprenticeship meant a welcome loosening of the rigidities of heredity; master and pupil (*ācariyo* and *antevāsi*) are often mentioned in the Pali texts. According to the later law books (e.g. the *Nārada-smṛti*), it appears that apprenticeship was in practice akin to domestic slavery.

Besides their economic functions, corporations held complete judicial authority over their own members. Guild bye-laws were considered as fully valid; and the royal government not only upheld them, but had to take them into account in framing its own regulations. Relations with the court were therefore rather close, and the more important guilds kept representatives of their own there. The common and most dreaded penalty for infractions of the guild laws was expulsion.

The *Kauṭṭilīya Arthaśāstra*, which may be taken to illustrate conditions in the post-Maurya age, gives increased importance to the guilds; they now served also as banks, receiving deposits at interest (at least for religious purposes). They even undertook some military tasks, in so far as the wealthiest of them kept bodies of troops, which could be summoned by the king. There was even a tendency towards a federation of trade unions under heads called *bhaṇḍāgarika*. But state control in the society depicted by the *Arthaśāstra* was much closer than in the times of the Buddha. Some handicrafts were state monopolies, such as mines, pearl-fishing, salt, coinage, manufacture of arms and of ships. The state also controlled and licensed the manufacture of liquor.

Moreover the state itself was active in the industrial field, with cotton, oil, and sugar factories. Convict labour was partly employed for the purpose. The same applied to the state spinning-houses, which yielded a steady output of textiles and clothes.

In fifth- and fourth-century Greece small and medium-sized industrial undertakings were beginning to develop at the side of artisan workshops at Athens and a few other centres, such as Corinth, Delos, Miletus, Samos, and at Syracuse and Massilia in the West. They were run by citizens or resident aliens (metics), who used slaves as well as free labour. These centres of production were few in relation to the vast area over which their manufactures were exported and profits were correspondingly high; moreover the competition between a large number of craftsmen was a constant encouragement to specialization and to improvement in production. Specialization on these lines is recommended by Plato and Xenophon, and it is attested in the pottery workshops, where modellers, painters, and stokers were working side by side.

All kinds of workshops and so-called *ergasteria* existed at Athens. They made metal goods in iron, copper, and bronze, such as arms, lamps, and miscellaneous utensils; they manufactured the leather which was produced at home or imported from the Pontus; they employed craftsmen, carvers and turners, to make jewellery out of precious metals or semi-precious stones or ivory; they wove cloth; and they produced painted vases. It was through the export of these manufactures that Athens was able to import not only raw materials, but also its grain and other essential supplies of food.

In the Hellenistic age the leading centres of artisan and industrial production moved eastward. In some of the older Greek colonial centres it was intensified, such as Ephesus with its marble, metals, woollens, and carpets, Smyrna with its marble and clay, or the industrial production of Rhodes. But in all the new countries, the Seleucid and Ptolemaic empires above all, industrial output was a feature; there was a multiplicity of factories at Alexandria, which could draw raw materials of all kinds from Asia and Africa. But this large number of new centres of manufacture and export, when added to the old ones, meant that each had normally to operate in a narrower field and adapt itself more closely to local tastes. Profits were more modest, especially in view of the tax-collectors' demands. Yet on the other side of the balance sheet there were larger home orders, to execute the great public works favoured by all Hellenistic rulers.

Nevertheless conditions were not the same in all areas. In Egypt, for example, the Greek dynasty took over the monopolistic system which went back to the days of the New Kingdom. Here practically the only producer, seller, buyer, and exporter was the state, which fixed the prices and selling margins both for agricultural products (oil, beer, etc.) and for linens, woollens, papyrus, unguents, and the rest.

In other countries the free workmen, son following father, were organized in corporations which transmitted the secret of certain crafts; and the state imposed a tax on their operations, even for the smallest and most humble undertakings.

We have a fairly good knowledge of the organization of Carthaginian production between the fifth and second centuries. They specialized in the standardized type of manufactures, which were easy to sell. Their factories excelled in naval construction, in metalwork, and in the working of gold, semi-precious stones, ivory, and glass. Some of these operations were in the hands of monopolies, others were freely carried out by artisans.

Italy came to be ruled by Rome, and the first Western provinces, which were founded by the end of our present period, were gradually being Latinized. But in all this area small industry continued, with roughly the same local markets as had been fixed in the pre-Roman period.

Rome's economy was mainly based on the city itself and the surrounding countryside. Its main output came from its kilns, from its metalworking, textile, and pottery factories, and from its goldsmiths on the Via Sacra. But there were corresponding developments of artisan working and small industry with regional significance at Ostia (mainly naval construction, as also at Ravenna and Misenum), at Sulmo, Pompeii, and Puteoli (iron and vases), at Capua (bronzes, scents, and pottery), at Cumae, the island of Aenaria, Tarentum, Canusium, Comum, Bergomum, Aquileia, and many other towns.

Rome did nothing to organize and protect the export of Italian manufactured goods to the provinces, but this did not prevent local centres from developing artisan and industrial operations with a very wide market.

We are told that the *collegia opificum,* the corporations of artisans, were preserved when the other corporations, which had degenerated into political clubs, were suppressed first by Caesar and then by Augustus.

3. THE DEVELOPMENT OF TRADE

Trade in India in the age of the Buddha was already highly developed, and we hear of merchant princes such as Anāthapiṇḍika, who was a generous benefactor of the young Buddhist community. In the towns trade centred in the bazaars, where shops (*āpaṇa*) and store-rooms (*antarāpaṇa*) were to be found. An exception was trade in perishable foodstuffs; this was carried out in markets situated outside the town gates.

Trade was partly by barter (on the lower level), and partly by money payment ('for fees, pensions, fines, loans, hoarded treasure, and income'). Finance had already gone beyond the cruder stage, for we hear of loans 'given on security of gold such as a ring' or a debtor's personal guarantee. We read of wives or children being pledged or sold for debt, and of IOUs or schedules of debt. Loans carried interest, called *vṛddhi.* Money-lending was approved as an honest calling along with tillage, harvesting, and trade.

Traders were organized, like the craftsmen, in guilds (*śreṇī*) led by headmen called *śreṣṭhins.* Anāthapiṇḍika was a *mahāśreṣṭhin,* i.e. the head of a union of merchant guilds.

The normal means of transport in India were bullock carts and pack animals (horses, oxen and buffaloes, camels in the north-west). Water transport also played a role.

The Buddhist texts allow us to infer the existence of several commercial routes, radiating from Śravasti to Rājagṭha, to Paithan and towards Sindhṛ and to the sea. Later on Megasthenes describes the Royal Road from Pāṭaliputra to the north-western frontier, the forerunner of the Grand Trunk Road, for a distance of about ten thousand stades (Strabo XVII, 2). The Maurya government did much to improve communications, and Aśoka's inscriptions are witness to the care he took over the security of the roads and amenities for travellers (by the planting of trees along the route, etc.).

In the time of the *Arthaśāstra* the carrying of goods was usually organized, for reasons of security, in convoys or caravans under a leader called *sārthavāha,* who was responsible both for the safety of goods and travellers and also for the success of the journey. Transit must have been much impeded by a suspicious police control (passes were required), but above all by fiscalism. Foreign merchants had to pay transit duties (*vartanī*) and tolls (*śulka*) at the frontier. But even in the interior of the kingdoms taxes were levied at several points on the roads, and octrois had always to be paid at the gates, which were strictly controlled by customs officers; the customs houses even contained detention rooms for merchants caught violating octroi rules. The only relieving feature of this ruthless fiscalism was that there was a government guarantee for losses in transit, which had to be made up by the local authorities concerned.

Greek commerce was considerably promoted by the circulation of coinage and by the invention of bottomry loans (capital lent by private individuals to merchants). But although till the end of the sixth century and also in part of the fifth the profession of merchant was regarded as respectable, in the ensuing period it was pursued by non-citizens or members of the lower orders of society and was therefore less highly esteemed. Moreover merchants did not have their own corporations and were not even a single recognized class. They were divided into wholesalers, retailers, and shippers, the last of whom sometimes had their own ship and sometimes a ship on charter.

Merchants also had to encounter many obstacles in their travels. Goods had to pass through the territories or the waters of several states, and duties were imposed on entry and exit. The continual wars, domestic and foreign, subjected trade to great risks. Laws varied greatly from state to state, though they were generally severe on debtors. State hoarding would often withdraw liquid capital from circulation, and there were frequent embargoes of a protectionist kind on both export and import.

In the Hellenistic period the merchants' field of action was substantially enlarged, at least in theory, by the opening of new territories through Alexander's conquests and by the fresh creation of large towns which served as markets for the sale and exchange of their wares.[6] The size of the new states was another advantage, since it reduced the number of frontiers. Moreover a considerable amount of precious metal previously stored in the Great King's coffers was now circulating in the form of money; and communications by land, river, and sea were being improved. It was true, as we have already pointed out, that the proliferation of industry in all big towns tended to limit the market for manufactured goods to the immediately surrounding areas. But it still remained essential to seek out the raw materials for industry in distant producing countries, if necessary with the aid of middlemen; and also to arrange for a regular trade in manufactured goods against foodstuffs and other prime commodities.[7] The main producing areas of these commodities were very much scattered. Cereals came from the Pontus and from Cyrenaica; timber from the Caucasus, Anatolia, and Lebanon, iron from the northern area of Anatolia near Sinope; gold from Colchis and Armenia; silver from Carmania; tin from Drangiana; copper from Cyprus; and bronze from Corinth, Delos, Chios, and Samos. Egypt (and certain other areas) had abundant supplies of salt; Lydia, Egypt, and Armenia of soda (nitrum); Palestine of asphalt; and Assyria, Babylonia, and Susiana of rock-oil (naphtha). The best-known producers of flax were Syria, Phoenicia, Cilicia, Babylonia, Egypt, and Amorgus; of wool, Cyprus, Phrygia, Galatia, Lydia, Ionia, and Achaea; of silk, Cos and Phoenicia; of cotton, Babylonia, Egypt and Phoenicia; of papyrus, Egypt, but Ptolemaic control on its export promoted the trade in parchment from Pergamum. Among the manufactures derived from these materials special reputation was enjoyed by Egyptian, Damascene, and Phoenician carpets and hangings; by Phoenician and Palestinian purple goods; by the dyes of Hierapolis, by Greek pottery; by Phoenician and Egyptian glass; by oriental perfumes (these were distributed through Cyzicus and Cyrene); and by the arms manufactured at Pergamum, Cyzicus, and Rhodes.

Some areas, however, had become less favourable to trade and business operations, mainland Greece being one example. There were still some cities of great importance, but the country grew more and more disturbed and impoverished by its wars; it was also ravaged by Galatian raids, and depopulated by the movements of emigration to the new cities inside the Hellenistic empires.

In Egypt we learn of many obstacles to trade. There were heavy customs duties on imported goods, as well as tolls, harbour and canal dues, and taxes on business. Monopolies or semi-monopolies controlled trade in salt, wine, oil, precious stones, ivory, papyrus, textiles, scents, and spices.

After the fall of the Tarquins, and once again after the Gauls had burnt the city in 386, Rome gradually extended its possessions, until after the expedition of Pyrrhus they comprised the whole peninsula of Italy. *Pari passu* with these conquests it extended the exercise of its rights over the adjoining seas. We can see this from a comparison between the various maritime treaties it made with Carthage between 509 and 278 BC. They show how Rome gradually acquired greater freedom for its trade, especially through Ostia, Misenum, and the other sea-board cities of Italy which had come into its hands.[8]

The conquest of Italy was followed by that of the western Mediterranean islands, Spain, north-west Africa, the Balkans, and the areas which earlier formed part of the Hellenistic empires. This political unification led to a growing unity of the Mediterranean in the economic sphere. But from these vast territories and from those beyond the frontiers, Rome under the Republic drew only such merchandise as was needed by its own city and by the Italian peninsula. This merchandise included grain from Sicily, Sardinia, Corsica, Spain, and Africa; salt fish and cheese from Spain, Gaul, and the Pontus; spices from Arabia; metals, wool, and hides from Spain and Gaul; timber from the Pontus, Asia, and Syria; ivory and various luxury objects from Arabia, Phoenicia, Syria, and Egypt; and slaves from Gaul, Germany, and the East.

These imports were systematically making Italy into a pauper country, living on the money it drew as tribute. Rome made no effort to balance them by guaranteeing monopolies for the export of industrial products from the city and the peninsula. It is true that some conquered cities, like Corinth and Carthage, were for a time destroyed. But in general the peoples and cities who became Rome's subjects were freely allowed to develop their commerce as they wished, and to build industries, serving more or less localized markets.

Such Italian goods as were exported came more from Etruria, Campania, and the Po valley than from Rome and Latium. A further feature of the period was that the competition of imported grain drove the Italian farmers to develop vine- and olive-growing, and also pasturage, at the expense of the cultivation of cereals.

The small industries of Latium and other parts of Italy had earlier been run by corporations of free artisans. These now generally became undertakings employing slave labour, although artisan working did not entirely disappear.

a. *Main Roads*

The history of commerce implies attention to the conditions of road and sea transport. For various reasons, including the number of their colonies, the Greeks were more accustomed to travel by sea than by land; and so far as roads were concerned, they took more trouble, especially in pre-Hellenistic times, with communications inside individual cities than with inter-city traffic. We have plenty of information about city streets in the period of the fifth and fourth centuries when the regular planning begun by Hippodamus of Miletus was being put into effect. This system is later found in many places in Miletus and other cities of Asia Minor, in the Piraeus at Athens, at Thurii, and at Selinus; and in the Hellenistic period it was copied at Megalopolis, Alexandria, Nicaea, Cnidus, and Priene. The streets were normally still fairly narrow; only in a few cases were they as much as 50 feet wide. Roads between cities, on the other hand, still very often lacked artificial bedding, and were more suitable for traffic by pack-animals than for carriages.

But in the Persian empire, and in the Hellenistic kingdoms which succeeded it, things were different. The great roads which the Persians had built for their armies and traders, and for the service of the post, were kept up by the Hellenistic rulers and extended on the lines the Persians had laid down. We can see this from a papyrus of 255 BC, of the time of Ptolemy II Philadelphus, which preserves a fragment of a 'post-book' recording despatches exchanged between the king and his minister of finance.

Roman roads were of largely artificial construction. The beds were of pommelled gravel sometimes covered with concrete; and the surfaces were paved with polygonal blocks to secure maximum life and minimum cost of maintenance. The technique began with the construction of part of the Via Appia in 312 BC, and was then extended rapidly as Roman conquests increased and the conquered areas became Romanized. These roads almost always formed part of a permanent scheme of planning based on pre-existing routes, which had come into being naturally through the movement of baggage animals and travellers on foot. They therefore followed lines dictated by the contours and by the need to avoid country subject to flooding. Daring bridges, cuttings, escarpments, and even short tunnels were built to ensure the uninterrupted course of these roads. Often they would encounter steep gradients in climbing the ridges of hills, and whenever possible they would drive in a straight line over part of their course. The carriage-way was normally between 8 and 13 feet wide, with a footpath running on a natural bed at each side. Posting stations were provided, and branch roads ran in every direction to the smaller towns. These great roads became one of the foundations of Rome's empire, ensuring the free movement of its armies and the regular development of its trade, communications, and postal service. They were maintained partly out of the receipts from tolls and partly at the expense of the towns through which they passed. The continually increasing number of itineraries were recorded in guide-books, and distances along the ground were marked by milestones. In Augustus' time we are told that an up-to-date catalogue was made on the 'golden milestone', which was placed in the Temple of Saturn at Rome in 20 BC. (Map XV.)

In respect of our present period it is sufficient to mention the following roads of the Italian network: (1) The *Appia*, started in 312 BC and built in sections in succeeding years, ran from Rome to Brundisium. (2) The *Flaminia* was started in 220, and went as far as Ariminum. (3) The *Valeria* ran towards the Adriatic Sea through the valley of the Aternus, then along the coast northwards to join the Flaminia at Fanum. (4) The *Salaria* ran along the valley of the Truentus and then south along the coast, as far as Brundisium. (5) The *Aurelia* coasted the Tyrrhenian Sea as far as Pisa and beyond. (6) The *Cassia* of the interior ran to Volsinii and Florentia, whence it branched off to Pisa and Bononia. (7) The *Aemilia* ran from Ariminum to Placentia and beyond. (8) The *Postumia*, started in 176 BC, ran from Genua to Placentia and then north of the Po to Aquileia. (9) The *Popilia* ran across Magna Graecia towards the straits.

China too took care to see that its main lines of communication were in order, for example the two roads across the Great Wall which allowed trade with the West, at any rate between the end of the third century BC and the beginning of the third century AD. These roads, like the Roman ones, were divided into appropriate stretches with a station at the end of each. The silk traders brought an account of their routes to the West, and Ptolemy was later able to make use of them in his work on Geography.

b. *Navigation and Piracy*

The history of the purely commercial vessel is different from the history of the warship, though the two are closely connected. From the fifth century onwards warships were made gradually bigger and stronger, with a corresponding increase in the number of rowers, so that they could carry on board both machines such as catapults and grappling-irons, and also a larger number of marines for fighting. (Pl. 22.) The normal ship consequently had between four and six banks of oars (some had as many as twenty), and it was accompanied by fast light craft and also by transport vessels (*naves onerariae*) to carry landing parties, food, and horses. Commercial ships, on the other hand, were built to much the same moderate-sized tonnage as before. But warships were not only used for naval actions; the threat presented by a fleet on the water was a guarantee of free navigation of the seas; or, conversely, a fleet could often prevent access by foreign ships to waters which a powerful nation wanted to keep for itself. In this context the naval and commercial treaties, dated 509, 348, c.306, and 278 between Rome and Carthage are of great importance. The presence of navies also made large-scale piracy more difficult, and pirates were in practice confined to areas where navies could not make their strength fully felt. In the Adriatic, for example, pirate ships were helped by the countless natural hiding-places offered them by the islands and the broken coastline of the eastern shore.

In the periods when powerful naval squadrons controlled the Mediterranean destitute men who sought a life of adventure had to find an outlet in mercenary service rather than in piracy. But with the extension of Roman dominion there was gradually less use for mercenary armies, while at the same time less need was felt for maintaining large navies. The result was a revival of piracy.

Meanwhile the limits of the known world, and with them the range of commerce, were growing all the time. For this the famous explorers were largely responsible, especially in the fourth and third centuries BC. Pytheas of Massilia voyaged in the Atlantic, and reached the British Isles and the coast of Germany; Nearchus travelled in the country between the mouths of the Euphrates and Indus; Androsthenes sailed between Arabia and India, and Eudoxus along the coast of Africa. There were others of the same kind. Constant efforts were also made, by means of harbour works and lighthouses, to make it easier for ships to put into land; the best-known examples are the Piraeus and the fourth-century Pharos of Alexandria.

During periods of war between great naval powers piracy took on a special function, because the combatant fleets themselves carried out piratical enterprises to harm their enemies, and on the fringe of operations there would be established nests of genuine pirates acting on their own, who were ready to take advantage of any favourable situation. We find this for instance during the struggle between Greece and Persia in the first decades of the fifth century, when the Delio-Attic league, after its victory over the Persians, had to clear the seas of pirates. During the wars of the Greek cities for hegemony in the fifth and fourth centuries pirate enterprises again appeared on the fringes of the zones of action.

Alexander's unification of political power subdued the pirates for a time, but they revived during the continuous struggles between the dynasties which divided up his empire. Indeed there were now pirate squadrons acting under orders of the Hellenistic rulers, just as they made use of mercenary armies. Their most notorious lairs were in Cilicia, Crete, and Aetolia.9 At the end of the third century and during part of the second the eastern Mediterranean

pirates grew weaker on account of the naval strength acquired by the Ptolemies, with their bases in Egypt and Rhodes. They revived later, especially
when Rome was fighting Mithradates, who had organized bands of pirates
to help him. In this way the whole Mediterranean was thrown into confusion.
The pirates ravaged the coastal districts, interfered with regular trade, and
paralysed the food supplies not only of the armed forces but of civilian
populations. Rome's war against the pirates lasted for many years and was
eventually completed by Pompey the Great in 67 BC. At this stage Pompey
tried to prevent any recurrence of the scourge by giving the pirates land and
trying to turn them into peasants. But his own son Sextus was responsible
for the resurgence of piracy for a number of years during the wars of the
Second Triumvirate. After this action was ended the pirates were exterminated.

In very early times the most famous pirates of the western Mediterranean
were the Etruscans and Carthaginians. But pirate squadrons were also active
in these seas in the fifth and fourth centuries, their chief enemies being the
Syracusans who wanted to protect their trade. From the third century Rome's
expansion encountered an obstacle in the piratical activities of the Illyrian
peoples, and regular military action had to be taken against them at various
intervals between 229 BC and the time of Augustus.

c. Coinage

Chinese coinage had its precursors, as in many other countries, in the use
of cowrie shells, their imitations, and the 'ant nose money' (*i-pi ch'ien*), which
appears to have been a degenerate form of imitation cowrie. Actual minting
began under the Chou dynasty and copper became for about a thousand
years the means for ordinary transactions. The first actual coins were the
bronze or copper spade coins (*pu*); originally they were actual agricultural
tools, which then degenerated into toys too small for practical use, and then
into legend-bearing coins, of which there were four main varieties. Their
dating is still doubtful, and their origin may go back as far as the beginning
of the Chou period; but their use became general only after about 500 BC.
In their latest forms they circulated till the end of the anarchy and the
unification of China by the Ch'in. The spades were a regional currency, and
187 mint names are known, mostly from states on the banks of the Huang-ho.
Minting was at first free and coins were merely a commodity for barter. The
principle of state monopoly for minting and of standardization of the issues
appeared rather late, perhaps for the first time in the state of Ch'in at the
time of its reform by Shang-chün along legalist lines. For a long time Ch'in
was alone in having a state currency.

Along with the spades, the knife coinage (*tao*) came into use, chiefly in the
rich mercantile state of Ch'i and other states on the Shantung peninsula, in
the seventh century BC or even earlier. At first they bore much resemblance
to the real tool ('early knives'), but then they spread toward the north and

north-west, taking the place of the spades in that region and losing the characteristics of a tool to assume those of a currency ('late knives'). Two main types are extant. The Ch'i knives were guaranteed (even if not actually minted) by the state, and bore a stamp indicating them as such.

The south, including above all its largest state Ch'u, had a quite different coinage of its own, consisting of a gold currency (*ying-huan*).

Spades and knives yielded to the round coins (*ch'ien*), having a square hole for tying them together in strings (the first 'cash'). This happened toward the end of the Chou period. But with characteristic conservatism in the former 'knives' territory the 'cash' maintained the monetary unit of the old Ch'i currency, the *huo* (denominations of 1, 2, 4 and 6 *huo*); while the ex-'spade' territory had as its unit the *chin*. The new round copper coin was the normal circulating medium for all ordinary purposes during the Former Han dynasty; for large transactions gold in *catties* was used.

During the short-lived Ch'in dynasty the round coin was called *pan-liang* and weighed probably 12 *shu*, i.e. half an ounce. Han Kao-tsu (202–195) abolished it as being too heavy and relaxed also the state monopoly of coinage, as being too closely connected with the totalitarian principles of the fallen dynasty; private minting was allowed and coins sharply decreased in weight. Shortly afterwards various measures had to be taken in order to increase the weight of coins; in 175 BC Wên-ti issued a *pan-liang* coin of 4 *shu*. The heavy expenditure for the Hsiung-nu wars necessitated other arrangements and in 118 a coin of 5 *shu* was issued, the legend of which also indicated its actual weight. After 113 minting became once more a government monopoly and this state coin proved to be very practical in use. The new currency was stable and lasted in use till the end of the dynasty and beyond.

We must not, however, lose sight of a general characteristic of Chinese coinage: its use did not go much beyond commercial transactions and failed to dominate public economy until the Ming period. State finance was reckoned in terms of money, but taxation in this period was mostly in kind, and so was public expenditure.

For Indian coinage we have to take into account the rules concerning weight and denomination set down by the *Dharmaśāstras*, but above all the coins themselves. The lists of weights and coins found e.g. in the code of Manu (VIII, 132 ff.) go to great detail, although a great part of it is mere theorizing without factual importance. The basis is always the *rati* (weight of a gunja berry: 0·118 g). The standard piece of gold is the *suvarṇa* of 80 *ratis*. The most important silver piece is said to be the *purāṇa* or *dharana*, of 32 *ratis*, and the copper piece is the *kārṣāpaṇa*, of 80 *ratis*. Each of them has various multiples and subdivisions. But actual use, as reflected in the Buddhist texts, seems to have known only one standard piece, the silver *āpaṇa*; it seems that when afterwards it went out of use it was called by the legal texts *purāṇa*, 'the old one'. The standard copper coin was really the *māṣaka*, of which sixteen went to a *kārṣāpaṇa*. As can be seen the ratio 1 rupee = 16 annas is very ancient.

The earliest Indian coins seem to go back to the sixth century at the earliest. They were purely Indian in weight and execution; and this coinage went on with little change for several centuries. No gold was minted, but silver and copper coins are extant in great numbers. Most of them are rather crude pieces of any shape (round, square, rectangular, etc.), stamped with a great number of devices (over 300 are known including the sun and various animals and symbols); they are called by the clumsy name of 'punch-marked' coins. Generally speaking, they are tribal in origin. Most of the silver coins correspond in weight to the *kārṣāpaṇa*; but there are numerous examples of double, half and quarter *kārṣāpaṇas*; only a very few minute silver coins correspond to the *kṛṣṇāla*, i.e. one-sixteenth of a *kārṣāpaṇa*. Copper coins cannot at present be reduced to a single standard, as their variety of weight is bewildering.

The punch-marked coins were the coinage actually current in the Maurya empire. But even before its rise, and chiefly after its disappearance, Iranian and then Greek influence began to be felt in what is now West Pakistan. The first coins of this type are thick, slightly bent bars of silver, stamped with wheel or sun-like designs, double on the large denominations and single on others. They go back to the last years of Achaemenid rule in the Indus valley, and are struck on the Persian standard (*siglos*, 5·601 gm), showing double, half, and quarter *sigloi*. The Athenian *drachms* too reached India, in the wake of the brisk commerce through the Persian empire; they were even imitated locally.

Slightly later north-western India felt the influence of the splendid Graeco-Bactrian coinage, which of course is a part (perhaps the most beautiful one) of Hellenistic coinage and not of Indian. Indo-Greek coins were at first purely Hellenistic in character and were struck on the Attic standard (mostly *hemidrachms*). But with some of the last Greek rulers the legends became bilingual and the Attic standard faded away, replaced by the earlier Achaemenid standard. In one way and another, Greek influence wrought a complete change in the form and metrology of coinage in the Indus valley.

A particular phenomenon of Greek coinage is noticeable in cities which lived under the political influence of Persia. Originally the gold and silver of Croesus was used for the empire of Cyrus and Cambyses. Darius I was the first to issue Persian gold and silver as a world currency. An official relationship was established between Greek silver coins of regular weight and composition on the one hand and Persian gold coins on the other. The latter, however, were part of a managed currency, containing metal of intrinsic weight lower than the value fixed officially by the government. So the Greek silver disappeared, and the Greek districts accepted a local invasion by depreciated Persian gold.

Mainland Greece and the Greek colonies, like the Roman world, were in

fact on a silver standard, and even when gold was struck the basis of calculation was still related to silver. Bronze coins in Italy, Egypt, and Carthage
retained the weight and composition which corresponded to their values
(Pl. 23). In other places such coinage represented defined fractions of a given
unit, and had a legal fiduciary value higher than that of the metal they contained.[10]

In fairly early times, especially at moments of crisis, tricks were played
with the coinage. Sometimes the government was speculating, sometimes
(as in the case of Persia) it wanted to stop melting by operators who made a
corner in coins, or to check the drain of gold to foreign parts. The state could
gain practical benefit from expedients of this kind when they were used
exceptionally and unexpectedly; otherwise they produced inflation of prices,
equivalent to a fall in the value of money, since the state was not in a position
to impose an artificial value as a permanency. Perdiccas III of Macedon
resorted to a debased currency to pay his army in time of war; so did Athens
in the long war against Sparta. The Ptolemies in Egypt followed their
example. The Roman government did the same during the Hannibalic war,
and again in 91 BC and during Sulla's dictatorship.

d. *Business Practices*

In Greek towns the central square or *Agorā* was not only the normal
meeting-place of the popular assembly, round which public buildings and
the principal temples were erected, but it also served as a market-place
where shops and movable counters were usually grouped according to the
type of commodity offered for sale. The quality of goods on the counters
was supervised by the *agorānomoi*, and the weighing of them by the *metrono-
moi*. The *Agorā* was also the place where the *trapezitai* or money-changers
congregated; and in various adjacent parts, embellished with porticoes,
fountains and the like, were the meeting-places of the countrymen who came
to sell or exchange their wares. As the citizen population grew, and with it
the number who would come in from the country and from other cities,
every city developed a number of specialized markets for the different types
of produce, especially for foodstuffs.

The same thing happened at Rome and the cities which Rome founded.
The central market split into a number of smaller ones, which specialized
in particular commodities, such as cattle, pigs, fish, oil, or wine. More
important sales, which brought together larger numbers of traders and a
greater volume of goods, were often organized in special parts of the market-
place, even in small towns; the dates for these were fixed in the calendar,
like the *nundinae* held every eight days in Latin communities. Often again
the towns lying along the main roads would provide quarters furnished with
wells and drinking-troughs, in which beasts of burden, and even flocks and
herds, could be stalled, as they had been in early times in the *Forum Romanum*.

In other respects transport of goods by land (though less so by sea or river) was made difficult at the outset by the fact that each state was so small. At every stage tolls could be exacted, or customs and excise duties on both imports and exports. Things became easier when the area of the average state increased. (Customs and excise were often the same thing in the earliest days of city-states, but they were differentiated later as empires grew bigger.) Yet even in these larger states freedom of trade could encounter obstacles and not only those imposed by transit and import duties (called *portoria* when exacted at harbours). The import of certain goods was limited or prevented by protectionist restrictions, or by monopolies which made the state or the priesthood (as in Egypt) the sole trader in a large number of commodities.

Individual states wanted to extend their own trade and impede that of rival or enemy cities. Naturally, therefore, the trade between two or more contracting states was governed by fixed rules. Although the absence of any unifying political organization made it impossible to arrive at any common 'commercial code', convention and community of standards brought into being a number of formulae applied to commerce on both land and sea.

The ancient world, we must remember, generally believed that foreigners and enemies were identical. It is therefore clear, even when we have no particular evidence, that the operation of trade over a wide area implies the existence of a number of rules about permits, safe-conducts, reciprocal benefits, and compensation when needed. These rules could be positive in the sense of allowing concessions based on definite treaties, but they might be restrictive, or even negative, as when entry or trade in particular commodities was prohibited in certain areas. Agreements of this kind were often the result of wars, when the victors at the time of signing peace would get guarantees of certain rights or privileges or monopolies or favours. Typical examples of commercial treaties are those made between Athens and certain allies, or between Rome and Carthage at various moments of their relationship, from which we can see the reciprocal concessions and prohibitions being gradually modified.

In the days of its expansion Rome was never an upholder of monopolies in sea-borne trade. All it did from time to time was to fix general rules governing access to its territories and harbours, and it was broadly speaking friendly to the freedom of the seas. It is true that with the extension of its possessions to all shores of the Mediterranean international rules became superfluous or fell into disuse.

In the period when slavery, and correspondingly also piracy, were at their height, the slave trade tended to concentrate on large ports, especially those like Delos which were regarded as free.

The port in antiquity can in fact be regarded as an entity almost distinct from the city it served. It could have its own magistrates, and it sometimes therefore acquired all the features of a free port. This is what happened to **Delos under Roman protection.**

e. *The Social Impact of Trade and Industry*

The growth of industry and commerce naturally bore a close relation to other historical conditions obtaining in different parts of the world, some of which were favourable and others not. During the Graeco-Persian struggles, for example, the political position of the Greek cities in Asia declined generally; and for a time their economic prosperity fell away too, to the advantage of the leading cities of the Greek mainland, such as Athens and Corinth.

At the same time victory over Carthage and Etruria put the Sicilian Greek colonies into the limelight, especially Syracuse and Acragas, and the prosperity of Syracuse mounted to greater heights with the creation of the empire of Dionysius I. A century later we find the situation profoundly altered. The great Hellenistic cities had taken the lead in the East at the expense of the mother country, and in the West the world power of Rome had entered the field.

But the growth of industry and commerce, which encouraged the formation of large fortunes in liquid wealth, had the additional result of altering radically the relations between the social classes. At the expense of the old landed aristocracy new elements rising from the middle classes were coming to power. Since a large part of the available wealth was in their hands, they were forming an aristocracy of money over against that based on landed estates, and were gradually detaching themselves from the class from which they were drawn. The rest of the middle class was moving progressively downwards to join the proletariat.

This phenomenon was general, and is found on the Greek mainland no less than in the colonies. At Carthage too history over centuries is based on the struggle between the land-owning class, who wanted peace, and the industrialists, arms manufacturers, and merchants, who wanted war as a means of enriching themselves by supplying armaments and by enlarging the city's empire and therefore its trade. In Athens Aristophanes informs us about similar trends for the decades of the Peloponnesian War.

The same development can be seen in the plebeian class at Rome. A minority of wealthy knights broke away, to share power with the nobles and even to swamp them: these knights had no interest in common with the impoverished residue of the middle class from which they sprang. In their hands was all the industry, commerce, and tax-farming; and often also the military commands with the booty they brought. In the end they used part of their wealth to acquire land, and became owners of large estates themselves.

4. SCIENCE

a. *Indian Beginnings*

Indian speculative thought reached the border of science, but crossed it only in a few cases. It can be maintained that some of the *śāstra* (treatises or manuals) in Indian literature show a scientifico-technological character, although a theoretical and abstract one. The *śāstra* literature is formally connected with the *Vedas* and consists almost entirely of commentaries, elucidating some ancient and brief text (mostly lost). They aim at giving the means for easier and more perfect execution of religious practices in their various aspects. Thus we have texts referring to every branch of knowledge: medicine, astronomy, mathematics, drama, grammar, lexicography, hippology, jewellery, and even theft. The problem of dating the single works is a formidable and hardly soluble one. Most of them belong (at least in their present shape) to a period later than the limits set to the present volume. We shall therefore mention only those which go back, at least with some probability, to the Gupta age or earlier. The *śāstras* of the major sciences (medicine, mathematics, astronomy) will be dealt with in their proper place. Of the minor sciences, we may list here the texts on archery (*Dhanurveda*), all of them late; hippology (*Aśvaśāstra*), of which several treatises of unknown date are extant; jewellery (*Ratnaśāstra*), etc.

b. *Astrology and Astronomy*

Before the coming of Greek influences post-Vedic astronomy is very little known. The influence chiefly felt was that of the *Jyotiṣa Vedāṅga*, which, moreover, was put into writing only during this period. The material underlying a Jain work called *Sūriyapaṇṇatti* (but not the work's compilation) may belong to the last centuries BC. In this the astronomy is still Vedic, but its cosmology is akin to that of the *Purāṇa*, with Mt Meru in the centre surrounded by seven stories; the central story is divided into four parts, of which the southerly one is *Bharatavarṣa* or India. One of the most famous astronomers was Garga, but the work attributed to him is a late compilation. From all this it is practically impossible to reconstruct the main lines of the history of Indian astronomy. Probably, however, one can speak of some degree of Babylonian influence, which came in through the Achaemenid provinces of the Indus valley.[11] This would be the origin of the concept and calculation of the Great Periods of stellar revolution, which appear in astronomical writings of the following period.

China has no real astronomical literature in this period. The main evidence about the extent of knowledge of this subject comes in the chapters on astronomy, the calendar, and celestial phenomena in the dynastic histories and other works.

One of the most famous texts is the *Hsia-hsiao-chiêng*, a farmer's calendar for the 12 lunations, of the mid-fourth century BC; at the beginning of our era this was incorporated into chapter 47 of the *Ta-tai Li-chi*. Of the same period or somewhat later are the earliest stellar catalogues, compiled by Shih-Shên, Kan Tê, and Wu Hsien: all three are lost. But from a work written in the eighth century AD, the *K'ai-yüan-chang-ching* of Ch'ü-t'an-Hsi-ta, we know that observations made in the fourth century BC had led to the construction of a catalogue of 1,464 stars divided into 284 constellations. The principal document still preserved is the chapter on astronomy (*t'ien-kuan*) in the *Shih-chi* of Ssu-ma Ch'ien (*c.*90 BC); it contains a list of the constellations, describes celestial movements and conjunctions, and offers interpretations of unusual phenomena. Astronomy, as always in Chinese history, was a state affair, closely connected with the rites of the great imperial cult.

As to the general principles, there was an ancient theory, enunciated for example in the *Shan-shu-wei-k'ao-ling-yao* of the first century BC, according to which the earth moves 30,000 *li* to the west after the winter solstice and 30,000 *li* to the east after the summer solstice; only at the equinoxes is it still. This meant that the earth is continually moving, but that man is unaware of the movement; so one might as well base one's assumptions on an earth which did not move. In the later phases of its development Chinese astronomy diverged completely from Greek. Greek was 'ecliptic, angular, true, and annual'; Chinese was 'equatorial, hourly, mean, and diurnal'. The Chinese did not observe 'the heliac passage of the star on the ecliptic', but they determined 'culmination and lower transits (i.e. meridian passages) of the circumpolar stars'.

'Just as the influence of the Son of Heaven on earth radiated to all directions so the hour-circles radiated from the pole'. In this period the Chinese constructed a complete system of equatorial divisions, defined by the points of intersection between the equator and these hour-circles. These divisions were the *hsiu*, which must be conceived as slices of an orange labelled by names of constellations, normally those of small magnitude; when the constellations are invisible, the *hsiu* are fixed by means of the circumpolar stars belonging to the slice in question. This solved the sidereal-solar problem, since the full moon is exactly opposite to the sun and therefore the sidereal position of the moon is opposite that of the sun. The 28 *hsiu* are grouped in the four celestial palaces (with the same names as the four seasons), to which was added a fifth (the Emperor, corresponding to the Pole Star). The core of this system goes back to the Shang astronomers, but we first find it complete in the period of Shih-Shên and Kan Tê. Its similarity to the 27 or 28 Indian *nakṣatra* is obvious, though it is hard to say whether this is a case of borrowing or of independent creation. A common origin in Babylonia has been suggested, but there is no certainty.

Some simple astronomical instruments were already known. One was the gnomon, a plain stick held in a perfectly vertical position, the length of which was in early times fixed at 8 feet. It is mentioned in the *Chou-li* (*c.*175 BC), which attributes the first observation of the summer solstice to the Duke of Chou in the ninth century BC. By a simple alteration, namely by inclining the stick in the direction of the pole, the gnomon is converted into a sundial. This appears to be a fourth-century invention, though its first mention is in the *Shih-chi* under the date 104 BC.

The calendar was fixed by purely empirical methods, but quite soon certain principles got established. The division of the year into 12 months was for a long time connected with the cycle of 12 animals, which was common in all eastern Asia. Later the Chinese discovered the period after which a tropic year and a lunar month coincide again; this is the Chang cycle of 19 tropic years corresponding to approximately 235 lunations, and is therefore identical with Meton's cycle; various other cycles were determined as multiples of this one. At the end of this period a beginning was made with the recording of conjunctions and occultations of stars.

The observation of eclipses continued. The true cause of eclipses of the sun seems to have been known as early as the fourth century BC, and is certainly mentioned in the *Wu-ching-t'ung-i* of Liu Hsiang (*c.* 20 BC). Predictions could be made on the basis of a cycle (*chiao-shih-chou*) of 135 months containing 23 eclipses. This was invented in the first century and we find an example of its use by Liu Hsin in the *San-t'ung* calendar of 7 BC.

Observations of novae and supernovae were made from early times with remarkable accuracy. The list of Ma Tuan-lin (thirteenth century AD) starts with the same nova of 134 BC which led Hipparchus to begin his stellar catalogue. We find the chroniclers normally noting the time, duration, exact position, brightness, and colour of these phenomena. Later the comets are described with great care, and the catalogue made of them in Chinese sources is the most complete which exists today.

Finally it is worth observing that the Chinese gave close attention to meteorology. Systematic records, especially of rainfall, were kept as early as the Shang period. The meteorological cycle—clouds, rain, evaporation— has already been mentioned in the *Chi-ni-tzŭ* of the late fourth century BC. We also have long lists of floods and droughts.

Astrological and astronomical science in Babylonia established new propositions, and improved on the formulation of those which had been enunciated in the preceding period. Greek and Latin writers speak of a famous Babylonian astronomer called Cidenas (Kidinim), who calculated the movements of the sun and moon; and there is no doubt that this period saw an advance in knowledge about the relations between the movements of these two bodies. It was claimed that they were in the same position relatively to one another every eight years; later the theory was improved by positing a cycle of 19 years and 235 lunations. Furthermore the correspondence between the 360 degrees of the earth's circumference and the subdivision of the solar day was now established (4 minutes = 1 degree); the constellations were reduced to geometric shapes; observation was made of the sidereal years based on the passage of the sun between the constellations, as well as of the tropic year resulting from the succession of equinoxes and solstices; and, among other things, the Babylonians enunciated the varying rate of the sun's passage over the ecliptic, due to the eccentricity of its orbit. Parallel with these discoveries went the development of astrological doctrines.

These concern the influence on human actions of the movements of the heavenly bodies and of their positions relative to one another; knowledge of the way these complex movements are going to succeed one another is thought to make it possible to predict the future. At the same time the Chaldean seers used other methods of divination. They drew a man's horoscope at the moment of his birth, and revealed the future destiny of every man alive. We find this in the *Anaphoricos*, a Greek work inspired by Chaldean sources, which was compiled about 100 BC and wrongly attributed to Hypsicles of Alexandria. This proves the spread of those theories in the Mediterranean world.

In Greek lands the progress already made by Thales and Pythagoras had also owed much to oriental influence. In the fifth century BC Greece had some outstanding astronomical scholars. Anaxagoras (*c.* 500–428), who was put on trial for heresy because he deduced from the fall of a meteor that the sun was mineral, had several discoveries to his credit. He established that the moon shone with reflected light, and explained the moon's phases, the causes of eclipses, and the stellar composition of the Milky Way. Oenopides, who is always called the discoverer of the oblique ecliptic, calculated the Great (Luni-solar) Year of 59 years of $365\frac{22}{59}$ days each, which gives an error of only 3 hours each year. Meton then posited the cycle of 19 years containing 235 months, which we have seen may have been derived from the Babylonians; 12 of the years had 12 months and 7 had 13, while of the months 125 had 30 days and 110 had 29; here the error is reduced to half an hour a year. Empedocles tried to establish the relative distances from the earth of the sun and moon. The Pythagorean Philolaus maintained that in the cosmic sphere, besides the earth, the main heavenly bodies, and the other fixed stars, there was a central fire, distant in a geometrical ratio from the orbits of these bodies and facing an uninhabited side of the earth.

In the fourth century Plato changed his ideas in the course of his thought. His system was at first geocentric, but he ended as a heliocentric thinker believing that the earth went round the sun.[12] Eudoxus, who had learned the results of astronomical observations made by the priests at Heliopolis, imagined the planets to be fixed in 27 ideal concentric spheres, all revolving round a fixed earth and each with its axis pivoting upon another sphere. This theory was taken up by Callippus, who increased the number of spheres to 34, and by Polemarchus and others, who increased them again to 56. It was accepted by Aristotle, who expressed it in material terms, substituting a mechanical basis for the geometrical one. On the other hand the two Syracusans Hicetas and Ecphantus maintained that the earth was the one moving body amid the fixed stars, and that there was a fire at the centre of the universe. This theory was similar to an early view put forward by Heraclides Ponticus, that around an earth rotating on its own axis revolved the sun, and around the sun Mercury and Venus; later however he maintained that Mars, Jupiter, and Saturn also revolved round the sun, a view taken to

25

(a) *Winged horse and birds, clay tile from a tomb. Early Han, third to second century BC*

(b) *Cervide figure from Pazyryk in the Altai. Leningrad Hermitage Museum*

(a)

[M.O.K.

(b)

[I.O.

26   *Bharhut: three Yakshinis*

[*photo Josephine Powell*   (a) II   [D.A.I.

27   *Sanchi, India: The North Gate*

   (a) (i) *Ensemble view from the interior;* (ii) *East pillar, inside top panel: the musicians*

   (b) *Façade of the Bhaja caitya, India*

(b)   [D.A.I.

(a)

[Alinari

28   *Athens: The Acropolis*
    (a) *General view with the Parthenon*
    (b) *The Propylaea seen from the West, 437–432 BC*

(b)

[Alinari

its proper heliocentric conclusion later by Aristarchus, and endorsed by Seleucus. In Sicily Pheidias and his son Archimedes treated of the relative sizes and distances of the heavenly bodies; and Eratosthenes of Cyrene devoted his *katasterismoi* to astronomical studies on the constellations, of a semi-mythological kind.

In the second century BC Apollonius Pergaeus, instead of using the theory of rotating spheres to represent the movement of the planets, invented the theory of epicycles, according to which each star revolved round an ideal point. This was developed by Hipparchus, who with the aid of appropriate instruments was able to identify 850 stars, of six different magnitudes, and to give each its celestial co-ordinates. He enunciated the inclination of the plane of the ecliptic (the precession of the equinoxes), and brought into being what was later known as the Ptolemaic system of the circulating bodies, each with a path related to that of another. He calculated the distance and size of the moon with an error of $1/10$. He also believed in the scientific value of astrology, which had undergone a period of great development in all the Hellenistic world through the spread of the old Babylonian theories, propagated by 'Chaldeans' who wandered from city to city.

An example of this development is the way in which these Chaldeans' ideas became amalgamated with others which various countries already possessed, especially on the subject of divination. We can see this in Etruscan religion, which in its later development seems to have been deeply tainted by recently imported oriental features (these are often wrongly held to be ancient and are connected with the problem of the origin of the Etruscans).

Another source for the import of oriental ideas into Italy lay in the Stoic philosophers, for their school had Hellenized discoveries which had originally been made in the ancient East. At Rome we find a certain degree of astronomical knowledge by the second century BC. For instance in 191 Acilius Glabrio perceived the defects in the system of intercalating in the calendar; and C. Sulpicius Galba foresaw an eclipse of the moon before the battle of Pydna. Here too the spread of the treatise *Anaphoricos* (mentioned earlier) made an important contribution; so did the astrological propaganda of the Stoics, and we may remember the judgement of St Augustine on the Stoic Posidonius, 'fatalium siderum adsertor'. In quite early times, indeed, the activity of these prophets was considered dangerous, and they were frequently expelled, for instance in 139. Although he was a pupil of Posidonius, M. Tullius Cicero was hostile to astral theories. But it was in his day that theories of this kind were spread abroad by Nigidius Figulus (d. 45), the Magus and astrologer who wrote his *Sphaera Graecanica* to show that the great heroes were metamorphosed into stars. This work had not a little to do with the fact that C. Iulius Caesar (who himself was expert in astronomy and astrology, wrote a *De Astris*, and reformed the Roman calendar with the aid of Sosigenes) was believed after his death to have been changed into a star.

c. *Mathematics and Geometry*

Chinese numeral notation, as described in Part I, was already finally settled. Starting from the first century BC we find also more complicated forms to express the numerals from 1 to 9, the so-called 'accountants' forms' (*ta-hsieh-tzŭ*), which were designed to make fraudulent alterations more difficult.

Chinese mathematical literature has its origins in a classic text, the *Chou-pei-suan-ching*, 'Arithmetical Classic of the Gnomon and the circular paths of Heaven', the first part of which may go back to the fourth century BC, though the second part is three or four centuries later. In the first part the properties of the right-angled triangle are already known, and Pythagoras' theorem is propounded but not demonstrated. The text shows also a knowledge of the use of the gnomon, of the circle and of several astronomic-solar principles. It makes practical use of fractions and of their multiplication and division, and even of square roots. Already at that early time Chinese mathematics clearly displays its arithmetico-algebraic and anti-geometrical outlook. Geometric properties depend on the number, and no interest is shown in abstract algebra; the Chinese never developed an algebraic notation. The text is remarkably free of mystical and magical elements.

The Chinese have always recognized the four basic arithmetical operations alone. It appears from a passage of the *Kuan-tzŭ* that the Pythagoraic table was not unknown. As a mechanical aid to arithmetic the counting rods (*ch'ou* or *ts'ê*) were used, and they are mentioned already in the fourth and third centuries BC.

Chinese metrology at first made use of variable measures, partly based on the human body. Later the decimal system became common, its chief champion being Mo-ti (*c.*330 BC); in 170 BC a memorial submitted to the throne already proposed the adoption of the decimal system for all measures; but for the time being the proposal was not accepted.

Some seeds of theoretical geometry are contained in the text of Mo-ti, but they were not developed; and geometry remained unknown. This serious gap represents the weakest point in Chinese mathematics.

Indian chronology is so incorrigibly fluid that it is extremely uncertain what stage mathematics (*gaṇita*) had reached during this period. Nevertheless we know that these centuries saw the birth of the positional arithmetic which is the foundation of all future advance. From the start the Indian system of numbers was strictly decimal. The earliest digits had no positional value; they are already found on Aśoka's inscriptions (third century BC), although the complete series is not attested in epigraphy before the second century BC. But the essential feature was already there, and it appears that the manual on metric called *Chandraḥ Sūtra*, attributed to Pingala (200 BC) implies a knowledge of the zero, though the latter is not actually named.

Our information about geometry is less vague. There have survived a series of manuals called *Śulvasūtra*, which give practical rules for the rite of *agnicayana*, the construction of an altar for Vedic sacrifice. The *Śulvasūtra* are a part of the *Kalpasūtras*, or more precisely of the *Śrautasūtras*, very condensed summaries of Vedic lore for use in schools. Seven of them have come down to us. The practical rules they contain presuppose knowledge of various geometrical operations, although the latter are not enunciated and discussed. There must, for instance, have been a practical knowledge of Pythagoras' theorem, of the transformation of areas, and of the doubling of squares. This last implies taking the square root of 2, the value of which is taken in the *Śulvasūtra* as 1·4142156 (1·414213 is the correct approximation).

The problems in advanced geometry which most interested the Greeks after 450 BC were the trisection of angles, the squaring of the circle, and the duplication of the cube. Hippias of Elis invented a curve, which he used not only for trisection of angles but later also for squaring the circle, and which was therefore known as *quadratrix*. Hippocrates of Chios, author about 450 of an early treatise on mathematics, although he failed to square the circle or to duplicate the cube, achieved notable results, for instance about the relation between the circle and the square on its diameter. Democritus of Abdera (460–370?), among his many works, wrote treatises on mathematics, though we know of them little more than their titles: he was concerned with surds, in connection with parallel sections of a cone, and also with the volume of cones and pyramids. The Pythagorean Archytas in his work on mathematics successfully solved the problem of doubling the cube; and Theodorus, the teacher of Plato and Theatetus, gave a definition of surds and of their main properties, which were later expounded in the tenth book of Euclid.

Plato (427–347) made no new discoveries or applications, but from the technical standpoint he attached enormous importance to geometry and arithmetic, and wanted statesmen to contemplate the nature of number and to study geometry out of pure love of knowledge. He preached the need for mathematical analysis, and his theories of classes and forms also contributed to throw light on the subject. Eudoxus of Chios (408–355) had two claims to fame, his theory of proportions, which could be applied to commensurable and incommensurable magnitudes alike (see Euclid, Book V), and the method of 'exhaustion', which proves by *reductio ad absurdum* the equivalence of two magnitudes between which no difference can be shown. A pupil of his, called Menaichmus, took up the study of conic sections.

About the end of the fourth century the *Elementa* of Euclid appeared in thirteen books, which because of the clarity of their exposition had a great future in all subsequent treatment of mathematics in schools, and were the continuous subject of commentaries. Euclid naturally made use of the propositions of his predecessors, expounding and improving them systematically. Books I–VI deal with plane geometry and the general theory of magnitudes, Books VII–IX with arithmetic, Book X with surds and in-commensurables, Books XI–XIII with solid geometry. Other works by Euclid have come down to us, treating of elementary and higher geometry and of applied mathematics (Phenomena, Optics, and the Elements of Music).

Aristarchus of Samos (310–c.230) intensified the application of geometrical processes and trigonometrical ratios to astronomy. Archimedes of Syracuse (287–212), who also studied in Alexandria, was remarkable for the breadth of his interests and investigations. He was an astronomer, a student of hydrostatics who discovered the Law of Floating Bodies, a mechanic who invented such things as engines of war and hydraulic tubes for pumps (water snails), but above all a mathematician. In geometry he did distinguished work in the measurement of curvilinear figures and solids. He was devoted to pure theory as much as to the practical application of mathematics, and wrote a large number of specialized treatises, several of which survive.

Eratosthenes of Cyrene (275–195), whom we mentioned earlier as an astronomer, was a friend of Archimedes and like him a scholar whose learning ranged over every field. Among other things he invented an apparatus with which he obtained results in duplication of cubes; and in his *Platonicus* he expounded the relations between philosophy and the science of numbers. Nicomedes invented the 'conoid' or 'cocloid', and Diocles the 'cissoid' curves for determining duplication of cubes and trisection of angles.

With Apollonius of Perge (d. 170) geometry attained the highest point which was possible before the use of algebra. His great work on conic sections has survived partly in Greek and partly in Arabic: of his many other writings, which formed part of the *Treasury of Analysis*, no trace remains.

The great astronomer Hipparchus of Nicaea (160–125) developed the methods of trigonometry. To the end of our period belong a number of specialist scholars: Hypsicles, who added a XIVth Book, on regular solids, to the work of Euclid; Persaeus, who studied spiral sections; Zenodotus, who analysed 'isometric' figures, planes and solids with equal perimeters and areas; and Theodosius of Bithynia, who examined the properties of the sphere.

We must also mention the Stoic philosopher Posidonius of Apamea (135–51), one of whose many writings dealt with definitions in elementary geometry, for instance the definition of parallels. His pupil Geminus of Rhodes wrote a general work on mathematical and geometrical disciplines.

d. *Geography*

The basic idea of Chinese geography is the earth considered as a square or nearly square plate, surrounded by the sea on every side, with the half-sphere of the sky above it. The whole is subject to the fundamental Chinese idea of a close correspondence between heaven and earth, between the movement of the celestial bodies and the development of mankind. A sort of *axis mundi* connects the whole and is represented by the emperor. Therefore China is the centre of the world; in earlier times it was even accepted as the world.

The oldest geographical text is the *Yü-kung* chapter of the *Shu-ching;* it purports to be a description of the dominions of the legendary emperor Yao, compiled by his minister Yü in order to show the proper places for digging canals and regulating the waters. Its main interest is therefore hydraulic and economic. In reality the text goes back to the fifth century BC and covers more or less the lands on the middle and lower Huang-ho. Being a section of a canonical text, the *Yü-kung* enjoyed widespread authority, but was soon overwhelmed by a still more famous text: the *Shan-hai-ching* (Classic of mountains and seas). The latter is an unequal compilation, where elements of positive geography are inextricably mixed with tales of fabulous monsters and of legendary populations. It is interesting to note that many of these fabulous beings are closely similar to those described by Herodotus, Strabo, and Pliny; their common origin seems to lie in India or Iran, perhaps even in Mesopotamia. According to Karlgren, the text belongs to the Han period, and in some portions even to the Later Han; but a good deal of its material seems to go back to the times, and perhaps to the school, of Tsou Yen (end of the fourth century BC). Geographical material is also found scattered in the fourth chapter of the *Huai-nan-tzŭ*, a collection of essays by various authors of the mid-second century BC. Another class of geographical writing, that of tales of travel, is opened by the *Mu-t'ien-tzŭ-chuan*, the partly legendary account of the journey of the Chou king Mu to the fairy Hsi-wang-mu in the Western countries. It was discovered in AD 281 in the tomb of a prince who had died in 296 BC; it therefore goes back to the fourth century BC.

Knowledge of geography became more and more a recognized part of science. Beginning with the *Shih-chi* of Ssŭ-ma Ch'ien all the dynastic histories include a section (*Ti-li-chih*) on the geography of the empire; often also some accounts of foreign countries are placed at the end of the biographical sections. The latter had their true beginning with the fateful missions of Chang Ch'ien (138–125 BC), who opened up the West to Chinese explorers, mostly envoys and merchants; and soon a vast literature arose on the subject. Hydrography too, after its first beginnings in the *Yü-kung*, took on definite shape with the original *Shui-ching* (Water Classic) of Sang Ch'in (first century BC), though this was soon afterwards lost.

Chinese cartography existed from an early age; the *Chou-li* refers to officials preparing maps of feudal principalities. The first mention of a map of a district incised on wood appears in 227 BC, in connection with an attempt at murdering the king of Ch'in. All extant maps were shortly afterwards collected by order of the first emperor Shih-huang-ti; they continued in existence for a long time after the fall of Ch'in. In Han times too maps are mentioned, e.g. on the occasion of investitures of feudal princes (117 BC) or of Li Ling's campaign against the Hsiung-nu (99 BC). In 35 BC an imperial general, on returning from crushing the Hsiung-nu chief Chih-chih in the far west, showed the harem ladies maps or paintings of his campaign (*t'u-shu*; the term is ambiguous).

In the fifth and fourth centuries the Pythagorean theory of the earth's sphericity was used to effect in explaining climatic phenomena and seasonal cycles. In the third century Dicaearchus and Eratosthenes gave attention to measurements of the earth and to construction of maps.[13] In this period historians and geographers, because of their journeys, were fond of including geographical or ethnographical digressions in their works: Herodotus did this, and after him Ctesias of Cnidus, Ephorus of Cyme, and among later writers Timaeus in the third century, Polybius in the second, and Posidonius in the first. For similar reasons the reports of the sixth-century Carthaginian explorers, Himilco and Hanno, were translated into Greek.

Alexander the Great took with him on his expedition a number of historians and geometers, such as Beton, Diognetus, and Amyntas. The result was a remarkable development in exploration, and similar journeys were undertaken under the Hellenistic rulers who followed Alexander. Part of the Indian ocean was explored by Nearchus, and later described by Simias and Agatharcides (second century); Androsthenes of Thasos explored Arabia, Dasius and Simonides the Nile basin, Patroclus the Caspian, Demodemus the regions of Scythia, and Megasthenes India.

The expedition against Carthage by Agathocles of Syracuse enlarged Greek knowledge of North Africa; the journeys of Pytheas of Massilia discovered eastern Britain, and also western Germany as far as the Elbe; about 120–115 Eudoxus of Cyzicus sailed along the coasts of Africa; in 95 Publius Crassus reached the Cassiterides islands; and finally the conquests of C. Iulius Caesar brought close knowledge of all western Europe.

All this gave great impetus to the production of the guide-books known as *periploi* and *periegeseis*. The one wrongly attributed to Scylax was composed about 340–330; and others were written by Timosthenes of Rhodes, Cleon and Nymphodorus of Syracuse, Demetrius of Callatis, Mnaseas of Patrae, the pseudo-Scymnus, Artemidorus of Miletus, and Alexander Polyhistor (with separate monographs on particular parts of the world). King Juba II of Mauretania wrote a treatise on Libya and Africa; and Menippus of Pergamum was the author of a *Periplus Maris Interni*.

The growth of geographical knowledge was also responsible, at the end of our period and the beginning of the next, for the production of two great works designed to make known all the world which was then in Roman hands. One was the *Geography* of Strabo of Amasia (60 BC–AD 25). The second was the *Commentarii* of M. Vipsanius Agrippa, based on a series of researches on the ground by Isidore of Charax and others, and leading to the construction of a great map of the empire set up by Augustus in Rome.

e. *Medicine, Anatomy, and Pharmacopoeia*

In ancient Chinese thought medicine is closely integrated with the other pre-scientific disciplines: cosmology, astrology, geomancy. The first medical text (apart from one famous passage in the *Tso-ch'uan*) is the 'Yellow Emperor's classic of internal medicine' (*Huang-ti nei-ching*). It is attributed to hoary antiquity, but goes back probably to the fourth century and is connected with Taoist speculation. It is divided into two parts (*Su-wên* and *Ling-ch'u*), both heavily interpolated in the Han period. According to this text, health is due to the harmony of *yin* and *yang*; illness is due to its disturbance. It gives prominence to acupuncture (perhaps the outstanding original feature of Chinese medicine) and rejects the incantations of the priest-doctor. It accepts the mysticism of numbers, but rejects religions. A very minute description of symptoms is given, but they are not distinguished from disease. Much emphasis is placed on the constitution of the individual and on environment; diet is given considerable attention, and this discloses the knowledge of some elements of dietetics. Knowledge of the pulse is well developed and diagnosis is usually made thereby.

The first treatise on Chinese pharmacology is the *Pên-ts'ao-ching*, attributed to the mythical emperor Shên-nung but probably belonging to the first century BC. It describes 365 types of drugs and shows a considerable knowledge of emetics, purgatives, and antipyretics.

The only real document on the practical working of Chinese medicine in this period is contained in a passage of the *Shih-chi* concerning the physician Ch'un Yü-i (fl. 167 BC). Upon his dismissal he submitted to the government a curriculum vitae followed by twenty-five medical observations and eight questions and replies on teaching, as it was then practised by oral transmission from teacher to pupil. He knew the five inner organs (heart, liver, lungs, spleen, kidneys), and there is a position of the pulse for diagnosis on each organ. The breath-power (*ch-i*) circulates through meridians (*ching*), sorts of force-lines which communicate between themselves by means of the vessels (*lo*). This pneumatic theory is completed by the influence of *yin* and *yang*, whose dominance and equilibrium follow the seasons. They must influence the patient without penetrating too deep. Therapeutics are eclectic; mineral and vegetable drugs in pills, decoction or infusion; physiotherapy, massage, acupuncture, and *moxas* on fixed points. Numerous diseases are known by name.

As everywhere else, Indian medicine has its origins in curative magic: several medical spells are preserved in the *Atharvaveda*, and their ritual use is explained in the *Kauṣikasūtra*. Pathology is characterized by a close relation between illness and sin. The latter results in consumption or organic waste (*yakṣma*). The *Atharvaveda* has a fair knowledge of the various kinds of fevers; but symptoms are not yet properly separated from illness, and most of the pathological terms apply to external phenomena. Cure was mostly by spells and incantations, although a crude therapy by herbs was not unknown; but even the herbs were employed chiefly because of their magical power. The Vedic doctor had a considerable knowledge of anatomy (even of the inner organs) and of physiology. The central theme of their lore was a close correspondence between the body and its several parts, and the cosmos and its divisions. Thus breath corresponds to the wind, the eye to the sun, etc. A pneumatic theory was developing, which reached its final shape with the classical texts of Indian medicine in the next period. One at least of the Late Vedic medical works, the *Bhelasaṃhitā*, is preserved; it appears to go back to the last centuries BC. A comparison of the *Bhelasaṃhitā* with the (later) *Carakasaṃhitā* makes possible a reconstruction of the original doctrines and knowledge which both texts trace back to Ātreya. The elements of their physiology are those of the *Yajurveda* and *Atharvaveda*. The pneumatic theory has its Hellenistic counterpart in the treatise *Peri Physeon* in the Hippocratic Corpus. Besides, the fundamental theory of the three elements of the body and the universe, which belongs to classical Indian medicine, finds its counterpart in the theory of Plato's *Timaeus*; and the connection between Indian and Greek medicine at the time of Plato and of the Hippocratic Corpus is attested by the references in the latter to Indian remedies and medical recipes, about which see later (Part III, Chapter XV).

Medicine in Greece of the late sixth century had made such advances that about 520 Democedes became the doctor of highest renown at the Persian court of Darius I. Again in the mid-fifth century Onesilus of Cyprus had a great reputation in the Oriental world, and at the beginning of the fourth century Ctesias of Cnidus was doctor to Artaxerxes II. At Croton, Rhodes, Cyrene, Cos, and Cnidus schools of medicine competed with one another for primacy; and empirical observation freed itself more and more from the practice of magic, though the latter was still important to Empedocles of Acragas. Among the Crotoniate school must be noticed Alcmaeon (early fifth century), who is credited with discovering the Eustachian tube and the optic nerves and was a pioneer in the important Greek studies on the working of the brain. Empedocles expounded theories on the derivation of blood from the heart,[14] on the importance of the pores in sensation and respiration, on the structure of the eye, and on the morphology which is common to hair and feathers. At the end of the fifth century Diogenes of Apollonia had a considerable reputation: he dissected corpses to study the vessels of the blood, and evolved the so-called 'pneumatic' theory.

The collection of writings which have most value for the study of Greek medicine in the fifth and fourth centuries is that attributed, for the most part with justice,[15] to Hippocrates of Cos. He had pupils throughout Greece, and was a man of great cultivation, discretion, and precision, considerate and humane towards his patients, as can be seen from the oath which he exacted from his pupils about the way in which they should pursue their profession. Hippocratic medicine was based on the premises that health depends on the harmony of the human body, on the proper distribution and balance of the elements which compose it. These elements were earth, air, water, and fire, each with its own characteristics—dryness, cold, moisture, and heat, and with its respective 'humours'—blood, phlegm, black bile, and yellow bile.[16] Hippocrates' work started from facts ascertained by direct observation, mainly by auscultation, from symptoms ('clinical signs'), and from the progress of diseases and the way epidemics spread. In this way he was able to formulate a number of clinical studies, of which more than forty are known to us, and to indicate the remedies needed to overcome the various types of disharmony between the elements and humours. In many cases he assisted the patient to reach and pass the 'crisis', leading on to recovery by means of appropriate diet, rest, baths, bleeding, or limited use of drugs. Many of his aphorisms have become a vital part of the wisdom of mankind.

The lack of systematic experiment in physiology, pathology, and anatomy prevented Hippocrates from reaching results in surgery as decisive as those he reached in medicine. He could do no more than give careful attention to wounds, fractures, and dislocations, as well as studying skeletons and the dissection of animals, especially during sacrifices and the taking of omens. The means at his disposal were certainly inadequate, but he brought meticulous preparation, and all the preparatory thinking one could wish, to bear on quite difficult operations, such as opening the chest for empyema, or trepanning the head.

At the beginning of the third century the most famous head of a medical school was Herophilus of Chalcedon, who practised at Alexandria and wrote a work on anatomy. This book won a great reputation on account of its general observations on dissection methods and also because of its descriptions of particular workings of the human body—nerves, eyes, the vascular system (Herophilus saw the relation between the heart, the circulation of the blood, and the rhythm of the pulse), glands, digestion and liver, reproduction, and bone structure.

A younger contemporary of Herophilus, also working at Alexandria about 258, was Erasistratus of Ceos, known mainly through Galen's criticisms. From these we learn that he in part followed traditional ideas, such as the pneumatic theory and the use of diet as the main element in cures, but that he also had progressive notions based on his various experiments. He studied the epiglottis, the lymphatic ducts, the anatomy of the brain and blood, and the action of the motor muscles and sensory nerves.

Another head of a school was Philinus of Cos, a pupil of Herophilus, who practised in the Serapeum about 240. He was an empiricist in outlook, but was disposed to over-value drugs and considered the cause of diseases, like anatomy, to be of secondary interest. The same tendency was shown by Heracleides of Tarentum (c. 100) and by Asclepiades of Prusa (130–40 BC), a follower of Epicurus who spent much of his life at Rome. The latter was an enthusiastic atomist, an orator and psychologist, and an inventor of

P*

remedies. He wrote a number of works on medicine, and had a close understanding of certain diseases, including dropsy, tetanus, and malaria. He
attacked the theory of 'humours', but strongly believed in the efficacy of
physical education. He used to describe perfect cures with the saying 'Cito,
tuto, iucunde' ('with speed, safety, and comfort').

It had been the presence of Greek doctors which started the rational
practice of medicine at Rome. The earliest was Arcagathus in 219 BC, who
earned the title 'carnifex' ('butcher') for his audacious surgery. Medicine
was regarded as a profession beneath the dignity of a Roman, so it was
predominantly practised at Rome by foreigners, mainly freedmen of Greek
origin: they were responsible for great advances, although they were opposed
by traditional politicians like Cato and his followers. At the same time,
however, the Romans showed strong interest in the practice of hygiene:
this went back to the time when the *cloaca maxima*, and the first aqueducts
and baths, were constructed, and when the corn supply and purifying of
water were brought under control. The Twelve Tables already laid down
that graves must lie outside inhabited areas; and the earliest drainage operations aimed at reducing the malarial districts. A series of laws regulated and
supervised the conduct of doctors, being directed particularly against
abortion, poisoning, and negligence towards patients.

Caesar set store by genuine doctors, and in his day any foreign student or
practitioner who took up residence in Rome enjoyed privileges and concessions, even Roman citizenship. Medical schools could come into being,
and in the next generation a well-known doctor was Augustus' physician
Antonius Musa, who cured him of a serious illness in 23 BC, and compiled
works about medicinal herbs.

The advance of medicine was accompanied, as we saw in the cases of
Philinus, Heraclides, and Asclepiades, by progress in pharmacology, which
is frequently mentioned in our sources. We are told of about 300 ingredients
which were made up in powders, pills, infusions, decoctions, tisanes, oint-
ments, and so on. They could be administered by the mouth, or in packs,
frictions, massages, baths, gargles, inhalations, or enemas. They included
purges, emetics, diuretics, and drugs to induce perspiration or sleep; or they
might be generally designed to rid the body of 'humours' which had gone
wrong.

f. *The Natural Sciences and the Origins of the World*

The Greek world gradually extended its knowledge of zoology and botany
as observation became closer, the known world grew larger, and the element
of fancy and story-telling got progressively discarded. Yet this last element
was slow to disappear: we must remember the fantastic animals described by
Ctesias about 400, and later by Megasthenes, and later still in the 'Paradoxical
Stories' of Antigonus of Carystus (born *c.*295–290). But all the time the

habits of particular types of animal were undergoing observation, as we see in Xenophon's work on hunting; and ideas were collected about the young of animals in the work written by Polybius about 380 BC. Considerable progress in zoology was made by Aristotle (384–322), particularly on account of his systematic approach. He catalogued about fifty species in his ten books *De Historia Animalium*; he then wrote a further five books on the reproduction of animals, and a further five on the parts of their bodies. He put marine animals in a class by themselves, paying special attention to their description, and gave similar treatment to insects and their metamorphoses.

Next in time should be mentioned the observations of Callimachus on birds and of Nicander on bees. Bees were also the subject of the *De Apibus* of C. Ilius Hyginus (37 BC), and of Virgil in his *Georgics*. About 20 BC Trogus Pompeius wrote on animals and plants, and he was followed by Juba II on various phenomena in nature, by the African Turanius Gracilis on zoology and botany, and by Trebius Niger on fish and other marine animals.

Meanwhile the study of botany had been markedly advanced, mainly by Aristotle's pupil Theophrastus of Eresus (372–287), who wrote an *Historia Plantarum* in nine books, with systematic description of various vegetables, particularly those related to agriculture. Other Greek writers were Phainias of Eresus, another pupil of Aristotle; Dicaearchus of Messana; and Nicander of Colophon, who wrote *Georgics*. Rome was influenced by the Carthaginian works on agriculture, for instance Mago's book, translated into both Greek and Latin. The Latin output included Cato's *De Agricultura* (he died in 149 BC), the three books of Varro's *De Re Rustica*, the *De Agricultura* of Hyginus published in 37 BC, and the *Georgics* of Virgil. Then the Sisennae (father and son) wrote on agriculture, and were followed by C. Tremellius Scrofa and Manilius Sura; Juba II wrote on euphorbia and the Etruscan Tarquitius Priscus produced a work on the flowering and colouring of plants.

Researches into nature gave a new impetus to speculation about the origins of the world. Bearing in mind the materialist monism of the Ionian philosophers and the spiritual outlook of the Eleatics, Empedocles of Acragas (490–430) advanced a new rationalist and mechanical explanation of the world. The four elements, or roots of the material world, were brought together by love or alternatively separated by hate; and so birth and death came to being. Anaxagoras of Clazomenae (*c.* 500–428) came to believe in dualism of a teleological kind. He held that there existed an infinite quantity of tiny elements, the seeds of things; that from their union or disunion birth and death were derived; and that the finest and purest of these elements constituted Mind, which gathered the world from the primeval mass of seeds by sending matter round in rotatory motion and so separating the various elements from one another. A third explanation was given by the Atomists, Leucippus of Miletus and Democritus of Abdera (460–370). Democritus supposed a Void, and thought it was moving Matter, composed of an infinite number of indivisible atoms, homogeneous in substance but variable in weight and size. In the eternal movement of atoms those of equal weight tried to unite with another to form various bodies, but when struck by others of different velocity they started to revolve and so created 'phenomena'.

Plato, above all in his *Timaeus*, gives an explanation which is a mixture of realism and poetry; it is largely enigmatic and is based on Pythagorean ideas. The Creator or Demiurge, the boundless and unchanging principle of the God, had in his work of creation to take account of three factors, Necessity, Reason, and Disorder (with the movement that Disorder brings). He created the spirit of the world, bringing the Cosmos, or organized world, out of chaos, and bringing rule and order from that which lacked both. This is the macrocosm, inscribed in a harmony of celestial spheres; and the microcosm or man is in its image, with his head a sphere, containing the brain in which his thoughts go round. The power of vision given by light and fire, and the power of touch given by the earth, are directly related to the other two elements, air and water. These elements can be conceived as geometrical shapes, earth as a cube, fire as a pyramid, air as an octahedron, and water as an eicosahedron; all can then be reduced to a set of triangles, and are interchangeable one with the other.

With Epicurus of Samos (341–271) we return to Atomism, and it had now developed more fully. Matter and the Void exist, and Matter is composed of atoms, simple particles of the smallest size, countless and indivisible. They are continually uniting and dividing; and where they fall into the Void with a swerving movement they collide, combine, and so form bodies, which later dissolve again into atoms. In the cosmic Void, which is infinite and incommensurable, there exist countless worlds, but of these we know but one, which is isolated from this Void around it. The worlds are born and move about without end, and in the vortex of these successive experiments nature has made our own world and man as he exists today. The soul consists of the lightest atoms. It cannot live without the body, nor the body without it: when the body dies, the soul dies too. Every body gives off images of itself, again composed of very light atoms, which impact on our senses and there form impressions. Sometimes these images combine, and it is then that errors of the senses and concepts of the unreal arise.

The theories of Epicurus were later modified in the works of pupils belonging to his school, for instance Asclepiades (130–40), who maintained that atoms could be divided. In the Roman world the greatest exponent of Epicureanism was the poet Lucretius (*c*.95–50 BC). Of his poem *De Rerum Natura* in six books, the first two books deal with cosmogony, the third with the theory of the soul, the fourth with perception, and the last two with the origin and history of nature and man.

g. *Philology*

Chinese lexicography had its beginnings in the works of commentators on the classics. Their collections of rare and obscure terms were the earliest examples of vocabularies. The first work of this kind is the *Êrh-ya*, attributed to Tzŭ Hsia, a pupil of Confucius, but really belonging to the second or first century BC. This glossary of terms in the classics is divided by subjects, the items being grouped together in nineteen sections.

Another incentive to lexicography came from quite another direction, the official reorganization of writing under the Ch'in emperors. Li Ssŭ's list of standard characters, the *San-ts'ang* (now lost), was also in itself a sort of dictionary, which aimed at completeness rather than at explaining difficult terms.

After the beginning of our era dictionaries and glossaries (and later encyclopaedias) took two main forms: either they were classified by subjects, on the model of the *Êrh-ya*; or they were arranged by 'characteristics' or 'radicals' of the character to be explained (later also by rhymes). The latter class was inaugurated by an etymological dictionary, the *Shuo-wên chieh-tzŭ* of Hsü Shen (*c.* AD 120). It is organized according to a system of 540 radicals and contains 9,353 characters, plus 1,163 doubles, i.e. 10,516 items in all. It is the ancestor of all the later dictionaries arranged on a key system, down to the famous *K'ang-hsi tzŭ-tien* of the early thirteenth century.

A place by itself was occupied by a dialect dictionary, the *Fang-yen*, compiled in the first two centuries of our era, but lost long ago.

Indian grammar (*vyākaraṇa*) has a long tradition. Its origin goes back to the post-Vedic treatises concerning the proper recitation and understanding of the sacred texts. Hence the particular care given to it, and the very high place that grammatical studies always occupied in the literary life of India.

The first treatise preserved and the most authoritative one is the *Astā-dhyāyī* of Pāṇini, belonging probably to the fourth century BC. As the name implies, it is divided into eight sections (*adhyāya*) and contains about 4,000 rules (*sūtra*). The first two sections set forth definitions and general principles; sections 3, 4 and 5 deal with nominal derivation; sections 6 and 7 give phonetic rules concerning junction (*sandhi*) of composites and derivative formations, with a sub-section on accent (*svara*). The last *adhyāya* deals with the *sandhi* of sentences. Pāṇini's rules are couched in the shortest and pithiest mode of expression possible: a few words only for each. The work is practically a series of algebraic formulae, very precise and exact in their meaning. They were meant of course only as a mnemonic help to oral teaching, which alone could vivify the obscure text.

The work of Pāṇini represents a landmark in the development of grammatical studies. It caught the language in the process of transition from Vedic to classical Sanskrit and dealt with all its minutiae, thus decisively contributing to fix it in that rigid and invariable shape which is peculiar to dead languages. The mentality which inspires it is thoroughly scientific, to a degree rare in India. Thus it was a revelation to the early European philologists, who adopted several of its leading ideas and some of its happiest technical terms.

Of course Pāṇini, in spite of his immense authority, did not say the last word on Sanskrit grammar. His great work was either too general or too short or too obscure on several minor points. Therefore a large body of commentaries arose. Pāṇini's foremost successor Kātyāyana is known only by name. But we have a work by Patañjali (not identical with the Yoga philosopher), the *Mahābhāṣya*, i.e. the great commentary on Pāṇini. It may be placed in the second century BC and is a discussion on the single *vārttikas* (elements of interpretation) of Kātyāyana. It is thus an interesting example not only of grammatical science, but also of dialectic discussion as practised in the Indian schools of that time.

The process of interpreting the ancient poets, especially the Homeric cycle, made the Greeks of quite early times want to explain words of particularly obscure meaning. They formulated 'glosses' on a wide variety of topics, ranging from straightforward formal grammar to analysis of philosophical doctrine. About 500 BC they came up against the problem of the origin of language. Heraclitus of Ephesus, followed later by the Stoics, thought language developed naturally (φύσει) while the Eleatics, followed by the Atomists, derived it from a convention among mankind (νόμῳ, θέσει). Etymology and similar-sounding place-names were used by historians from Hecataeus onwards as evidence for reconstructing historical events.

Grammar and correct use of words may be said to have started with the observations of Protagoras of Abdera (*c*.480–410). To him goes back the recognition of the three genders, the formulation of precise rules about the appropriate moods of verbs to use in particular forms of sentence (imperative for command, optative for request, interrogative for a question, affirmative for reply), and the identification of irregularities in inflection of verbs. Synonymous words were studied by Prodicus of Ceos (*c*.470–400), and style together with phonetics by Hippias of Elis. Investigations of this kind, and also comparisons between the dialects, soon became of general interest, as we see, for example, from the frequent mention of them in Herodotus' *History*.

In the fourth century the problems went deeper. For instance Plato examined the origins of poetry, aesthetic criticism, and exegesis; he also analysed the parts of speech, substantives and verbs, and made a study of such matters as the origin of language and etymology. The *Cratylus* is our main source on the latter topic: Plato derives words from expressive-sounding elements which developed by convention.

Aristotle too devoted thought to the origins of poetry and other types of literature. He also analysed parts of speech, letters, syllables, conjunctions, nouns, verbs, inflection, and prepositions. But his work may be called the end of general philological studies with a theoretical basis, which gave place in the Hellenistic age to a number of distinct types of grammatical investigation. These included linguistic and literary phenomena, the various types of style, the lives of writers, and the history of literature. Athens and the older centres of culture had in this period the aid of the great libraries, above all those at Alexandria and Pergamum. But while at Athens the favourite field of study was on critical editions of early authors, especially Homer, and at Cos Philetas was writing on miscellaneous problems (*Atakta*), Philetas' pupil Zenodotus of Ephesus (325–260) was starting the series of complicated studies centred on the library at Alexandria, of which he became the first librarian in 282. Alexandrian work was based on analysis of the language and style of particular authors. With this they prepared editions designed to get rid of alterations to the text; and believing that language originated by convention, they studied the various dialects, the etymologies of the words they used, and the exact way in which they were written. To reconstruct texts they freely used the criteria of analogy, harmony, and proportion, and produced general lexicons as well as volumes on particular authors and dialects.

In the linguistic field the main works of the Alexandrian librarians were as follows: Zenodotus produced a Homeric lexicon; Callimachus composed a history of literature (the *Pinakes*) and a number of 'glosses' on place-names; Aristophanes of Byzantium, who invented both the theory of 'analogy' (on which inflection is held to follow rational rules) and also the 'diacritic' signs used in editions, edited a dictionary which took account of dialect variations; and Aristarchus of Samothrace wrote on parts of speech and on the value of analogy.

Meanwhile the Stoics, starting with Chrysippus of Soloi (280–206) had a line of their own. They still believed in the natural origin of language, and with the aid of phonetic symbolism they worked on the possibilities of onomatopoeic or direct imitation, on likenesses and contrasts, on the theory of grammatical forms, and on etymology. But the laws they formulated were capricious, and were severely criticized by the Alexandrians.

Another school was working at the same time at Pergamum. The principle of Crates of Mallus, who wrote a famous Attic lexicon about 168, was the theory of anomaly, or grammatical irregularity. An age-long argument, with exaggeration on both sides, resulted between Analogists and Anomalists, ending with the creation of a definitive theory of grammar which took account of the concrete data accumulated by the advocates of both theories. The dispute later found its way to Rome when the Stoic Panaetius (180–110), a member of the Scipionic circle, took up residence there.

The first effort to reconcile the Pergamenes and Alexandrians was made about the middle of the second century in the etymological researches of Apollodorus of Athens. An attempt was also made to reconcile the theories of the Stoics and Pergamenes when Dionysius Thrax, a pupil of Aristarchus

born at Alexandria, founded the school of Rhodes. Dionysius wrote a famous
school-book on grammar, which was continually re-edited and remained the
standard work for a thousand years, though the paradigms it offered were
sometimes arbitrary. It was divided into six parts, reading, etymology,
analogy, exegesis of poetical writings (images, glosses, and content), criticism,
and judgement.

There were certain later modifications to Dionysius' scheme. Asclepiades
of Myrleia (150–50), who came to Rome from Alexandria with Pompey,
reduced the treatment of the subject to three parts: linguistic technique,
history, and criticism (or exegesis). His pupil Tyrannio of Amisus (100–
26 BC), who also came to Rome, had four divisions: reading, textual criticism,
exegesis, and criticism of the subject matter. The arrival of these grammarians
in Rome had a most important effect on the beginnings of Roman study of
philology, although the foundation of this had been very different, seeing that
it was concerned with Latin language and literature rather than with Greek.
A number of Latin writers on philology deserve mention. The tragedian
Accius (170–*c*.90) gave attention to the orthography of long vowels and the
transcription of Greek terminations. The Lanuvian Stoic L. Aelius Stilo
Praeconinus (150–90), who lived first at Rhodes and taught both Cicero and
Varro, supported the natural origin of language and placed great importance
on syntax. M. Antonius Gnipho, the Celtic tutor of C. Iulius Caesar, wrote a
work *De Sermone Latino*. Stilo's pupil M. Terentius Varro (116–26), the
author of many works on grammar, was an eclectic between the Analogist
and Anomalist schools, since he believed that the artist might depart from
traditional rules: we possess his twenty-five books *De Lingua Latina*, published after 25 BC, which start with an introduction and then proceed to
etymology, inflections, constructions, and syntax. Nigidius Figulus (d. 45 BC)
wrote a work called *Commentarii Grammatici*; Santra about 50 BC published
De Antiquitate Verborum; and L. Ateius Praetextatus (died after 29 BC)
produced collections of glosses. Nor should we forget Caesar's own philological writings.

In later times the Alexandrians gave attention to Latin by the side of
Greek. Tryphon in Augustus' day was mainly concerned with syntax; and
he was followed by Didymus (65 BC–AD 10), by Philoxenus of Alexandria,
who studied the roots of words, and by Juba II, who made etymological
comparisons between Greek and Latin.

NOTES TO CHAPTER IX

1. Dr P. Oliva emphasizes, however, that Greek culture survived Persian conquest in Asia
Minor, and that we may therefore doubt whether it was really in danger of being destroyed,
even if the Persians had been strong enough to conquer mainland Greece.

2. Except, Professor F. M. Heichelheim notes, that we can recognize the influence of Hellenistic techniques.

3. Professor C. Danov maintains that the exploitation of slave labour was a primary factor in the development of Greek agriculture from the end of the fifth or beginning of the fourth century BC, as it was also in contemporary China. For the view that the use of slaves in agriculture has been underestimated throughout Greek history see M. Finley, *Slavery in Classical Antiquity* (Cambridge, 1960), pp. 53 ff.: *contra*, A. H. M. Jones, *ibid.*, p. 3. It is very doubtful, however, whether slave labour was productive of technological developments, which are the subject of Professor Pareti's present section.

4. In his *Georgics* Virgil does not touch upon the labour force at all. Varro's treatise indicates that the purely slave-owning farms had made considerable progress since the days of Cato. According to the latter, the basic nucleus of workers on the villa consists of slaves, but there are also various categories of free workers, and the relationship between them and the landowners (e.g., share-cropping) apparently still has many features of the patriarchal relationship of the dependent client to his patron. According to Varro slaves play a fairly important part. Free landless labourers and artisans are employed on small farms, and traces of the old relationships (e.g., the exploitation of enslaved debtors) have been preserved, in his words, only in the provinces. It is only simple peasants, he says, who work the land themselves. (E. M. Shtaerman.)

5. The same period saw considerable achievement in the carving of gold. Professor C. Danov calls attention to the treasure recently discovered at Panaghiuriște (in the region of Plovdiv), for which see D. Končev, *Neue Denkmaler antiker Toreutik* (Prague, 1956), p. 717.

6. As Professor C. Danov points out, the main centres in the Hellenistic period were in the East—Alexandria, Seleuceia, Antioch, with Rhodes also playing an important role. The centre of gravity of commerce no longer lay in mainland Greece and the Balkan area: see below, Chapter X, pp. 468 ff.

7. The pseudo-Xenophontine *Constitution of Athens* has a fascinating passage (II, 7) on the variety of Athenian imports during the late fifth century BC.

8. But there are scant signs of any Roman mercantilist policies throughout the Republican period: see H. H. Scullard, *A History of the Roman World 753–146 BC* (second edition, London, 1951), pp. 218 ff., pp. 244 ff. There was an advance in Italian industry in the late fourth and third centuries, and it was Italian, rather than Roman, merchants who led the way in promoting commerce with the East in the period of the great Roman conquests. See also Part III, pp. 737 ff.

9. In the Black Sea too, as Professor C. Danov emphasizes, pirates were a constant menace to the corn trade.

10. Athens about 450 imposed a uniform system of weights and measures on its empire, and Athenian 'owls' became the recognized coinage (though some other issues continued). Professor F. M Heichelheim also notes the establishment of 'world-wide' currencies at various points in this period, such as the 'Attic' coinage under Alexander and the Successors, the 'Phoenician' coinage of the Ptolemies, and the more or less 'Attic' Roman *denarius* of the second century BC.

11. Cf. O. Neugebauer, *The Exact Sciences in Antiquity* (second edition, Copenhagen, 1957), p. 166.

12. Professor Pareti had no opportunity to set out the evidence for this view. The *Timaeus*, a late dialogue, has no passage which unmistakably supports it. The heliocentric doctrine is generally thought to have been first advanced by Aristarchus of Samos (third century BC). See p. 414.

13. Eratosthenes (*c.*275–194) was the first systematic geographer. Though his system was of course erroneous, and indeed was much criticized in antiquity, he made fairly accurate computations of the earth's circumference and of its distance from the sun and moon.

14. The true nature of the circulation of the blood was of course not discovered in ancient times.

15. The view that a substantial part of the 'Hippocratic Corpus' is the work of Hippocrates himself is strongly contested by Professor A. Lesky and by many other scholars: see C. Singer in *Oxford Classical Dictionary* (1946), s.v. 'Anatomy and Physiology', 'Hippocratic Corpus', and 'Medicine'. The inconsistencies between different sections of the Corpus are indeed very marked.

16. The classic treatise on the 'humours' was that attributed to Polybus, supposedly Hippocrates' son-in-law. Both this and also Polybus' *Sacred Disease* had influence on medical theory and practice until well into the nineteenth century, and even now are responsible for much medical terminology.

CHAPTER X

PUBLIC ADMINISTRATION, POLITICS, AND SOCIAL CONDITIONS

I. CHINA

a. *Political Theory to the third Century BC*

Chinese polity was to a large extent influenced by philosophical thought, its currents and controversies. Conversely, Chinese philosophy since its very beginning in the sixth–fifth centuries BC was strongly conditioned by sociological preoccupations and was mainly political in its aims and problems. Thus it is difficult to separate politics from philosophy, and we cannot avoid a certain amount of repetition in dealing with Chinese thought both in this and in the following chapter. We may, however, simplify matters by leaving to our account of Chinese philosophy the description of those political theories which exerted no considerable influence on the history of the country or on the development of its institutions. We therefore deal in this chapter with two systems only: Confucianism (*ju-chia*) and Legalism (*fa-chia*).

At the foundation of Confucius' thought (551–479) was society as it existed in his times, i.e., the feudal structure as it had developed during the decadence of the Chou kingdom; the men to whom he addressed himself were the gentlemen (*chün-tzǔ*). He accepted this society and within its frame tried to build up a conservative polity based on a high moral standard. Man ought to act in society not for any profit, but only because he thinks it right and proper, and therefore morally obligatory, to act in a given manner, even if his action cannot be crowned by success. It follows from this that righteousness is the leading idea of the political man. The school of Confucius, and foremost among them Mencius, worked out these simple principles into a coherent system. Humanity should be regulated by the five relationships: affection between father and son, respect between ruler and subject, love between husband and wife, affection between elder and younger brother, loyalty between friends. This is what differentiated man from birds and beasts. No universal love, but a graduated scale of affection and respect. The state is based upon it and represents a moral entity. It follows that the ruler ought to be a moral man and to act only according to a strict standard of morality. It is a fundamental postulate of Confucian political theory, never demonstrated but always asserted, that the moral conduct of the ruler and the example he sets imply a material power of their own, which compels his subjects to follow his lead and to behave according to morality, i.e. according to Confucian rules and precedents. A properly constructed state needs no actual laws, no police, no tribunals; the moral example set by the ruler is sufficient for all practical purposes. If violence and crime prevail, the fault lies usually with the ruler, whose example is not lofty and compelling enough. And if the ruler is utterly bad, he morally ceases to be a ruler, and the people has the right to rebel and to depose him. Hence a sharply drawn distinction between legitimate ruler (*wang*) and tyrant (*pa*).

Another aspect of Confucianism is that the political ideal is sought for in the hoariest past, in the golden times of the mythical rulers Yao and Shun. Thus Confucianism is not exactly a conservative theory; it is a revolutionary one of a peculiar kind, viz. one which tries to abandon the present and the near past and to work back to remote antiquity; the latter in itself is largely fictitious, being but an ideal reconstruction by the Confucians, thrown back into the past.

In the field of sociology and economics, the main conception of Confucianism is the *ching* (square field) system, which has been described above; although petrified in an absurdly rigid and schematic form, it may really go back to a hazy recollection of collective soil-ownership in the Shang period.

Of course these principles too often clashed with the stern reality of the terrible suffering, bloodshed, and crime of the Warring States period. Some adaptation to actual conditions was attempted even within the Confucian school. This was chiefly the work of Hsün-tzŭ (third century BC) who, starting from the postulate (diametrically opposed to Mencius) that man's nature is intrinsically and potentially evil, asserted the necessity of rules of conduct (*li*). This conception of *li* (ceremonies, rites, customary rules of living and of social intercourse) became afterwards an all-important element in the practice of Confucian life. Although their need is postulated from a purely utilitarian point of view, the *li* are no positive laws; they are merely a code of moral and social behaviour, compliance with which is compelled by moral feeling, the example of the ruler, and public opinion, but never by penal sanctions. That was a step which Confucianism, even in its most rationalist wing, never took.

But another school arose, which took its stand exclusively upon the actual conditions of the time, without any thought for abstract morality or for the examples of the past. They reflected the changing society of the Warring States, in which the gentleman class was slowly killing itself off in unceasing warfare, and two political elements only were left to face one another: the rulers and the peasantry (towns and town life practically counted for nothing). Those harsh times required a high degree of organization and of military or quasi-military discipline, if a state was to survive at all. Therefore the Legalist school, whose last and greatest theoretician was Han-fei-tzŭ (third century BC), held that man's nature is intrinsically bad and that he cannot be expected to act socially if not under the spur of reward and the threat of punishment. Antiquity and its tradition have no practical importance. 'As conditions in the world change, different principles are practised' (*Shang-tzŭ* II, 7). The state must be governed by a clear, precise, and severe set of laws (*fa*), which must explain in detail to the subjects what ought to be done, and the reward and punishment for doing or not doing it. The ruler has the power and authority (*shih*) to punish and reward. He is under no necessity to be nearly superhuman, as the Confucians would have him; he merely needs the statecraft (*shu*) necessary for finding and handling an efficient staff to carry out his orders. In a word, the Legalist ideal is that of a despotic, authoritarian, and even totalitarian state. The conflict between Confucianism and Legalism was a fundamental one; it was a clash of idealism and realism, of feudalism and absolutism, of ethics and practice, of optimism and pessimism.

The first serious instance of putting Legalist theories, indeed any political theory at all, into practice, was in the fourth century BC in the north-western state of Ch'in. There Shang Yang (d. 338), being appointed minister, re-organized the machinery of the state strictly according to Legalist ideas. He set down the principle of mutual responsibility, by which the people was organized into groups of families who were responsible for the good behaviour of any of their members and suffered collective punishment in case of a crime or transgression. Agricultural labour was compulsory. On the other side, collective land-ownership began to be broken up and private property was favoured. Economy was subjected to a sort of state planning. The aristocracy was greatly diminished in power and practically disappeared as a class. Severe, even cruel, laws regulated every activity of the people. The army was reorganized. The territory of the Ch'in state was divided into thirty-one districts (*hsien*), ruled by governors appointed by the king and removable at will. In other words a military authoritarian state was built up, which in the long run proved to be the strongest of all. Its victory was accompanied as a matter of course by the victory of the political theory that had shaped it.

Thus it came about that the new Chinese empire founded by the ruler of Ch'in in 221 BC was built upon Legalist principles. Indeed, it was but the extension to the whole of Chinese territory of that organization which had been the peculiarity of Ch'in for more than a century and had given it victory over all its rivals.

b. *The Organization of the New Empire*

Yet in the position of the head of the state there was something that went far beyond the strictly utilitarian tenets of the Legalists. The new emperor was the heir of the Chou kings and of their sacred paramountcy. His very title (*huang-ti*) went back to the legendary emperors of high antiquity. He held the mandate of heaven (*t'ien-ming*) to rule the earth and was the head of the state cult (at least potentially, because Shih-huang-ti did not stress overmuch this aspect of his power). Thus a ruler conceived according to tradition was the head of a novel form of state. This traditional conception of the supreme position of the emperor became one of the strongest permanent elements in Chinese society. The emperor held his authority directly from heaven. Later on it came to be accepted that his mandate was not irrevocable; but if the emperor was weak or bad heaven could withdraw it and transfer it to another dynasty. The symptom of the changed will of heaven was the success of a new pretender to the throne; the actual transfer of the mandate was later formally expressed by a religious ceremony by which the last representative of the old dynasty handed over the insignia to the founder of the new one. This was a convenient theory for explaining and justifying usurpation; it also acted within certain limits as a corrective to the sacral conception of the emperor. In some aspects the latter's authority extended even to heaven, inasmuch as he could and did confer titles, and promote or demote lesser gods; the Chinese extended to heaven the bureaucratic régime of their own country. The emperor could only be one: 'as there is only one sun in the sky, so there is only one ruler on earth'. He was at the centre of the cosmogonic conception of the world (All Under Heaven, *t'ien-hsia*), and conceived foreign countries only as an outer ring of 'barbarians' of less than human status. The emperor thus came to be regarded as a real *axis mundi*, and the Chinese heaven-willed state assumed some of the formal aspects of a theocracy.

Feudalism was wholly abolished, and so were local autonomies. The aristocracy, or whatever was left of it after centuries of war and the first emperor's wholesale deportations, lost all power. The new state was divided into thirty-six (later forty) provinces (*chün*). These were governed by prefects (*shou*); but the local levies were commanded by a general (*wei*) directly dependent upon the central government. The latter was highly centralized; its proper functioning took a heavy toll of the ruler's capacities for work. The ministers were only his executives and did not form a cabinet. Foremost among them were the two state ministers (*ch'êng-hsiang*), the Commander-in-chief (*kuo-wei*), the Chief Judge (*t'ing-wei*), and the Chief Inspector (*yü-shih ta-fu*). A powerful unifying drive led to far-reaching changes. Weights, measures, the laws, and writing were made uniform throughout the empire. The triumph of the Legalist school was complete and the Confucians were cruelly persecuted; their writings, and indeed all books except those treating of technical matters, were banned and destroyed. Although trade was beginning to flourish with the cessation of wars and of insecurity along the roads, the economic policy of the Ch'in government followed the principle of favouring agriculture and repressing trade. Whatever its merits and demerits, this policy was followed with greater or lesser consistency throughout Chinese history down to the nineteenth century.

The reaction of almost all classes of the population against the iron rule and the exasperated centralism of the Ch'in swept away that short-lived dynasty and marked a step back on the path hitherto followed. The Legalist system was rejected, and the stigma attaching to it as a result of its association with the hated régime prevented any serious recovery; the *fachia* lingered on obscurely and died out in the course of the second century. But the Legalist collapse did not give victory to Confucianism, and the reign of the first Han emperors was the triumph of empiricism over doctrinaire political theory.

c. *Politics under the Han*

Feudalism had revived during the civil war of 207–202. It represented not so much a *revanche* of the old ruling class, as a revival of the traditions of local autonomy. The new Han dynasty accepted the fact, but saw to it that this dangerous return of feudalism was gradually emptied of any threat to the unity of the empire. They divided the fiefs into small units, granting the larger ones to members of the imperial family, and enjoining the division of the inheritance among all heirs; and lastly they withdrew from the princes the actual administration of their territories, placing it in charge of imperial officials who merely paid the revenues to the titular incumbents. At first the empire appeared as a motley and irrational mosaic, consisting partly of provinces under direct rule, partly of feudal states. But by the time of Wu-ti (141–87), the last revolts having been suppressed, the provincial bureaucratic administration covered the whole country; political feudalism (i.e. feudalism in the proper meaning of the word) died a natural death, to be revived for a short time and in different circumstances only about the middle of the seventeenth century.

The empire was now ruled by officials who could be promoted, dismissed, and transferred at will by the government; that is, by a bureaucracy. The only rivals they found were the families of the empresses, the Lü in the early second and the Wang in the late first centuries B C. The new ruling class owed their positions not to noble birth, but to ability, patronage, or both. The fact that high officialdom was at times nearly hereditary in one family was marginal and not essential to the new system. Its recruiting had its basis in the famous edict of 196 B C. This enjoined on governors and local officials to send young people of promising talents to the capital, to be educated there with a view to further employment. Step by step upon this basis a scheme was built, which eventually resulted in the Chinese state examinations, whereby access to administration was by means of public competitions on literary subjects. After the middle of the second century B C Confucianism triumphed at court, and in 140 it secured an edict excluding from public service the followers of the most important rival schools, and above all of Legalism. This meant that only men trained in the Confucian lore of the classics could accede to high office. The bureaucracy, and with it the whole state, became Confucianized. This was at first a rather peculiar Confucianism, as we shall see later. But Chinese tradition and the Chinese state (in so far as it was national, not dominated by foreigners) never swerved from this path until the beginning of the twentieth century. In this way a characteristic figure came into being: the literatus, an official Confucian scholar, who was usually at the same time a land-holder on a fairly large scale; his landed property belonged to him partly as member of a family belonging to the ruling class and partly as a normal reward of high office. Ch'in legislation was abrogated and the principle of mutual responsibility was formally abolished.

But in spite of everything the victory of Confucianism was more apparent than real. Confucian morals were paramount, but the administration of the empire was not brought back to the feudalism of the early Chou times (the classical antiquity of the Confucian school); it went on the path traced for it by Shang Yang, Li Ssŭ, and the other Legalist statesmen. The result was a harmonious blend of morality and practice—a Legalist organism directed by Confucians in a Confucian spirit. Legalism was dead, but its great creation, the centralized bureaucratic empire, was adopted by the rival school and with its help lasted for two thousand years.

Han administration was mainly a development of Ch'in. The emperor was theoretically absolute. Gradually, however, a convention developed by which the emperor did not usually take the initiative in issuing an order, but merely expressed his approval or disapproval of measures proposed to him by his chief ministers or other high officials. This considerably lightened the burden on the ruler, while safeguarding his control of state affairs if he was strong enough to exercise it; otherwise power tended to slip into the hands of the bureaucracy.

The emperor was flanked by an advisory council (*t'ien-i*), modelled on the legendary institutions of antiquity and including the Three Dukes (*san-kung*), the Nine Ministers (*chiu-ch'ing*), and other advisers summoned from time to time. Central administration was conducted by the twelve above-mentioned officials. The Three Dukes were the Counsellor (*ch'êng-hsiang*), the Commander-in-chief (*t'ai-wei*—the post was mostly vacant), and the Chief Supervisor (*yü-shih ta-fu*). The last office became the nucleus of that highly influential and beneficent institution, the censorate; it supervised all the branches of the administration and had the privilege of submitting memorials directly to the emperor. The Nine Ministers included a mixture of political and court officials. The only ones among them who were entrusted with general administrative duties were the *t'ai-ch'ang*, in charge of relations with the tributary barbarians; the *ta-li* or *t'ing-wei*, chief judge; the *ta-ssŭ-nung*, general tax collector; and the *shao-fu*, in charge of the Privy Treasury of the emperor. Each minister had at his disposal an assistant (*ch'êng*) and several subordinate officers (*ts'ao*). Official correspondence soon increased to such a bulk that the emperor Wu-ti had to organize four secretariats for coping with it. The Chief Secretary (*shang-shu ling*) was normally an official of lesser rank; but he was in closest attendance on the emperor and was usually the actual medium through which the latter shaped his policy. His importance therefore increased rapidly and excited the jealousy of the bureaucracy.

The empire was divided into provinces (*chün*). Their number went on increasing, by conquest of new territories or by the partition of unduly large units; at the end of the dynasty they numbered more than a hundred. The governors (*t'ai-shou*) held full administrative, judicial, and military powers, and exercised them through six offices (*ts'ao*), modelled upon those of the central government. A good road network and an efficient postal system (*t'ing*) ensured regular communications between centre and provinces.

Taxation was chiefly in kind, and only secondarily in money; officials received half of their salary in kind and half in cash. The basis of all revenue was the land tax, which was proportionate to the cultivated area, the unit being the *mou* (piece of land yielding about 30 litres of grain). The grain was stored and sold, or otherwise employed locally, and only a portion was sent to the capital. Money taxation included a personal tax (*suan-fu*) on every male adult; a military tax for any conscripts not called out; and revenue from the salt, iron, and strong liquor monopolies. When these were not sufficient, the sale of office was widely resorted to. The Privy Treasury of the emperor was supported by its own system of taxation (on markets and shops, on children, on princes *per capita* of their subjects; also revenues of the private estates of the emperor). It was a rigid and unwieldy system, in which the only taxpayer of any importance was the peasant.

The art of war was the foremost occupation of the Chinese nobility in early Chou times (Pl. 24, a), and it soon became the subject of theoretical treatises. The earliest extant is the *Sun-tzŭ-ping-fa* (Master Sun's Art of War), written in the state of Wu by a contemporary of Confucius, about 500 BC. It is precise and matter-of-fact, but is concerned with strategy and tactics only, and not with technique. Slightly later (beginning in the fourth century BC) is the *Wu-tzŭ*, written by Wu Ch'i of the Wei state. Other manuals were composed in the Han period.

The early Han period saw remarkable developments: the introduction of the crossbow (Pl. 24, b) and the perfecting of siege warfare. The crossbow (*nu*) was an import from northern Eurasia. Although wall crossbows and cavalry crossbows were not unknown, it was a typical infantry weapon, whose use entailed a change in infantry tactics. The disciplined bodies of crossbowmen, formed in three lines, offered an insuperable resistance to the nomad mounted archers, whose weapons they heavily outranged. The crossbow was a standard weapon with a most ingenious release mechanism of fused iron, consisting of three parts pivoting on two axes. It was usually cocked by the foot. We possess several originals of the Han era and a substantial number of good copies of the Ming period. Its use appears to go back to the fourth and even fifth century BC, and by the second it was in common use; an important memorial by Ch'ao Ts'o dated 169 BC concerns the utilization of crossbows and crossbowmen. The Tun-huang documents show that the crossbows were preserved in special magazines and classified according to the weight necessary for cocking them.

Heavier machines of war were *arcubalistae*, cocked by means of a winch; multiple-bolt *arcubalistae* are mentioned in the last year of Shih-huang-ti (210 BC) and were perfected by Chu-ko Liang (*c.*225 AD). Trebuchets (worked by a heavy counter-weight) are mentioned. *Petrariae* existed since the time of the Warring States and were much in use under the Ch'in, the Han, and afterwards.

The Han army was in principle based on a militia system; but actually few recruits were called out and its core became the Imperial Guards, organized in two 'armies' and consisting mainly of professional soldiers. In case of war on the frontier, the Guard was not usually sent there, but levies were raised locally or in the neighbouring provinces. It was a slow and inefficient system, which was unable to keep the barbarians outside the Great Wall. The standard weapon of the Han infantry was, as we said above, the crossbow. Such was the superiority it conferred on the imperial troops that for a certain period export of the trigger mechanism was severely prohibited. In case of offensive expeditions into the steppe the main arm was cavalry, organized in companies of 100 men (*tui*) and regiments of 1,000 men commanded by colonels (*hsiao-wei*). The commissariat was primitive and badly organized, and the hardships caused to the peasants in collecting grain and transporting it to the field army were always the source of much oppression and discontent, and sometimes of revolt. For this reason stable garrisons were supposed to grow their own food, on land specially granted to them and tilled by squads of soldiers. This is the origin of the military colonies (*t'un-t'ien*), fairly akin in nature and organization to the Roman ones. Their first beginnings go back to the conquest of Kansu in 121 BC. Their complete and typical form is due to Chao Ch'ung-kao (*c.*60 BC).

d. *Social conditions*

Chinese society at the beginning of this period was still a purely feudal one in the political and economic meaning of the word. It included three main classes: aristocracy, peasants, and slaves. The main concerns of the nobles were sacrificial ceremonies and warfare. The land belonged to them, but of course the princes of the several feudal states claimed rent and corvée from their aristocracy. The peasants were hereditary tenants of the fields they tilled; this tenancy could not be sold nor transferred to others. They had to pay dues to the aristocracy in grain, cloth, and labour. Actually their life was not far better than that of the slaves. The latter were mostly prisoners of war or their descendants; they had two main functions, household work and the tilling of the fields (although there are some doubts on this second point). But the intensive farming of northern China, with its horticultural aspects, was not conducive to a real slave economy, like that developed in Italy in late republican times.

The wars of the fifth–third centuries BC caused a progressive impoverishment and decay of the aristocracy, as well as a considerable diminution of the hereditary slaves. Aristocracy as such ceased to exist and their lands passed into the possession of new social elements, rich peasants and merchants. Land was and remained for a long time the only effective form of investment. Thus people disposing of large amounts of cash invested it in land; and not being able or willing to cultivate such large areas themselves, they let it out to tenants at a high rent. The owners kept on their estate some members of the family to supervise their tenants, but themselves usually lived in the nearest town. Lesser cultivators became clients and protégés of the big land-owners. The latter enjoyed not only the prestige and influence conferred upon them by their wealth, but even functioned *de facto* as tax collectors. These wealthy proprietors became gradually the centre of all social, political, and educational life; bureaucracy was mostly drawn from their ranks, since only men of substance could afford the means for imparting to their sons the education and training needed for passing the state examinations successfully. Thus Han society revolved around the two poles of the rich land-owners and of the mass of the tenants.

Landless labourers always had the possibility of migrating to less inhabited regions; and indeed the Han period witnessed a most intense colonization of the southern Chinese space by northerners. Social pressure resulted thus in the expansion of the Chinese people southward.

The tenants were always living nearly on starvation level, and being without reserves were at the mercy of any natural calamity or increase of taxation, easily fell into debt to the town merchants, and sank deeper till their lot became unbearable. The result was then one of those peasant revolts which so often characterize periods of social stress throughout Chinese history.

Slavery in the Han period still existed, but mainly as a household institution. The origin of slaves was now mainly from convicted prisoners (who became state slaves) and from peasant children sold by their starving parents in times of distress. Slaves imported from abroad were merely a luxury in the houses of the richest. But on the whole it is calculated that slaves accounted for less than 1 per cent of the whole population during Han times.

The market towns (*shih-i*) and townspeople played an increasingly important role in economy, but not in politics. They were strictly under the control of the government, and no beginning of corporate life or of administrative autonomy was apparent. There was no industry on any large scale, but craftsmen were supported by the government. The most important elements in the towns were the merchants. They acquired an increasing economic influence, being favoured by the expansion of territory, by the betterment of communications, and by the resulting increase in trade. Their wealth and their usurious exploitation of the peasants' indebtedness made them exceedingly unpopular, and they usually became the first target of any peasant revolt. But also Han Confucianism considered them as enemies of the cultivator, as social drones, as responsible for monetary devaluation and for the subversion of rural economy. Thus they were regarded with suspicion by the government, and repressive laws were passed against them from the very beginning of the dynasty, by means of heavy taxation, exclusion from office, and sumptuary regulations, but the effects of these laws on the strength and compactness of this class were scanty. Other means for curbing the merchants' activities were the state monopolies and the so-called Equalizing Granaries (*p'ing-ts'ang*), introduced by the Han and later perfected and enhanced by Wang Mang. The monopolies were attacked on moral grounds by the Confucianists, but were defended on the ground of expediency by the greatest economist in

Chinese antiquity, Sang Hung-yang. The proceedings (*Yen-tieh-lun*, Discourses on Salt and Iron) of this famous debate, held about 86–81 BC, are one of our major sources for the economic history of this period.

2. THE NOMAD SOCIETIES OF THE STEPPES

Steppe society is historically linked with nomadism. But recent research has shown that nomadism, at least in the case of north-eastern Asia, is a secondary development due to ever-increasing differentiation between two forms of agriculture: a full-time one on fairly fertile soil with a sufficient water supply, and a marginal one on a meagre soil with little water, which with its ever-diminishing returns eventually compels the local tribes 'to neglect the use of agricultural resources and to develop as an alternative the use of pastoral resources. It was only when this diverging specialization had been carried to a certain point that the marginal steppe society ceased to be marginal and committed itself definitely to the steppe. Having reached that point it was ready to take advantage of a steppe technique of horse usage in order to increase the efficiency of life within the steppe environment' (O. Lattimore, *Inner Asian Frontiers of China*, p. 59). The early Chinese were not in contact with horsemen; these begin to be mentioned only after *c.* 500 BC. The process sketched above thus attained maturity about that time.

The main features of the new society were indeed the paramount importance of the horse, and of cattle as the main source of subsistence. Agriculture became a part-time operation (mostly left to women), to be used only in order to gain some fresh vegetables as a supplement to meat and milk. Later even this limited agriculture was abandoned, and the necessary products were gained by bartering with or raiding the cultivators on the border. This was the stage of pure nomadism.

In nomad society the land has no importance, with the exception of the grazing rights on it. Wealth is measured in terms of cattle. On this economic basis a society grew up, whose pattern is uniform throughout the steppe areas. It has been defined by Vladimirtsov as nomad feudalism, although the term is not a very happy one. Its structure is aristocratic. A hereditary ruling class of cattle-owners is at the top, with their private retainers specially bound to them by contract; then the free men, i.e. the mass of the nomads, bound to the nobility by ties of blood and of economic dependence; lastly the slaves, usually prisoners-of-war from the sedentary peoples. No higher political organization is normally developed, and the clan, or at the most the tribe, is the highest unit. Only in times of stress a tribal confederacy may come into life under some outstanding chieftain, and this may give origin to what Grousset aptly called an 'empire of the steppes'. The normal course of events is then a series of victories over the sedentaries, going as far as the conquest of a more or less substantial portion of their lands. In this case the nomad aristocracy move into the conquered territory and live on the fat of the land, gradually allowing themselves to be assimilated by the superior culture of their subjects. They lose contact with their own poorer tribesmen, who have remained in the steppe. Then the political band snaps or becomes obliterated and the confederacy dissolves in a sort of social dust. Then, after a more or less long period of disintegration and of relative peace and inactivity, the same cycle can start all over again. As seen from the point of view of the cultivators in the fertile lands to the south, the result is a series of cataclysms, of eruptions from the steppe at irregular intervals of centuries, with masses of nomad horsemen overwhelming the frontier defences with dire consequences for the agricultural states which bear the brunt.

The first important nomad state in Asia, or at least the first one about which we have sufficient information, was that of the Hsiung-nu. Its rise was contemporary with the unification of China and the foundation of the empire, and probably there was some socio-economic connection between the two events. The political structure of the Hsiung-nu is known from the Chinese sources. The latter gave to their chief the title of *shan-yü* (a word of uncertain meaning) or *ch'êng-li ku-t'u shan-yü* (the first four characters seem to transcribe a proto-Turkic term *tengri-qut*, majesty of heaven). Under him were the Wise Kings *t'u-ch'i* (proto-Turkic *doğri*), of the right and of the left, that of the left being in principle the heir-apparent. Below them were two *ku-li*, kings of the left and of the right, the two great generals (as above), the two great governors (as above), the two great *tang-hu* (as above), the two great *ku-tu* (as above), the chiefs of 1,000, of 100, and of 10 men. It was a politico-military organization which reproduced the form of an army drawn up for battle, facing south. This pattern is met with in most of the later empires of the steppes. The same can be said of the dichotomy of the people into two wings or halves, which was usually the starting point for a growing political estrangement and for the dissolution of the state into two rival ones.

The religion of the Hsiung-nu was shamanism, in which the foremost place was occupied by the cult of Tengri, heaven. Their way of life was that of the nomads, with limited semi-annual migrations between summer and winter pastures. Their formidable military power was represented by the masses of horse archers, wielding the composite bow; and their skill of born and bred hunters and cattlemen was more than a match for any regular army of the sedentary peoples. Their favourite tactic was the sudden attack and nimble retreat, without committing themselves to hand-to-hand fighting before the adversary was exhausted by the rain of arrows and was manœuvred into unfavourable positions, where he could be ridden down without difficulty. This military supremacy of the nomad over the armies of the southern and western agricultural countries became a truism to be experienced again and again, till the coming of fire-arms spelt the end not only of the supremacy, but even of the military importance of the mounted archers.

3. INDIA

a. *Administration and Politics*

India had no unitary tradition, no systematically selected bureaucracy, no state organization independent of and more lasting than the dynasty. Thus we cannot speak of a linear development of Indian administrative institutions. There was no continuity. Every founder of a kingdom created a new organization of his own. Of course this was usually done on the traditional pattern; novelties were eschewed and the influence of political and legal thought was always strong. But the fact remains that no administrative structure was permanent and none lasted after the collapse of the dynasty to which it belonged. This makes the history of Indian institutions something quite different from that of Rome, China, and even of Egypt and Assyria-Babylonia. The lack of a historical literature is also a great hindrance; inscriptions are a poor substitute, and the fairly numerous works on political and legal theory, however important, fail to give us a really satisfactory picture of the historical development of the various institutions.

The first authentic account of the working of the administration in a large Indian state is found in the fragments of Megasthenes, the ambassador of Seleucus I at the court of Chandragupta Maurya. It is a rather one-sided description, not free from misunderstandings, but it has the all-important advantage of describing what was the actual practice, and not the theoretical organization prescribed by the *śāstras*. The king was not only the titular head of the state, but also the chief of the government, which he directed personally. Because of this his daily routine was very heavy and he had to attend to business even while having himself combed and massaged. He was the centre of a magnificent and large court and appeared in public only in great state and with rich pomp. But his rule was based on systematic suspicion; not only did he employ an army of spies, as was always the tradition in India, but he was always surrounded by a bodyguard of armed women, who watched the access to his inner apartments and accompanied him when he appeared in public. The chief executives under him were a body of counsellors and assessors, who had the main responsibility for choosing subordinate officials.

Pāṭaliputra, the seat of Chandragupta's government, was a large city, with a length of 80 stades and a breadth of 15; its walls had 64 gates and 570 towers. Its administration was placed under a sort of municipal board consisting of six committees of five members each (*astynomoi*). These committees took care respectively of the artisans; of foreigners; of birth and death registration; of trade, weights, and measures; of the municipal manufactures; and of the sales tax (10 per cent). Some subjects were reserved for the united body of all the six committees. Such were the upkeep of public buildings, regulation of prices, and the care of markets, harbours, and temples. Of course, this administration was a strictly authoritarian one. As in China, so too in the

Mauryan empire, there was no local autonomy. The capital and the other cities too were under the rule of the king's officials; and no local bodies, not even the merchants' guilds (*śreṇī*), played any role in it. Generally speaking, town life was of but little importance. During this period there were in India but two cities that held a high rank and played any substantial role in history. They were Pāṭaliputra, the capital of the kingdom of Magadha and of the Mauryan empire; and Takṣaśilā (Taxila), the chief centre (but by no means the only one) of the successive foreign dominations in north-western India. Another town of importance, but only on a regional scale, was Ujjayinī. Not only is it well known from the literary texts, but recent excavations have brought to light a part of the ancient city, with its strong clay walls reinforced by iron beams. Other ancient cities that have been excavated are Kauśāmbī and Ahicchatrā, both in Uttar Pradesh.

Provincial administration in the Mauryan empire was directed by a regular hierarchy of functionaries, beginning with the governors (mostly princes of the blood) of the few large units into which it was divided. The districts were entrusted to officials (*agoranómoi*, probably a mistake for *agronómoi*), whose main concern was with land measurement, and with irrigation and the distribution of canal waters. Other supervisors were in charge of agriculture, forestry, timber works, foundries, mines, and roads. Of the army we shall speak later. The country seems to have been flourishing and happy, and the soil of northern India, being less exhausted than today, gave bountiful crops, with two harvests per year. Famine was practically unknown. Wars made no great difference, since (according to Megasthenes) the cultivator was considered 'neutral and inviolable', and was strictly left alone by marching and fighting armies. Trade was very brisk and was carefully protected by government. Economy was under a measure of state supervision; at least government was actively participating in it by conducting manufactures of its own and by keeping in its pay as state servants the merchant sailors on the rivers.

To a slightly later stage of the Mauryan empire belongs the information that can be gleaned from the inscriptions of Aśoka and Buddhist literary sources relating to that period. The huge empire, covering the whole of India with the exception of the southernmost tip, included some autonomous states (mostly in backward areas) but was as a whole still directly ruled by the king. It appears that he was assisted by a sub-king (*uparāja*; his brother Tissa) and by the heir-apparent (*yuvarāja*). There was also a chief minister (*agrāmātya*) and a council (*pariṣad*). The territory was divided into a few great viceroyalties, ruled by princes of the blood; we know the names of four of them: Taxila, Ujjain, Tosali (Orissa), and Suvarṇagiri (central India). Under the viceroys were the provincial governors (*prādeśika*). Farther below there were three groups of officials: district prefects with chiefly judicial powers (*rājūka*), district finance directors (*yuta*), and officers in charge of town administration and of reviewing the administration of justice (*mahāmātra*). Among the latter were the superintendents of religious and moral affairs (*dharma-mahāmātra*), and of women (strī-adhyakṣa-mahāmātra). Cities were governed no longer by committees, but by a single mahāmātra; provincial capitals were under the joint administration of the prince-viceroys and of mahāmātras. The local judiciary was entrusted to town judges (nagara-vyavahāraka). There was a sort of diplomatic service, i.e., a body of envoys (dūta). And, last but not least, there were the all-important and always present informers of the police (prativedaka). A good deal of care was bestowed on public works and chiefly on the water supply (kūpa, udapāna), the gardens (udyāna), and the botanical gardens. They were under the general charge of a vrajabhūmika. The smooth working of the huge machinery was ensured by quinquennial and triennial circuits of inspection (anusaṃyāna), conducted by the three above-mentioned classes of officials. The main concern of Aśoka's administrative policy seems to have been that of ensuring a continuous and intimate contact between the government and the subjects. In this as well as in his religious policy Aśoka stood quite isolated, and Indian governments of later days were content with a much smaller degree of interference with the way of life and opinions of their subjects.

The system of administration of the Śuṅga dynasty was a continuation of that of the Mauryas, with a much looser organization. Provinces were ruled by prince-viceroys who bore the same simple title of rājan as the king. Feudatory families had the right of issuing coins at the principal cities.

The foremost theoretical work on politics is the Arthaśāstra traditionally attributed to Kauṭilya or Cāṇakya, the minister of Chandragupta and the real founder of the Mauryan empire (an interesting parallel case to Chin Shih-huang-ti and Li Ssŭ). The authorship of Kauṭilya has been challenged by many scholars and the date of composition of the Arthaśāstra has been pulled as far down as the fourth century A D, although everybody agrees that the materials on which it is based may be much earlier. In any case it seems safer not to take the Arthaśāstra as a manual of Maurya administration. The political system to which it refers is a constellation of smaller or larger states, not one huge empire. We can assume therefore that it represents the political theories current in post-Mauryan times, i.e., in the last two centuries B C.

The form of government described in the Arthaśāstra is absolute monarchy. The king's authority is full and unchecked by the necessities of expediency and custom. He is, however, advised by a council (parisad) of the highest officials (mantrin). These had at the same time executive functions, being each in charge of a department of government. Under them work the sannidhātr (treasurer) and the samāhartr (collector-general). Under the ministers stood the directors of departments, or superintendents (adhyakṣa). Government kept in touch with and controlled public opinion through a well-organized system of spies and secret agents (gūḍapuruṣa). The basic element of the state was the village, whose economic and social life was to follow fixed rules laid down and enforced by the government. For survey and land-revenue purposes five or ten villages were grouped together under a revenue and police

(a) [Alinari

(b) I [Alinari

29 *Athens:*
    (a) *The Theseum, c. 449–444 BC*
    (b) *The Erechtheum, c. 421–405 BC:*
        (i) *North portico,* (ii) *Caryatid porch*

(b) II [Alinari

(a)

30   DORIC TEMPLES I

(a) *Sunium, temple of Poseidon,* 444–440 *BC*

(b) *Agrigento (Acragas), Sicily, temple of Hera Lacinia,* c. 460 *BC*

(b)

(a)

[B.F.M.

31 DORIC TEMPLES II

    (a) *Segesta, Sicily,* c. 424–416 *BC*

    (b) *Paestum, temple of Poseidon,* c. 460 *BC*

(b)

[B.F.M.

(a)

32 (a) *Epidaurus, the Greek theatre,* c. *350 BC*
    (b) *Phlyakes masque, Taranto, National Museum*

(b)

officer (*gopa*). These were in their turn supervised by the provincial finance officers (*sthanīya*).

Bureaucratic work was to a large extent carried out in writing, and the *Arthaśāstra* gives rules both for account-keeping and letter-writing. Finance was based on the land-tax, consisting in a fixed share of the produce, plus varying additional demands; various devices are prescribed for raising additional revenue in times of stress. Officials are paid by the exchequer according to a fixed scale.

As was pointed out above, the state is not conceived as an all-embracing unity as in China, but as an element of a political constellation, with the would-be conqueror (*vijigiṣu*) at the centre surrounded by a circle of actual or potential allies and enemies. Politics was strictly a practical statecraft on a power basis and with no element of morality in it except the material welfare of the state, or of the king (which was the same thing). War seems to be the normal condition of international relations, and peace in its several varieties is only a means of escaping conquest or of preparing for it.

The question how far the precepts of the *Arthaśāstra* were followed in actual practice is a moot point; but some influence at least on the administrative titles of later times cannot be gainsaid.

Lastly, it should be noticed that republics and republican states have little place in the *Arthaśāstra*; as a matter of fact the republic was but a minor form of polity. It was limited to some well-defined areas on the north and northwest and seems to have been slowly decaying, although republics continued to exist at least till Gupta times.

The ideal figure of the sovereign in Indian literature requires some comment. There was no conception like the Mandate of Heaven in China. The highest ideal was that of the *cakravartin*, the conqueror of the universe, who finds his moral justification only in the way in which he discharges his duties. He is bound to uphold moral and civil justice (*dharma*), to be beneficent and pious, and to rule for the welfare of his subjects only. But he remains an idealized and isolated figure, deeply individualistic like everything Indian. The very concept of dynasty is strange to Indian thought (but not to the semi-historical lore of the *Purāṇas*); so is also the state as an entity transcending the king who rules it.

b. *Political and Social Theory*

Religious and social law (*dharma*), as distinguished from administration and politics (*artha*), is the subject of a special class of literature, the *Dharmaśāstra*. Several texts are extant but, as usual, it is difficult to determine which of them were compiled during this period. The only one of which this can be assumed with some degree of likelihood is the *Manava-Dharmaśāstra* or *Manu-smṛti*; its authorship is attributed to Manu, the first man. This work exerted an enormous influence not only on later legal thought, but on the institutions and social life of the Indian people at large.

The *Manu-smṛti* recognizes four sources of law: the sacred scriptures (the *Vedas*), the legal books (*smṛti*), the customs of holy men and the inner feeling of man about what is just and unjust. It is interesting to note that Kauṭilya, possibly in conscious opposition, places the royal edicts uppermost, followed in order by custom, contract, and sacred law. But for Manu too the power of punishment (*daṇḍa*) of the king is the supreme guarantee of the law. Criminal law is based on the gradation of punishment not only according to the gravity of the fault, but also according to the caste of the offender; Brahmans are always let off more lightly and are in no case subject to the death penalty, however heinous their offence. The caste system is by now well established and the *Manu-smṛti* gives it the full weight of its sanctity. The scale of punishment is harsh, death in various forms (some of them outrageously cruel) being imposed even for minor offences. Mutilation is often resorted to. The role of the witness in both civil and military law is all-important, but as a rule women and the men of the several castes should give evidence only on behalf of people of the same class. In serious cases, however, and when other evidence was lacking, any witness was accepted in court, or else there was trial by ordeal. The tribunals were to be presided over by the king himself, or in his absence by a learned Brahman appointed by him, assisted by three counsellors who were normally Brahmans versed in the *Vedas*.

As can be seen, the Brahman is everything in Manu's society; he is teacher, priest, judge, minister; he is also a member of the *dharma-pariṣad*, the body appointed by the king as a standing legislative commission. Manu's rules for the *śūdras* are very harsh and they are treated little better than slaves. Still, the system has not yet complete rigidity, since Manu admits inter-marriage between males of higher and females of lower castes (*anuloma*) without loss of status for their progeny; the opposite case (*pratiloma*) is forbidden, and if it occurs, any issue goes to form a special caste. The whole caste system was in this period undergoing a twofold process, of a growing rigidity and seclusion between the castes and of a large increase in the number of mixed castes. Manu explains the latter as due firstly to marriage between different castes, and secondly to members of the upper castes being degraded on account of not fulfilling their sacred duties (*vrātya*). This is of course but a convenient convention for explaining the ever-increasing number of sub-castes, arising specially from guild-like associations of people following similar arts and crafts. It served also the useful purpose of incorporating into Hindu society foreigners (traders or conquerors) and the primitive jungle tribes; and this has remained one of the features of modern Hinduism.

Caste was as a matter of principle disregarded in the Buddhist and Jain communities; even where they are mentioned, the *kṣattriyas* invariably take precedence over the Brahmans.

Alongside the caste system there ran the broader distinction between free men and slaves. Slavery in India existed since the earliest period. In Vedic times prisoners-of-war of both sexes belonging to non-Aryan peoples were reduced to slavery, and their very name (*Dāsa*) came to indicate the slaves (like Slavs in Europe). In the time of the Buddha (*c.* 500 BC) slavery was diffused in the north Indian monarchies. But although several large estates were partially tilled by slave labour, this type of economy seems never to have played any substantial role in Indian agriculture. Most of the slaves were employed in household work. It also appears that even the Buddhist monasteries owned slaves, who were employed in menial duties for the community. Slaves were such by birth, by sale (mostly by indigent parents), by capture in war, or by penal sentence. At a later time, Kauṭilya dedicated a whole chapter (III, 13) to them. Besides life slaves, he knows of a new category, that of slaves for a definite term. The rules he sets down are on the whole slightly more humane, chiefly over protection of slave girls. It appears that the institution of slavery, through economic causes, went into a slow decay after the break-up of the Mauryan empire.

Another social subdivision was that of the four *āśramas*, or patterns of material, religious, and spiritual life, conceived as successive stages in human existence. They make their appearance in this period and play a great role in the *Dharmaśāstras*. They are: (1) *brāhmacārin*, the young student who goes to live in the home of a teacher in order to learn from him the sacred texts; (2) *gṛhastha*, the grown-up married man and head of a family, who conducts the domestic ritual; (3) *vanaprastha* or *bhikṣu*, the elderly man, who lessens, though he does not entirely interrupt, his sacrifices and his family ties, and retires to the forest to lead a life of restraint and self-denial and to meditate on the significance of the sacrifices; (4) *sannyāsin*, who renounces his family, his sacrifices, the world, and his caste and leads a life of absolute austerity as a wandering ascetic, in order to meditate on the absolute. This last *āśrama* was a later addition to the first three and was always the chosen refuge of thinkers who felt dissatisfied with the Brahmanic ritual. Of course, the *āśramas* were purely voluntary, and as such were on a quite different plane from the castes, which were inborn and therefore inescapable.

c. *Warfare and Military Institutions*

One particular but important aspect of life in ancient India (as elsewhere) was war. As a matter of principle, war was the duty and privilege of the *kṣattriya* caste; it formed their religious obligation (*dharma*) and no other caste was supposed to take part in it, although in actual practice this rule was not strictly observed, chiefly in the case of infantry. Being reserved to a professional hereditary class, warfare soon became an elaborate art, with conventions and rules to be observed by every warrior. It tended thus to assume a ceremonial character, although the presence of foreigners on Indian soil, who were not bound to observe the rules, prevented its growing into a rite like that found in Aztec Mexico. Still, the result was a general trend toward obsolescence in military technique, and this goes to explain why nearly every foreign invasion of Hindu India was successful in its first impact.

An Indian army was traditionally composed of four arms (*caturaṅga*): chariots, elephants, cavalry, infantry. It is noteworthy that out of an old Indian war game our modern game of chess was developed; its European terminology mostly comes from Persian, but its Persian name, *śatranj*, is merely a transcription of *caturaṅga*. According to Megasthenes, the armed forces of the Mauryan empire were supervised by six committees of five members each: one for each arm, plus one for the commissariat and one for the navy (i.e. river craft, mainly used for transport only). The total force was 600,000 infantry, 30,000 cavalry, 9,000 elephants; the number of chariots is not stated.

Chariots were the foremost arm for the Aryan warrior of Vedic times, and the Mahābhārata war was principally a fight between charioteers. The Vedic chariot was a simple wooden structure with two wheels on a wooden axle, drawn by two horses (rarely four) attached on either side of the pole. It carried usually two persons only, the fighter and the driver. Later the vehicle became larger, heavier, and slower. It still formed a conspicuous part of Porus' army in his fight against Alexander; his chariots accommodated six men (two shield-bearers, two archers, two driver-fighters). In the Mauryan army they carried two men-at-arms and one charioteer. But chariotry had already become insignificant as a war weapon; and it gradually went out of use (as everywhere in Asia) during this period, except for ceremonial purposes.

The elephants formed the shock element of an Indian army till the end of the Middle Ages. They were the typically Indian contribution to the history of warfare. From India they were taken over by Alexander's successors, in whose time the possession of elephants was a decisive element of military potential; and thence they came into the Carthaginian army. An elephant carried usually three archers beside the driver. Their great drawback was that, if wounded, they would be seized by panic, and carry confusion and destruction into their own ranks.

Cavalry was comparatively a late-comer, in India as everywhere else. It was hardly known in the Vedic and Epic period, and seems to have been introduced in India chiefly through contact with Achaemenid Iran on the Indus. It became all-important after the wars with the Śaka and Parthians in the decades before and after the beginning of our era, and then became the backbone of the army. In Mauryan times cavalry technique was rather primitive, neither stirrup nor saddle nor bit being known. But then it rapidly improved: saddle and stirrups appear in the Sanchi reliefs (end of this period), with an anticipation of about 500 years over the rest of Eurasia. The main weapon of the horseman was the spear; horse archery of the central Asian type was not popular in India, and this was another element of weakness as against nomad invaders.

Infantry were enrolled in large masses but had little training and discipline. Their status went on deteriorating after the Vedic age and they were no match for the chariots in early days, and for cavalry later. Their chief weapons were the bow and the lance.

The Mauryan army was a standing and professional one. It received regular pay from the government, and its only duty was to fight. The army depicted by the *Arthaśāstra* was rather different, including troops bound by hereditary loyalty (*maula*), mercenary troops (*bhṛta*), soldiers of the guilds (*śreṇibala*), allied troops (*mitrabala*), deserters or contingents exacted from a defeated enemy (*amitrabala*), and forest tribes (*āṭavi*; chiefly as scouts). There was even a sort of medical corps.

Indian tactics seem to be mainly characterized by the importance of forts. Siege warfare plays a great role in Indian history along with pitched battles. Alexander's campaign on the north-western frontier is an instance in point; also the *Arthaśāstra* deals with the subject in some detail. Simple war machines such as large stone-throwers are mentioned, but the battering-ram appears to have been unknown.

The queen of Indian weapons was the long-bow, made of bamboo, horn, or metal, shooting arrows of reeds and iron. Archery was the chief accomplishment of the warrior and of the king. Defensive armour was worn from an early period; its chief forms were mail and the long and narrow infantry shield.

4. PERSIA

After the reign of Darius I, who had given the Persian empire its greatest extension and laid the foundations for making it into a concrete whole, his successors could not find a way to prevent its deterioration and decline; indeed they often, though unwittingly, accelerated their empire's fall by their own behaviour. By making themselves into absolute rulers of the oriental type they became estranged from their subjects; they were kept aloof in their palaces by a rigorous system of etiquette, making it difficult even for their own wives to approach them and impossible for anyone to see them except when the people prostrated itself before them at great ceremonies. This state of affairs fostered court intrigues, conspiracies, and outbreaks of violence. Official inscriptions show us how the absolute power of the sovereign was justified. The appeal was to his race (he was a Persian and an Aryan), to his family (he was an Achaemenid and descendant of Achaemenids), to his outstanding position as King of Kings, and to the extent and populousness of his dominions, which included countless peoples of many races.

But the Achaemenids were unable to overcome the irresistible dualism which divided the Iranian and Zoroastrian portion of their empire from the rest. They could not quell it by religious intolerance along lines dictated by the Iranian policy of theocracy favoured by the Magi, which increased the discontent of the subject peoples. Tolerance, on the other hand, antagonized the priesthood of the Iranian nation. In any case there were racial considerations preventing cohesion: the dominant Iranian race was too small numerically in comparison with the mass of other peoples in the empire. From the time of Xerxes (486–465) there were many periods of intolerance, accompanied by great harshness towards subjects either guilty or suspected of back-sliding, such as the Egyptians and Babylonians: one example is the severity shown to the admirals of the Phoenician fleet after their defeat by the Greeks at Salamis. This, however, does not exhaust the reasons why Cyprus, Caria, parts of Anatolia, Egypt, and other peripheral areas tried to break away. A further source of trouble was the formation of centrifugal groups among the fiefs, which controlled their own armies, mainly consisting of mercenaries; it was easy for satraps to revolt, given the amount of military and adminis-trative power they possessed. Moreover the whole history of the Achaemenid empire, from the 'Persian Wars' to Alexander's conquest, proves the weakness of its gigantic but ill-organized army: defeated again and again by the Greeks between 480 and 469, it was shattered at Cunaxa in 401 by 10,000 Hellenic mercenaries, who were then able to return to their homeland almost without loss; and Alexander was able to confront it in confidence, though at the outset he possessed only 40,000 men and 160 ships. The fact was that as early as the fifth century the most solid force in the Persian army consisted of Greek mercenaries, just as the core of the fleet was composed of Phoenician vessels; but the latter were in practice no more effective than they had been in 480. In 469, for instance, they refused battle at the Eurymedon.

Under Xerxes and his three successors the kings of Persia were already giving up boasting of their warlike enterprises on their sepulchral inscrip-tions. They preferred diplomatic to military intervention; to be more exact, their policy was to divide, and so to weaken, rival nations by financing one faction against another in a way which would further their own interests. The careers of Alcibiades, the Spartan Lysander, Conon, Evagoras of Salamis, and Epaminondas, together with the history of the Corinthian War, contain abundant elements to support this account of Persian policy; and another telling point is Alexander's accusation that the Great King had suborned murderers to cause the death of his father Philip.

The Achaemenid dynasty showed remarkably little interest in intellectual or scientific developments or in unifying the culture of their empire.[1] The sporadic achievements in this field were due to the priests (for example the completion of calculations about the calendar) or to single individuals. Simi-larly no concrete or deliberate initiative by the government was in the main responsible for the cultural relations which existed between Iran and India on the one side, and Greece on the other. These were mainly caused by spon-taneous forces reacting on one another in the countries on each side of the borders of the empire; and a further factor was the existence of mercenaries and other Greeks, who lived for extensive periods as individuals or as parts of communities in Persian countries (apart of course from those in the Greek territories under the control of the Great King). As regards artistic borrowings the essential cause was employment by the Achaemenid kings of Greek work-men, who transplanted their methods into Persia and later made Persian methods familiar to their own countrymen. Scientific and cultural borrowings

took place through the intermediary of individual Greeks, above all the doctors, like Ctesias, who lived in Persia in the service of the king or his satraps—
these last had not infrequently married Greek wives. In this way they also
made contact with India, whose cures and other branches of medical science
were already known to them. At the same time religious and philosophical
ideas passed between Greece and Persia, not least because there were Persian
students at the school of Plato.

After his conquest of the Persian empire Alexander, followed by his successors, attempted to build on to the foundations of Greek culture, although
he also drew suggestions and instructions from Achaemenid methods when
evolving his own. Yet he was not successful in laying bases on which Greek
and Persian civilizations could be blended into a single and lasting whole. One
reason was that he and the Successors found themselves facing two markedly
different worlds, one in the borderlands where the Persians had previously
been overlords, the other in the Iranian homeland from which the overlords
had sprung. Hellenization was relatively easy in the western portions which
in later times were firmly held by the Seleucids and Ptolemies, and in the
intermediate areas of Babylonia and Mesopotamia, where civilization had
prevailed from ancient times; it was also possible in Bactria (in the extreme
north-east) where Greek culture lasted for two whole centuries after the
country's separation from the Seleucid empire by Diodotus about 246 BC,
and was brought to an end only when the land was captured by the Scythian
hordes. But Hellenization penetrated much less deeply in the Iranian areas
which lay between these two extremes. Achaemenid traditions and institutions
were too strong, and these were combined with resistance from Zoroastrian
religion and the Magi. Moreover the races of this region remained separate
from 'Outer Iran', that is to say from Iranian peoples such as the Scyths and
Sacae of the areas round the Caspian, who were always ready to invade. To
them was due the formation of the new independent state of Parthia, created
by Arsaces the Scyth.

This new kingdom in the process of its continual expansion became the
heir to the Persian empire three-quarters of a century after that empire had
disappeared. It never succeeded in reaching the old Achaemenid frontiers;
but it attained such success that it became not only a barrier against nomad
attacks but was the one formidable enemy of Rome, which was trying its best
to rescue and promote Greek culture in the East and to impede Parthia's
westward advance. At the end of the first round of contests between these
powers, which falls within the period of this present chapter, Rome under its
general Crassus was defeated at Carrhae in 53 BC; and even Augustus, who
later set himself the task of salvaging everything possible in Greek civilization
in the East, did not feel confident enough to take decisive vengeance. Yet even
at this period the quarrels between the kings, princes, and nobles of Parthia
were a great aid to Roman diplomacy, which took strenuous action to intensify
these conflicts and make use of them in the interests of Rome.

5. THE GREEK WORLD

a. *Evolution of Politics after 500 BC*

Two tendencies, antithetic to each other, were common to all Greeks; and both were an important cause of the exhaustion of Greek vigour as well as preventing any lasting success attending any attempt at national unity. One tendency was shown in the efforts made by individual cities to establish empire over others: the second is marked by the desire of every *polis* for freedom undiluted and unqualified, making it resist every attempt to dominate it from outside. These tendencies gave rise to a third, which is also found throughout Greek history, namely a rigid and uncompromising attitude towards political ideas; and this frequently exacerbated the internal affairs of the different cities. There were therefore frequent wars between the Greeks, both in the mother country and in portions of the colonial areas where they had acquired supremacy over the natives; and these wars were exhausting to Greek populations and economic resources.

It is true that methods of warfare in those days limited the number of casualties in land actions. Cavalry were little used, the main reliance being placed on the heavily armoured and slow-moving hoplite; pursuit was very difficult, and siege operations were slow. Even so we hear of bloody battles such as Delium, Leuctra, and Chaeroneia. Moreover losses in naval campaigns were normally very high: in Athenian history one has only to remember the Egyptian expedition in the days of Pericles and the Syracusan expedition in the days of Alcibiades, as well as the battles of Arginusae and Aegospotami. In any case the disastrous effect of wars was not felt only in the numbers of killed, or of heavily wounded who were rendered unfit for work, or even of prisoners or displaced persons. One has also to reckon with the cost of war to individuals and to cities, especially in the provision of naval equipment; and also with the destruction of crops and trees, the abandonment of the fields, and the famines that resulted. There were many epidemics; the farmers and middle classes, who served at their own expense, were gradually impoverished; people were exiled in lands far from their homes; and sieges were pressed ruthlessly to the point at which the population starved. Three tendencies were becoming more serious all the time, each of them draining the life-blood of the population and retarding social progress. The first was a growth in the number of mercenaries; the second a revival of colonial emigration, due (as was mercenary service) to poverty and unemployment; the third was the enslavement of large bodies of Greeks who had been made prisoners, though it is true that their servitude was normally only temporary owing to the great efforts made for their redemption and the willingness of purchasers to accept ransom.

But the passion for freedom and the continual effort to build an empire over other cities, these two inborn characteristics of the Greeks, can be seen even better in the failure of every attempt at any lasting political union. One or two efforts did succeed, at least momentarily, in bringing larger political organisms into being. But they were precarious and incomplete; and each one owed its origin to the threat of foreign domination—by Persians or Carthaginians, Etruscans or Sabellians, Macedonians or Romans. Against the Persians, for instance, we find the Ionians of Asia Minor uniting under the leadership of Aristagoras of Miletus; the Athenians receiving support from the Peloponnesians; later the two Attic leagues; the Theban league of Epaminondas' time; and then the confederate Greek leagues formed by the Macedonians Philip II and Alexander. All these are successive phases of the same effort at unity which was imposed on mainland Greece by the Persian danger; and all were led by men who were actually or nominally in the position of tyrants. In the same way many of the Siceliotes came together under the leadership of Gelon and Theron against the Carthaginians, and we find the same phenomenon in the days of Dionysius I, Timoleon, Agathocles, and Pyrrhus. Many of the Italiotes too, came together to resist the Lucanians and Iapyges, and also the Sicilian threat from Dionysius I and Agathocles; they sought a unifier from abroad to help them in their task, Archidamus or Cleonymus, and Alexander or Pyrrhus from Epirus.

But union never lasted longer than the continuance of the danger, and was sometimes dissolved before the danger was over. Every time the irresistible particularism of Greek politics reasserted itself. After this sort of thing had happened again and again—and every attempt at unity had failed—many of the most representative figures in Greece came even more firmly to regard a small city as being the inevitable model on which the Greek political unit should be based. Plato thought the right size was about 5,000 citizens, Aristotle put it at not more than 10,000. Yet Aristotle was the teacher of Alexander, who achieved political union, short-lived though it was, in so great a part of the civilized world.

The same particularist forces were responsible eventually for weakening the Amphictionic Leagues. Every imperialist power which belonged to one of these would conceive the idea of making itself the sole director, and would gain support from groups of subordinate powers. So the struggle to acquire a majority of votes on the Amphictionic council led to continual wars and provided a field for the most bitter political propaganda. The Amphictionic Leagues therefore never carried out for any length of time even the main task for which they had been formed, namely that of avoiding wars between league members. We hear, for example, of three 'Sacred Wars' fought for the control of Delphi.

It goes without saying that the stability of leagues whose basis was more purely political (the *Koinai*) was for the most part even more precarious. More than the religious leagues they were at the mercy of the ups and downs of political events, and there were continual jealousies and struggles connected with attempts by one state after another to acquire hegemony within the

Q*

alliance. As time went on individual member-cities, which had originally enjoyed equality of status, would react against the most powerful member of the alliance if it was trying to reduce them to subjection. The history of the Delio-Attic League provides an example.

The most lasting leagues in early times were the Thessalian, Peloponnesian, Boeotian, and the two Athenian confederacies; and in later times there were the Achaean and Aetolian Leagues. But all had a troubled history and an erratic process of development, since despite their frequently sincere intention of acting in concert, they all had to recognize that unity was an ideal practically unobtainable by part of the Greek race. We see this very clearly in connection with peace treaties concluded at the end of a conflict between great powers. They would swear oaths to remain at peace for ever, or at any rate for 100 (or 50 or 30) years; but they were then almost invariably ready to break the compact, sometimes after a very short interval, rather than attempt to iron out any unexpected difficulties or submit to any loss of what they considered to be their rights.

b. *The Poleis: Basic Constitutional Elements*

Almost every Greek city-state had three basic constitutional elements, the Popular Assembly, the body known as the Boulé, and the magistrates. But in each state these institutions possessed peculiar features and were organized in an individual way.

The Assembly of the people had much less part to play in oligarchic cities, where it was convened relatively seldom: the direction of affairs was entrusted almost wholly to the other two organs of government—and of course also to the royal power, if this still existed in any form. In any case the 'people' was reduced to small dimensions in cities of this kind, since persons under a fairly mature age, or who did not possess a given census, or who belonged to certain supposedly unworthy professions, would all be excluded. Moreover in order to exercise his right to speak a man had to obey very exact rules of precedence. In democratic cities almost completely opposite assumptions prevailed. There the theory was that every adult citizen could take part and speak at any of the frequent meetings of the fully sovereign Popular Assembly, though in practice it was true that the less well-to-do people who lived on land at a distance from the city were not always in a position to exercise their full rights.

The Council (Boulé), Senate (Gerousia), or other smaller assembly had of course more importance relatively to the Popular Assembly in oligarchic states than in democratic. In oligarchies the *primores* who exercised power tended to form a small senate (only twenty-eight members at Sparta), with a long term of office, membership being sometimes for life. Consequently their policies were stable, being dictated by tradition and by the overriding interests of the class to which the members belonged; and their powers, especially in judicial matters, were very wide. Democratic cities, on the other hand, made their Councils large, kept down the duration of membership (normally limited to a single year), and restricted the Council's powers.

The fundamental differences in the position of magistrates in the two types of régime were less striking, though here too there were variations in the way magistrates came into being and in the names and particular functions they were assigned. Certain features were general: magistrates were annual, collegiate, and responsible, and were therefore liable to render account of what they had done; they were not arbitrary officers, but were there to execute the duties laid on them by the assemblies.

It is, of course, impossible to give an account of all the idiosyncrasies found in the changing political organizations found in so vast a number of *poleis*, which varied from the closest and most restrictive oligarchy of *gamoroi*, through moderate oligarchies and democracies, to the most unbridled form of demagogy. The histories of these cities were too different for any definite rules to be laid down, and the most diverse distribution of landed and movable property prevailed among them. Moreover, we must reckon with the strong individualism of the Greeks, who could not be persuaded for long to respect a régime imposed from above or to surrender the particular experience of politics they had acquired in their own right. So there were great variations. In some oligarchic cities, such as Sparta, the number of families of *homoioi*, who had at the outset possessed equal allotments of land, grew disastrously smaller in the course of time: the original 8,000 Spartan citizens with full rights had become, by stages, 2,000 in the early fourth century, 1,000 in the time of Aristotle, and 700 in 241, thus justifying the revolution of Cleomenes, who brought the number back to 4,000. Other cities, though equally conservative in their outlook and so equally insistent on minimum ages and census qualifications for the exercise of political rights (both active and passive), none the less took account of movable as well as of landed property in calculating the census. In them, therefore, power was not confined to the landed nobility, but was a prerogative of the rich in general.

In democracies every citizen had *isonomia*, full equality of rights both active and passive. So everyone could speak in the assemblies, and could become a counsellor or magistrate (though a minimum census was sometimes retained for treasury officials, and military experience was demanded of generals). To make all this possible for the less well-to-do, pay was instituted for magistrates and members of the Boulé (*misthophora*), just as the provision of free equipment to the army had made it possible to recruit from the poorer classes. But in places and periods in which democracy descended to demagogy, greater extremes were reached. Magistrates were selected by lot, a ticket entitling pay was issued to those who took part in assemblies and juries, and the poor were recompensed for judging and attendance at public spectacles, so that they could interrupt their work without suffering personal loss.

We have explained earlier how archaic Greece, and later still more the Greek colonies, allowed foreigners not only to reside but to obtain citizenship.

The consequences of this could be extremely significant when special tribes
or other units were created for the new citizens (*Neopolitai*), for instance when
one city received a large influx of persons who had previously lived elsewhere.
In the classical period this situation was even more variously handled than
before. In Sparta, for instance, xenophobia was the ruling force: but at
Athens the number of resident aliens (*metoikoi*) was growing all the time. There
were merchants, artisans and industrial workmen, political refugees, artists
and men of letters, and pupils of various schools; moreover people engaged in
definite branches of commerce and industry could settle in the city to the
point at which they became a substantial element in the population when
measured in terms of economic potential, labour, or productive output. They
paid taxes and performed military service for the city whose guests they were,
in the same way as citizens; and like citizens again, they were protected by the
courts and could take part in cult acts and attend schools. But they were
usually prohibited from owning land, and they could not exercise either active
or passive political rights. We are told that a law of Pericles, which later
worked against its own author on account of his union with Aspasia of Miletus
and the son she bore him, declared that only the son of two Athenian parents
could be regarded as a citizen. Moreover only in rare cases was citizenship
granted to *metoikoi*.

At one moment régimes of an oligarchic tendency would be in the ascendancy, at another those of democratic outlook; and the main reasons for this
short-lived predominance lay in the more important historical events, such
as wars (especially national Greek wars) or the rise and fall of tyrannies and of
imperial cities. In the Greek peninsula before the Persian Wars the supremacy
of the Peloponnesian League had set its mark on a period in which oligarchic
ideals were triumphant. But after the victory at Salamis, Athens, the main
author of that victory, came to the fore, having already taken important steps
in the direction of democratic concepts; and in the period which followed, the
successes of the maritime and imperial policies of Themistocles and Pericles,
combined with the formation of the Delio-Attic League with its national anti-
Persian programme (at least at its outset), were a fundamental cause of the
development and spread of democracy.

When it became obvious that Athens was being defeated in its thirty-years
war with Sparta, there were repeated attempts at oligarchic restoration in the
cities of the empire; and these were carried to a conclusion after the decisive
defeat in 404. But the oligarchies imposed by the Spartan Lysander also
collapsed with the decline of Spartan power, while democratic ideas were
once more spread by Athens and by the city which had destroyed Spartan
hegemony, namely Thebes.[2]

c. *The Individual and the State: Tyrannies*

It would be a great mistake to attempt to establish a direct relationship in
Greece between oligarchies and over-emphasis on the individual, and between

democracies and under-emphasis. In no city was it perhaps so difficult to set up a single man as ruler as in oligarchic Sparta, where there prevailed the myth of equality and equilibrium between the *homoioi*; in no city was it so dangerous for anyone to make the attempt and in none was it so rare that an attempt was successful. In democracies, on the other hand, and in cities where the *demos* was seeking to free itself from control by cliques of nobles, tyranny would find a fruitful field because the masses were bound to seek for leaders. Social conflict indeed is one of the commonest backgrounds against which the tyrants of the fifth and fourth centuries came into being. At the same time these tyrants, open or disguised, were adept at showing they could interpret and realize the peoples' longing to free themselves from the power of their enemies or to accomplish some dream of imperialist expansion.

On the other hand, imperialism permitted the formation of great fortunes, and through these new men would come to power. They would combine with military leaders in opposition to the tyrant and would intrigue against a smooth succession, which might be already difficult to achieve owing to the existence of rival claimants. In this way tyranny would be overthrown; and the same would happen if a tyrant risked a war to consolidate his power and reputation, and then was unsuccessful. Even if the price of liberation might be the loss of the city's imperial power, many citizens would be concerned to see that tyranny, once overthrown, could never revive. Various means were adopted to this end, such as propaganda designed to demolish the myth of the man of genius, by asserting that his successes were due not to himself but to his people; or the deliberate and simultaneous elevation of personages who were all remarkable but in a single field only, one being an eloquent politician, another a competent general, and a third an invaluable financial expert. A less logical, and therefore less efficient, means was the institution known at Athens as ostracism and at Syracuse as petalism. Ostracism consisted in a vote in the Popular Assembly, at which every voter wrote on a potsherd the name of the politician he considered most dangerous; the man who received most votes had to go into exile for ten years. In fact this system finally enabled the most skilful aspirants to power to eliminate their most threatening rivals. We are told that in 417 Hyperbolus asked for a vote of ostracism in order to break the power of Nicias and Alcibiades, but that in the outcome he was himself removed, while the other two were elected generals.

The complete eradication of tyranny was always difficult. If an empire created by a tyrant collapsed, it was often followed (as happened in Sicily) by the rise of a number of lesser tyrannies in the cities which had been liberated. Similarly the fall of a tyranny did not render the city in question immune from this form of government later, since tyrants arose whenever there was an appropriate situation and a suitable man: once again there is the case of Syracuse, where the rule of the Deinomenids was followed, after some interval of time, by Dionysius I and his son, and later by Agathocles. Two cities of completely different outlook, Sparta and Thebes, after the magnificent successes achieved by Lysander and by Epaminondas and Pelopidas, were prepared to regard those commanders as supermen who merited divinity.3

But there are a number of other ways in which a study of the relationship between state and individual in the fourth century, and of the obvious consequences of this relationship, will help us to understand the radical changes which converted the world of *poleis* into the world of monarchies.

During the fifth century most of democratic Greece followed the example of Athens in setting the interests of the state above those of individuals. But after the fall of Athens and of its political ideals the centralizing force of the *polis* suffered a progressive decline, and the individual came to enjoy a greater measure of freedom. This meant that he was inclined to concern himself largely with his own well-being and with ways of increasing it, and to take as little interest as possible in the problems and needs of the community. It is true that the state had to obtain money, among other things for the payment of citizens who were beginning to show reluctance to take part in public duties; taxation, tolls, and customs duties were all heavily increased, and besides this the rich had to pay contributions towards the liturgies (which included the trierarchy for the construction and equipment of warships, the choregia and gymnasiarchy for the upkeep of dramatic and gymnastic festivals, as well as the provision of torch-races, public banquets, and sacred embassies). But just because they were not interested in public office and preferred to attend to their lands, their commerce, and their industries, most rich men did not feel themselves aggrieved by these payments: they were finding it fairly easy to make large profits. In addition the state came to the assistance of those citizens whose individualist attitude made them reluctant to be distracted from the pursuit of their own undertakings by the performance of military service. Large numbers could be exempted by the increasing employment of mercenaries, which was also the simplest means—now that colonization was no longer available—of ensuring a livelihood to unemployed persons, exiles, and the like.

There are other clear consequences of this general decline of the state and of the lack of enthusiasm to assist the *polis*. Public duties were not performed even when pay was granted; assemblies were increasingly smaller, being attended only by the unemployed and by persons of little account; there was less philanthropy; and there was a falling-off in the number of marriages and births. Not a few philosophers met this situation by working out a panacea in the form of novel and ideal constitutions, full of unpractical logic and abstract ideas which made it impossible to put them into effect. More practical minds, like those of Xenophon (*Hieron* and *Cyropaedia*) and Isocrates (*Ad Nicoclem*) took the view that a strong form of government was needed, of the kind that could only be provided by a monarchy or tyranny. And in fact there was a fairly general resurgence of tyranny, rather like the rise which had occurred two centuries earlier. We know of about 130 tyrants in this period: they are found in the western colonies, in Thessaly, at Corinth and

Sicyon, at Pellene in Achaea, at Lesbos, in Cyprus, in the Pontic cities, and many other places. This was one of the preludes to the transition which was soon to be made from the age of city-states to the age of the Hellenistic monarchies.

d. *Hegemonies*

Cities. We shall now attempt a brief and generalized history of the great hegemonies which appeared one after another in Greece, calling attention to the imperialist outlook which was their common failing. Western Greece we shall pass over, but there too the same story was true.

Pausanias the Spartan had attempted to exploit the victories over Persia, to which his city had made a powerful contribution, by building a Spartan empire outside the Peloponnese while proceeding to liberate further Greek areas from foreign rule. But he had neither support from his government nor co-operation from the allied navies. From 478 the direction of the fleet, and the same programme of liberation, was taken over by Athens; the credit for this belongs mainly to Aristides, who created the Delio-Attic League with its centre and treasury at Delos, its operations depending on the provision by the allies of either naval squadrons or money contributions for common purposes. Then, however, imperialist aims, which had not been diminished by the fall of the Peisistratids, divided the Athenian leaders, together with the factions supporting them in their alternating periods of power, into two groups. Aristides and later Cimon wanted war to the death against Persia and friendship with Sparta: Themistocles, Ephialtes, and later Pericles (after the disastrous failure of his first plan of simultaneous action against Persia and the Spartan League) preferred to come to terms with Persia. And in fact peace with Persia was concluded in 449, to prepare the way for the contest against Sparta for hegemony over all Greeks, including the Greeks of the West.

But this latter policy altered the basis of the Delio-Attic League, because the allied contributions, which had been fixed in relation to the continuance of the Persian War, were now, after peace had been made, put into a reserve fund, or else used to embellish Athens and provide it with the means to fight its rival. The pretext was that Athens was really protecting the allies against dangers of every kind. Naturally not all the allies, especially the stronger cities or those in a position to revolt, were sympathetic to Athenian pretensions; but when Samos revolted in 440/439, it received no outside help, and was therefore defeated and disarmed. The allies were gradually transformed into subjects; the Athenians, though ruled democratically at home, used oligarchic methods abroad.[4] The annual contributions from the allies, now converted into tribute impositions, were paid to Athena in its Parthenon; and law-courts for the allies were set up in Athens to guarantee the loyalty of its new subjects. For 'defensive' purposes 'cleruchies' of Athenian citizen-soldiers were sent out to allied territory; and all the time the empire was being enlarged by new conquests, while Athens did its best to intervene in the affairs of western Greece and to detach allies from Sparta and generally weaken its power. But after twenty-seven years of almost continuous war Athens fell, ruined by the bloody defeat inflicted on it beneath the walls of Syracuse, by the revolts of its subjects, and by the offensive carried on by the Spartan Lysander with the help of Persian gold. For the next thirty years a new hegemony was established under Sparta, this time of oligarchic rather than democratic sympathies.

But this hegemony, too, though it was a source of admiration and interest to many politicians, historians, and philosophers (including some Athenians like Xenophon) was to prove short-lived. The former subjects of Athens, who had helped to bring it into being, expected that they would really receive the freedom which the Spartans had promised; but they then found that they had simply changed one master for another, and therefore were anxious to dissolve the hegemony and follow their own devices. But this was not the only factor. Sparta was culturally incapable of leading Greece, and at this particular moment it also seemed unworthy to do so, because it had won with the help of Persian gold. Moreover it had emerged from the war with its internal structure seriously dislocated, since the conquest of an empire had made it impossible to preserve the 'Lycurgean' ordinances unchanged. The Spartan state had to procure economic means of a kind to which it was not accustomed, in order to maintain the fleet needed to rule the seas. Equality between the *homoioi* had now become a plain lie; some had grown extremely rich, while others had lost their lots and with them their rights of full citizenship. The struggle between Ephors and kings, and between the two royal houses, impeded every action; the Spartan armies were not developing techniques which could match those being perfected elsewhere; and without Persian aid the Spartan navy, so far from growing stronger, could not even act as an adequate defensive force. When Lysander was seen to be preparing a revision of the constitution, which might have brought some relief, he was sent abroad in what amounted to exile, and his attempt was frustrated.

But above all Sparta did nothing to retain the sympathy and loyalty of its new allies (or subjects), to whom it had promised autonomy and freedom from Persia. Instead of granting autonomy it laid claim to a tribute of 1,000 talents; and in every city, as well as imposing the rule of oligarchic factions, which inaugurated a reign of terror in their greed for vengeance, it stationed a Spartan garrison under a 'harmost'. As to its second promise, it is true that, to prevent the dissolution of the hegemony, it did renew the war against Persia; but the Great King financed the rebels who fought at Coronea in 394, the same year in which, also assisted by Persia, the Athenian fleet built by Conon defeated the Spartans at Cnidus. So in 387/6 the Spartan Antalcidas, to check the growing power of Sparta's Theban and Athenian adversaries, made peace with the Persian king, recognizing his ownership of all the cities of Asia Minor and Cyprus. Sparta undertook to get this Diktat accepted by all cities of the peninsula, which were by yet another show of empty words declared to be autonomous, and in which Sparta once again installed oligarchic factions and stationed, by force, garrisons of its own troops.

All this led to the breakdown of the Spartan hegemony. A revolt by the Thebans against Spartan occupation of the Cadmea was the beginning of the next hegemony, that of Thebes, which in 379 assumed once more the leadership of Boeotia. It then made an alliance with the naval power of Athens,[5] and with Jason, the strong ruler of Pherae in Thessaly. The victory of Leuctra in 371 enabled it to turn all the Spartan garrisons out of central Greece, to invade the Peloponnese, and to detach large areas away from Sparta by giving assistance to the movement in favour of democracy. But it proved impossible to carry on this new Theban hegemony after the deaths of the two great men who had created it, Epaminondas and Pelopidas: so it too collapsed quickly. Although the régimes it imposed were democratic and not oligarchic, it worked always through force and the promotion of faction; and when one of its two great founders tried to give a definite measure of autonomy to the cities, his plan was frustrated. Theban dominion had come into being through the victories of its two great generals and their armies; and when these two disappeared from the scene, the cohesive force behind the régime, which did not consist in any ties of a moral kind, was gone. Meanwhile another army, the Macedonian, seized the chance of making itself more powerful than the Theban, by improving on the reforms of Pelopidas. Revolts multiplied, but the most decisive was that of the Phocians, who occupied the temple of Delphi: the ensuing Sacred War (356–346) provided Philip II with his opportunity to intervene; and so began a new hegemony in Greece, and one of fundamental importance in history.

Philip of Macedon. Philip had created a strong army by bringing to perfection a combination of light-armed peltasts and heavy-armed phalangites. He annexed Epirus and Illyria to his empire, captured the Greek cities of Amphipolis, Potidaea, and Methone as bases for his fleet, and occupied the gold mines of Pangaeus. During the Sacred War he took the side of the Thebans, Locrians, and Thessalians against the Phocians, Athenians, and Spartans; and after defeating his opponents he occupied Delphi and rearranged the Amphictiony to suit himself. Then, after many other achievements which there is no need to list here, and after overcoming the final resistance of his enemies at Chaeroneia in Boeotia in 338, he was elected general of a new 'Koinon synedrion' of the Hellenes at a Panhellenic congress held at Corinth. In this new league all cities preserved their internal institutions, but each provided forces proportionate to its size for the war by land and sea which was the proposed aim of the league, and which was in fact begun in 336, though it was then interrupted by the king's death. This war against Persia had been broken off by the Athenians when they were in control in 449: Sparta had resumed it to no effect between 400 and 394; and Gorgias, Lysias, and

Isocrates had proclaimed it at the great Olympic meetings of 392,388,and 380, but their appeals had found no response. It was a great task in the national interest; it justified the new league's existence, and its leadership by the most powerful Greek state of the day. But it was not the only thing that Philip's league was intended to achieve. Macedonian hegemony gave concrete effect to the internal autonomy of the cities, which up till then had been promised at the outset of every hegemony, only to be disavowed very quickly thereafter. It was this same autonomy which Demosthenes prized with so exact an assessment in his political programme, at the time when, in desperation and already too late, he prepared to organize a 'free confederacy of Greek states'.

e. *Characteristics of the Hellenistic monarchies*

Alexander's empire, and the collection of Hellenistic states which carried it on, extended over wider areas and over peoples more numerous and varied than the Persian empire which preceded it and to some extent prepared the ground: in its turn it opened the way for the Roman empire, which in both area and population was larger still. In the unified form achieved by Alexander this was a much shorter-lived empire than its predecessor or its successor; but its importance for history and civilization was immense, on account of the prolonged influence exercised by the Hellenistic political organisms which it generated.

It was essentially due to the differences in method of the Successors, and to their personal ambitions, that Alexander's great empire split up. But in addition the states into which it split went on disintegrating, because the many little cells represented by the autonomous Greek cities could only with difficulty be controlled by the state on to which they were grafted; furthermore there were dissensions between Greeks and natives, and several regions were inclined to separatism. So foreign invasions and the Roman conquest can be regarded as the logical effect of the collapse rather than its operative cause.

One of the main features of Alexander's system, to some extent carried on by the Hellenistic dynasts too, was to transplant large numbers of Greeks to the East, as well as promoting the exchange of commodities and cultural ideas between the Greek and Oriental sections of the lands he had conquered. The result was an impressive phenomenon, a *koiné* between the two races and cultures, though one in which Hellenization of the eastern peoples was generally more marked than was Orientalization of the Greeks. [6]

Something has been said already of the inevitable revival of the monarchical ideal among fourth-century Greeks. Of this ideal Philip II was the incarnation, as leader of a powerful army and as the man who proclaimed a Panhellenic enterprise against Persia. The first period after Alexander's death was one of adjustment, in which the desire to preserve the great founder's legacy in a united form was in conflict with the tendency of the Successors to build up dominions of their own. [7] From this period emerged three major states, those of the Lagids in Egypt, the Seleucids in Asia, and the Antigonids in Macedonia; but, particularly inside the second of these, smaller dynasties arose at different times, such as those of Pergamum, Bithynia, and Pontus; and others, such as the Parthian kingdom, were created when areas once Seleucid got detached. In this last type of case the ruling elements were Hellenized orientals: otherwise the basis of all these monarchies was Graeco-Macedonian, with some oriental influence.

Meanwhile monarchy persisted in the Balkan peninsula, not only in Macedonia, but in peripheral regions such as Epirus, Illyria, and Thrace; and in Sicily the new group of tyrants like Agathocles and Hieron II assumed the title of 'King', with the consent of their subjects.

Here we must pause to consider some of the features of these monarchies which derived from Alexander's empire. The king, beloved of the gods, is an expert and brave soldier, the true and legitimate leader of his army, credited with a many-sided virtue (*areté*) which makes him a sublime and heroic figure. He is the only law-giver, directing and protecting the life of his state in full awareness of the weight of his duties, and looked to as lord and benefactor of his subjects. Usually his eldest son succeeds him, but he has the right to prefer another member of his family, using his own unfettered judgement on the point; and he can associate his successor as co-regent with himself to prepare him for full succession. Although originally these kings did not favour undue personal parade, and liked wearing Macedonian dress, their dignity could only be shown to the world if they also wore a diadem. They were surrounded by their faithful friends and courtiers, and also by their generals: all of these became their counsellors (and at times they had to put up with their intrigues), as well as serving as a class from which major dignitaries such as military commanders, ambassadors, and ministers were drawn. Although they used native personnel in local administration and to some extent preserved the pattern of the former satrapies, for all higher and more delicate jobs they employed Greeks, at least alongside the natives; and these were an organized bureaucracy, who were commonly fairly leisurely in the performance of their tasks.

In every country the king owned vast domains of every kind, which were largely worked by masses of slaves, serfs, or dependent labour. To the income from their rents he added the yield from taxation, the main element in which was the annual *phoros* imposed on every inhabited centre; and eventually there was a poll tax on every human being and head of livestock, a tax on the produce of the land, and customs duties, excise, and corvées. From this revenue the king had to meet the expenses of his court and officials of his army and donatives, and of his patronage of artists, writers, and so on.

The difficulties of administering these vast multi-racial states were later increased by the existence of regions which were under special government and required peculiar treatment. These included peoples retaining their traditional kings, who were in fact vassals and whose 'gifts' were really no better than tribute; secondly peoples of minor importance ruled by dynasts;

thirdly supposedly autonomous peoples, who sometimes still preserved a tribal organization; and lastly the Greek cities.

Alexander had founded Graeco-Macedonian colonies in various parts of his new empire.[8] These were independent states, whose task was to provide the government with fortresses at strategic points and commercial centres, as well as to spread Greek culture and language, and to give land and a livelihood to large numbers of impoverished and vagabond Greeks who had left their own cities. These colonies, with their defensive walls, their temples dedicated to Greek gods, their democratic institutions and magistracies of Greek type (including tribes, demes, popular assemblies, councils and so on), and their autonomous administration, were so many islands of the Greek race amid alien territory. They paid a modest tribute to the king; they accepted a garrison and sometimes control by an *epistatēs*; and if they became capitals of the new Hellenistic states they were the seats of the king's court, though naturally they did not concern themselves with foreign policy.

These colonies were later multiplied in number by individual Hellenistic rulers. Sometimes they were set down in existing native 'cities', whose populations lived together with the Greek settlers under conditions similar to those of *metoikoi* in Greek cities (the same was true of natives permitted to reside in colonies founded where no city had existed before). The status of many of these natives, whose origin was semi-servile, was improved in time, as their economic position and their degree of Hellenization increased, and as they gradually contracted ties of marriage with the colonists: eventually they could obtain access to the citizenship of the *polis*. This situation was of obvious importance in promoting Hellenization within the empire, a process which we have already seen to have been more significant than the effect of Eastern influence on the Greek population.

The army of a Hellenistic state consisted normally of a permanent core of paid Greek and Macedonian soldiers, who provided the king's bodyguard and the garrison troops. These could constitute the hoplite phalanx, now relatively lightly armed, and the squadrons of heavy cavalry. To meet emergencies native troops could be mobilized, in which case their civil status was enhanced; and in addition use was made of Greeks scattered over the king's territories in military colonies, or of mercenaries either recruited individually or offering their service in regular units under their *condottieri*. In general the Hellenistic states did much to promote military technique, for instance in organizing a strong and fast-moving cavalry arm, in their employment of elephants acquired from India and of artillery machines both in the field and for siege operations, and in their building of large warships. (Pl. 22, b.)

When the chequered period of the Hellenistic monarchs is viewed as a whole, down to the time when the most easterly regions got detached and Rome gradually conquered the remainder, it appears as above all a period of peace, which worked to the distinct material advantage of the countries concerned. In some the existing development was preserved and advanced, in others a start was made from scratch. Hydraulic works were revived and improved, additions were made to the road system, and harbour services were brought into line with current needs. Care was taken over the cultivation of vines and olives where climate permitted; and there was supervision of grain production and also of afforestation. Though there was no uniform system of standards, more money was put into circulation: and this did much to promote trade, when combined with the network of roads inside the Hellenistic countries, and with the attention paid to the caravan routes connecting these countries with central and east Asia, and to the sea routes starting from the northern parts of the Red Sea and the Persian Gulf. Although these routes were run by foreigners they gave new impetus to Hellenistic economy, by opening new outlets for exports and making possible the import of silk, cotton, ivory, costly woods, pearls and precious stones, spices, scents, and so on. Governments exercised a watchful control over all this trade by laying their hands on large stocks of exportable goods acquired at low prices, even if this meant keeping the standard of living of the natives at an unduly low level.

f. *The Areas of Seleucid Rule*

Conditions in the various Hellenistic states were rendered different by geographical and racial factors, by divergent theories of government, and by the relative importance of the Greek element in the population and the degree of Hellenization that had been achieved. In broad outline, therefore, we must take each of the larger areas in turn, starting with the Seleucid countries in Asia.

The Seleucid kings owned very large domains, cultivated by serfs, and paid a great deal of attention to all aspects of their administration. They were not, however, excessively concerned to centralize the government of their very numerous and diverse subjects, and did not impose heavy taxes upon them. This very large territory with its many races did not lend itself to uniform methods; and the returns from taxation were high enough without any need to make its rate particularly onerous.

The sole founder of this dynasty was Seleucus, a man who had shown himself not averse from Alexander's ideas of fusion between Graeco-Macedonians and natives: he had not copied the other generals after their leader's death in at once renouncing his marriage, and had kept the Syrian Apama as his wife. Moreover his successors had continued his policy of founding Greek cities with characteristically democratic constitutions; he himself had founded at least fifty-nine. Yet little was done to combine these cities in a single whole with the multi-racial native towns; the latter were governed by oligarchies and were reduced to poverty as well as being deprived of their legal liberties. It was to the Greek *poleis*, together with the Greek soldiers and officials, that the general level of culture and the prevalence of Hellenism were due. The racial admixture of the non-Greeks with one another was only in small measure the result of rural settlements formed by the transplantation of peoples such as Hebrews, Persians, Mysians, Galatians, or Carduchi.

On the coast of Asia Minor as far east as Pontus and Cilicia there had been clusters of Greek colonies before Alexander's time, and from them Greek culture and language had penetrated the interior to Mylasa, Pergamum, Tralles, and Sardis. Under the Successors new cities came into being at Antigoneia (later called Nicaea), Docimium, and Synnada. Then the Seleucids refounded Celaenae with the name of Apamea, and established settlements at Laodicea on the Lycus, Themisonium, Antioch on the Maeander, Seleucia and Antioch on the borders between Phrygia and Pisidia, and several other places; meanwhile veteran colonies grew up at Peltae, Thyateira, Nacrasa, Blaundus, and Magnesia by Sipylus, and Lysimachus founded Lysimacheia on the neck of the Chersonnese.

The autonomous states of the region were equally active in their colonization. In Bithynia we find Zipoetium and Nicomedia; as well the kings of Pergamum built Philetaireia, Attalia, Gergitha, and Eumenia, and at times taxed all their colonies severely. In the third century no less than fifty of these Graeco-Macedonian settlements in Asia Minor can be counted: they completed the early ring of Hellenic colonies, and were for the most part placed in the hills just inland from the coastal districts. One can easily see how important the whole chain of Greek cities was in furthering the spread of Greek ideas, language, religion, and trade: goods were exchanged above all through the flourishing cities of Ephesus, Miletus, Magnesia, Smyrna, Pergamum, and Rhodes; and the results of the whole process are attested by Greek inscriptions throughout the region, by syncretism between Greek and native cults, and by archaeology. Yet native languages, though they were driven out into country districts, still survived; and the cult of the ancient gods was still carried on, especially in central and eastern districts, where Hellenism made marked progress only in Roman times. To judge from literature, the most important cultural centres were still those in the older Greek lands. Cos was the home not only of a flourishing school of medicine, but also of poets and philologists of the school of Philetas; Samos was the birthplace of Duris, Asclepiades, Aristarchus, Conon, and Epicurus; and other poets and scholars came from Ephesus (Zenodotus), Rhodes (Antagoras, Apollonius, Hieronymus), Lampsacus (many Epicureans), Byzantium (Moero and others), Perge (Apollonius), and so on.

In the two sections of Syria Hellenism progressed at very different rates. It went ahead far more rapidly in the north, where the Seleucids had their seat of government; in the south, a region most of which in any case was controlled by the Ptolemies for about a century, progress was relatively slow. In northern Syria the old Greek colonies attained some cultural importance, for instance Soli (the home of Aratus, Chrysippus, Crantor, and Philemon) and Mallus (which produced Dionysiades); but there was additional colonization by Macedonian veterans and Greek immigrants as early as the Succession period, when Antigoneia, Apamea on the Orontes (first called Pella), and Alexandria on the Issus were founded. Under the Seleucids the region became virtually a Greek country, and local place-names were replaced by Greek: it was then that the capital Antioch, with its port Seleucia, was founded, and later came Laodicea, Seleucia, Apamea, Europus and Amphipolis on the Euphrates, Cyrrhus, Beroea, Chalcis, Arethusa, Maronea, Larissa, Leucas, and other cities. This was a land richly endowed by nature, and the Hellenistic rulers endeavoured to increase its production of cereals, oil, and wine, to develop its orchards, and to build roads for the promotion of trade. The religion and art of the country, and still more its literature, reveal an impressive admixture of cultures. The court of Antioch attracted a collection of scholars and philosophers from all over the Greek world, such as Aratus, Hegesianax, Euphorion, Erasistratus, and Lycon. Members of the royal family, such as Stratonice, daughter of Antiochus Soter, were patrons of literature; and the town, with its great library, became a most important centre of Greek civilization, showing all the peculiar features of Hellenism in its materialist, sceptical, and cosmopolitan outlook, including a great delight in novels and fanciful romances. Strabo compared it as a cultural centre with Athens and Alexandria. Scholars of local origin, such as Posidonius of Apamea, were not lacking; and it was here, too, that in later days the apostle Paul came to make the teaching of Christ accessible to the Hellenistic world.

The Hellenization of southern Syria, though less deep, was still significant. Greek influence had been felt before Alexander's day, and can be seen in the philhellenism of Strato II, king of Sidon from 373 to 362. The Successors founded here a Graeco-Macedonian Dodecapolis, of which Gadara, Dion, and Pella (Berenice) were the best-known members. Tyre was repopulated by Alexander himself after its siege, and he also sent settlers to Gaza. The Seleucids colonized Samaria; and the Ptolemies during their occupation of the country founded Philadelphia, Philetaireia, Arsinoe, and Berenice, making use to some extent of the peculiar methods of government which they employed in Egypt. In the Jordan valley there existed a Greek Dodecapolis in Pompey's time, and there was a Tripolis on the sea-coast. But the process of Hellenization was hampered by political disaffection, combined with the peculiarities of the indigenous Semitic culture, especially that of the Hebrews; and the intrusion of Ptolemaic methods was a further complicating factor.

In Mesopotamia, Babylonia, and Susiana, where civilization had flourished for thousands of years and where the population was high, it would be natural to think that there was little room for colonies and small chance of Hellenization succeeding. Nevertheless the Alexandria founded by Alexander at the mouth of the Tigris and the Macedonian settlement at Carrhae (Harran) in 312 were followed by a number of Seleucid cities. Seleucia-on-the-Tigris was their new capital, and they also founded Anthemusia, Antioch Arabis, Antioch in Mygdonia, Apollonia east of the Tigris, Edessa, and Ichnae, as well as the Euphrates cities mentioned above. In this area it may be that Hellenism received more from the civilizations of antiquity than it gave—in religion, for example, and in the sciences, astronomy and astrology: yet we find works written in Greek by scholars who were born in Mesopotamia and neighbouring countries, such as Berosus of Babylonia or Diogenes and Seleucus of Seleucia.

In these countries, too, as in all districts of the Seleucid empire (including those farthest to the east) parties of Greeks were allowed to settle outside the regular *poleis*. They often travelled, traded, and acquired land in organized groups, which made a significant contribution to the spread of culture and to economic and intellectual progress.

Indeed even beyond the Choaspes, in the most easterly districts he had conquered, Alexander founded several stations along the caravan routes and garrison posts on the frontiers, for example the five cities which bore his name (in Margiana, Sogdiana, Areia, Bactria, and Arachosia). The Seleucids founded, or refounded, several more: Europus (Rhagae) and Ecbatana in Media; Antioch in Persis; Achaia, Charis, Calliope, Hecatompylus, and Soteria in Parthia; Antioch in Margiana; and others besides. It is true that these farthest districts, as has been stated earlier, were soon separated off from the Seleucid domains, but the process of Hellenization left its mark there, and in Bactria it was revived by the new dynasty over the century 246–150 (*circa*). Even the Parthians did not show themselves hostile to Hellenism: at the time of their victory over Crassus they still liked to recite Greek plays at their festivals.

g. *Egypt, Macedonia, Western Greece*

The greater part of the Nile valley, which unlike the Seleucid dominions had a homogeneous native population, belonged to the royal domains. It was let out in plots, but the farmers were left no freedom: they were obliged to till given areas and raise certain crops, and their produce was impounded until the next year's seed together with their rent and taxes had been withdrawn from it, which left a very small amount for the labourers to live on. In the rest of the country too there was a rigid state economy with an infinite number of controls, in order to ensure that the country produced export goods (cereals, wine, and oil) in the maximum quantity and at the minimum cost. The state monopolies laid down rules of production: for instance oil must not be extracted in privately owned presses, and must be handed over to officials at a price fixed by the state. The principal industries were also monopolies.

For a long time past Egypt had had the Greek trading station of Naucratis: Alexander added the Greek *polis* of Alexandria, by the side of which the Ptolemies built Ptolemais, as well as several commercial factories on the Red Sea coast. One cannot, however, speak of any large-scale foundation of Greek colonies comparable with that in certain Seleucid countries. The creation of *poleis* would have diminished the absolute powers of the kings in a part of their territory. But if the Lagids were reluctant for this, they were at great pains to preserve the racial integrity of the ruling house and never fully learned the native language; this may explain their readiness to grant a privileged status to Greek settlers, both in the cities and elsewhere.

Greeks in the cities lived on free and autonomous territory. But Alexandria contained the royal abode, and from the first allowed 'metic' inhabitants, particularly the native population of the pre-existing settlement of Rhacotis and also the Hebrew community. These all took on a wide measure of Hellenization: an effort was made to impede mixed marriages, but some degree of infiltration proved inevitable. A number of natives obtained the citizenship, though a more frequent outcome was discord and rioting. But many Greeks lived in other places than the three cities, either on their own or in groups. They might be state officials, or traders in other towns, or possibly *cleruchs* settled as soldiers on the land, which became their private property although their heirs were tied to it for the future. The Greek settlers in Egypt were the party of order, from which the officials were drawn. They provided the regular and essential establishment for the army, which in time of war was expanded to include Greek mercenaries: native recruits were employed only on menial tasks. In the course of time, however, the various classes of soldiers became less distinct, as was inevitable in view of the small number of Greeks and the high native population. Moreover in the light of these proportions it is not surprising that native cults and language survived, nor that the Hellenization of other races (represented, for instance, by the Greek writings of the Egyptian Manetho, or the Greek translation of the Bible for use by local Hebrews) was fairly often accompanied by the opposite phenomenon, namely the absorption of Greek elements by the natives. The centre of Greek intellectual life, recognized of course also by the Ptolemaic possessions outside Egypt in the Cyclades, Cyrenaica, and the semi-Greek areas of Cyprus and southern Syria, was Alexandria; and there were built the vast and famous Library, the second library in the temple of Sarapis, and the 'Museum' with its arrangements for salaried artists. At the court of the Ptolemies, who were often enthusiastic patrons of literature, there was always a large circle of scholars and artists drawn from countries inside the Ptolemaic empire and from all other parts of the Greek world. Under the first Lagids there were Theodorus and Hegesias from Cyrene, Demetrius of Phalerum, Hecataeus of Abdera, Zenodotus of Ephesus, Straton of Lampsacus, Philetas of Cos, Euclides of Alexandria with his mathematical school, and Herophilus of Chalcedon with a school of medicine. In the time of Ptolemy Philadelphus (258–247) Alexandria was the home of a large group of poets, some belonging to the 'Pleiad', such as Alexander of Pleuron, Callimachus of Cyrene, Dionysiades, Philiscus, Lycophron, and Sosiphanes. Under Ptolemy Euergetes (246–221) the list included Apollonius of Perge, Apollonius of Rhodes, Conon of Samos, Dositheus of Pelusium, Dioscorides, and Eratosthenes and Lacydes of Cyrene.

Macedonia was of Hellenic origin and was fairly well in unison with the spiritual and literary movements going on in the Greek peninsula. There were naturally only a few Hellenistic Greek colonies in the area, such as

Cassander's foundation at Antipatreia in his southern Illyrian dominions, and that made by Antigonus Gonatas at Antigoneia in Paeonia. Greek influence received a severe setback on the coast of Thrace, where several colonies were overwhelmed by the Celtic invasion of 279. The artistic and literary centre of the Macedonian empire was of course at its court; and for some time under Antigonus Gonatas there was a circle of scholars and artists: these included the poets Alexander of Pleuron, Antagoras of Rhodes, Aratus, and Nicander, the philosophers Bion, Menedemus, and Persaeus, and the historian Hieronymus of Cardia.

At this period the Greek elements in Magna Graecia were in continuous retreat before the Sabellians, and until the time of the Roman conquest it was only foreign aid that preserved them. These then were clearly not times in which art and thought could prosper as in previous generations. It is believed that at the beginning of the fourth century Croton, the second Greek city of the district after Tarentum, could put only 2,000 citizens under arms.

In the Greek part of Sicily the situation was much less disastrous than in Italy. Indeed the Sicilian Greeks enjoyed a new period of prosperity under the empire of Agathocles, which extended at some moments over practically the whole island. Equally beneficial, though confined to a portion of eastern Sicily, was the long and peaceful reign of Hieron II. Under his rule the climate was clearly favourable to science and the arts: whereas before his day there was a continual exodus of intellectuals from the West—such as Leonidas of Tarentum, Lydus of Rhegium, Timaeus of Tauromenium, Boeotus and Theocritus of Syracuse—in Hieron's time we find some of them, like Timaeus and Theocritus, coming back again. Moreover Syracuse in these years could take pride in the genius of its citizen Archimedes; and once again it became one of the greatest cities of the Greek world, not only as an intellectual centre but as a home of riches and trade.

h. *The Greek Peninsula*

Meanwhile the little *poleis* and the federations in the Greek peninsula still continued with their republican institutions inside a world of monarchies both great and small. They were kept in political subjection, although they were always ready to start abortive and short-lived revolts. Their social and economic conditions, together with their population levels and military potential, were worsening all the time.

The decline in commerce came about because the task once performed for Mediterranean trade by the ports in the peninsula had now been taken over by those in Egypt and Asia Minor. The actual Aegean trade tended to be monopolized by Rhodes and Delos, and the mainland cities did not own sufficient tonnage to overcome this competition. Moreover the routes of navigation had changed, leading now to the great new ports, which soon included Rome. The industries of older Greece were still on a small scale, resembling artisanship, and could not stand up to the competition of the large factories built in the Hellenistic countries. The prices at which wine and oil could be bought in these empires were so low that production for export from Greece often became futile; but it was increasingly necessary to import grain, and this had to be bought at high prices. In this way famine, unemployment, and major economic disasters became frequent; and even social revolution was a common phenomenon (the most serious example indeed was seen in traditionalist Sparta), made easier by the abolition of pay for officials, which restored *de facto* power in democratic cities to the well-to-do bourgeoisie. As the only means of escaping such upheavals men would leave their homes in Greece to become members of the rising *poleis* in the East or to enrol as mercenaries in the service of the new empires. But this of course led, when combined with other results of poverty (such as a decline in marriages, exposure of children, or an increased death rate), to gradual depopulation of the country. Another partial remedy was devised in the constitution of new federations on a larger scale, avoiding the main defects found in the older leagues: the two new leagues we have chiefly in mind are the Aetolian and the Achaean. They were the only organizations large enough to be able to put a significant army in the field, given the immense forces belonging to the new empires. Their main feature was genuine autonomy of the individual member-states in their internal policy and the discarding of all possible imperialist ambitions: external policy was co-ordinated by the decisions of a central council with a general at its head, and the members of this, in numbers proportionate to the importance of each member-state, were appointed each year by the General Assembly of all citizens. This assembly met at fixed intervals in cities which were chosen for each occasion.

But from the cultural standpoint the centre of peninsular Greece remained at Athens. Indeed during the half-century lasting from the death of Alexander to the imposition of more severe Macedonian rule, and particularly under the government of Demetrius of Phalerum (317–307), Athens was still the centre of the whole Greek world. During those fifty years philosophers of almost every school were teaching there: the Peripatetics from Theophrastus to Straton; the Cynics under Crates; the Stoics under Zeno; Epicurus in person; and the Academy under Xenocrates and Polemo. There were orators like Demetrius, Deinarchus, Demochares, Stratocles, and Philiscus; historians such as Diyllus, Demochares, Timaeus, and Philochares; and writers on the history of art like Xenocrates. Meanwhile Menander, Philemon, Diphilus, Philippides, Apollodorus, and Posidippus were writing for the theatre; and there were epic poets such as Antagoras and Aratus, not to mention a number of tragedians belonging to the so-called 'Pleiad'.

Later, however, while the great Greek cities of the East were attracting more people to their courts and their learning, Athens in the period of its subjection (263–228) withdrew more into itself. This was the result of the philosophy prevalent at the time, which was largely sceptical and pessimistic;

and the habit persisted even after the city recovered its freedom. Yet the language of Athens was becoming the Hellenistic language: it spread far enough to become the officially recognized language of half the known world.

It is commonly said that in contrast to the *polites* of earlier times the Hellenistic age provides us above all with the 'cosmopolites'. But these concepts need precise definition. The Greeks, it is true, had been divided into a large number of cities down to the time of Philip and Alexander: but the same is true, in broad terms, of the Greek peninsula and part of western Greece down to the Roman conquest, and even later. When Aristotle wrote his *Politics*, at the height of Alexander's conquests, his ideal was still the small *polis* of Greek tradition; and when the Greeks and Macedonians became masters of the world, each of the colonies they founded in the East was still given the old municipal constitution of the *poleis*.

As to cosmopolitanism, though some philosophers arrived at the concept that all men are naturally equal, that was not the normal way of thinking of the Greeks and Macedonians who conquered the East. One proof is the fact that Alexander's plan for fusion of Greeks with natives died with him: the conquerors always regarded themselves as a privileged people. The Ptolemies, for instance, according to Plutarch, were never prepared to speak the Egyptian tongue. So Greek cosmopolitanism of the Hellenistic period must certainly in general be understood in a different sense. Greeks of all regions had for long been accustomed to get involved in the politics of empires, in commercial enterprises, and in warfare (particularly as mercenary soldiers). After the conquests and colonization achieved by Alexander and his successors they found themselves even more heavily involved, and were adopting other peoples' ways of life, at the same time as they were feeling themselves to be 'citizens of the world' because the whole world belonged to them. A 'cosmopolites' for this generation simply betokened a member of the 'Greek world'. Anyone who spoke no Greek, even if he was a subject of a Greek state, remained in Greek eyes a 'barbarian'.

So there was no very great process of levelling between Greeks and non-Greeks. Even the levelling among Greeks themselves was neither complete nor real, since they were still separated into a multiplicity of autonomous *poleis*. In addition the profound and subtle differences of outlook between the various Greek areas still persisted. The Greeks of the peninsula and the West were still a turbulent people, always in the throes of political strife and the problems of defending their own cities: their feelings and tastes are in contrast with those of the Greek world in the great Hellenistic states, where politics revolved round the king's government, and where the artist became once more a part of the court, as he had been in times long past. There was always an essential difference between Athens, where philosophers of all schools and outlooks met and argued, and Alexandria or Pergamum, where the scholar or scientist predominated; between Athens again, where 'New Comedy' was born, or the Sicily which produced Theocritus, and on the other hand Alexandria the home of libraries, where patient philologists and biblio-philes catalogued, collated, annotated, and published the various ancient texts.

6. THE ROMAN WORLD

a. *The Republican Constitution and Social Conditions to* 390 BC

We have already spoken of the causes and history of the fall of regal power at Rome; as well as of the earliest collegiate magistracies, a 'praetor maximus' and a 'praetor minor' (from *prae-ire*, i.e. 'leaders'), which were supported by lesser offices. In times of exceptional crisis power was given, for the duration of a campaign or for six months, to a dictator, aided by a 'magister equitum'. The fall of the foreign kings had grave results in the economic and social fields. Hegemony over Latium, which the monarchy had been responsible for establishing, was now lost; and agriculture deteriorated because it became impossible to maintain the expensive drainage works built by the Etruscan princes. The people were compressed into a narrow area of land which had to be carved up into lots so small that starvation levels were common; both sea-borne commerce and the transit trade across Latium were brought to a standstill, with the result that there was a shortage of gold and also of raw materials for the nascent industries. The patriciate, however, had formed itself into a closed caste, and was able to assert itself. Its power came from the possession of large landed estates and of clients attached to each individual and family; moreover it had all the magistracies, priesthoods, law-courts, and army commands in its own hands.

The *plebs* gradually got divided into two sections, which sometimes col-laborated but at other times did not. One consisted of the richer plebeians, often clients or retainers of the patricians; and this section wanted political equality, that is to say parity in voting and eligibility for all offices. The other section were the owners of inadequate plots of land, together with men who were entirely landless and unemployed, whose claims were essentially econo-mic and social. These two factions carried on the battle; but the first, although they could always count on support from the second, were sometimes careless of the interests of their allies.

The first armed secession of the *plebs* in 494 led to the creation of 'tribuni plebis', two in number, who were private magistrates of the plebeians and took on the protection of their order. They were declared 'sacrosanct', in that the plebeians bound themselves with an oath to defend their inviolability with all force at their command; and to them were added as treasurers two plebeian 'aediles' known as Ceriales. The tribunes presided at assemblies of those plebeians who were enrolled in tribes (the later *Comitia Tributa*), and in 492 this assembly obtained allowances of corn from the government in order to meet a famine. One of the most pressing demands, resulting from the recur-rent land-hunger, was for division among the plebeians of the unnecessarily large plots of *ager publicus* occupied by the patricians. This the patricians resisted to the death, and executed in 486 the praetor Spurius Cassius who had declared himself in favour of a redistribution.

Between 482 and 471 a new system of 'centuries' was introduced, in the effort to detach the rich plebeians sharply from the poor.9 The population was divided into centuries, grouped by census qualifications into five 'classes', outside of which were the centuries of the 'Knights' drawn from the 'primores urbis'. The system was so arranged that in the *Comitia Centuriata* the centuries of the knights and those of the first class (in which the rich plebeians were enrolled) comprised more than half the total voting units. In reaction to this the number of tribunes was raised in 471¹⁰ to five and in 457 to ten, the numbers corresponding to the number of classes, with each one of which, since they differed in census and in aims, a tribune or tribunes were to be linked: but this move had little result. In 456 the plebeians successfully carried a plebiscite redistributing the public land on the Aventine, with compensation for the dispossessed patricians. For many years, beginning in 462, the patricians conducted resistance to a proposal to appoint *Decemviri* to produce a written code of laws; and such a board was finally appointed in 451, all other magistracies being suspended for a year. When at the end of the year only ten tables had been drawn up it was agreed to appoint a second college for 450, this time with half its members plebeians; but after they had drafted two further tables they ran into opposition from both patricians and plebeians (for opposing reasons), and their operations were interrupted by violence. The result of this work was a set of laws befitting the archaic conditions of a people engaged in a backward type of agriculture and possessing very severe conceptions of law and morals. Yet they achieved the passage of a law preventing a capital sentence on any citizen without a judgement by the people, a principle reaffirmed in 449 by one of the laws passed by the praetors Valerius and Horatius to the effect that no magistrate could pronounce sentence of death without the possibility of 'provocatio' (appeal to the people). Another law of these praetors declared anyone who inflicted injury on a tribune or any other plebeian magistrate to be 'outside the law'.

In 445 C. Canuleius proposed to abolish the prohibition on marriages between patricians and plebeians, and after heated debate the proposal was carried. Another proposal was for the election of one patrician and one plebeian praetor every year; but decision on this was postponed until the end of the war then in progress, and in the next year (444) the election of praetors¹¹ was suspended. Instead their power was given to 'tribuni militum', whose numbers (3, 4, 6 or 8) varied from year to year according to the needs of the wars simultaneously being carried on against many foreign states; these were chosen for their technical abilities from among the patricians, but from the end of the century plebeians were elected too. Meanwhile, to avoid irregularities in the assessment of census qualifications, which affected enrolment of the classes and the determination of fiscal and military obligations, the patricians instituted new officials called 'censors', who had to take census every four or five years. In 421 plebeians were included among the *quaestores aerarii*, who kept the state treasury; and in 406 the military *stipendium* was fixed at a rate which allowed the poorer plebeians to provide their own arms and to avoid complete ruin in the long and frequent wars of the period.

A word may here be said about Rome's foreign relations and the methods it used to maintain the new hegemony it established in central Italy in the fifth century. After the Latin Coalition had been defeated, Rome in 493 made a defensive alliance with the Latins on terms of equality (the *foedus Cassianum*), but with the command reserved for Roman generals. This meant that Rome's conquests to south and east were common to the two parties to the alliance; and from this originated the concept of 'Latin colonies', and also the form taken by these colonies, in which the two peoples took part with equal shares. The Hernici, with whom a further *foedus* was concluded in 486, were admitted as a third party. But later, when Rome had to defend itself unaided against the Sabines and Etruscans, and then passed over to conquer Sabine and Etruscan territory, it was natural that purely Roman colonies should be founded, with settlers enrolled in Rome's 'rustic tribes'. So the new hegemony was uneven: Rome's power was absolute in Etruria and the Sabine country, but in the south it held a condominium with other peoples.

b. *Constitutional and Imperial Changes to the First Punic War*

The siege and sack of Rome by the Gauls in 390 (Roman chronology; the Greeks said 387/386) not only involved the loss of most of its army and the burning of its streets, but was followed by the revolt of many allies. These included both the Etruscan, Volscian, and Aequian towns with the colonies which held guard over them, and also many of the Latins and Hernici. These people, who had begun to be afraid of their powerful ally and were anxious to forestall the danger of being transformed into satellites, thought the sudden collapse of Rome's prestige provided a good moment for breaking away and revising their treaties. It was Rome's good fortune that a certain number of cities and colonies remained loyal, for these not only formed a defensive ring but erected barriers which broke the territorial continuity of its enemies.

So Rome took up again with vigour its work of imperialist conquest, and after half a century, about 325, it possessed, directly or indirectly, the whole of central Italy. Its dominion ran on the Tyrrhenian side from Sutri and Nepet in the north to Nuceria in the south, on the Adriatic side from the Aternus valley to northern Apulia. It was the achievement of men like L. Furius Camillus, and of the others who assisted and carried on his work, to conceive a vast new system of organization, in which all older methods of treating allies and defeated enemies, hitherto used empirically and without discrimination by the Romans, were employed together on well-defined principles. It was essential to prevent cities which had been brought into Rome's orbit from rebuilding political or military coalitions against the mother city. At the same time it was important to relate the treatment of each individual city to the services or harm it had done to Rome, and to make each realize that its legal and material position was not fixed for ever but could be changed for better or for worse, depending on the city's future behaviour. So the various forms of status were arranged like the rungs of a ladder, which one could go up but also go down. It was also desirable to interpose regions of one type between those of another, so as to encourage emulation and frustrate hostile combinations; and the Roman citizens who had been settled individually ('viritim') in conquered areas had to be given security by the foundation, alongside them, of compact colonies, which were ready to defend their neighbours and safeguard Rome's possession of the territories in question. But the most important task was to bind conquered peoples to Rome by ever stronger ties, and to enlarge the actual nucleus represented by the dominant element, in proportion to the size of its dominions. This problem Rome handled in the most liberal and humane manner possible.[12] The peoples who showed themselves most friendly and who were most akin to Rome in race were gradually admitted to full Roman citizenship; but for loyal peoples of relatively different race a new experimental method was devised, under which their autonomy was in part respected and they acquired a sort of half-citizenship. This latter method did not infringe the structure of the ruling power, which preserved full initiative in the political and military spheres. These various forms of status must now be examined in greater detail.

The first grant of Roman citizenship to an ally was that made by Camillus to Tusculum: the first settlement of Romans on conquered territory in the first sixteen *tribus rusticae* probably goes back to 495, and in 318 the twenty-seventh such tribe was formed. In these tribes there were also enrolled the inhabitants of any existing communities (such as Tusculum, Aricia, or Lanuvium) which had been granted Roman citizenship. In *tribus rusticae* which possessed no town, and in areas where the nearest town was too far away, Rome established villages where meetings, markets, and religious ceremonies could be held. These were called 'conciliabula', and to them were added 'fora' along the main roads. Both types of foundation were often the nuclei from which new towns came into being.

Along with the tribes there was a new set of colonies, both Roman and Latin. The former were originally situated inland as well as on the coasts, but in later times they were generally maritime. They were composed of Roman citizens, settled sometimes in places where a previous community had existed and sometimes on fresh sites; in return for the duties of defence undertaken by their citizens they were excused ordinary military service. These citizens, though always regarded as part of the Roman people, enjoyed some measure of autonomy; and they had their own magistrates, modelled on those of Rome, with limited functions in the administrative, financial, and judicial spheres. The name of 'Latin colony', in contrast, was given to a town formed of non-Romans, or of Romans who elected to take part in it. The latter was possible

(a)

[Alinari

33   *The 'Ludovisi Throne', mid-fifth century BC, Rome, Terme Museum*

    (a)   *The birth of Venus*

    (b)   *Woman burning incense*

    (c)   *Flute player*

(b)   [Alinari   (c)   [Alinari

34   GREEK SCULPTURE

(a) *The charioteer, bronze,* c. 474, *Delphi Museum*

(b) *Pallas Athena, after Myron*

(c) *The Athena Lemnia by Pheidias, Dresden Museum (the original head is at the Municipal Museum, Bologna)*

in early days, since Latin colonies enjoyed greater autonomy, and this seemed to imply a more favoured status at a time when full citizenship did not, as it did later, include a mass of advantages and privileges. The condition of these colonies, therefore, was analogous to that of the 'cives sine suffragio' mentioned below. For to the most friendly cities Rome would not send colonies but would give a reward for their services; and of these, though all were called 'municipia', some had full citizen rights and others were made 'sine suffragio', implying that their inhabitants could not vote at Rome or become Roman magistrates. They were autonomous, with their own magistrates and councils, and to a large extent their own judicial arrangements; and they had rights of *conubium* and *commercium* with Rome (*ius Latii*). It was only later that this favoured status became in practice a diminution of rights.

The peoples who remained as *socii* were bound to Rome by treaty. Some had 'foedera aequa', treaties made on the basis of equality, with defensive obligations but with the right to make peace and war on their own, although they were bound to give passage through their countries to Roman armies. The peoples in question were few in number, and were for the most part far away from Rome. Some had to provide assistance in agreed quotas, on land and sea. But most *foedera* were 'iniqua', unilateral instruments devised in Rome's interest without any attempt at equality. These allies were obliged to furnish military contingents brigaded as auxiliary troops under Roman *praefecti*; they were not allowed to make war or new alliances; and they were bound to accept Roman arbitration if they were involved in disputes. Apart from the *socii* there were peoples bound by *indutiae* or voluntary truces; and there were others standing in the general relationship of *amicitia* (friendship). The permanence of the latter relationship varied, but it normally included the obligation not to help Rome's enemies.

We now turn to the domestic reorganization which Rome underwent during this half-century. The Gallic disaster had reopened the struggle for a definition of the respective powers and functions of patricians and plebeians, with the plebeians reviving their assault on the patrician monopoly of magistracies and high offices. Their demands were from the first acceptable to enlightened patricians like Camillus, and they formed the background to the attempt at tyranny made by M. Manlius Capitolinus. After the tribunes had pressed them with fervour over a period of ten years, they at last resulted in the passage of the Leges Liciniae Sextiae in 367. These reduced debts, limited to 500 *iugera* the amount of public land which a single family could hold, and brought to an end the *imperium* of the *tribuni militum*. Once again two annual chief magistrates were appointed on the lines of the earlier praetors; but there were significant modifications, and it was now possible for plebeians to hold the office. The new magistrates, who were called 'consules', were a regular college, in which each member had equal rights with the other and could veto his colleague's action (*intercessio*); each was empowered to summon the senate or the people in order to get guidance; and both could be absent from Rome in the conduct of war, since the administration of justice in the city was entrusted to a new officer, the *praetor urbanus*. At first, it is true, the patricians by mobilizing their clients and creating riots were able to prevent any plebeian being elected for a number of years after 366. But in 356 we find the first plebeian dictator, and in 351 the first plebeian censor; and plebeians and patricians held office in alternate years as *aediles ceriales*, deputies of the consuls for policing the city, supervising markets, guarding the treasury, and so on. This drew the plebeian *aediles* into the regular state machinery, and gradually the tribunes were incorporated as one of the organizations of the state proper. They were allowed to summon the senate, and to speak and make formal proposals at its meetings; later on plebiscites ratified by the senate were recognized as equivalent to state laws.

Camillus is also credited with the reorganization of the army, in which the phalanx was replaced by the more flexible 'manipular' order of battle. This was a criss-cross formation in three lines, each provided with different types of weapon suitable to the men's age and the task they had to perform. Technical considerations instead of wealth determined a man's place in the field.

The wealthy plebeians, it is true, were concerned with obtaining equality with the patricians inside a constitution which remained an oligarchic stronghold of the rich, nobles and plebeians alike. Yet some measures were also taken to help the lower classes. In 357 the interest on loans was lowered, and in 352 debtors who had fallen into arrears were given advances from state funds. It was all too little for the people who were engaged in fighting Rome's wars for the possession of central Italy, with their own livelihood disappearing in the process. After the failure of an army rebellion designed to seize the Campanian lands a series of plebiscites were passed in the same year (326). According to Livy these laid down 'that loans at interest were prohibited, that no one could hold the same office until ten years had elapsed, that one man could not hold two magistracies in the same year, and that both consuls could be plebeians'. The same author declares that this year 'was for the Roman *plebs* like a second beginning of liberty, because imprisonment for debt was brought to an end'.

Meanwhile the progress of conquest led to constitutional change. The assembly of the people in their centuries was becoming less representative of the will of all citizens, because many of them lived far away from the city. At the same time the consuls were often out of Rome for long periods on campaigns. It was therefore inevitable that direction of public affairs should be centred on the senate, a body which was composed of the best men from all factions, chosen conscientiously by the censors, and which was in a position to ensure stability and continuity of policy. Senators were mainly drawn from the richest and most illustrious patrician and plebeian families, those which produced generals and diplomats, law-givers and administrators. Yet the hardening of tradition tended to produce a uniform type among their members, and there came into being a governing oligarchy grouped round a small number of families. This frustrated the initiative of individuals and put a curb on any move in the direction of dictatorship, but it also weakened the power of the magistrates, who were already too few in number to cope with the growth of business and the new tasks that were constantly arising.

For the increase in political problems was accompanied by new problems of an economic kind. Deforestation, with the resulting erosion of the top-soil, was changing the character of the districts nearest to Rome from arable land to pasture, and it became essential to conquer new lands for the production of cereals. At the same time bronze coinage was circulating more widely, and with it the standard of well-to-do living was rising but the poorer classes were encountering higher prices and mounting debts. This last was in part compensated by the outlets for employment opened by the revival of transit trade and of small industry.

At the turn of the fourth century the political struggle had revealed three main parties at Rome. The first, which at this time had its typical representative in Q. Fabius Maximus Rullianus, was narrowly patrician and intransigently conservative, opposing all fresh concessions to the *plebs*. The second, a moderate party represented by Appius Claudius, favoured an outright census qualification for the exercise of political and civil rights, and was therefore prepared to grant a place among the privileged classes (at this time composed in the main of landed proprietors, both patrician and plebeian) to newly rich men who had made fortunes in commerce and industry: for traditional reasons, however, religious offices were to be confined to the old nobility. The third party was composed of illustrious plebeians like Q. Decius Mus. It aimed at using the plebeians, of whatever social standing, to break the *optimates*, and was prepared to uphold the claims of the humblest among the *plebs*.

During the censorship of Appius Claudius, and during his consulship later, the social position of the poorer classes was significantly improved by their employment on the construction of the Via Appia and the Appian aqueduct. Moreover the better-to-do members of the *plebs*, who because they had no landed property had been confined to the lowest census class and were not enrolled in tribes, now secured enrolment in the tribe of their choice and in the census group which corresponded to their actual economic status in society. This enabled the state to tax them proportionately, and it was a measure particularly favourable to sons of freedmen; many of these were foreigners of good family who had served as slaves in the noblest and richest houses in Rome, and they were therefore the best-educated and most active section of the plebeians.

The aristocrats led by Rullianus, who was censor in 304, managed to limit the influence of these new citizens by confining them to the urban tribes, the argument being that such persons were essentially residents of the city. This enabled the aristocrats to preserve their freedom of manœuvre in the use of their clients in the rural tribes. Yet it did not prevent a certain amount of new recruitment to the governing class, as we see from the career of Cn. Flavius (son of a freedman called Annius), who was successfully elected to various magistracies and became a senator in reward for his services as a *scriba* of Appius Claudius. He had drawn up a list, for all to consult, of the *dies fasti* on which justice could be obtained; and he had produced a pamphlet containing the *actiones* or procedural rules for legal suits, which had hitherto been the secret property of the pontiffs and had been employed by them as they pleased.

The power of the people and their *comitia* to limit the arbitrary decisions of magistrates went on growing, as did the penetration of the plebeians into the various offices. From 362 some of the *tribuni militum* in the legions had been appointed by popular vote: in 321 the number was raised to twelve, and in 311 to sixteen, out of the twenty-four tribunes in the four legions. In the same year, 311, the *duoviri navales* were also chosen by the people. In 300 the tribune Q. Ogulnius and his brother Gnaeus secured the opening of religious offices to the plebeian order: the colleges of pontiffs and augurs were each raised to nine members, of whom four pontiffs and five augurs were plebeians. Also in 300 a *Lex Valeria* prohibited the flogging or execution of a citizen without appeal to the people.

Yet these reforms were not enough to make the constitution democratic. It was essentially the rich plebeians—the new nobility of wealth, including men serving in the cavalry at their own expense—who secured election to military commands, wrested offices and privileges from the nobility of birth, and won support at the *comitia*. These *comitia*, because the citizen body was so scattered over territories far from Rome and because the ordinary citizen had no right to propose measures or even to speak, became increasingly less representative of the broad interests of the masses. It would be wrong to regard the last struggles between patricians and plebeians before the First Punic War as phases in a class conflict between rich and poor: such a conflict did exist, as we have shown, but it has left little definite mark on history. In reality the patricians and plebeians who were contending for power were both members of the richer classes; and the outcome was not a victory by one section over the other, but the formation of a dual power composed of the senate, where the old nobility still had the upper hand, and the *comitia*, dominated by the most powerful among the plebeian families. By and large the Roman state was now a plutocracy, whether its rich rulers were nobles or plebeians.

The poorest classes in the *plebs* were increasingly forgotten, and were left to fight their own battles. Their hardships must have reached extreme heights if despite state intervention to relieve the famine of 299 and the plagues of 295 and 293, and despite fines and other penalties imposed on usurers, the struggle broke out again with such violence that in 287 the *plebs* seceded. Q. Hortensius succeeded in placating them by securing that the senate would give its preliminary ratification to all *plebiscita*, which thus assumed the force of laws. The first plebiscite which automatically became law in this way was one in the interests of the poorer classes, cancelling certain debts and reducing others. But the future operation of Hortensius' measure mainly favoured the rich plebeians, the class which in 280 succeeded in getting the first plebeian censor elected.

The rise to power of this new nobility of wealth had its effect on the economy in general, and it contributed to the constructive effort which put Rome on the same level as the greatest powers in the Mediterranean, now that it was mistress of the Italian peninsula. One indication of this rapid development was the appearance of silver coinage from the Roman mint in 269.[13] Other effects were seen in the constitutional field, such as the growing estrangement of the chief magistrates from the senate. Now that wars were being fought over long periods at a great distance from Rome the practice was started of prolonging commands beyond the period of a year; and this made the magistrates increasingly independent of the senate, though it also enabled the senate to saddle them with the blame for any defeats. At the same time the senate was more effectively than ever becoming the motive power in the state. It was the only organ capable of exercising some continuity in policy and overcoming the consequences of the annual rotation of consuls and *praetors*. It was also the great repository of technical experience, gained through the variety of fields in which its members had commanded or otherwise operated. In the end the senate claimed the credit for every victory and every achievement, and thus enhanced both the measure and the permanence of its own prestige.

Meanwhile Rome's methods of exercising dominion were undergoing a gradual change. When in 264 the great political organism of the Roman state and its allies covered the whole peninsula from Pisa and Ariminum to the Straits of Messina, only about a quarter of this area comprised citizen territory and land directly owned by Romans, one-tenth belonged to Latins and to Latin colonies, and all the remainder (a territory three times that of the *ager Romanus*) was in the hands of 'allies'. This undoubtedly indicates an alteration in the 'ladder' system. Grants of Roman citizenship and the creation of *tribus rusticae* had been halted; Roman colonies were becoming less frequent; and there was an increase both in the amount of territory confiscated to become *ager publicus* and in the number of treaties of alliance. In part at least the change was due to three things. Different races, whose assimilation would be a slower and more difficult process, were entering the great political organization; certain peoples desired a wider measure of autonomy; and many of the newcomers lived so far from Rome that the benefits of Roman citizenship would for them have been negligible in practice. The new policy was to orientate the diverse and distant peoples of Italy upon Rome by making use of existing treaties of alliance and by breaking up the old political leagues. So began the cultural and political unity of the peninsula described in Chapter VII.

c. *The Punic Wars*

From the start of the campaign in Sicily the cities of that island which had joined Rome either voluntarily or under compulsion were made to provide regular supplies and troops for the war. They were in any case already accustomed to paying tribute to the dominant power, which before the Roman intervention was in most cases Carthage, though some cities were tributary to the Mamertines and others to Syracuse. When, therefore, both during the war and after the peace of 241, Rome made a provisional settlement of the conquered portions of the island, which were administered by one of the *quaestores classici*, it deliberately placed the cities on a lower footing and avoided any policy which might have tended to equate victors with vanquished, such as founding colonies, granting citizenship either wholesale or selectively, or employing Sicilians in the army. On the principle that cities were to be treated in a way which reflected their conduct during the war, some remained in a treaty relationship and were exempt from tribute, a second class were 'liberae et immunes', though obliged to furnish a tenth of their produce, and a third class, called 'decumanae', were made to provide the tenth free and further 'tenths' against payment. Finally, on the land confiscated from cities which had revolted, since Rome was unwilling for the present to allow Roman citizens to settle there, plots of land were relet for rent to the former owners, the cities in question being called 'censoriae'.

These arrangements could be varied in detail, and were so on many occasions. The first was in 227, when after conquering parts of Sardinia and Corsica and dividing them up into only two categories of community (*decumanae* and *censoriae*), Rome made a definitive settlement of all three islands as 'provinciae'. To the four praetors with *imperium* existing at that time (two urban and two *peregrini*) a further two were added, one for Sicily and the other for Sardinia/Corsica; and the district in which they exercised command was called a 'provincia', because that word denoted each magistrate's specific sphere of power. But the new praetors had exceptional powers in comparison with the old. They combined the military functions of a consul with the judicial functions of a praetor; they were exempt from collegiate restraint, since there was only one for each province; and they had absolute control over property and persons, there being no tribunician veto, no *intercessio*, no *provocatio*. So Rome had renounced any policy of uniting the people of the two large islands with the Italian nation. Instead of following the generous plan laid down by Camillus it was applying to its conquests outside the peninsula the methods of the Carthaginian 'eparchies'.

The long and hazardous course of the First Punic War, fought so far from home, did much to alter the lives and aspirations of Rome's subjects. For many years the armies were in contact with civilized peoples of a different culture, learning to speculate, to spend their money, to use their leisure, and to purchase possessions: all these new habits were making their characters different and more refined. The bolder among the small proprietors, when they returned to find their holdings untilled or mortgaged or sold, were not prepared to become peasants again and perhaps fall to the status of day-labourers: they embarked on a more adventurous existence as travelling *negotiatores*, or as something like pirate sailors. The great landed proprietors, for their part, once they had swallowed up these smallholdings by fore-closure or purchase and had arbitrarily taken possession of large tracts of *ager publicus*, became the owners of vast *latifundia*; and these they preferred to use for pasturage or arboriculture, employing for this purpose the slaves acquired as the result of war and piracy. Meanwhile the rich plebeians—and also such nobles as possessed liquid assets—not only found occasion to increase their stake in commerce and light industry, but also took up such occupations as piracy, money-lending, tax-farming, army services, trade in distant countries, and traffic in slaves.

The *comitia* of the people acquired unexpected importance in the course of these years. In 264, for example, in alliance with the consul Appius Claudius Caudex, they pressed for the despatch of assistance to the Mamertines; in 241 they insisted on reopening the discussion about peace terms; and similar activity can be seen later, in 223, when they allowed C. Flaminius the honour of a triumph refused him by the senate. On the other hand the selfish policy of the senate must have been in the ascendant during much of this period. Only thus can we explain Rome's failure to make extensive grants of citizen-ship to its allies, who were contributing with so much of their life-blood to its wars and conquests—and its application of so illiberal a method of govern-ment to its provinces, which became the 'praedia populi Romani'.

Even when its conquests on both sides of the Po left it, inside the peninsula itself, with very large areas of public land for disposal, the official policy was not to distribute it in individual assignments to needy citizens, but to get money for the treasury by letting it out to the native inhabitants, as had been done with the lands of *censoriae civitates* in the provinces. In 232 this policy was violently opposed by C. Flaminius Nepos, who carried a plebiscite dividing among members of the Roman *plebs* the lands south of Ariminum which had been taken from the Senones and Picentes. About fifteen years later the same Flaminius passed another plebiscite forbidding senators to possess ships larger than were needed to carry produce from their own estates, 'for all traffic by senators was regarded as unworthy'.

A new spirit is evident in Roman politics during the quarter of a century when Publius Cornelius Scipio (Africanus maior) and the senatorial faction supporting him were normally in power. It is visible in 202, when terms were dictated to Carthage after its defeat. No new provinces were created in Africa, and Scipio refused to accept the proposal of his counsellors to destroy the city of Carthage and demand the surrender of Hannibal. Instead Rome established a balance of power between the small state, which was all that was left to Carthage, and the Numidian kingdom of Masinissa, enlarged to its original dimensions, both of them recognizing the alliance and protection of Rome. So we get a return to the old ideology, an extension of supremacy through alliances with states recognizing Rome as the head. It was not only a more generous conception than that of direct rule of provincial territory (or of colonies, to use modern terms): it also avoided the military effort involved by the latter policy of holding down conquered countries by armed occupation, and it allowed former enemies the opportunity to collaborate with Rome in the cultural field and to defend their own countries from barbarians invading from remoter zones. The same policy was followed, under the leadership of Africanus and his friends, when in 196, after the defeat of Philip V, Macedonia was allowed to remain as an allied and independent state, reduced to its original position in relation to Greece, but able to fulfil its function of civilizing and perhaps even annexing the countries of the northern Balkans. The programme corollary to this was one of giving freedom to the Greeks and recognizing their freedom for the future. It is true that this was regarded by many Romans as a means of preventing the formation of great powers in the Balkan area which might challenge Rome itself, and of promoting instead the development of a large number of tiny Hellenistic states with a balance of power, all friendly and looking towards Rome. Yet Rome was in no way aiming at direct rule of a provincial kind, nor at a protectorate in which it would be automatically involved. In the minds of T. Quinctius Flamininus and his supporters it was a disinterested policy and a moral one. Moreover the same principles were applied when the Seleucid kingdom was defeated and dismembered, for here too Rome made no effort to impose direct rule.

But Africanus also showed himself conscious of other unresolved problems in the political and social organization of Rome. One was that of the citizen proletariate, who may be said to have lost their natural protectors, the tribunes of the *plebs*, from the time when the senate succeeded in attaching these officers to itself. The poverty of this proletariate was in strong contrast with the wealth of the state, and with that of the senatorial aristocracy and equestrian bourgeoisie. Africanus promoted a number of corn distributions, and dispensed land to his veterans in Spain, Sicily, Sardinia, and Africa. He also carried laws for large-scale individual assignations of land in Bruttium, Lucania, and Apulia, confiscated from allies who had revolted during the Hannibalic War; and he settled other groups of landless men in new Latin colonies, or as reinforcements to older foundations, or in a large group of new citizen colonies on the coasts of Italy. In addition he tried to meet the complaints of those richer citizens (knights and freedmen) who felt that their political status was unequal to their census qualification and that their businesses were suffering because they were not given adequate public recognition. The senate under his guidance allowed well-to-do freedmen enrolment in any tribe they chose, and granted the knights reserved places at public shows. He also gave attention to the fundamental problem of the Latins and other Italian allies. Their complaints concerned first the halt in grants of Roman citizenship to their cities and peoples; secondly, the Roman monopoly of military commands, provincial governorships, and ambassador-ships; and thirdly their own inability to share in tithes, customs revenues, and other provincial taxes, or even (to any significant extent) in war-booty, which was not divided among the soldiers but went to the treasury at Rome. To these Scipio made some answer. He founded a large number of Latin colonies, into which Italian allies were admitted; he granted Roman citizen-ship to the inhabitants of Formiae, Fundi, and Arpinum; he allowed the Campanians to be enrolled as Roman citizens once more, a privilege they had lost in 211; and he made no resistance to the settlement in Rome of 12,000 Latin families who secured Roman citizenship thereby, nor (probably) to Latin families sharing in Roman colonies.

d. *The Age of Cato*

The appearance in politics of a strong individual line like that of Africanus was repugnant to the rigid senatorial oligarchy and to its interests. His phil-hellenism and his idea of achieving a Roman empire by means of alliances and by a synthesis between the Italians and other Mediterranean peoples appeared a mistaken view of politics both to these oligarchs and to 'new men' like Cato[14] who had been incorporated into the oligarchy and became its most intransigent defenders. To such men the 'Graeculi' of that day were the people really responsible for the moral decline of their Roman imitators, being the prototypes of 'levitas', with all manner of vices elegantly blended in their characters. The Scipionic policy seemed to sacrifice all the permanent advantages which Rome's victories might have secured for the state and for its business classes. Lastly, the oligarchs were not willing to allow one family group among them to become dominant, and for the individual at the head of this group to be regarded as a man out of the ordinary, an arbiter who imposed his own judgement on the rest. The method adopted to bring about Scipio's fall was the same as that employed against Pericles at Athens. First they ac-cused his most loyal supporters, and then his own brother Lucius, of various irregularities; finally in 184 their great opponent left Rome in anger and re-tired to one of his villas.

In the next decades a number of factions contended for power and carried on the broad process of constitutional development. They were personal and family groupings without settled programmes, subject to sudden changes of direction in the course of their temporary alliances and arbitrary blends of policy. In broad terms there were three main groups, the Scipionians, the Catonians, and a middle party, though each was constantly evolving. But the real embodiment of this period was Cato, and it was he who was most re-sponsible for everything that followed. His influence on events was especially felt in the early and most decisive years, namely the decade 180–170, but it continued right down to his death in 149.

R*

Cato made no real effort to solve any of the problems which had confronted Africanus. He was concerned only to undo Africanus' work, even though this might make some of the problems more serious than before. He punished with great severity several thousand people for being members of religious conventicles where the Bacchanalia were celebrated, on the ground that they were conspiring against the state; and he brought to trial and execution another unfortunate group of persons who were accused of causing a plague by spreading poison. He thought he could improve the people's morals by doubling the taxes on luxury goods. Moreover he purged the senate, removing from it seven of his political opponents, and excluded from the equestrian order anyone who was prevented by physical disabilities from riding a horse. Yet at the same time he was using gangs of slaves to till his estates and was calling attention to the value of slave labour in his writings, as if there were no hosts of unemployed free men. In addition he opposed every grant of citizenship to the allies.

This period saw the beginnings of the harsh imperialism which drove the provinces to their first revolts, put down with bloodshed. The new set of allies were treated without any consideration, in the firm conviction that it was far more convenient and more profitable for the state and its ruling oligarchy to reduce them to the status of provinces.

To achieve greater stability and loyalty among the new allies Africanus had arranged to give power inside republican states to oligarchic factions, and had seen to it that in monarchies the rulers should be men on whose pro-Roman outlook one could rely, because they had lived at Rome and been in contact with the more powerful families there. But putting this system into practice required statesmanship of the kind Roman politicians neither possessed nor desired. It meant avoiding entanglement in an endless series of crises, each more violent than the last, in the course of the struggles between the pro-Roman oligarchs and their democratic opponents, the latter always ready to give support to anti-Roman powers. It meant taking care to see that kings, like Masinissa and Eumenes II, could not indulge their dreams of expansion in a way which upset the balance of power desired by Rome. It was also essential to keep an eye on each dynasty at the moment of a succession, since a new ruler might bring great changes.

A fresh Macedonian war broke out when King Perseus gave support to the democratic movements and popularist factions in Greece. After he had been finally defeated at Pydna, his conqueror, L. Aemilius Paullus, in the consequent settlement of the country, was made to apply a principle which derived from a compromise between the parties in the senate. The monarchy in Macedonia and Illyria was brought to an end, and the two countries were dismembered politically and economically. Cato's ideas were put into effect in that a *vectigal* was imposed as if the territories were being annexed; but Rome avoided the responsibility and burden of provincial occupation, and the military and administrative duties this would have implied. In this way

Macedonia was divided into four republics, with an absurd prohibition on intermarriage and the purchase and sale of land between members of one republic and another: trade in salt and shipbuilding materials was also forbidden. The inhabitants of Illyria too were divided into tributary and non-tributary states, the former being further subdivided into three distinct groups. In the Greek districts, loyal allies received additions of land, but the territories of the remainder were still further reduced by the formation of small autonomous states between them and their neighbours. The Achaean League was compelled to send a number of suspect persons to Rome as hostages. Finally, fierce reprisals were taken in Epirus, where many cities were sacked and razed, the inhabitants being reduced to slavery.

The war had also had repercussions in Asia, and the consequent measures taken by Rome reveal the same harsh spirit of imperialism. Rhodes and Pergamum were deprived of territory, while Rome gave help to states wanting to attack them: and humiliations were heaped on them, as when Eumenes II at Sardis was compelled to hear his enemies accuse him of every sort of crime in the presence of a Roman legate.

For about 25 years (180–155) this imperialist policy could still be checked, and sometimes reversed, at the hands of Africanus' party and the moderates. But the latter were tending to concern themselves more with detail than with major changes of principle; and after the death of Ti. Sempronius Gracchus, who had been the most energetic supporter of pacification, the younger generation, accustomed now to elegant living, but freed from all inhibitions, found a very young leader in P. Cornelius Scipio Aemilianus. These new Romans, used to the bowing and presents, the prayers and laments, of Greek and Eastern kings and ambassadors, suddenly found themselves heavily engaged with peoples who were ready to defend their liberties at any cost and any sacrifice. This unexpected revival of enemy opposition, which the Romans quite underrated, was the more wounding to their pride in that each new war began with severe and bloody defeats of their legions; and it was undoubtedly one of the main reasons for the violent action now taken by Roman generals. More than at any other time in Rome's history they showed an absence of all humanity in putting down revolts, making use in their diplomacy of the kind of trickery and perfidy which is all too often shown by conquerors conscious of their overwhelming power and of their destiny to rule.

The most important results of this imperialism are too well known to require attention here. In 148/7 Macedonia was unified territorially again but reduced to provincial status, being obliged to pay tribute and furnish mineral and agricultural supplies to Rome. In 146 Greece saw its great port and industrial city of Corinth—an object of jealousy to Roman business men and a centre of democratic influences—sacked and completely destroyed, the population being sold as slaves and the territory made into *ager publicus*. Other Greek cities received various forms of treatment related to their behaviour during the 'Achaean War'. Some districts were attached to the

province of Macedonia; several cities became tributary with oligarchic constitutions and a ban on the reconstitution of the leagues Rome had dissolved;
others were made 'liberae et immunes' with various types of treaty, of which
that with Athens was the only one on terms of equality.

The same thing happened in Africa. Rome had failed to give Carthage
proper protection against the growing claims of Masinissa, and Cato carried
on his obstinate campaign against the danger of a supposed Punic revival.
After a heroic defence the city was taken and destroyed, amid scenes of
barbaric massacre and rapine; and curses were pronounced over its area
against anyone who should try to inhabit it again. Its territory, up to the 'fossa
regia', became a province.

But the growing severity of Roman imperial methods had its most tragic
results in the older provinces. We must briefly recount what happened in
Spain and Sicily. When Scipio (later Africanus) relinquished his command
in Spain, having completed the work of his father and uncle, the two provinces established in the country were given a 'ladder system' with communities of different status like those in Sicily and Sardinia (*civitates foederatae*,
liberae, and *stipendiariae*, together with Roman domains). In general, however,
conditions were more generous than those in Sicily, mainly because the number of cities in the more privileged categories was quite high. There were also
already several *vici* in Spain inhabited by Italians, which like Roman colonies
were available to Romanize the country and to raise its communities gradually
to the upper rungs of the 'ladder' on the Italian model. A further point was
that Scipio had intended Roman commands in Spain to be held for long terms,
in order to promote friendly relations with a native population which was
proud and devoted to its liberties. But the senate in fear of providing opportunity for a possible dictator adopted the system of annual commands, and
also reduced the occupation troops below the level of safety. So the changing
policies of governors, the conflict between the desire for expansion and the
small forces available to effect it, and the lack of contact between rulers and
ruled, all led to discontent and rebellion. The first revolts were largely quelled
in 179 by the wise action of Ti. Sempronius Gracchus, who bound the population by treaties so clear that future governors could not misinterpret them,
and also distributed presents and land in generous measure to the poorer
classes, to the extent of founding mixed towns of Romans, Italians, and
Iberians. After his day peace lasted for a quarter of a century, but then increased severity led to further revolts. In vain M. Claudius Marcellus laboured
to restore order: in 151 the despatch of L. Licinius Lucullus, with the young
Scipio Aemilianus as his assistant, signified the whole-hearted application of
Rome's methods of terror and exploitation. So the war with Viriathus blazed
into fury, ending with the terrible punitive expedition into Lusitania and
neighbouring areas in 138/7; and after heroic resistance Numantia capitulated
at discretion to Aemilianus in 133, any inhabitants who had not committed
suicide being sold as slaves, and the town like others being razed to the ground.

Its policy of imperialism undoubtedly gave Rome the direct rule of most of the world, but in the end it provoked, in Italy as well as outside it, the series of crises which mark the closing period of Republican history.

e. *Political and Social Problems under the Gracchans*[15]

The ease with which slaves could be acquired at low prices in the period of conquests, and the small cost of their upkeep, led the owners of *latifundia* and of medium-sized estates to prefer slave to free labour. On the other hand the unbearable conditions of slavery caused its unfortunate victims, especially those who were born free, to dream of liberty and plan revenge. They were regarded purely as tools, and were the property of their masters, who had rights of life and death over them and who could exercise any form of cruelty without intervention by the law: and a master was entitled to compensation if a third party did harm to his slaves. In general they were treated brutally, packed into *ergastula* in chains, branded like beasts, fed on inadequate food of the cheapest kind, and kept half-naked. When they became old or infirm they were sold again. Beaten almost to death, they were made savage by seeing the rich and luxurious lives of their masters, whose avarice made them shut their eyes when slaves provided themselves with food and clothing by robbing another's property. Many of these slaves remembered being free and even powerful, but they despaired of acquiring the *peculium* needed to redeem their liberty. Yet when herded together in gangs they became conscious of their power, and as the only tillers of the soil they knew what advantages their masters derived from their labour. In the harshest periods of imperialism there must have been constant revolts here and there, although our sources allude to them rarely and then only in the briefest terms. At the beginning of the second century we hear of a revolt at Setia in 198, another in Etruria in 196, and a third in Apulia in 185. In 139 the praetor P. Popillius Laenas had to attend to trouble of this kind, and between 142 and 138 some revolted slaves on estates in Bruttium carried out a series of murders. All the time that Roman forces were kept occupied by the great revolt in Sicily, from 136 to 132, there were lesser risings in Rome itself, and at Minturnae, Sinuessa, in the mines of Attica, and at Delos; and in Asia Aristonicus used rebel slaves to lay waste the country far and wide.

In these convulsive outbreaks against land-owners the slaves often found natural allies in other outcasts of society, who, although they too were victims of the *latifondisti*, might well have been regarded as enemies of the slaves. These were the small countrymen, now landless, men whose estates had been swallowed up by the *latifundia*: the slaves were the principal obstacle to their leading at least the life of wage-earners on the land, and were therefore looked on as the ill-omened instrument by which *latifundia* were further developed. Yet a common misery and despair united slaves and rural proletariate in their resistance; and they must often have supported one another in the way we find them operating together later in the Servile Wars in Sicily and in

Spartacus' rebellion.[16] In this way a social rising against the rich took on also an anti-Roman political aspect, its authors regarding the Roman conquerors as responsible for all their misfortunes.

The *Lex Rupilia* of 131, passed after the bloody and ruinous First Servile War, attempted to put Sicily on a new footing. The *latifundia* were to be broken up, new lands were to be brought under cereal cultivation, the volume of slaves was to be reduced, and limits were to be set to the numbers of landless men. Lastly the natives were to be granted a measure of autonomy, especially in judicial matters, in order to allay the hostility towards Rome. The effects of the more enduring portion of Ti. Sempronius Gracchus' work were already being felt, even though it was in the very year of his legislation that he fell— a victim to his own mission.

The first step taken by Tiberius was in the field of agrarian reform. His bill as first drafted aimed at the re-enactment of an ancient limitation (never abrogated) on the amount of *ager publicus* which could be occupied by an individual, and at the recovery, and subsequent distribution to the needy, of amounts occupied illegally or in excess of the quota. Generous provisions were offered in addition: for example, amounts over and above the 500 *iugera* could be claimed in respect of grown-up sons, compensation was given to ex-owners for any improvements they had carried out, and occupied land once reduced to its proper dimensions was to be held in full ownership. The proposal could not, of course, be agreeable to the diehards: they lost property thereby, and part of the proletariate on which they counted for their electoral manoeuvres would disappear from the city. But in its essence the reform, which benefited Italian allies as well as Roman citizens,[17] might have been carried out (as indeed it was, even after Tiberius' death) without any violent convulsions, if the *optimates*, relying on the distortion which had taken place in the tribunate's function, had not obtained another tribune, M. Octavius, to interpose his veto. Tiberius reacted by having Octavius deposed by the *comitia* and another tribune elected in his place. He was accused of violating the sanctity of tribunes and of aiming at tyranny; the attacks grew in strength, and eventually led to his destruction, when he presented himself for re-election to the tribunate in the following year with an enlarged programme of a frankly political kind. In the debate about the use of the property and land left to Rome by Attalus III of Pergamum, Tiberius proposed that the decision should be taken by the people, thus reclaiming for the people and the magistrates functions which the senate had usurped. He furthermore intended to propose an extension of *provocatio* and the introduction of knights to the jury-courts. In this crisis the senators established an entirely illegal procedure, used by them on many occasions later to get rid of an opponent without recourse to regular trial. Tiberius was declared a public enemy ('hostis'), and the senate constituted itself a court-martial which pronounced the 'senatus consultum ultimum'.

The second Gracchus, Gaius, had started with a political plan designed to give himself the support of a coalition containing other malcontents, namely the knights and the Italian allies, besides the urban *plebs*. In 125 his ally, the consul M. Fulvius Flaccus, proposed a law to grant citizenship to the Latins and allies: though rejected by the senate this provoked lively agitation among the Italians, and an increase in the numbers of *peregrini* registered in the census had to be allowed. After securing a law permitting tribunes of the people to be re-elected, he was himself elected tribune for the first time for 123. His legislation opened with two plebiscites, one excluding any deposed magistrate from holding office during the remainder of his life, the other prohibiting condemnation without appeal to the people. Then he went on to a number of *leges*. One was a *Lex Agraria*, restoring full powers to the triumviral commission, which now resumed the recovery and assignation of *ager publicus*. Then there was a *Lex Frumentaria* for the benefit of the urban *plebs*, and thirdly a *Lex de Comitiis* governing the drawing of lots to decide which centuries should vote first. For the equestrian class he secured reserved seats at theatre performances, compensation for *publicani* who failed to gather the tribute which the state had farmed to them against advance payments, and the reorganization of provincial statutes (*Leges de provinciis*) in a manner which suited equestrian interests, with the addition of a *Lex de Asia*. Meanwhile Gaius opposed the cession of Phrygia to Pontus, and supported the extension of Roman conquests in Gaul in order to increase the areas in which Roman businessmen could operate. Gaius was then re-elected for 122, and proceeded, at the expense of the senate, to secure the passage of a *Lex Iudiciaria* putting knights as well as senators on the courts for cases of extortion (*quaestiones repetundarum*); a number of less important laws were also passed about these courts. At the same time he caused a colleague to propose a law for the foundation of colonies overseas, on provincial soil, starting with one called Iunonia at Carthage; other colonies were founded at Tarentum and Capua, and Gracchus constructed roads, warehouses, and markets. But while he was in Africa attending to the foundation of Iunonia, the *optimates* counterattacked by denouncing him as sacrilegious for including in his new colony lands which Scipio Aemilianus had placed under a curse. They also tried to deprive Gaius of his support from the Italian allies by causing the tribune M. Livius Drusus (the Elder) to propose laws in the allied interest. Meanwhile the knights, who had got what they wanted from Gaius, were already tending to make common cause with their old opponents.

Gaius met this attack by attempting to prove that there was no sacrilege, and also by proposing Roman citizenship for the Latins and Latin franchise for the Italians. But his opponents convinced the urban *plebs*, and the citizen body in general, that they would suffer greatly from the passage of such a bill. In the outcome Gaius was not re-elected tribune for 121, and the consul L. Opimius proposed the abrogation of all Gracchan laws. Gaius now surrounded himself with armed bands, and could not prevent one of his opponents from being killed during a public meeting: the result was the passage of the *senatus consultum ultimum* against him, his own death, and the execution of 3,000 of his followers. So the Gracchan reforms perished in bloodshed. Yet the grave problems his legislation had been designed to solve—the problems of the proletariate, the allies, the provincials, and the slaves—remained wide open, and the danger was great.

f. *The Democratic Revival*

The quarrel between the two sections of the governing class, senate and knights, broke out again on many occasions, though it would then be composed when the interests of the two bodies coincided once more. The most characteristic instance of the process began in 111, when war was declared on Jugurtha to punish him for the massacre of Italians who had contributed to the defence of Cirta; and it was necessary to put the economy on an emergency footing. One expression of this moment of concord was a new *Lex Agraria*, bringing together all earlier provisions, and attempting to reconcile divergent interests by arranging for the sale of the remaining *ager publicus* to any bidder. This closed the agrarian question for the time being. But the Jugurthine war revived the quarrel between knights and senate in an even more venomous form. The former wanted to conquer tracts of Numidia in order to enlarge the field for business interests, while the *nobilitas* were accused by their opponents of carrying on the war too half-heartedly because Jugurtha had bribed them. The friction grew gradually more serious, and it was then successfully exploited by the plebeian C. Marius, legate of the victorious new general Q. Caecilius Metellus (later Numidicus). Marius claimed the successes won as his own, attacked Metellus for not having allowed him leave to return to Rome at the proper time to present his candidature for the consulship, and then, with support from the knights and the people, obtained both the consulate for 107 and the command in the war, which was still not decided. In the ensuing action Marius found an able and impartial collaborator, especially in diplomatic matters, in a noble called L. Cornelius Sulla (later Felix), who was his quaestor; and the war ended with the capture of Jugurtha and the partition of Numidia, on the Scipionic model, into two states allied to Rome, a solution avoiding any increase in Rome's military burdens. But in the course of the war Marius began to use a new recruiting system of his own devising, which allowed proletarians to volunteer and receive pay. This absorbed practically the whole force of landless men of military age, and was therefore a long step in the direction of solving that particular social problem; it also made possible the creation of a standing army, with well-trained and competent soldiers serving for long terms. The new army admittedly tended to attach itself to those of its generals who had won most glory and who offered them the best prospects, rather than carrying out policies which were best in the interests of the state. It therefore provided a foundation for the gradual growth in extraordinary commands by dictators and commanders (*imperatores*).

(a)   [Alinari

35 *Olympia, Temple of Zeus, Olympia Museum*

   (a) *Eastern pediment, Zeus presiding over the sacrifices before the competition between Pelops and Oenomaus, c. 457 BC*

   (b) *Western pediment, Apollo, c. 457 BC*

(b)   [B.F.M.

36 *Athens, the Parthenon, scenes from the Panathenaic procession,* c. 435 *BC.* [B.M.
    London, British Museum

37   *Scopas, Greeks and Amazons, detail from the frieze of the Mausoleum at Halicarnassus,*
      c. 350 *BC. London, British Museum*

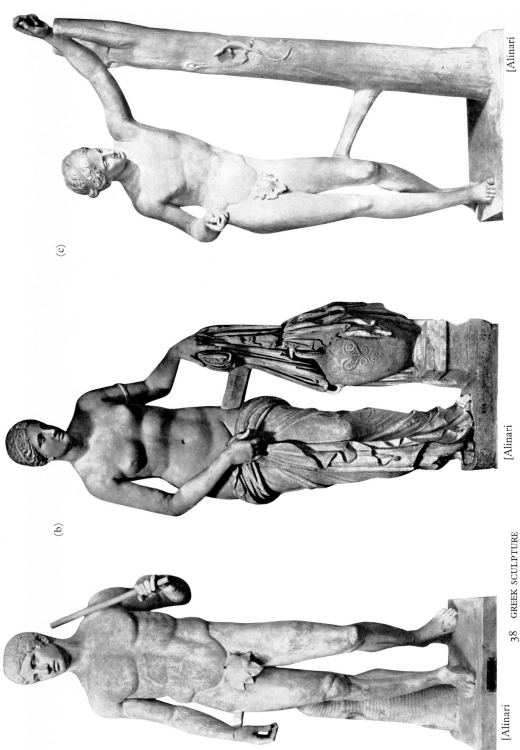

[Alinari]

(a)

(b)

[Alinari]

(c)

[Alinari]

38   GREEK SCULPTURE
(a) *After Polycletus, 'The Doryphorus' (or 'Lancebearer'). Naples, National Museum*
(b) *After Praxiteles, 'Aphrodite of Cnidus'. Rome, Vatican Museum*
(c) *After Praxiteles, 'Apollo Sauroctonos'. Rome, Vatican Museum*

The Jugurthine war was hardly over when Marius, after winning a second consulate for 104, obtained the command against the Cimbri, Teutones, and Ambrones. In the years 104–101 he defeated these tribes several times and annihilated their main forces, securing in the process new areas for commercial development and enormous hordes of slaves for the landed proprietors. Meanwhile his association with Appuleius Saturninus, tribune in 103, helped him to renew his consulates year after year and to secure lands for his veterans.

But the military effort required to meet the barbarians had brought internal stresses which complicated a situation already acute. Recruiting needs had led the government to order the manumission of all slaves who had once been free allies; and this brought a flood of requests from slaves and also protests from such land-owners as were affected. So in some areas the order was not carried out; and there followed slave revolts at Nuceria, Capua, and above all in Sicily, where Rome had to face a regular war (the second Servile War, 104–101). After it was over the victorious commander M'. Aquillius took care to break up the *latifundia* and to transform landless men into peasant proprietors, an operation which led to the prosperity and high levels of agricultural production found by C. Verres during his governorship of the island in 73–71. At the same time as the Servile War there was a campaign against the pirates, whose refuges were mainly in Crete and Cilicia; and this resulted in the formation of two new provincial areas, Cilicia and Pamphylia.

Meanwhile Marius, as we have said, had since 103 been in alliance with that year's tribune Appuleius Saturninus, enabling the latter to launch a large-scale attack on the senate and to lay before the people a programme of laws in this sense: an example is his *Lex de Maiestate*, a regular Sword of Damocles hanging over the head of every Roman citizen in that it punished with death anyone who had offended the majesty of the Roman people. Another law, proposed by the tribune Atinius, gave tribunes the right of proposing *sententiae* in the senate, and consequently of sitting in that body. Saturninus was now allied with C. Servilius Glaucia, who some years earlier had carried as tribune a *Lex Servilia Repetundarum*. Their combined authority was such that even when Saturninus was a private citizen in 102 the censor Q. Caecilius Metellus Numidicus could not expel them from the senate against the opposition of his censorial colleague, who was afraid of the people's reaction. In the next year (100) Saturninus secured another tribunate, while Glaucia obtained the praetorship and Marius his sixth consulate. This enabled Marius to carry the provisions he needed to reward his veterans. One such provision he simply assumed arbitrarily, when he granted Roman citizenship to 1,000 veterans from Camerinum for their services in the field. A plebiscite put forward by Saturninus was opposed not only by certain senators (despite the fact that any who did not swear to observe its provisions were threatened with expulsion from the senate and a fine), but also by many of the people, who maintained that only the allies would benefit from it. Nevertheless he obtained the required majority for it by bringing to Rome a mass of country voters in the rural tribes, who did not refrain from violence. The bill gave Marius' veterans lands in Sicily, Achaea, Macedonia, Corsica (where there was a 'Colonia Mariana'), and in the Po valley where the Cimbri had been defeated and where the Latin colony of Eporedia was now founded. Money was voted for the recovery and purchase of the land; and Marius was allowed to create a given number of Roman citizens in each colony.

But the price Marius had to pay for this assistance was dear. He was asked to support Saturninus' candidature for a third tribunate in 99 and Glaucia's candidature for a consulate in the same year. At the consular elections the popular party murdered an opponent of Glaucia, after which Saturninus and Glaucia together with the voters from the rural tribes occupied the Capitol. The senate passed the *senatus consultum ultimum*, calling on the consuls, of whom Marius was one, to take appropriate measures. The position of Marius was very delicate: he disapproved of the illegalities and violence of his supporters, but he wanted them to be brought to book by legal means and not by the procedure involved in the *senatus consultum ultimum*, which was no less violent and illegal than their own behaviour, and which would make him appear to be the executioner of his own friends. While he was seeking a way to gain time, the opposing party shut Saturninus and his supporters into the senate house and there put them to death. So Marius became a scapegoat, attacked no less by the popular party than by the patricians. He had been a great soldier, but he was not born for politics and was quickly ruined when he tried to engage in them. For the time being he went into retirement, leaving the city for a 'legatio libera' in Galatia.

After the popular leaders had been killed and Marius had retired into private life outside Rome, the immediate step taken by the senate was to invalidate Saturninus' laws, including that assigning lands to Marius' veterans. A strict control was imposed on the behaviour of the knights in the provinces, and the creation of new provinces, which would have favoured equestrian interests, was avoided: for instance no action was taken to annex Cyrenaica, left to Rome by Ptolemy Apion. New restrictions were placed on the grant of citizenship to the Latins and Italians, and those whose claims were doubtful were excluded by a law of 95.

Then in 91 came an important event, namely the attempt of the tribune M. Livius Drusus (the Younger) to achieve reform not through the victory of a single party but by agreement among all interested classes to bring about a general improvement in conditions. The government and the jury-courts in extortion cases were once more to be in the hands of senators only, but in return the senate would at one blow admit into its own ranks the best among the *equites*. They would also surrender all *ager publicus* occupied in excess of the legal amounts so as to ensure a livelihood, in Italy as well as overseas, to the mass of proletarians who could be made smallholders once more. Drusus thought it right that the most deserving and honourable of the knights should become senators and share in the government and the courts, but they in turn would have to sever their duties and aims from those of the businessmen. The landless citizens had little chance, during the period of peace through which Rome was passing, of finding a solution to their economic problems through recruitment in the army; and Drusus maintained that they should be given immediate relief by distributions of food, and more permanent support by land assignations. Their contribution to the settlement must be to give up their opposition to the grant of citizenship to the Italian allies, who were all the time giving their lives for Rome in the field, but whose franchise rights, recognized as early as Camillus' day, had been disputed and whittled down over two centuries. On the other hand the richer Italians would have to resign themselves to surrendering excessive and illegally held portions of *ager publicus*, in order to solve the proletarian problem. To carry this plan into effect Drusus proposed all the necessary laws and other provisions. Naturally every class showed itself ready to take what favoured its interests, but each rejected what it was asked to concede. The diehard senators and the equestrian class as a whole, together with their respective clients among the *plebs*, broke with Drusus, and suspected him of aiming at tyranny. In the autumn of 91 he was attacked by the consul L. Marcius Philippus and defended by the orator L. Licinius Crassus: subsequently, on the pretext of unfavourable auspices, his laws were annulled. After he had retired to his house he was assassinated by an unknown hand, and the senate instituted no inquiry.

Drusus naturally had close relations with the Italians, but it is certainly false to accuse him of responsibility for the Social War that followed. War had been preparing for a long time, and it was not his proposals but their abrogation which clearly provided the occasion. There followed, even during the war, a number of other measures against anyone who favoured allied claims; and children of unions between Romans and Italians were to be made in all circumstances non-Roman. But already during the year 90 the senate, with a furious conflict on its hands, began to revise its attitude. First they passed a *Lex Calpurnia* which enabled citizenship, in two new tribes, to be given to deserving veterans and soldiers in the field; we know that Cn. Pompeius Strabo made use of this law to give Roman citizenship to thirty Spanish cavalrymen. A block grant of citizenship was then made to the people of Tuder; and finally by a *Lex Iulia* the number of tribes in which loyal Italian allies or deserving soldiers could be enrolled was increased to ten. In 89 Pompeius Strabo gave Latin rights to the Transpadani; and then laws under the names Plautia Papiria gave citizenship to the Cispadani between the Rubicon and the Cottian Alps, and to all Italians south of the Rubicon who had remained loyal and 'who made a request for the grant within sixty days'. (Pl. 23, a.) The Italians were defeated in the field but were in fact victorious, for they had obtained what they sought. Yet the war had cost 300,000 lives, and the army emerged from it disorganized and disordered. In consequence new agrarian measures became necessary, as well as action of a financial kind, such as a reduction in the weight of the *as*.

The new citizens, however, were relegated to the last tribes, which in practice were never called on to vote. P. Sulpicius Rufus now passed a bill distributing them among all the tribes, and this enabled him to bring a mass of new citizens back to Rome and persuade them to vote, amid scenes of violence, for another bill transferring the command of the Mithradatic War from Sulla (to whom it had originally been assigned) to Marius. There followed Sulla's march on Rome and Marius' flight to Carthage; he and eleven of his supporters were declared *hostes*, and arrangements of a summary kind were made to restore the constitution. Sulpicius' measures were rescinded, and with them the provision that plebiscites must be given automatic approval by the senate in advance. The *comitia tributa* lost all importance, their function passing to the *comitia centuriata*. It was agreed to introduce 300 knights into the senate, to diminish the power of the tribunes, and to grant a remission of debts.

As consuls for 87 Sulla left at home two men whom he hoped would prove evenly balanced, the moderate optimate Cn. Octavius and the anti-senatorial L. Cornelius Cinna. But they quickly moved in opposite directions, Cinna carrying on the work of Sulpicius and preparing the way for the return of Marius with support from the new citizens, Octavius defending the rights of the senate with support from the original citizens and from certain tribunes. Cinna, who wanted Sulla to be put on trial for condemning the Marians without allowing them *provocatio*, was expelled from the city. But forming a coalition of new citizens, townsmen in Latium, and the garrison troops in Campania, he joined the returning Marians, and with these forces captured Rome. Diodorus says that when they became masters of the city Marius and Cinna, with their supporters, decided to put their enemies to death so that their own rule could be peaceful. So began vendettas and purges; homes were ruined, and men put to death without trial; revolutionary courts were indeed held, but with the inevitable accompaniment of delation and inquisition. Sulla's laws were abrogated, his houses were destroyed, and the senate was made to declare him a *hostis* along with such followers of his as were still alive. Companies of freed slaves committed such outrages that it was found necessary to massacre them. For the next year (86) Marius and Cinna were consuls, but within a few days Marius died and so Cinna was in effect left master of Rome, to nominate himself consul for both 85 and 84. But he revealed no complete or rational plan. Revenge continued, and the support of the knights and people was canvassed by the repeal of certain laws. Monetary measures were passed of a type which, in Sallust's words, mean that 'copper was paid out instead of silver'. Cinna was then stoned to death by his soldiers in their refusal to embark on an expedition against Sulla.

Sulla now returned victorious from the East, defeated the Marians, and entered Rome with the city's destinies in his control. His first act was a wholesale massacre of the conquered soldiers together with the proscription (in an initial list) of 40 senators and 1,600 knights. Then, on the proposal of the *princeps senatus*, L. Valerius Flaccus, he was nominated dictator 'for as long as he wished'. This was not the type of dictatorship which had fallen into disuse at the end of the Second Punic War, nor was it modelled on Greek tyrannies or Hellenistic monarchies. It looked back to the ancient Roman concept of elective kings, and specifically to the example of Servius Tullius, who according to tradition had actually given Rome the idea of a republic and had later expressed his intention of abdicating. Moreover Sulla's momentary evocation of that monarchy establishes a logical connection between it and the later conception of the *imperator*, no matter what political formula was used to justify a Roman emperor's rule.

The senate, which had now become the preserve of a few dozen families, both patrician and plebeian, and which in fact consisted of only about a hundred members,[18] was to be made the central guiding force in the state, providing the supreme courts of justice and controlling all legislation. But it was radically overhauled. Five hundred knights from the army and the professions (but excluding businessmen) were admitted, and its members were ensured for the future by granting membership not only to persons elected to the higher magistracies, but also to ex-quaestors. Having thus secured a permanent place in the senate for 'the better' among the Equites, Sulla showed no favour to the greedy class of speculators who formed the main body of the equestrian order. He put a stop to their excesses in the collection of tribute, excluded them from serving on the courts, and forbade them to exercise privilege betokening their dignity. The lot of the people Sulla tried to improve, not by expensive and degrading distributions of corn, but by giving employment on great public works, by fixing maximum prices, by reducing debts and regulating interest rates, and finally by granting land to 120,000 vererans. He also allowed the people the satisfaction of electing the consuls, but he put an end to the distortion of the tribunician power. The tribunes lost their rights of veto, their position in the *cursus honorum*, and the powers of summoning the senate or of presenting proposals to the people which had not received prior senatorial approval. They became simply defenders and patrons of the people, and in this way Sulla frustrated any attempt to establish dual control by his new senate and by the people.

From the allies who had newly become citizens he took away neither their citizenship nor their voting rights. But he was harsh in his treatment of any who had assisted the Marians, their lands being confiscated for distribution to his veterans along with such *ager publicus* as was available to him from other sources. He increased the number of magistrates, the quaestors from eight to twenty and the praetors from six to eight; but he raised the minimum age for holding each post, and set an interval of ten years before a man could hold a second consulate.[19] He also suppressed the censorship; but his major measure in this field was a *Lex Cornelia de provinciis ordinandis* which firmly distinguished the purely civil powers of consuls and praetors during their year of office in Italy from the military commands they were to hold outside Italy as proconsuls or pro-praetors in the ensuing year.[20]

Finally, he attempted by a large range of laws to check the moral and political corruption he was convinced was affecting the life of his day. These
laws were severe and detailed, amounting to a complete revision of the criminal code. Sulla also avoided military operations abroad as far as possible, kept
a check on any of his supporters who might subvert the constitution, and
carried out important public works. Then, without transmitting his power
to any successor, he voluntarily abdicated (February, 79, is a likely date),
and retired into private life.[21]

g. Caesar's Consulate—the Ascendancy of Pompey

Sulla's retirement left his constitution at the mercy of events, and of
party struggles and individual ambitions. The first signs of a breakdown
came when Cn. Pompeius Magnus, now in alliance with the powerful family
of the Metelli, secured a triumph which Sulla had refused him. The Metelli
were among the supporters of Sextus Roscius, falsely accused by Sulla's
treacherous freedman Chrysogonus and defended by the young M. Tullius
Cicero, whose success was a signal event.

Of the two consuls for 79 Q. Lutatius Catulus was a Sullan and a friend
of the senate: the other, M. Aemilius Lepidus, was a Marian who had crossed
to Sulla but had then resumed his old allegiance. Lepidus went round
haranguing the mob with promises to recall the proscribed and to wrest land
away from the veterans in order to give it back to the dispossessed owners.
Naturally the latter were induced to revolt, and trouble broke out on the land
at Faesulae. Lepidus, his consulate now over, united the rebels together
with certain scattered leaders of the Marian party, and sent an ultimatum
to the senate. That body at last decided on resistance, declared Lepidus a
hostis, and pronounced the senatus consultum ultimum against him. They
found it a simple matter to tear up the Sullan constitution and give the
young Pompeius an extraordinary imperium in Italy. The defeated rebels
crossed to Sardinia, where Lepidus died: then under the command of
Perperna they passed on into Spain to join hands with another Marian who
had established himself there, namely Q. Sertorius.

By making a treaty with the continually rebellious Lusitani and then
extending his activities to Celtiberia and the Nearer province, Sertorius had
built in Spain a fortress for the Marian movement, with an organization which
followed in the footsteps of the elder Scipio Africanus, Ti. Sempronius
Gracchus, and M. Claudius Marcellus. His halo of greatness, fearlessness,
and moderation brought him the support of the 'sacred societies', and he
was able to organize, on the Roman model, a powerful army of natives with
Italian commanders and subordinate officers. Among the natives, whom he
governed through Italian magistrates, he spread the conception of democracy,
aiming at the voluntary Romanization of the entire population in a single
whole with the Italian settlers, with both groups on the same political and
social level. This could be made to serve as the fulcrum of a new organization

in the Roman world, taking the place of the plutocracy which was in persistent charge of Rome. The Italian nucleus was now reinforced by the arrival of Perperna's forces, and Sertorius created a senate to advise the magistrates, and not a degenerate body like the senate at Rome. At the same time, in order to prepare the native chiefs for their new role he opened a school of Graeco-Latin culture for them at Osca (Huesca). Pompeius Magnus was now sent against him with exceptional proconsular power, but with scanty means. By threats and other forms of pressure he obtained from Rome the necessary reinforcements, and Sertorian resistance was broken by military attack, promises of an amnesty, and Perperna's treachery, the last leading to Sertorius' murder. Sertorius' organization collapsed, but his work endured: in Caesar's words 'Pompey reaped what Sertorius had sown'. Pompey continued the measures of relief in Spain and its Romanization, with a charter of freedom to Osca, the foundation of Pompaelo, grants of citizenship to loyalists, and many other measures. To this was due the loyalty of the country and its rapid adoption of Roman ways.

Meanwhile at Rome, despite the trouble-making of individual politicians, there was a gradual movement towards conciliation, aiming at restoring the tribunician powers removed by Sulla. The recent entry of 500 knights to the senate had made its policy less rigid; and it was also felt that by making the tribunate once more a step in the *cursus honorum* one could prevent any excessive combination between the tribunes and the poorer sections of the *plebs*. Moreover by now everyone was conscious of the losses Rome was incurring, and the grave peril it was in, from the continuance of political and social struggles. Of the latter there was now an example in the rising of Spartacus. Although this was not supported by slaves from the towns, the rural proletariate (especially that resulting from Sulla's confiscations) broke into revolt at the same time and made common cause with the rebellious slaves.[22] Italy had to suffer a devastating war, which lasted three years (73–71) before it was put down by M. Licinius Crassus.

But at the last moment Crassus found part of his credit snatched from him by the arrival from Spain of the victorious Pompey, who routed a band of Spartacist survivors. The two generals with their armies, keeping close watch on each other, marched as far as the line of Rome's *pomerium*, where they agreed to form a kind of 'duumvirate' and demanded the consulate for 70. When this had been granted, they proceeded to revise the constitution in a manner which favoured the equestrian class, to which both had originally belonged, at the expense of the senate. Probably aided by the propaganda of their future colleague in the triumvirate, C. Iulius Caesar, who was then simply a *tribunus militum*, they restored the tribunate of the *plebs* to its former position and also had censors elected once more: the latter revived the *lectio* of the senate (expelling sixty-four members) and of the knights, and also completed the first census since the extension of the citizenship. Particular problems of a controversial nature were once again reviewed. The

Sullan system of exclusively senatorial juries, since the senators had abused it, was brought to an end, and the jurors were now to be one-third senators, one-third *equites*, and one-third *tribuni aerarii* (mainly younger members of the senatorial families). Persons convicted of electoral corruption were debarred from office for ten years. The consuls announced that, to use Pompey's words, 'the provinces were ruined and plundered'; so the system of farming tithe-collection at Rome was revived. Meanwhile the embezzlement case against the member of the nobility who had governed Sicily from 73 to 71 was ably prosecuted by M. Tullius Cicero (who undoubtedly exaggerated), and it gave convincing proof of the need for reform. Even though immediately thereafter the new juries showed partiality in favour of an embezzler from the equestrian class, it was clear that under Pompey's leadership the breakdown of the Sullan system had brought social equilibrium. The knights were the basis of the new system, but the democrats from the people were satisfied and the senate had not lost all its power. Subsequent events make it impossible to suppose that Pompey aimed at an out-and-out dictatorship.

The victorious Eastern campaign of L. Licinius Lucullus resulted in a temporary ascendancy of the conservatives at Rome. Then, however, the news arrived of the mutiny of his troops, corrupted by democratic propaganda, and of the inevitable renunciation of his plans for further conquests. A reaction in favour of the anti-senatorial party began, and it was given powerful impetus by the return of C. Iulius Caesar from Spain, where he had been pro-quaestor. Caesar supported in the senate a series of popularist bills which certain tribunes were putting forward in the interests of the people: and he himself made propaganda in favour of granting full citizenship to the Transpadani, who at the time had only Latin rights. The tribunician proposals, which were strongly opposed by the conservatives, had a fourfold aim. Loans to foreign ambassadors in Rome were prohibited: a bribery law was directed not only at candidates at elections but at their lackeys (the *divisores*); the senate was forbidden to grant dispensations from the laws unless 200 voters were present, the people's right to intervene being still preserved; and governors were obliged to publish, at the outset of their tenure of office, the *edictum perpetuum* containing the rules by which they would be bound.

But Caesar's main support was reserved for a number of proposals by A. Gabinius. These included such matters as prohibition of exorbitant rates of interest; but the most important concerned the command in the war against the pirates, and led to a decision based on a scheme prepared in 100 BC by Marius but never put into action. The senate designated Pompey as commander, and gave him *imperium maius* for three years over all the seas and adjoining coasts, with 25 legates, 500 ships, up to 20 legions, and the use of the funds controlled by the quaestors at Rome and of the societies concerned with collection of provincial tribute. Once again Pompey showed no ambition to become dictator, but completed his task in three months instead of three years.

The result was that in 66, while Pompey was still in Cilicia attending to the settlement of the defeated pirates as peasants, the tribune C. Manilius Crispus proposed that he should be given 'imperium extra ordinem' without limit of time, to finish the war with Mithradates and to have the right to make war and peace at his will or to declare peoples enemies or allies of Rome. The majority of the *patres*, though they had not the courage to act in accordance with their views, were hostile to this *imperium*, which by its enormity in time, in space, and in powers seemed like a straightforward dictatorship—or at any rate could prepare the way for one. Cicero was then urban praetor, and he opposed the timid senators in his speech *De Imperio Cn. Pompei*: he maintained that the generalissimo would become a constitutional figure again once his task was accomplished, and cited the names of four illustrious statesmen who were standing ready to support his case. But Cicero was not alone. The bill was supported also by Caesar, who had less reason than any man to favour the dictatorial aims of another, since he was in secret preparing the way to dictatorship for himself. Pompey, although his work in organizing conquered or newly allied territories had the most important historical consequences, was above all proud of his military abilities, having always had the good fortune to overcome enemies who had already been weakened by his predecessors in command. He was often in a position to make himself dictator and seize the reins of government, but this pride made him regard the exceptional powers with which he had been invested as simply giving him a military task to accomplish and as lapsing once the task was done. For a few years Cicero thought he might become the 'princeps' guiding the state in alliance with the senate. But much more realistic were those senators who saw in him as a young man, and still again as an old man, the sword that was needed to free them from their dangerous adversaries.

h. *The Implementation of Caesar's Programme*

After Pompey's departure for the East the *equites* lost their leader, and the popular party had a period of revival, marked in the elections for 65. Two *populares* were successful for the consulate, Caesar for the aedileship, and Crassus for the post of censor. But the *optimates* ousted the two consuls-designate by accusing them of bribery, and there ensued a popularist conspiracy about which, since it never came to fruition, our evidence is tenuous and self-contradictory. The most probable reconstruction of Caesar's plan is that Crassus was to assume the dictatorship with Caesar as his *magister equitum*, and that when senatorial resistance had been broken the two deprived consuls-designate would be restored to their positions, while in the Trans-padana, Spain, Mauretania, and Egypt partisan groups would have been supporting revolutionary action aimed at changing the constitution. When the conspiracy failed, the popularist leaders tried to salvage everything possible. The tribunes proposed unsuccessfully that Caesar should be sent to give Egypt, which had been left to Rome as an inheritance, its provincial organization; and Crassus was equally unsuccessful with a proposal to grant full citizenship to the Transpadani. Meanwhile Caesar as aedile kept himself in the public eye by spending heavily on great shows to delight the *plebs*. Then having made sure of his support, he committed acts of audacity such as the restoration of Marius' trophies, which the Sullan party had overthrown, and the prosecution under the *Lex de Sicariis* of some of the most notorious agents of the Sullan persecutions.

In 63 it was undoubtedly Caesar who inspired another unsuccessful proposal, a new agrarian bill put forward by the tribune P. Servilius Rullus, under which practically all existing *ager publicus* was to be requisitioned to provide a stable livelihood for the landless population and relieve congestion in the city. At this point Caesar obtained the dignity of *pontifex maximus*. His next move was to prompt the tribune T. Labienus to accuse of *perduellio* certain senators who had carried out *senatus consulta ultima*, decrees which in Caesar's view were illegal. Here too there was no practical result, but Caesar achieved a moral victory by getting the *optimates* put on their defence.

It was about this time that L. Sergius Catilina struck out a political line of his own, pressing his candidature for the consulate, which was to serve him as a jumping-off ground for a dictatorship. He was assisted by some of the conspirators of 65, but no longer had support from Crassus and Caesar. His programme involved the exclusion of the oligarchs from offices and priesthoods, the remission of debts in Italy, the revision of the judicial system, and the redistribution of wealth, as well as financial measures, sumptuary legislation, and other such matters. But when his third attempt on the consulate failed, he gave up legal methods and attempted to put his programme into effect by force. Cicero, consul for 63, succeeded in having the *senatus consultum ultimum* passed against the conspirators; and as a result those who had been imprisoned were strangled, and an army took the field and annihilated those who had left Rome. Caesar, who had been designated praetor for 62, naturally took the view that the procedure was illegal in that no citizen could be condemned without a proper trial, involving an appeal to the people. But no one at the time succeeded in proving that Caesar was privy to the conspiracy. Cicero did not even try to do so, and no value can be attached to the story which he tried to put about later, after Caesar's murder.

As praetor in 62 Caesar continued the battle with the *optimates*, often without carrying his actions to a conclusion but being satisfied if he could damage them in the face of public opinion. Naturally they counter-attacked. He was accused of participating in a riot and suspended from his office, but he was then reinstated since he was clearly not guilty. He was then accused of complicity with the Catilinarians; but he was acquitted once he had appealed to Cicero's own evidence in his favour, and he then took legal proceedings against his false accusers. Crassus had meanwhile retired to Macedonia in nervousness at the news of Pompey's homecoming (though this was subsequently postponed); and Caesar was left as sole leader of the popular factions.

When Pompey finally returned to Italy in January 61, he disbanded his army, thus justifying the view of Caesar who had denied that Pompey wanted to become dictator. Caesar persuaded Crassus to come back and make his peace with Pompey. Then he proceeded very late to a governorship in Spain, but in a few months succeeded in improving the administration and extending Rome's dominions.

While he was away the difficulties between Pompey and the senate grew sharper. Pompey was closely linked with the equestrian order: the senate's suspicions were played on by L. Licinius Lucullus, who felt slighted on account of his replacement by Pompey in the conduct of the Mithradatic War. Pompey failed to obtain either land for his veterans or the ratification *en bloc* of the decisions he had taken in Asia. Consequently when Caesar returned from Spain in 60 and found both Crassus and Pompey in political low water, it was a simple matter to bring about a complete reconciliation between the two and to become himself the third and most influential member of a secret coalition (the so-called First Triumvirate), with the object of exercising all possible force to overcome the nobility. With the support of his two allies Caesar secured the consulate for 59: and this enabled him, with the co-operation of tribunes and other magistrates, to unfold the first parts of the combined plan, while his consular colleague Bibulus retired, at least in appearance, into contemptuous inactivity. When the senate refused to entertain his proposals, Caesar had them passed by the people, the most important in the early period being a *Lex Iulia de Repetundis* to improve the moral standard of provincial government, with heavy penalties for violation, and two agrarian laws. The latter distributed to veterans (who were not allowed to sell their allotments for twenty years) the surviving portions of *ager publicus*, certain other lands purchased by the state, and the *Ager Stellatis* and *Ager Campanus*, these last confiscated from the nobles who were occupying them. In addition Caesar had Pompey's Eastern settlements ratified, and arranged for the *publicani* to recover sums equivalent to the amount they were out of pocket over their payments for farming the taxes. At the same time he tried unsuccessfully to win over Cicero, who since 64–63 had crossed to the optimate party and was now deploring the activity of Pompey, now linked to the popular side by family and other ties. By a proposal of the tribune Vatinius, who was taking his lead from the triennial command conferred some years earlier on Pompey, Caesar was given the government of Illyricum and later of Gaul for five years; and at the beginning of 58 he began his proconsulate, while political strife and intrigue continued to be rife at Rome. In April 56 the triumvirs, at a conference held at Luca, decided that Crassus and Pompey, after holding the consulate in 55, should be proconsuls for five years, while Caesar's extraordinary power was prolonged to the same terminal date as that of the other two. In this way he hoped to get his two allies out of Rome and prevent their acquiring an advantage over himself; but though he succeeded with Crassus, who was subsequently killed at Carrhae in 53, it was otherwise with Pompey, who remained in Italy at the head of his army and became free of his family ties through the death of his wife Julia, Caesar's daughter. With Crassus' death the triumvirate became a duumvirate, and Pompey began to follow a line of his own, seeking a concordat between *equites* and senate under his own domination. The senate now granted him a prolongation of his five-year *imperium*; and this, if implemented, would have made it possible for him to become arbiter of the state, and to eliminate Caesar as a political force when the latter returned as a private citizen.

There is no need here to dwell on the events of the Civil War, or on Pompey's death and the destruction of his party. But we must say something about the way in which Caesar gradually established his power and put his constitution into effect during his brief periods of residence at Rome. He was there first in 49 after having, in absence, been elected dictator for the first time; then again in 47; then in 46, when he was sole consul for five years (later extended for ten years more in 45); and finally during the last months of 45 and the first months of 44, being elected dictator and perpetual censor on 4 February of the latter year. Several times he refused to alter the character of this dictatorship by assuming the title of king, though his enemies spoke of his 'adfectatio regni'. Yet there is no evidence that he intended, like Sulla, to bring his power to an end; indeed, though he was in no hurry about the particular steps to be taken in the matter, he was preparing to make his sister's grandson, C. Octavius, his successor, and secretly adopted him by a will drawn up on 13 September 45.

Once he had become head of the state instead of head of a party, Caesar did not desire the ascendancy of any faction, whether noble senators or rich knights or lower classes; nor did he want the struggle between factions to continue, for he had made himself the arbiter between them. With this in mind he reduced the powers of the senate, altered its composition, even opened its doors to a few provincials, and regarded *patres* and *equites* as equals so far as the dignity derived from their census qualifications was concerned. Yet he would not have knights outnumbering senators on the juries, and he was anxious to prevent the wealth of the knights from becoming inordinately large. Moreover, although in every way he met the fair demands of the *plebs* in the economic sphere, he prevented them from forming associations which might open the way to conspiracies, riots, and divisions within the state; and he imposed a rigorous control on the numbers of poor people who had a prescriptive right to state relief and bounties. Reviving the application of the 'ladder' system, he wanted provincials, by stages, to become Roman citizens; and meanwhile there was to be greater justice in provincial government by the transformation of the old type of military governors into responsible officials. The position of Italy became less privileged; it was made into a single nation, with all its communities receiving the same status, but the provinces were to be raised gradually to the Italian level. He gave preference neither to the East, where he tried to strengthen Hellenization, nor to the West, where he wanted to accelerate Latinization. He conceived that the two civilizations, Greek and Latin, were capable of being welded together into a higher synthesis among the classes of highest culture and in the capital city of Rome, and that this capital could become a majestic and monumental metropolis where the cultivated people resided and spoke both languages. Greek and Roman civilization must then be harmonized and blended in the artistic field as well.

i. *The Imperial Conceptions of M. Antonius and of Augustus*

As early as the archaic period the Romans had regarded their first king, Romulus, as the son of Mars, received into heaven as the god Quirinus, and their second king, Numa, as inspired in his legislation by the nymph (or Camena) Egeria. When exceptional individuals began to appear, men like Scipio Africanus, Sempronius Gracchus, Marius, or Sertorius, whom foreigners were readily prepared to regard as divine beings superior to the ordinary run of men, it was natural that many of them, like Sulla, should believe their actions to have been assisted by divine agreement, attested by predictions, prodigies, dreams, and the like; and that others, like Caesar, should attach special importance to the legendary traditions linking their families with gods —in Caesar's own case with Venus Genetrix. But though even Cicero was ready, in his *pro Marcello*, to declare that Caesar was 'deo simillimus', and the senate erected a statue to him with the dedication 'Caesari semidio', Caesar never claimed recognition as a god in his lifetime. His apotheosis came only after his death through the wish of the Second Triumvirate, who by this means pointed the way which his designated heir was to follow. The way marked out by Marcus Antonius was very different.

Antonius was a loyal supporter of Caesar's conceptions of dictatorship, and had a contempt not only for the republic but for all compromise forms of constitution. He was convinced that ruling the empire required an iron hand; he had no more confidence in the traditional system of dictatorship than in the imprecise concept of a 'princeps' formulated by Cicero. In the East, moreover, he was no longer in daily relations with the senate and people of Rome. These were the factors which first impelled him to adopt a more personal concept of the ruler, one conflicting with traditional Roman ideas, but later on he was even more decisively influenced by the Eastern environment in which he lived. He was in contact with peoples who from the distant past had been accustomed to be ruled by all-powerful princes, whose subjects looked to them as veritable gods on earth and were permanently in a relationship which implied servile veneration and obedience. Antony came from a family boasting descent from Hercules and had physical characteristics which Cicero described as 'gladiatorial'. In 41, when he landed at

Ephesus at the moment of the Dionysiac festival, he was greeted as the 'New Dionysus'. But the real turning-point in his policy came about through the bold action of a remarkable Egyptian queen, Cleopatra, who prevailed on him to make a 'hierogamia', a divine marriage between herself, identified with Isis and Aphrodite, and Antony, identified with Dionysus-Osiris. The divine marriage took on very human features later, with the birth of three children who were set alongside the son which Cleopatra claimed she had borne to Caesar. In a famous ceremony at Alexandria Antony, who had already rounded off Cleopatra's possessions with lands belonging to Rome, announced the territories of which the four children of Cleopatra would become rulers under their mother's protection; and it is certain that at this moment the triumvir had been plainly converted into an absolute ruler of half the Roman empire, and was ready to become 'dominus' of the whole in the event of his victory over Octavian. He was bound by 'personal' ties to the Alexandrian 'Queen of Kings': and she, by means of the children she had borne him, was ruler of another autonomous and allied empire, to which were assigned Roman provinces and states once allied to Rome. This was not the Caesarian idea, but a complex new conception half-Roman and half-Pharaonic.

Before he became Augustus in 27 BC, Octavian's policy was made up of a series of contingent struggles, and there is no need to recall its evolution in detail. At the outset he was the rival and enemy of Antony who had seized the leadership of the *populares* and was putting obstacles in the way of his obtaining the adoption and inheritance left him by Caesar. At one moment Antony tried to crush him, at another to put him in a subordinate position. In the next stage we find Octavian raising his own army, reaching agreement with the Caesaricide D. Brutus (who, like Cicero, saw in him the 'princeps' ready to draw his sword in defence of their rights), and taking the field against Antony, who had now been declared a *hostis*. But the accord with the senate was short-lived. Octavian soon concluded a new triumvirate with the Caesarians Antony and Lepidus, after having entered Rome with an army and secured the consulate by force. Once the 'imperia maiora' which the triumvirs had assigned to themselves had been confirmed by law, Octavian was associated in the bloody proscriptions and sentences carried out against anti-Caesarian elements (Cicero included), and in securing Caesar's deification; then he took part in the war which overcame M. Brutus and Cassius, the two most powerful murderers of Caesar. A number of fresh partitions of the area under triumviral control were arranged, in partnership with Antony and Lepidus, and later with Sex. Pompeius. But the elimination of first Lepidus and then Sextus led to a duumvirate and so to the decisive struggle for sole mastery between the two survivors. So we come to Antony's fall, to Octavian's reorganization of the East, and to the final triumph he celebrated in 29.

For a year and a half, from the later part of 29 to the beginning of 27, although he abolished the office of triumvir and assumed that of consul, Octavian still held absolute power 'per consensum universorum . . . rerum omnium'. He was *imperator* for life; he held the position of *princeps senatus* and in virtue of it called himself 'princeps' in the Ciceronian sense of chief citizen; and he possessed the *ius auxilii* in addition to the inviolability of a tribune. In this period he provided for his veterans, and held a *lectio senatus*, expelling 168 members and introducing fresh blood, which was of use in the future. On 10 January 27 he resigned all his abnormal positions: 'I transferred the state from my own power into that of the senate and people of Rome'. But on 13 January he received the name 'Augustus', a word of religious significance indicating his sanctity; and in the outcome, to use his own words once more, 'I was superior to all in *auctoritas*, but I had no greater power than those others who were my colleagues in the magistracies'.

In fact his outstanding *auctoritas* depended on his accumulation of offices, on the fact that those offices were repeated over many years or even for life, on the extended functions of office which were granted to him and not to other holders, and on the positions of dignity reserved for him alone. In this way the whole life of the state passed under his guardianship, control, and direction; and it was always open to him to take on new functions or to modify, even radically, his earlier settlements and definitions of his position.

He was clever enough to induce the senate and people of Rome to restore to him piece by piece all the extraordinary powers he had formally resigned, and to do so officially and of their own free will. The senate and people were under the illusion that all the power of the *princeps* was legal, because it had been conferred by themselves in accordance with republican practice. They imagined too that they retained for the future the unfettered right to impose a new settlement at the death of this particular ruler, although in fact they lacked the military or economic means which would eventually be needed if they were to offer opposition either to the present or to future *principes*. Augustus was consul down to 23: but his power was nothing like that of an ordinary consul either in its duration or in the authority he wielded, seeing that he commanded all the armies and possessed the right to choose his own colleagues. In 27 the empire was divided into imperial provinces, in principle those which required substantial military forces, and senatorial provinces, mainly those which were peaceful and prosperous. This left Augustus in almost exclusive control of all operations in the provinces containing legions, but he also secured the right to intervene at his discretion in those provinces which in theory were entrusted to the senate (and through them to proconsuls). When finally in 23 he replaced the consulate by a proconsulate, his power was not comparable with that of the normal pro-consuls who governed provinces for a single year. He received, for one ten-year period after another, exclusive and complete rights over military, civil, and judicial matters in all the imperial provinces; and he also had discretionary rights of a general nature in Rome, Italy, and the senatorial provinces, which last could be transformed into military provinces if he wished it. In the same year 23 the senate conferred on him, in place of the partial attributes of a tribune which he had acquired earlier, the full tribunician authority, thus guaranteeing the sanctity of his position. But he had little to do with the ordinary annual tribunes, who were subjected to the veto of their colleagues and whose activity was limited to Rome: Augustus' tribunician power lasted until his death, was immune from veto, and gave him the right to oppose any decision of the senate and magistrates throughout the whole empire. Add to this accumulation of magistracies with extended powers that in 22 Augustus was given charge of the corn supply; that in 21 he was enabled to superintend the fire services; and that in 12 BC, on the death of Lepidus, he acquired the office of *pontifex maximus*, giving him control of all religion. It becomes clear that he had gradually concentrated unlimited power within his grasp, with each element in the power being delegated to him by separate conferments originating with the senate and people.

Moreover in his time the republican magistracies and institutions were transformed to the point at which they retained nothing from the past but their names. Though at first the *comitia* of the people still elected some categories of magistrate, many candidates for the higher offices were suggested by Augustus, whose wish was tantamount to a command. Later the prerogatives of the people were cut down, and a lead at elections was conferred on an assembly consisting of senators and knights, who cast their votes first. The senate itself, several times purged in order to get rid of Augustus' opponents as well as of unworthy members, was gradually reduced in number to 600, with its composition arranged according to Augustus' principles. Furthermore its work was gradually confined simply to the ratification of decisions already taken by a kind of junta, the 'consilium principis', composed of members of the imperial family, certain faithful friends, and a few senators and knights of proved loyalty.

Down to this time most of the important officers had been drawn from the senatorial class, and had not been paid. But to govern a few of the imperial provinces (including the vital province of Egypt) and look after some of the services he directed, Augustus chose officials from a new bureaucracy drawn from the equestrian order, with titles such as *praefecti*, *procuratores*, or *praesides*. All were paid a stipend related to their duties, and they became responsible to the *princeps* for what they were doing. The house of Augustus, containing his confidential servants, became the seat of government, and it also was the meeting-place of the *consilium principis*. (Other aspects of Augustus' reforms are considered in Part III, in relation to the way in which they were later developed.)

39

(a) *After Lysippus, Mars at Rest.*
   Rome, Terme Museum

(b) *'The Pugilist', third century BC.*
   Rome, Terme Museum

(a) [Alinari

(b) [Alinari

40   *The Victory of Samothrace, second century BC. Paris, Louvre*

NOTES TO CHAPTER X

1. But the administration of their empire was entrusted to a body of civil servants who used the Aramaic language and writing and were established wherever the Achaemenid dynasty was in power. It is this which explains so much of the cultural relations between the Hellenic, Babylonian, Indian, and Iranian countries. The use of the Aramaic language and culture, and the cultural exchanges, are attested particularly in India by the development of Kharoṣṭhī writing (see Chapter VIII, p. 377) which presupposes the adaptation of the Aramaic alphabet to an exact phonetic analysis of language, an analysis which characterizes ancient Indian philology. These exchanges are again attested by the use among the Persians of a Babylonian medical manual, and the obvious influence of similar works on a part of Indian medical tradition independent of their classic rational doctrine. (*Journal Asiatique*, 1952, pp. 299 etc.).

2. Soviet historians consider the events of Greek history in the late fifth and fourth centuries BC as the result of a crisis in the Greek city-states. The development of slave-owning relations in the more advanced of these city-states accentuated sharply the contradictions between various groups of free men as well. The internal social struggle was closely linked with the foreign wars. Moreover, it is precisely at this time that areas hitherto backward began to develop. But their course of development had specific features in view of the crisis in the city-state system. All this had a significant effect upon the complex interaction of events at that time, the intensity in the relationship between different social groups, which found expression in the existence of various philosophical schools. (E. M. Shtaerman.)

3. Professor C. Danov considers that a sharp distinction should be made between the earlier and the later Greek tyrannies. Professor Pareti is of course distinguishing between the seventh- and sixth-century tyrannies, the largely economic causes of which are outlined in Part I, pp. 300 ff., and those which began with the early fifth-century Deinomenids at Syracuse. It is an entirely tenable view that all the Syracusan tyrants—Gelon *c.* 500, Dionysius I *c.* 400, and Agathocles *c.* 300—came into power for similar reasons.

4. Professor Pareti means, of course, not that Athens ruled its subjects through oligarchies (in fact the norm, if not the rule, was that its cities were governed by democracies), but that Athens did not use democratic means to determine league policies. Yet it is arguable that the democratic elements in the cities were contented with Athenian rule: see G. E. M. de Ste Croix, *Historia*, 1954-5, pp. 1 ff.

5. Between 377 and 355 Athens had constituted a new confederacy of maritime states.

6. The author does not touch at all upon the problem of the social roots of Hellenism, or the degree to which slave-owning of the type found in antiquity was diffused in the various Hellenistic countries, or the relationship between this and the forms of exploitation that prevailed in the East. In Soviet historiography the problem of the relationship between social-economic and cultural 'Hellenization' (as later with 'Romanization') is considered very important and has frequently been the topic of specific discussions. See *Vsemirnaya istoriya* (*World History*), Vol. II, Moscow, 1956, pp. 231-5. (E. M. Shtaerman.)

7. There were many such attempts. One rather more permanent than the rest was the kingdom established in Thrace and north-western Anatolia by the thorough though harsh administrator Lysimachus. He was defeated and killed by Seleucus I in 281, but most of his dominions were incorporated into Macedonia rather than Syria: the Chersonnese (Gallipoli) fell temporarily to the Ptolemies.

8. Already his father Philip had colonized extensively after his conquests in Thrace, Philippopolis (near Sofia) being one of the most permanent of his foundations.

9. Roman tradition, in the main, ascribed the establishment of the centuries to Servius Tullius, king in the mid-sixth century. But both the date and the motive for their establishment are highly controversial, and it is unlikely that further light will ever be thrown on the question. For a summary of conflicting views see H. H. Scullard, *A History of the Roman World, 753–146 BC* (second edition, London, 1951), Appendix 3.

10. These and other dates in the early republic are for the most part those given by Livy.

11. Tradition anachronistically calls the praetors 'consuls', using the name adopted in 366; and for the same reason the succeeding *tribuni militum* are said to be 'consulari potestate'.

12. Professor Ch. Th. Saricakis protests against the use of words such as these (cf. 'moral', p. 482 below) to describe Roman foreign policy. He cites E. Täubler, *Imperium Romanum*, (Leipzig, 1913, esp. p. 239) for the view that Rome was purely selfish throughout. He is right to emphasize that from the late third century onwards Rome showed a brutality which shocked contemporary Greeks (cf. Polybius, XI, 5, 6) and an unscrupulousness in diplomacy which has shocked most later generations. Yet its earlier policy in Italy, though doubtless conceived in its own interests and consequently amoral, was remarkably far-sighted: it was not unreasonable (see the words attributed to the emperor Claudius by Tacitus, *Annals*, XI, 24) to claim that its liberal treatment of conquered tribes and cities, in its early period at least, was the foundation of its long-lived dominion.

13. In a classic paper H. Mattingly and E. S. G. Robinson, *Proceedings of the British Academy*, *1933*, argued that the regular Roman *denarius* did not appear till 187. But Dr Mattingly subsequently (*Journal of Roman Studies*, 1945, pp. 65 ff.), showed that the date given by Professor Pareti is that of the first silver (*drachmae*) issued by the Roman mint.

14. For the particular views of Cato, which are perhaps here made too egoistic, see above, p. 361, note 12.

15. In connection with the reforms of the Gracchi, the author mentions the importance of the development of slavery, but after this no attention at all is paid to its role in social history, which determined the course of political history as well. Yet it is sufficient to compare the data of Cato and Varro to observe that during the last centuries of the republic the share of slave labour increased *vis-à-vis* that of other forms of exploitation (employment of landless labourers, share-croppers, etc.), although the latter (particularly the exploitation of clients, debtors, and small tenants) continued to exist, especially in the larger agricultural—but not cattle-breeding—estates. Their role varied in different parts of Italy. (E. M. Shtaerman.)

16. This is argued more fully by Professor Pareti in *Storia di Roma*, III, pp. 295, 492, 694. Professor Ch. Th. Saricakis calls attention to the criticisms recently made by J. Vogt, *Abhandl. Mainz.*, 1957, p. 54.

17. This is a controversial point. Professor Pareti follows the account of our main source (Appian, *de Bello Civili*, I), but there is reason to doubt whether any but Romans were offered allotments (see E. Badian, *Foreign Clientelae* (Oxford, 1958), pp. 169 ff.). In any case, non-Roman proprietors complained that their land was being seized by the Gracchan commissioners.

18. The normal number of senators before Sulla was 300, but it may be that civil war and proscriptions had heavily reduced this number by 81 B C.

19. Professor Ch. Th. Saricakis points out that here Sulla was only reiterating an ancient law (Livy, VII, 42, 2—342 B C).

20. This was the view of Mommsen and of most historians before recent times, but it has little ancient authority: see J. P. V. D. Balsdon, *Journal of Roman Studies*, 1939, pp. 57 ff. It is certain, however, that Sulla imposed stringent rules about the conduct (as distinct from the tenure) of provincial commands.

21. Professor C. Danov contends that Professor Pareti gives too favourable an account of Sulla and minimizes his 'reactionary' tendencies. Sulla's main aim, we may agree, was to restore the 'authority' of the senate, both against the *plebs* and the tribunes who courted them, and against ambitious senatorial generals; and this was a traditionalist aim. Yet the measures Sulla used to attain it were novel; and his economic measures, though rigid and perhaps unimaginative, were far from pleasing to the rich. So little so that J. Carcopino, *Sylla ou la monarchie manquée* (Paris, 1931), was able to maintain (probably wrongly) that Sulla was hostile to the senate and simply concerned to perpetuate his own régime.

22. See above, p. 361, note 17.

CHAPTER XI

RELIGION AND THE EVOLUTION OF PHILOSOPHY

I. CONFUCIANISM AND TAOISM

CHINESE religious life in this period is mainly a continuation of that of the feudal period. But with the consolidation of regional states, and still more with the formation of the empire, religious life, or at least its formal expression in the cult, assumed an increasingly official character; and it became, in the words of Granet, an administrative religion. The state cult itself grew more and more formalized. It lost the larger part of its religious content and became a highly developed ceremonial with strict rules; the countryman's everyday religious life, on the other hand, concerned as it was with agriculture and with ancestor worship, never ascended to a higher level. These conditions were not conducive to any sort of philosophical thought. When the latter took place about 500 B C, it came from quite another direction, and played a much more significant role in China than religion could ever have done. It has been rightly said that 'the place which philosophy has occupied in Chinese civilization has been comparable to that of religion in other civilizations' (Fêng Yu-lan).

From its inception, and ever after, Chinese thought was chiefly moral and political in its aims, with a sociological undertone; metaphysics and formal logic were not an original component and never played an outstanding role. This is the main characteristic of ancient Chinese philosophy, the period of the 'Hundred Philosophers' (c. 500–200 B C). It was a magnificent flowering of philosophic thought, one of those god-graced periods in the history of a nation, in which suffering, and political and economic chaos, is matched by the brilliance of spiritual achievement. The principal schools, according to the classical list proposed by Ssŭ-ma T'an (second century B C) and modernized by Fêng Yu-lan, were the following six:

(1) The school of the literati (*ju-chia*), descended from K'ung-tzŭ (Confucius, 551–479 B C). A man of high birth, Confucius passed his life as a travelling adviser to the feudal princes, and then as the head of a flourishing private school of ethics. His teaching career was long and influential, but nothing in it seems to justify the enormous success enjoyed by his teaching after his death. It seems that no actual writing by Confucius is extant, with the exception, perhaps, of his share as editor in the *Ch'un-ch'iu* annals of the Lu state. His thought is best known from the *Lun-yü* (Analects): a collection of his utterances compiled by some immediate or mediate disciples. His

cultural basis was the Classics (*I-ching*, *Shih-ching*, *Shu-ching*), of which he was the first expounder and which for him were the root of all knowledge and rule of life. He conceived himself solely as an interpreter of this old traditional role, 'a transmitter, not an originator' (*Lun-yü*, VII, 1). This was true from many points of view, but in several other respects it was only a cover for the introduction of a new, severely ethical ideology. Of his political philosophy we have already spoken. He had a highly moral, but none the less aristocratic conception of social relations. He was aware, of course, that actual practice was very different from ancient theory, and this is the reason why he and his followers insisted upon the need for making things and functions correspond to the ideals attached to them by their names; this they called the 'rectification of names' (*Lun-yü*, XIII, 3). Individual morals are based on the idea that man ought to act rightly because this is a categorical imperative (*i*) and not because of the hope of any advantage (*li*). The consequence is that man must act, but without any thought for success or failure. The value of doing what he ought to do lies in the doing itself, and not in the external result. Only fate (*ming*) can decide the issue. The all-important thing is to be aware of the existence of fate, or of the decree of heaven (as Confucius himself seems to have understood the term) and to act accordingly. For him the inner law (*tao*) of the phenomenal world was a moral one.

The school of Confucius did not come into the limelight during the first century or so after the death of its founder. It lived in obscurity and received its real impetus only from the work of Mencius (Meng-tzǔ 371–289 BC). Mencius represents the idealistic trend in Confucianism. Starting from the postulate that human nature is intrinsically good, he maintains that man has in himself the four beginnings (humanity, righteousness, propriety, wisdom) and that he is capable, and therefore bound, to develop them. He fought bitterly against both the hedonism of the early Taoists and the indiscriminate love of Mo-ti, which he maintained was something artificial and imposed from without, while Confucius' graded relationship meant a human good-heartedness that developed naturally from within man's nature. Hence also the all-important imperative of Mencius' political theory: the state exists in its own right and is a moral institution, carrying out a moral task.

The realistic wing of the Confucian school was represented by Hsün-tzǔ (*c.*298–238). In contrast with Mencius, he held that human nature is originally and intrinsically evil, and that everything that is good comes only from man's conscious effort against his tendencies and towards culture. Social relations are based mainly on two particular aspects of the old conception of customary ceremonies toward the ancestors; these are the *li*, as a norm of social behaviour, and music as a means of furthering social harmony. Up to a certain point, Hsün-tzǔ's ideas move on lines that are parallel with Legalism; and it is noteworthy that the chief exponents of Legalism, Han-fei-tzǔ (theory) and Li Ssǔ (practice), were both disciples of Hsün-tzǔ.

(2) The second main philosophical school was that of Mo-ti or Mo-tzǔ,

who probably lived in the second half of the fifth century BC. His thought is opposed to that of Confucius in so far as Mo-ti denied the validity of tradition-al lore and its usefulness. His own background was not the aristocracy of the gentlemen-scholars, but the warrior class (*yu-hsieh*). His anti-Confucian criticism lies mainly in the field of practical ethics: he maintains that Con-fucian morality is harmful to society and to mankind, and above all he rejects the Confucian idea of the six graded relations as the basis of all society, and substitutes for them the conception of all-embracing love, an idea that was but an extension of the professional ethics of the knight class to which he himself belonged. It is, however, characteristic of the general Chinese 'this-world' attitude that this lofty principle is upheld mainly on utilitarian grounds, in view of the good ensuing from it for society at large. It is not an emotional love, but a purely intellectual one. In contrast with Confucius' agnosticism, Mo-ti upheld the existence of a supreme god—who loves all men and whose will is that all men should love each other. These tenets were expanded further by the later Moists, who introduced a large element of dialectic and went far towards creating a system of logic and epistemology.

(3) Another philosophical school was the one which we usually call Taoism. A sharp distinction must be drawn between Taoism as a philosophy (which is theoretical and early) and the Taoistic religion which is quite practical in outlook and aims and arose much later. Taoist thought is mainly a form of escapism; a philosophy of men who recognized human society as bad and therefore abandoned it and its struggles, and turned to seclusion in mountains or in other natural solitudes.

The earliest thinker of this school was Yang Chu (perhaps fourth century BC). His theory is a sort of egotistical hedonism: 'though he might have profited the whole world by plucking out a single hair, he would not have done it'. It was each man for himself. This, the earliest phase of Taoism, was limited to a desire to preserve life and avoid injury, and was later followed by a second one in which, escape not being always possible, an attempt was made to reach at the inner laws according to which things develop and change in this world.

A later stage is represented by the most puzzling and much discussed work of Chinese philosophical literature, the *Tao-tê-ching*. It is attributed by tradition to Lao-tzŭ, an older contemporary of Confucius. But the evanes-cent figure of Lao-tzŭ is, in all likelihood, unhistorical, and the book may date from the beginning of the third century BC. It is mainly a discussion about the *tao*, conceived as the unnameable, the ultimate principle that lies beyond shapes and features and is the beginning of heaven and earth. It is the absolute underlying principle, beyond good and evil, not amoral but super-moral. The *tao* includes the invariable law of nature, according to which when a thing reaches one extreme, it reverts from it to become its opposite. Man should know the laws of nature and act according to them. 'If one intends to achieve something, he starts with its opposite, and if he wants to retain anything he admits in it something of its opposite.' The other main conception is *tê* (power or virtue). *Tao* being the origin of all things, each thing obtains something from the universal *tao*, and this something is called *tê*. The *tê* of a thing is what it naturally is. Life should abandon itself to *tao* and *tê* and activity should be much reduced (non-action, *wu-wei*), avoiding all over-doing and unnatural strain. The resulting political theory is that 'the empire is gained by remaining constantly in non-action. As soon as one becomes active, one is unable to gain the empire. How do I know that this is so? By this: the more taboos and prohibitions there are in the empire, the poorer the people will be. The more useful implements the people have, the more state and dynasty will be in confusion. The more cunning craftsmen there are, the more bizarre contrivances will spring up. The more laws and ordinances are promulgated, the more thieves and robbers will there be.' (*Tao-tê-ching*, 57; trans. Duyvendak.) This means anti-statalism; it is a theory reminiscent of Max Stirner and anarchism.

About the same epoch, these theories were brought to their logical con-clusion by the composite work traditionally attributed to Chuang-tzǔ (*c.* 369–286 BC). Man's chief purpose is the achievement of happiness. A relative kind of happiness can be reached by the free development of our nature through the use of our inborn ability (*tê*). Natures are not uniform, and every attempt to make them so conduces only to grief, and therefore Chuang-tzǔ is utterly against any formal government and maintains that the best way to govern is by letting people strictly alone (by non-government). But there is another, higher happiness, which comes only from recognizing the relativity of the nature of things and identifying man with the Whole. Thus knowledge alone leads to ultimate happiness, and only the true sage, the spiritual man, can be perfectly happy. This can be achieved by the gradual recognition of all distinctions as mere conventions, which from the viewpoint of the *tao* are relative and not absolute. This is true also of the greatest distinction of all, that between life and death. The sage merely needs to be one with the Great One, which is unthinkable and unspeakable. The end of knowledge is its own abolition, it is no-knowledge. The practice can be summarized in the two words: do nothing (*wu-wei*); in the sense of acting wholly spontaneously and naturally, without any conscious effort. 'By doing nothing there is nothing that is not done' (*Tao-tê-ching*, 48). The perfect man does nothing and the great sage originates nothing—they merely contemplate the universe. Taoist thought at this stage is therefore a mystical scepticism with a strong anarchical element.

(4) The so-called School of Names (*ming-chia*) was composed of logicians, often misnamed sophists. The Chinese language is constitutionally not adapted to organic logic of the Aristotelian type. Still the problem of the relation between the name (*ming*) and the reality implied by it (*shih*) led to subtle, and sometimes even captious, disputes of a quasi-logical character. The foremost teachers of this school were Hui Shih (*c.* 350–260 BC); and

Kung-sun Lung (*c.* 284–259 BC). The latter, by emphasizing that names are absolute and permanent, developed an epistemology which came very near to the Platonic universals.

(5) With the *yin-yang* school we are moving into another field. It hails from the para-technical circles of occultists (*fang-shih*) and geomancers, whose main purpose was the practical one of finding or causing a favourable combination of natural forces for any enterprise. The meanings of the two opposite and complementary terms *yin* and *yang* have been explained in Part I. The theory built around them was a line of thought that later merged with a similar one, that of the Five Elements (*wu-hsing*: water, fire, wood, metal, earth), into what can be considered as a single school. Its main representative was Tsou Yen (third century BC). It gave a well-balanced cosmology and a series of practical precepts meant to place man's behaviour in harmony with nature, as the only possible path to success and happiness. Later on the theory of *yin* and *yang* was connected with the hexagrams of the Book of Changes (*I-ching*), probably an old diviner's handbook. Its influence in court life and even in the conduct of state affairs was at times very large, but of course this semi-magical lore can hardly be called a philosophy.

(6) Legalism (*fa-chia*) was mainly a school of political thought, and as such has been chiefly dealt with in the preceding chapter. Its chief theoretician, its synthetizer though not its founder, was Han-fei-tzŭ (d. 233 BC). We may recall that the Legalist philosophy of history was the only one which did not regard the past as the precedent and model for present behaviour.

This luxuriant expansion of philosophical thought underwent a process of simplification, but also of impoverishment, with the events that led to the foundation of the empire by the Ch'in and its final organization by the Han. Legalism met with disaster and was practically suppressed. Moism and the School of Names petered out. The *yin-yang* school ceased to lead an independent life and at first merged (at least to a great extent) with Confucianism. This left Confucianism and Taoism alone in the field. While the latter, being anti-statal, soon became a philosophy for disgruntled officials and retired politicians, Confucianism after several vicissitudes became the official ideology of the Han state. Its victory was complete by the second half of the second century BC.

But Han Confucianism was something very different from the teaching of the old sage, and it also differed from the later developments of the school. Its chief representative was Tung Chung-shu (179–104 BC). He was the theorist of the Han empire and also a great statesman; the first beginnings of the Chinese state-examinations system owed a great deal to him. His cosmology is a blend of Confucianism and of the *yin-yang* theories; according to him, the universe consists of ten constituents: heaven, earth, *yin* and *yang*, the Five Elements, and man. The waxing and waning of *yin* and *yang* are at the basis of all processes of nature and also of changes within the social order. Politics and the action of government should be modelled on the pattern of the four seasons. History itself is brought into this system, the changes of dynasties being influenced by the movements of a cycle of three colours: black, white, and red. It was also Tung Chung-shu who gave a final form to the theory of the mandate of heaven (*t'ien-ming*) and incorporated it into his philosophical system. He stressed the superhuman position of the emperor, thus supporting the authoritarian trend of the institutions. At the same time the circles around Tung Chung-shu introduced into Confucianism a great quantity of pseudo-scientific and even magical practices.

It can thus be seen that the rich variety of thought of the Warring States period gave way, if not to a synthesis, to a form of eclecticism. Tung Chung-shu was essentially an eclectic. The unknown authors of the interpolated chapters of Chuang-tzŭ and Hsün-tzŭ, which probably go back to the Early Han, were also eclectics. The best representative of this trend of thought is perhaps the *Huai-nan-tzŭ*, a collective work with a strong leaning toward Taoism.

The religious content of Chinese philosophy in general and of Confucianism in particular is very low by our standard. Under the Han the official cult was a state religion, one of the main concerns of government, urban in character and under the tutorship of the literati. Religion itself became bureaucratized. The emperor could and did prescribe a cult for new deities and demote gods to a lesser rank for state ceremonies. The state's bureaucratic system projected itself into heaven. The official cult of the ancient agrarian gods of the earth and of the crops, which had fallen into oblivion during the Warring States period, was restored by the Han; but the gods lost all reality. The various earth deities were synthetized into a single one, the Sovereign Earth, while the August Heaven (*huang-t'ien*) was dismembered by the Ch'in into several figures: the Green, Yellow, Red, and White rulers. To these the Han added the Black ruler, thus completing the number five as a counterpart to the Five Elements. This cult was more and more localized on five sacred mountains, of which the T'ai-shan in Shantung was the most famous. The imperial sacrifice on the T'ai-shan became the most august, elaborate, and costly rite of the official religion, and only six rulers in Chinese history were able to perform it. The foremost practical aspect of the state religion was perhaps the calendar, and determining it was one of the most jealously guarded imperial prerogatives.

In the private religion of the upper and lower classes the cult of the ancestors took such a place that it became the real mainstay of Chinese religious life. But in the official practice this too became a dematerialized, symbolic, abstract rite; a simple commemoration without any feeling of personal communication.

All this was not enough for the religious needs of the people at large.[1] Although the average Chinese is utterly 'this-worldly', there was still a natural yearning for some emotional uplift of the soul, for something that could give consolation to the simple man, for that heartfelt solace which the dry as dust state-cult or the cold moral norm of the Confucianists could not give. This was particularly true in times of anarchy, economic depression, and civil war, when the farmer turned from his present hopeless conditions toward something which could give him at least a glimmer of hope beyond this life. The only element of mysticism in this period was supplied by Taoism; not by the philosophy of Lao-tzŭ and Chuang-tzŭ, but by the mass of popular beliefs and superstitions that go under the same name. But these trends lived an underground life, and it was only during the Later Han period that they took the shape of sectarian movements, through which they ended by becoming a true religion. For the rest, Chinese everyday spiritual life was to a more or less extent dominated by the belief in spirits (*kuei*), sometimes beneficent but more often impish or even malignant, and by the all-present need of taking into due account the underground currents of supernatural forces, i.e. geomancy (*feng-shui*).

2. RELIGION AND PHILOSOPHY IN INDIA

While in China the philosophic values ignore or exclude the religious ones, in India philosophy starts from religion[2] and for a long time is intimately connected with it. While in China philosophy is 'this-worldly' and centres around society, the state, and their inter-relations, in India it is metaphysical and individualistic. The innermost natures of the two great Asiatic civilizations, partly conditioned by climate and environment, are therefore quite different.

About 500 BC religious life in India had not yet gone far from the Vedic stage. The Vedic ritual was more or less followed by the Brahmans, sole performers of its complicated sacrifices. Thus we have evidence that the highest rite of all, the horse sacrifice (*aśvamedha*), reserved for a great king and conqueror, was occasionally performed and in any case highly regarded. In keeping with the spirit of the sacred texts, there were no temples as yet, but only open-air altars. But, apart from the reform movements of which we shall speak presently, the practice of religion and above all the mythology as a living belief came to be gradually modified by the non-Aryan substrata of Indian society; and this process grew stronger as it kept pace with the advance of Aryan civilization southward. The libation (*yajña*) of the Aryans, usually of *soma* into fire, was slowly supplanted by the offering (*pūjā*), originally consisting in the anointing of the image and in any case including a strong element of ritual purification.

Thus the priestly and naturalistic Vedic religion underwent an insensible change. The old deities, too indefinite and too closely connected with natural phenomena, were replaced in popular favour by the earth gods, often theriomorphic and with a dominance of feminine deities. Varuṇa, Agni and the rest vanished out of the horizon of practical worship. Only Viṣṇu and Indra remained. To Viṣṇu local heroes like Kṛṣṇa and Vāsudeva and local gods

s*

like Nārāyaṇa were assimilated. The cycle of Kṛṣṇa is already a major factor in the great epics; even more so is Rāma, the central figure of the *Rāmāyaṇa*, another hero of northern India who was later equated with Viṣṇu. On the other side the terrific aspects in southern religiosity came to be typified in Śiva, the god of destruction, while the numerous Mother Goddesses merged into Durgā or Kālī or Pārvatī, the feminine counterpart of Śiva. With the epics, i.e. during the last few centuries of this period, the fusion between Aryan and non-Aryan elements is complete. The *Vedas* are still regarded as sacred texts, but the living religion is something new; it is Brahmanism.

Secular thought went on building on the base laid by the early *Upaniṣads*. The later *Upaniṣads* develop still further the ideas of *karman* as the human act that automatically produces its own retribution in the next life; of *ātman*, the individual principle, and of its essential identity with *brahman*, the world soul, the essence of the universe. But a shifting of emphasis comes in with the introduction of a strong deistic element, i.e. the exaltation of Viṣṇu or of Śiva (usually called Rudra) and with the beginnings of an emotional devotion (*bhakti*). Some hints of early philosophical conceptions of the Sānkhya type are not lacking. Typical in this respect is the *Śvetāśvatara Upaniṣad*, which has been said to usher in Hinduism. These elements increase with time, and the modern *Upaniṣads* (some have been compiled as late as the sixteenth century) are but a very secondary appendage to devotional literature.

Philosophical thought in the *Mahābhārata* is difficult to date, since that huge encyclopaedia grew slowly in piecemeal fashion in the course of centuries. By far the most important text is the *Bhagavadgītā* (Mhbh. VI, 23–40). It is a short poem of 700 *ślokas* in eighteen chapters, in which Kṛṣṇa assuages the doubts of the hero Arjuna, who cannot bring himself to fight against his friends and relatives on the opposite side. What Kṛṣṇa sets forth is a philosophy of action. Man must act according to his law or duty (*dharma*); but he must consider neither success nor failure nor reward; his action must be completely desireless. Salvation is obtained by three paths. The first two are the path of action (*karmamārga*) and the path of knowledge (*jñāna-mārga*). By the desireless act man enters the way of knowledge. But the latter is completely obtained only by meditation, and meditation is efficacious only through its special technique (*yoga*). Through *yoga* man reaches the highest of the three paths, that of emotional devotion (*bhaktimārga*). Many developments of later thought are included *in nuce* in this short beautiful poem: early *Sānkhya*, *Yoga*, the devotion to Kṛṣṇa. But above all the historical importance of the *Bhagavadgītā* is enormous; it became, and still is, the most popular and most commented-upon text of Hinduism, taking the place of the sacred *Vedas* in living religion. By its very vagueness and composite content, it is admirably suited to the introduction of new trends of thought by means of commentaries.

This leads us to the origins of classical Hindu philosophy. As always in India, the historian is handicapped by the utter uncertainty of chronology (even of a relative one) and by the anonymity of the texts. Later tradition distinguishes six philosophical systems (*darśana*), coupled two by two: *Vendānta* and *Mīmāṃsā*, *Saṅkhya* and *Yoga*, *Nyāya* and *Vaiśeṣika*. Of these, only *Vendānta* and *Sāṅkhya* are philosophies in the complete sense of the word, the other four relating to partial problems or to techniques. Making all due allowance for the impossibility of fixing even approximate dates, we may perhaps assume with some reason that *Sāṅkhya* and *Yoga* had their beginnings in this period. The case of *Vedānta* lies on another plane; it is mainly the linear descendant of Upanisadic thought, and the problem is one of drawing the frontier between the two. But in any case it will be safer and sounder to give a connected account of the six *darśanas* in Part III, because it appears that by the end of the Gupta period they were already fixed in their main outlines.

The main test of orthodoxy is the recognition of the sacred character of the *Vedas*. Beyond this pale, we are outside Hinduism. The first currents we meet with, as a sort of borderline case, are the sceptical and materialistic trends, which are one of the inborn ingredients of human thought. They did not much come to the fore in India. Still, some disjointed schools of this sort did exist, though they are known mostly from quotations in polemical writings of other schools. Such were the Ajñānikas or agnostics, who denied the possibility of knowledge itself. Then there were the Cārvākas or Lokāyatas, materialists who maintained the complete dissolution of man after death into the five elements, and the identity of the *ātman* with the body; they denied the existence of God, the sanctity of the *Vedas*, the law of *karman*; for them, therefore, there is nothing to be released from, and the only aim in life must be its enjoyment. There were also the Ājīvikas or fatalists, founded by Makkhali Gosāla, a contemporary of the Buddha. He maintained that the world exists because of the cohesion of the five elements (earth, water, fire, air, and life), and this meld is determined not by *karman* but entirely by blind fate (*niyati*). The cycle of deaths and rebirths (*saṃsāra*) is therefore predestined, and nothing that man does can influence it. Release is not elimination, but the non-manifestation of the eternal *saṃsāra*; it is, therefore, impermanent.

The arid formalism of Vedic religion, as we have said, provoked reactions from several quarters. In the case of the *Upaniṣads*, this reaction managed to keep within the very elastic bounds of orthodoxy and it merely contributed another spiritual facet within the old frame. But with the two reformers who lived about 500 BC, this reaction broke all bounds and resulted in the foundation of two new religions: Jainism and Buddhism.

a. *Jainism*

According to tradition Jainism was derived from a long line of teachers (*tīrthakara*), of whom the last but one, Pārśva (eighth or seventh century BC?), may have been a historical person. This was certainly the case with the last of the series, Vardhamāna, later called Mahāvīra (Great Hero) and Jina (Victorious One)—he died *c.* 477 BC. Unlike the Buddha, therefore, he was no originator but the continuer of a tradition, to which he added much, but not over-much, of his own. The Jain religion, to which he gave shape, is essentially an ascetic one. It reposes on a theory which denies the absolute validity of knowledge and recognizes solely its probability (*syādvāda*, the theory of 'may be', i.e. of looking from some point of view). There are two correlative and eternally independent categories, the conscious (*jīva*) and the unconscious (*ajīva*). The conscious corresponds almost to an individual soul. The unconscious is all the remaining things: matter (*pudgala*), space, time, qualities, etc. The innumerable *jīvas* are by their own nature eternal, omniscient, untroubled; but their junction with *pudgala* in the shape of action (*karman*) troubles this purity. The only way to restore this purity and to attain isolation (*kaivalya*), which means salvation, is through a life of utmost rigorous asceticism. In this the prohibition of taking life in any form plays an outstanding role. The main external feature of Jainism is the monastic order, a flexible and yet closely-knit institution that has allowed the Jain religion to continue in existence to this day; it is supported by the community of 'hearers' (*śrāvaka*), who, by a virtuous life, prepare for a future re-birth in which they may enter the strenuous career of the ascetic. No God is recognized: the Hindu deities are considered as impermanent and can be released from *saṃsāra* only if they are re-born as men and turn ascetic. In Jainism as well as in Buddhism man stands alone—he is the only shaper of his destiny and release can come only from his own efforts.

Jainism possessed a body of traditional lore, which had grown up in the course of centuries: it was sanctioned and fixed (according to tradition) in a council said to have been held in the third century BC at Pāṭaliputra under the presidency of Sthūlabhadra. But the Jain canon was only put into writing much later. Jainism never became a faith of the masses because of the terrible severity of its life, its conservatism, and also because it found no Aśoka; it was limited to definite circles (mostly wealthy traders) and, although it spread throughout India, it never went beyond its frontiers.

b. *Buddhism*

According to most modern scholars Gautama Siddhartha lived *c.* 563–483 BC. Born at Kapilavastu in the aristocratic republic of the Śākya in northern Bihar, he lived the luxurious life of a young nobleman until he felt impelled to abandon it to seek a means of release from *saṃsāra*. After he had forsaken as useless the terrible austerities which he had tried in the first place, he later, meditating under a tree at Bodh Gaya, found illumination (*bodhi*) at last. He preached the Law (*dharma*) for the first time at Sarnath near Benares; and henceforward the Illuminate (*buddha*), as he was called, taught and lived his doctrine until he died at the age of eighty at Kuśīnāgara. As far as we can reconstruct his teaching (he never wrote a line), it is based on the following essentials: there are four Noble Truths: (1) existence (the *saṃsārā*) is misery; (2) attachment (*tṛṣṇa:* thirst) the cause of existence; (3) misery can be ended by the elimination of attachment; (4) there is a path to the destruction of attachment: this is the Eightfold Path of right faith, speech, action, livelihood, mind, meditation, resolution, and view. In investigating things, the smallest unit we can reach is the *dharma* (properly the 'law' whereby their nature and condition are regulated), which is an irreducible factor of existence. The *dharmas*, and therefore the phenomenal world, have no existence, nor does a soul or individual principle (*ātman*) exist. Buddhism is also atheistic, in the sense that the gods of the *Veda* are impermanent and bound to the *saṃsārā* (as in Jainism) and can anyhow be of no help in obtaining release. Salvation means the attainment of *nirvāṇa*— a condition which can only be defined negatively; it is the absolute state where all distinctions of life and death, good, evil, knowledge and non-knowledge, cease to exist.

The main external feature of the Buddha's teaching was the institution of a monastic community, ruled by severe rules, living on alms and supported by lay believers. Every monk and nun, and they alone, could strive towards the attainment of *nirvāṇa* by the path shown by the Master. Thus the triad, the Buddha, the Law (*dharma*), and the Community (*saṅgha*) is the mainstay of the new religion.

After the death of the founder his community developed slowly, as just one sect among many similar ones in north-eastern India. The utterances of the Buddha were collected by his disciples and their descendants and were first put into some shape at the so-called first council, in the first half of the fifth century BC. A second council was held at Vaiśālī, in the early fourth century BC, but their account is untrustworthy, and the historicity of the event itself is not beyond doubt. It was during this council that the first split occurred between the Elders (Sanskrit *sthavira*, Pali *thera*), who claimed to be the authorized depositories of the tradition, and the Western monks, who seceded and convened a rival council; hence the name *Theravāda* for the first school and *Mahāsāṅghika* for the second. The conflict was mainly on points of discipline; but later doctrinal differences arose as well, and the number of schools went on increasing. Tradition mentions eighteen schools, but this is a sacred and therefore fictitious number. Anyhow, the schisms did not impede the decisive expansion of Buddhism from a local sect into a pan-Indian religion, thanks to the enthusiastic support of Aśoka. Not only did the king become a devout Buddhist, but he took serious and efficient steps to spread his faith throughout the whole of India and even outside it; his bilingual Greek-Aramaic inscription, recently found at Kandahar, is perhaps the most eloquent sign of his zeal for morality and orderliness. One mission, headed by his brother Mahinda, was sent to Ceylon, which was soon completely converted and became the stronghold of Buddhism in the south.

The Pali recension of the Buddhist canon, which tradition ascribes to a legendary third council convened by Aśoka, was introduced into Ceylon and received its final shape there in the last years before our era. It is written in Pali (a dialect which may have been spoken in Magadha), and is divided into three 'baskets' (*pitaka*): *Sutta* (Sanskr. *sūtra*), containing the word of the Master, i.e. his speeches and teachings; *Vinaya*, the monastic rules; *Abhidhamma* (Sanskr. *abhidharma*), a miscellaneous section of apparently later origin, which came to contain most of the philosophical doctrines. Of course this huge collection contains material of various origin, reflecting the opinions of the Buddha's disciples and their successors, and the discussions that took place in later generations. The Pali canon is that of the *Theravāda* school; but the missionaries were not particular about language; they put their texts into the tongue of the country in which they were preaching, and thus we also have fragments of canonical writings (chiefly *Vinaya*) in Sanskrit, Prakrit, and in an Indian dialect that underwent a thorough process of Sanskritization, and is known as Hybrid Sanskrit. But most of the non-*Theravāda* literature is now preserved only in Chinese and Tibetan translations.

Although the Śuṅga dynasty, which succeeded the Maurya, returned to Brahmanic orthodoxy and did not favour (though it did not hinder) Buddhism, about the beginning of our era Buddhist monasteries and monks were fairly widely spread throughout India. There was never, however, a central organization: not only was every monastery independent of the others, but the superior in each place had no authority beyond the administrative sphere. There was hardly any doctrinal control, and the only disciplinary court competent to judge a monk was the community of his brethren.

3. RELIGIOUS AND PHILOSOPHIC IDEAS IN PERSIA

In the fifth and fourth centuries the Zoroastrian religion lost its exclusively dualistic character. This was because the old gods (and in particular the western ones—Mithras, Anahitā, Verethreghae and Vayū), which had been preserved in popular worship, gradually recovered their importance and extended their influence at the expense of Ahura Mazda, who had been imposed by Zarathustra. However, the opposition between the powers of the Spirit of Good and the Spirit of Evil was accentuated, while the Magi supported the pessimistic conception of 'Zervanism': this made Zervan the Supreme Being, while Ahura Mazda and Ahra Mainyu are his two sons working against each other, with Mithras acting as a moderator between them. Herodotus was familiar with the Persian cults and sacrifices of his own day, offered to the sun, moon, earth, fire, water, and wind; just as he also knows of bloody sacrifices which had been forbidden by Zoroastrianism. Other ancient rites, which had already been outlawed, also returned, such as the use of the intoxicant 'haoma', though it had now been made less noxious; moreover the funeral rites of Zoroastrianism began to lose some of their rigidity.

The religious policy of the Achaemenid kings sometimes underwent sharp changes, such as the time Xerxes (486–465), in his anger against the revolt of Babylonia, forbade the cult of Marduk. But it tended in the main to religious tolerance, of which the Persian attitude to the Jews is an example. They allowed the Zervanism of the Magi, the Mithraic mysteries, the Anahitā cult (authenticated under Artaxerxes II, 404–358), and the use of sacred images.3 At the same time they were discovering the ancient myths on early man, on the primordial king, the fights between heroes and dragons, and so on. In philosophy the influence of Greece on Persia and of Persia on Greece is apparent in the time of Plato, who had Persians among the pupils at his school; from them he was able to get greater information about Zoro-astrian dualism.

Graeco-Persian religious syncretisms were of course at their fullest development when Alexander and his successors were ruling the Iranian countries. Nor did things change sensibly when certain lands about 247 got detached from the Seleucid empire, and were formed into the Parthian kingdom of the Arsacids (cf. Part III). These syncretistic ideas persisted into the Mithradatic kingdom of Pontus even when it was ruled by Mithradates Eupator, the great enemy of Rome, whom apocalyptic prophecy identified with Mithras, come down to earth to combat Ahriman—probably the beginnings of the Hellenized Mithras mysteries. (For the development of the *Avesta* cf. Parts I and III.)

4. THE HEBREWS

The first example of a 'diaspora' or dispersion of the Hebrew people took place, as we have seen, with the transplanting of conquered Jews into the countries of their conquerors. This happened in 732 under Tiglath-Pileser III, in 722 under Sargon II, in *c.*700 under Sennacherib, and in 597 and 586 under Nebuchadnezzar: the Jews were transplanted to agricultural colonies on the Lower Euphrates and to the city of Babylon, from which 50,000 survivors were repatriated in 539 by Cyrus the Great. But real Diasporai, following one after another, occurred above all in the time of Alexander the Great's successors. In this period the Hebrews were scattered in vast numbers throughout the Mediterranean basin; the movement was both voluntary and under compulsion, and is recorded by various writers who were conscious of this phenomenon. One of the countries to which they made their way (or in which they were forcibly settled) was Egypt, where indeed they had already taken roots under Jeremiah in the sixth and in Elephantine in the fifth and fourth centuries. The Diaspora was most marked during the vicissitudes of Palestine under Antiochus IV (Epiphanes) and Pompey, just as we find it repeated later under the Flavians and Hadrian. When the Romans, in the middle of the second century BC, supported the independence of Judaea, a Judaean (*Oracula Sibyll.*, III, 271) boasted that his compatriots were

scattered throughout the world, on land and on sea. The places to which
the Jews went from choice were, naturally, the great ports and commercial
centres: in some places they lived in their own quarters, in others they were
dispersed. In Alexandria, where the Jewish colony was always very numerous
and particularly so during the period when the Ptolemies occupied Palestine,
the figure of 100,000 Hebrews is given. However it is not impossible that there
were a million Jews in Egypt, since Jewish emigrants may well have out-
numbered those who had remained in Palestine. If we take into account
their spirit of kinship, ability in affairs, and the distance which they kept
between themselves and other people, it is easy to understand the strength
which these people represented to the ancient world.

The political and legal position of these Hebrews was very uncertain. In
some respects, undoubtedly, they were given various privileges, but from
another standpoint they were there on sufferance, regarded with suspicion,
and sometimes the victims of riots and persecutions. Violent popular mani-
festations of anti-Semitic hatred, followed by a reaction from the Hebrews,
often brought sharp intervention by the government; but in other places
and times we find a kind of fashion for Jewish usages, accompanied by a
tendency on the part of the Gentiles to accept Jewish customs and faiths.
Governments, however, were not always tolerant of this proselytizing.

The use of Greek (see below) by large groups of Jews in the Diaspora
facilitated proselytizing, which was pursued with tenacity and skill among
people of all ranks and achieved success in all districts. The majority of the
new disciples remained, however, at the level of sympathizers, perhaps
because circumcision, which was indispensable for becoming fully Jewish,
was a distinct obstacle for pagans. In any case, the difficulties for pagan
followers of Judaism were great because of the irreconcilable conflict between
the exclusively monotheistic conception of the Hebrews and the polytheistic
state-cults. These differences were already serious for relations between the
Jews and the cities which sheltered them, despite their recognition of Jewish
national religion; they were much more so when they affected the family
and public life of catechumens, who were full citizens of their respective
cities. We see this trouble beginning in 139 BC, when the Jews were first
expelled from Rome for making converts there.

Caesar showed particular benevolence towards the Jews, and created a
special legal status for them which survived in its broad outlines into later
times. The Hebrew 'ethnos' was considered similar to a corporation, with
an ethnarch, protected by Rome, at its head; members of the Diaspora were
allowed to belong to it and to preserve the national religion. The Roman
state dispensed them from military service, and from attending tribunals on
the sabbath; and they were allowed to administer their own property. It is
certain that the Hebrews of the Diaspora, from all their main centres, maintained most active relations with Jerusalem on religious matters. All Hebrews
sought to go to the temple at Jerusalem on great occasions as it was considered

the one true place of worship, although of course each local community had synagogues with its own leaders and men who had accepted a religious calling. The Hebrew community in Rome was very large. It is calculated that there could not have been less than 30,000 Jews at the time of Christ: there were several communities independent of one another, each provided with an autonomous council, and with meeting places for prayer. The attempt by the high priest Onias IV to erect a new temple at Leontopolis in Egypt was exceptional; it lasted a short time and the attempt was not repeated.

While the Hebrews in Palestine were subject in turn to the influences of Seleucid, Ptolemaic, and Roman domination, the scribes were giving their religion a new direction. These men had become interpreters, teachers, and preachers. They were devotees of the Law in its most meticulous applications, adhering both to its letter and to its allegorical meanings, stubbornly holding themselves aloof, 'separated' (Pharisee), from idolatrous Hellenistic thought. They pushed to its extreme the theory of the transcendent and unknowable God; and they developed the conception of celestial mediators, the various categories of angels who shielded God from any contact with the world, though He had always been ready to intervene to preserve the faithful and would always do so in the future. These ideas were mostly developed in the second century BC before, during, and after the period of the Maccabees, in the *Books of Esther, Judith*, and *Tobias*; at the same time poetic psalms celebrated the greatness, goodness, and justice of God, which would make Israel rule the world. Other works of apocalyptic type, such as the *Book of Daniel*, prepared the way for the advent of the Messiah who would found an empire, an empire ruled by the Almighty and no longer by alien races. The *Books of Enoch* (first century BC) belong to the same period and order of ideas. The attempt to maintain the purity of the tradition and the Law was, however, easier in Palestine than in any of the areas of the Diaspora. There, at least among the more educated classes, there was bound to be much give-and-take with native ideas; comparisons and syncretisms were made between the Hebrew religion and other religions. This happened very early and on a large scale in two areas.

In Asia Minor and in pre-Maccabean Palestine the meeting with local cults was almost inevitable. They had in common the use of the epithet the 'Highest' (*Hypsistos*), a name applied to the indigenous Attis; there was Sabazios whose name evoked the Sabbath; there were similar rituals for purification, and an analogous conception of a guardian angel who would guide its own charge to the seat of the blessed after his death.

If we leave out Parthia, the second area where an important meeting of religions took place was Egypt, and in particular Alexandria. There the Greek language was in such common use among Hebrews that for the understanding of their own Sacred Books they preferred to use the Greek translation, the earliest parts of which appear to go back to the times of Ptolemy Philadelphus. Later, when the inaccuracies of this translation were noticed (they are easily explained by the difficulty of transferring the peculiar Hebrew conceptions and forms of expression into a language such as the Alexandrian Greek *koiné*, which has a completely different structure), this version was gradually removed and no fewer than three other translations were substituted in the Imperial period.

The blending of religious ideas was natural enough in such surroundings; and there was an obvious likeness between the ideas of the Prophets and the 'Scriptures' in general on the one hand, and those of the philosophers and of Greek 'mystery' works on the other—although the Jews were wedded to the belief that the latter derived from the Hebrew. Such a tendency was naturally opposed by a party whom we may call 'particularists'; but the resulting arguments ended by provoking the formation of several Jewish-Pagan sects who were strongly at variance with one another. The comparisons and syncretisms were not without strong support in the Hebrew camp, for instance in the work attributed to 'Rabbi Qoheleth' (*c.* 200 BC) or in the 'explanation of the Mosaic laws' (at the beginning of the second century) by Aristobulus, who was both a Jew and a peripatetic philosopher, or in the 'Book of Wisdom' by the pseudo-Solomon. But we find this tendency above all in the writings of Philo (*c.* 30 BC—*c.* AD 40) whose clarity and influence on later works caused him to be known as the Jewish Plato. Philo, an expert on the Bible and also on Greek philosophy, wrote works expounding the *Pentateuch*, defending Judaism (*Moses*, and *An Apologia for the Jews*), setting forth a religious philosophy (*On the Contemplative Life, On the Liberty of the Sages, Treatises on Providence*, etc.), and other works of a historical type (*The Embassy to Caligula*, the *Contra Flaccum*). His theories were of great importance in creating an atmosphere in which the Christian idea could develop. They mark an intermediate stage between Plato, the Bible, and the Fathers of the Church: these last continued to use his works which, though clear and frequently enlivened by imaginative and creative lyricism, are long-winded and weighed down by a parade of technical terminology. His greatest aim was to attract pagans to Judaism because, according to him, the revelations of Moses, by explaining the creed, had made it possible to attain the true philosophy which Pythagoras, Plato, and Aristotle had drawn from Judaism. His thought is not always consistent, either on the nature of the matter with which God eschews all relationship, or on that of the beings intermediate between God and this matter. The word (*logos*) used by God to create the world coincides with the neo-Pythagorean word *logos*, and Philo deals at great length with this great mediator with God. According to him the conflict between the spirit and the flesh is fundamental: morality consists in destroying sin, but as in Platonic ethics, there is no true virtue without faith and the intention of serving God. Biblical history is dissolved into allegories and becomes a series of myths. Philo's idea of science is Platonic. Fundamental Jewish ideas, such as the Messiah, do not interest him much.

It is clear that the proselytizing of the Palestinian Pharisaic Judaism and that of the Hellenistic Hebrew gnosticism led towards different lives, but both developed because both found minds and hearts quick to accept them. Jewish propaganda was not regarded favourably by frivolous people because the austerity of its rites, its simplicity of dogma, and the purity of its ethics were not designed for ordinary people. Yet the fervour of their propaganda for the unity of God, and the virtuous nature of their lives, drew supporters. But the Hebraic gnosticism of Alexandria had many more followers since it did not demand that pagans should abandon their traditional culture; indeed this culture was actually essential to it.

So we can conclude that the most important consequence of the Jewish Diaspora was to effect some breach in the exclusive national religion which had been the fundamental characteristic of the old Israel, and so to make easier the transition to the universal Christianity of later years.

5. GREECE

a. *The Rise of Scepticism*

The political separatism of the Greeks, even after their common adoption of the Homeric-Olympian élite divinities, steadfastly retained the original variety of religious ideas and pantheon from region to region. In every colony religious practice was altered and diversified through the adoption of local cults or syncretism with them; and cities which came under the hegemony of another were affected by the cults of the ruling power. Mythology was continually modified by the unrestrained licence of poets; and the gods of one people became heroes among other people, and changed their genealogies. The lack of a powerful priestly class common to all Greeks made it impossible to control these variations, while the contrast between the refined conception of divinity maintained by philosophy and the banal, often immoral, 'lives' of the gods, humanized by the poets, was too strong. All this and a gradually increasing individualism helped to diminish the various state-religions in the minds of the more educated, while the misfortunes of wars loosened the hold of the traditional gods, who had been vaunted as defenders of the cities (*poliad*), on the minds of the poorer classes. The educated classes shocked the ordinary people by paying attention to the theories of an Anaxagoras (according to whom the sun was nothing but 'one huge incandescent stone') or to the atheistic ideas of some sophists; or by tolerating the dramatists' parodies of certain myths; and, on occasions, perpetrating acts of sacrilege such as those blamed on Alcibiades' circles, the mutilation of the Hermae and the parodies of the Eleusinian mysteries. On the other hand the rough and primitive religious attitude of the common people, teeming with superstitions and fatuous magic practices, irritated the more educated classes. We are able to follow the development of this complex phenomenon particularly at Athens and in the period of the long war to the death with Sparta (431–404 BC).[4]

The outbreak of the war was bad enough; but when it was followed by the
early disappointments, and then by anti-democratic moves which were still
unavailing to avert the final collapse, it may have seemed to the Athenians
that the disasters they had suffered were a punishment inflicted by outraged
divinities. So a sharp and violent reaction in the field of religion was inevitable.
Then the lack of interest and scepticism which the ruling classes showed
towards the old religion of their fathers, the contempt and the parodies, the
irreverent confiscation of sacred treasures, the obvious agnosticism of
Protagoras, the astonishing claims of Anaxagoras, the atheism of Diagoras
of Melos, the parodies and criticisms in Euripides, greatly aroused the anger
of the people. Trials and sentences followed against the unbelievers: Anaxagoras (432), Alcibiades (415), Protagoras (411), Diagoras (411). Euripides also
ran into trouble.

In the meantime the religious feelings of the mob also found an outlet and
satisfaction in the introduction of pathetic, orgiastic, and violent new cults
derived from Phrygia (Cybele, the Great Mother, Sabazius), from Cyprus
(Aphrodite and Adonis), from Egypt (Ammon), from Thrace (Cotytto and
Bendis). Initiation into the Orphic and Pythagorean secrets or to Demeter's
mysteries at Eleusis, or to those of the great Cabeiroi on Samothrace, became
commoner than ever.

Faced by this revival of religious feeling and the tendency towards new
superstitions, the upper classes, though scornful of these excesses and in
private indifferent to them, adopted in public an attitude of recognition:
sometimes they were attracted by the charm of the Dionysiac cult, like
Euripides in the *Bacchae*, his last tragedy.5 Between these two trends, the
scepticism of the upper classes and the superstitions of the *demos*, stood
Socrates, the man who dealt the heaviest blows against the Sophistic movement, and whose thought inspired all later generations of Greeks. Of his
religious beliefs and martyrdom we shall speak later.

b. *The Greek Religion and Hellenistic Conquests*

The conquests of Alexander the Great in the East, and the subsequent
creation of a number of new Greek states, did not bring chaotic consequences.
In general the oriental cults and their temples underwent no great vicissitudes. There were some disagreements between the Egyptian priests and
the ruling Ptolemies, under Ptolemy I, IV, and VIII; the Seleucid attempts
to confiscate the temple treasures in 210 and 187 provoked reactions; and
there were the inevitable difficulties with the monotheistic Hebrews, particularly when Antiochus IV determined to Hellenize their cults. But on
more than one occasion Alexander had found himself defending the local
religions and priests against real or alleged abuses by the ruling Persians; and
from that time on the cults of the Eastern peoples were generally respected
and their temples enriched.

For the Greeks themselves direct contact with so many exotic cults did not seem to create great difficulties. It was easy to invent or deduce new identifications between many such cults and the Hellenistic pantheon; for others the way was open for their introduction into Greece, where the list of divinities became like a book without end.

Never did the Hellenic cults, at any rate in Eastern countries, appear more splendid in their works of art, their temples, their votive offerings, and their festivals; for they helped to glorify the new Greek cities which were being founded in those lands. Nevertheless, believers felt that the traditional religion of *poliad* (protecting *polis*) divinities was not able to fulfil the more refined service that was now demanded of it—of satisfying human feeling and guaranteeing happiness after death. Intimate forms of worship were gradually confined to a few of the more cherished figures such as Zeus, Dionysus, and Asclepius; and to these was added Tyche (Fortune), to whom Aristotle and thereafter the Epicureans had already given recognition.

The new practice of deifying Hellenistic sovereigns, which took different forms according to areas and habits, ended by weakening still further the concept of gods in human form. Various essential factors brought about the new practice: the revival in Greece of the hero-cult to include 'men of distinction' and 'founders'; the example of Egypt, the only oriental dynasty whose divine nature was a dogma; and the admiration and adulation given to the great benevolent rulers. From these emerged the bold theories of Euhemerus, who in his 'Sacred History' held that even the traditional divinities were in general only great human figures, the kings of old who had been deified.

Everything appeared to push the educated people towards new concepts of divinity—loftier, more monotheistic, more intellectual—and so to lead them to take refuge in syncretistic movements.

c. *Religious and Philosophic Syncretism*

While, as we shall see, ancient Greece remained to the fore in philosophic progress, religious changes were pioneered by the new Greek lands of the East. Religious feeling, even if it was unsatisfied, was not dead among the Greeks: neither among the philosophers, who argued about a single god, a *nous* or a pure act which gave movement to the world, a being beyond imagining, a governor of the Universe; nor among the people, who in the depths of their superstition had recourse to fortune-tellers, questioned the oracles, were initiated at the Mysteries, and frequented foreigners' temples.

On this state of affairs were superimposed the new syncretistic trends from the East, both from Egypt, where the government had sponsored a flourishing cult of universal character based on native traditions, and from Syria and Chaldea, where what seemed vague ideas evolved by Greek philosophers were given embodiment in the astrological theories of those countries.

In Egypt Ptolemy Soter, in order to give religious unity to his Greek and Egyptian subjects, transferred the cult of Osiris Apis (or Serapis, as the Greeks called him) from the old native capital of Memphis to the new capital of Alexandria, where Isis was already being worshipped. Serapis was a miracle-working god, who had revealed himself to the king. He procured the salvation of the faithful after their deaths; and he alone dominated the whole world—in the heavens, the earth, the sea, and in hell. He embraced the whole of humanity. He was a god who contained in himself all the Greek and Egyptian gods so that none could supersede him; he could place them all in a great subordinate pantheon; and he allowed himself to be worshipped by the priests of all peoples. Linked with the belief in after-life and with the doctrine of the Mysteries of Demeter which had been taken to Alexandria and called Isiac (by the syncretism of Demeter with Isis) the Serapis cult spread in Egypt and beyond it wherever the Nile merchants went.

The syncretism which spread to the ancient Greek world from the Seleucid zones was in contrast astral in base. For some time in Greece there had been a tendency, indirectly influenced as well by the East, towards coalition between astronomical and philosophical studies, leading to a pantheistic astral doctrine within which the Greek divinities were identified with the stars worshipped by the Syrians and Chaldeans. From Pythagoras and Plato down to Aristotle the tendency to identify the stars with divinities became ever sharper; and for the first time, in the *Epinomis* attributed to Plato, the planets take the names of the traditional gods. Later, when Alexander had conquered the Syrian and Mesopotamian world, Syrian and Chaldean astrologers began to tour Greek lands; and the Babylonian priest Berosus, for example, set up a school of astrology at Cos. So it is not surprising that in Stoic theory, evolved first by Eastern philosophers, like Zeno, who had migrated to Greece,[6] a pantheistic concept of the universe predominates. Stoicism combines all that the Greeks succeeded in evolving on their own account with what the East had taught them. It was a spiritual religious doctrine, according to which worship could consist only in understanding of the divine nature.

Not all minds of course were able to reach the heights of Stoic theory. The Greek populace were content to see the astrologers, particularly the charlatans who had come from the East, as magicians, and in their dazzling theories to fall ever deeper into vulgar superstition.

In the meantime genuine Pythagoreanism, which had been dying for centuries, still existed in some form in the Orphic-Pythagorean Mysteries, and in the so-called 'Pythagorean life' of asceticism. These ideas, linked with others borrowed from Plato, Aristotle, and the Stoics, were developed until they formed the creed of a neo-Pythagorean school at Alexandria. This school maintained that, while corruptible matter is governed by necessity, God is transcendent and unknowable, and that the intermediary between God and man is formed by the *logos*. The relation between the gods of the past and the one God lay in the fact that they were particular and local expressions of Him. The neo-Pythagorean faith was spread by regular missionaries, preachers, and comforters, many of whom came from among the Cynics. They assisted in teaching the young to live; they prepared men for death; they sought to give all men an assurance that their hopes were firmly grounded in a just future after death, the other life being an appropriate reward for a man's deserts in this one; and they set themselves to satisfy the religious feeling of mankind. The actual ceremonies of these cults were striking and attractive: they resorted to fortune-telling, magical mani-festations, music, the recitation of mysterious and incomprehensible phrases, acts of purification and expiation, and public confessions with declarations made in writing. According to these neo-Pythagoreans the soul is subjected in hell to various purifications, and, depending on the degree of purity achieved, returns to earth in the form of a plant, an animal, or another human being; life is a brief second and should be lived in purity.

Of another syncretistic trend—the Hebrew-Hellenistic—we have spoken earlier.

d. *Systems of Cosmogony*

We have seen (Chapter IX) how in the course of the fifth century in Greece, and particularly after the successful result of the 'Persian Wars', there was a lively development in scientific research; in mathematics and astronomy, in biology and medicine.[7] From these researches sprang a keen new impulse to study the origins of the world; Empedocles of Acragas (*c.*490–430), was said to be a pupil of the Pythagoreans, as well as of Parmen-ides and Anaxagoras. He was of noble birth and took an active part in the political life of his city before withdrawing to the new foundation of Thurii and then going on to the Peloponnese and to Athens. He was a highly religious mystic, famous as a worker of miracles, a pioneer in many kinds of literature and science, and regarded as the founder of Sicilian rhetoric. He wrote an historical poem and, perhaps, a medical treatise; he was an expert on meteorology and hydraulics; but his fame rested above all on two philosophic poems which indicated his attitude towards scientific experiment, towards the materialistic Monism of the Ionians, and towards the spiritualism of the Eleatics. In the first poem of about 2,000 lines 'On the Nature of Things' he gives a new rational and mechanical explanation of the world. The four elements, which he calls 'the roots of things' are fire, light, earth, and water. These can never die, but they are variously blended by love which tends to unite them in the 'Sphere'; and at this point the cosmic cycle enters a stage of calm and of not-being in the perceptible world. Hate, on the other hand, tends to divide the elements and when it succeeds they are no longer compounded in any particular object. The being of things is therefore given by the antithesis between love and hate, and endures in the cosmic periods intermediate between those in which one or other of these forces is temporarily dominant. In the other poem, 'The Purifications', he propounds the mystico-religious aim of showing men the fundamental aspirations of the human soul, overflowing (like Xenophanes) all anthropomorphic and polytheistic concept of divinity, and believing (like Pythagoras) in the immortality of the soul and its purification in metempsychosis through successive human and non-human existences. From this belief it followed that man must purify himself, and must respect the beings, plant and animal, which marked the stages in the progressive rise of the souls they entertained, souls which were indestructible and of divine origin.

For Anaxagoras of Clazomenae, Leucippus, and Democritus, see above, pp. 421 f.

e. *The Sophists—Socrates*

Faced with the irreconcilable contradictoriness of the various systems put forward to account for the world which surrounded them, the Greeks were assailed by the doubt, already advanced by Parmenides, whether the senses could give more than subjective truth; and Heraclitus even questioned human reason. So some men tried to attain a form of cognition surer than that provided by the senses: others adopted a scepticism of a more or less absolute kind, or reconciled themselves to a truth which was relative. Indeed this relativism which was apparently established in cognition seemed to make itself evident in many other fields as well. In religion, for instance, anthropomorphism had been overthrown by Xenophanes; and his polytheism gave place to the idea, admittedly tenuous as yet,[8] of a single divinity, like the *nous* of Anaxagoras, though some people began to demand proofs of the very existence of any divine power. The same tendency is found in ethics and in law. It was now established that every people was governed by different laws and customs. Some thinkers therefore set up as superior to all else a common natural law, the law of the strongest and the weakest; others disputed this, and insisted on the distinction between man as a social being and animals. Finally what was one to make of dialectic, when every day one could see, in assemblies and law-courts, how oratorical skill, by the process of suggestion, could overthrow justice?

So the Sophists grew up, at first identical with the orators, but assuming decisive importance in the evolution of Greek thought and writing. They attracted to themselves the young men who were eager for advancement, and who were captivated by the audacity of the new propositions and the sparkling character of the dialectical debates. The speakers were grandiloquently called 'sophistai' or wise men (experts); but after Socrates and his diatribes this name acquired the derogatory meaning of 'tricksters', just as a fallacious or specious piece of reasoning was called a 'sophisma'. Even now, when so many centuries have intervened, many people repeat the view taken by their contemporary detractors that the Sophists misdirected Greek thought and made it sceptical, empty, formal, and amoral.

This judgement contains something of the truth, but it is greatly exaggerated. There were great and small Sophists, some harmful, some harmless; and there was never one general sophistic theory, but rather a number of Sophists of differing views possessing certain features in common. These features included contempt for the metaphysics of earlier days, confidence in their own power of reasoning, a desire for novelty which was sometimes exaggerated and arrogant, and (to some extent at least) a significant tinge of scepticism. Yet the Sophists were not always harmful, and in any case they had other qualities. They toured the country, and for a fairly modest fee would give young Greeks of the better families a kind of instruction which had never been provided before, teaching them to express themselves and defend their theses and opinions. They made known the doctrines of philosophers and the discoveries of scientists, and they opened men's minds to the finer issues of philosophy, ethics, logic, and aesthetics. It was in the sophistic movement that the mind of Pericles, the drama of Euripides, and the scientific history of Thucydides were fashioned; and it was this movement which evoked the thinking of Socrates, promoted study of language and grammar, and spread abroad an interest in the exposition of ancient texts and in the history of their transmission.

The sophistic movement started simultaneously among the East Greeks (those of the Hellespont and Asia Minor) and among the Greeks of Sicily. It acquired a close connection with the new ideas in Rhetoric, and so made its way to mainland Greece and Athens, where, like the Encyclopaedism of the eighteenth century, it acted as a leavening influence on all thought and literature. Two of the greatest Sophists deserve a mention.[9] Protagoras of Abdera (480–410) lived his life journeying round the Greek lands, especially to Sicily, to Thurii, where he drew up the legal code, and to Athens, from which he was probably banished during the oligarchic reaction of 411. He made large profits from his teaching, and wrote discourses, such as the 'Case for a Salary', together with various treatises. But his main philosophical work was entitled *Truth*, and it contained his two famous maxims: that on the relativity of knowledge ('Man is the measure of all things, of being in so far as it exists and of not-being in so far as it does not exist'); and the maxim about the impossibility of proving divine existence ('About the gods I can say nothing, neither that they exist nor that they do not; many things prevent one from knowing, such as the obscurity of the problem and the shortness of human life'). Protagoras was accused of having taught his pupils to 'make the worse cause appear the better', and it seems true that his oratory attempted to convince his hearers of the conclusion he set out to prove, even when this conclusion was unfair. Yet it remains the case that he imparted ethical instruction to his pupils, and did so lavishly. He taught by giving examples, some allegorical, others evidential or explanatory; he was effective in making his hearers commit pieces to memory; and he supervised debates in which one side would contradict the other.[10]

Prodicus of Iulis on Ceos (*c.*470–400) came to Athens as an ambassador and took up residence there. He liked to study the precise value of terms and the validity of synonyms, and Plato mimicked this passion of his. In ethics he upheld the old traditional ideas, in his *Horae* he told the pleasant story of Heracles at the cross-roads, giving exhortations to domestic and public virtues in so orthodox a fashion that Socrates used to call him Master.

Simultaneously with the anti-democratic reaction which engaged many young Athenians of noble family in 411 and 404 there was a reaction against all the characteristic culture of the democracy, and especially against sophism —which had been this culture's pivot. The uneducated masses too were ready to regard sophism as the cause of all corruption and of all their ills, and consequently to strike at its most vulnerable flank, namely its religious scepticism. The symbol of this crucial phase in the struggle of thought was Socrates, who had personally involved himself amid the various currents of opinion in a way from which there was no drawing back.

Socrates (470–399), the son of a sculptor and a midwife, had been given some small education, but was deeply devout, especially in respect to the god of Delphi. He had given up his father's craft and was content with the very modest standard of life allowed him by his tiny patrimony. He devoted himself wholly to the mission to which, since his boyhood, he had been drawn by divine inspiration—by a voice (*daimon*) within him which urged him on[11] at every stage. This mission consisted in teaching about what was truly good and in improving men who were like himself. He had no organic system; and he was not a Sophist in the sense in which the word was then used; for he ran no regular courses and claimed no pay from his hearers. He used to stop and discuss in any place with anyone who willed, from the noblest Athenians down to the sons of slaves; and the argument about 'what each thing really is', conducted with great dialectical skill, inevitably led his interlocutor to confess his ignorance, at which point the process of rational reconstruction would begin.

We have no direct acquaintance with Socrates' doctrines, which he did not leave behind him in written form. We know them through the statements of his pupils, who often dressed them up in various ways. Xenophon weakened their force and Plato heightened it, as befitted these two men's intellectual powers and personal views. In general one can at least regard as Socratic that of which we have agreed testimony from pupils whose outlook was different.

Socrates did not concern himself with problems of natural science. He was interested in man as a rational being, a being whose good consists in knowledge. But to achieve knowledge one must not rest, as the Sophists did, on opinions derived from sensations, which are changeable, relative, and conflicting. Rather one must, by means of argument, eliminate from the data of the senses everything that is contingent and individual, so as to reach a definition of the essence of each thing—to discover its universal 'concept',[12] which is the truth acceptable by all men and not by an individual alone. This is the inductive process by which an examination of many just things, or many beautiful things, or many trees, leads one to define what is 'just', what is 'beautiful', what is 'a tree'.

Applying this principle of cognition to the Good, Socrates asserted that the Good consisted in Knowledge, in organizing one's behaviour and directing one's search for happiness in a rational manner, rising above impulses and opinions to be guided by the 'concepts'. The greatest ill afflicting humanity is ignorance. We must act well because to do so is useful (and some pupils, like Xenophon, stopped at this proposition because their mentality did not allow them to go further), and still more because it is pleasing to the gods, the intelligent authors of an ordered world and of ethical concepts with divine and absolute value, concepts useful to mankind. These are the old concepts which have been handed down. In this way human morality consisted for Socrates in obedience to divinity and in living with divinity; and it was this that constituted the loftiest and most lasting part of his teaching.

But there was also a part which was more of an innovation and which tended to supersede the traditional religion. Although he never disowned the ordinary furniture of mythology, and even declared he was a worshipper of the sun and the moon, Socrates was in fact subverting the religious ideas of the city. The 'daimon' to which he continually alluded, and which may have been, as Plato implies, simply conscience, was, in the end, partly because of the exaggerated language of some of his pupils, believed by outsiders to be a new independent divinity, introduced by the philosopher without the permission of the people. There began an obtuse opposition, of which as early as 423 Aristophanes was a mouthpiece in his *Clouds*; yet for another quarter of a century the philosopher was able to continue his discussions and mode of life undisturbed. But when the new democracy was established after the overthrow of the oligarchic 'tyrants', accusations and hatred were poured on Socrates as the teacher of Alcibiades, Critias, and many other young aristocrats to whom the country's ruin was ascribed. With the agreement, in all good faith, of a citizen named Anytus, a man who wanted Athens to have concord at home, Socrates was in 399 accused of corrupting the youth, of not believing in his country's gods, and of introducing new divinities. It was thought that he would defend himself, but he declared that he was innocent and that he deserved to be maintained at public expense in the Prytaneum; moreover he affirmed that he had no fear of death, because his disciples would carry on his work. He was condemned to death by a small majority. It was thought that he would make his escape from the prison, which was not well guarded; but he would not do so, and instead drank the hemlock. His voluntary martyrdom brought sublimation to his doctrines. Within a few years all Greece was filled with Socratics; and Plato, Xenophon, and the rest were competing with one another to give clear exposition of their master's thought and to glorify his martyr's death.

No less than five schools appeared as off-shoots of Socrates' teaching and propounded their own systems. A few words may first be said about four of them, which were of minor importance and linked Socrates with pre-Socratic features: longer treatment will be reserved for the fifth school.

The Megarian school and the very closely related school of Elis developed the Socratic dialectic of the Concept, combining it with certain propositions of Parmenides, and using Zeno's method to put forward a general thesis and refute objections. To Euclides of Megara the only reality lay in changeless and incorporeal entities, and the world of sense was illusory. Good was unchangeable: it was reason, and God, and the only concept which had existence.

The Cynics were led by Antisthenes of Athens (*c.*440–360), a pupil of Gorgias and Socrates, and later by Diogenes of Sinope (d. 323), who was known as the 'mad Socrates'. They maintained, against Socrates, that cognition consisted in sensation, that there were no definable general concepts, and that only the individual was real and possessed an existence which could be intuited. Virtue was the one Good, making us like to God: all the rest, art and science, pleasures and pains, were indifferent matters. Man, they thought, must renounce all forms of culture which did not conduce to virtue. He must return to the state of nature, abolish social distinctions, and reduce his material needs, thus making happiness consist in misery. These theories were upheld not only with words and writings but by the practical example set by Cynics who lived squalid and miserable lives, and appear to have influenced proletarian and social revolutionary movements during the following centuries.

Directly opposed to the Cynics were the Cyrenaics or hedonists, who were indifferent to the religious problem and concerned themselves only with ethics. They maintained that the true good of man consisted in the mental and physical pleasure generated by sensations. But although man must savour this pleasure he must keep such freedom as enabled him to possess pleasure and not be possessed by it.

But these lesser schools, which largely differed from Socrates, remained for some time isolated and smothered on account of the overwhelming success of Plato and Aristotle. Only later, as we shall see, did they develop and expand under new forms.

f. *Plato and the Academy*

Aristocles, called Plato (428–347), was of noble Athenian family and had learned to write poetry as a boy. He always remained a poet at heart, but later was taught by Cratylus and, from 407, by Socrates, the latter of whom he loved as if he had been his son. After Socrates' death he stayed in Megara, perhaps then in Egypt, and then in southern Italy, where he was friendly with the Pythagorean Archytas and others. He then spent some time in Syracuse. His political career in democratic Athens had been brought to an end on account of the oligarchic views of his family,[13] and he thought he might be able to bring to reality at Syracuse his perfect constitution, which may be an idealization of the constitution of Sparta. But he was unable to convince the Syracusan ruler Dionysius I. So he returned to Athens and opened a school in the gymnasium of the Academy, where he taught first mathematics and later on philosophy. Pupils came from every part of Greece, and his discussions with them enlarged his knowledge on various matters, including the ideas of scholars in distant lands; these pupils were very numerous, drawn mostly from influential families. After two more fruitless attempts to impose his 'constitution', now brought up to date, on the Syracusans, he returned to his Athenian school until the time of his death.

Plato was a man of very great culture, learned in the various philosophical systems of his own day and of the past, and he possessed notable artistic ability in both speaking and writing. He had enormous success in carrying the Socratic doctrines to perfection. The theory of 'concepts', which Socrates had confined almost entirely to ethical thought, was extended by Plato to the whole world and was transformed, with essential features drawn from other schools, into the Theory of 'Ideas'.[14] This meant that for him there were so many universal ideas, incorporeal, eternal, and intelligible, which corresponded to the various types of object. They were conceived by the divine worker (*demiourgos*) as single entities in a hierarchic system, and were given actuality by Him within the formless matter of the original chaos, this being the way in which He created the world of perceptible nature, which consists of a number of copies of the ideas. The human soul, the higher element in which, namely reason, is the work of God, once upon a time had direct knowledge of the ideas. But when it was united with a body it forgot them, and only with great labour, through the experience of the senses, can it remember them, subject to limitless possibilities of error.

Plato agreed with Socrates that knowledge led to virtue and to happiness. But accepting Orphic and Pythagorean views of life after death, he added that the whole process must serve as a preparation for the after-life, because the soul, after a series of more or less painful reincarnations, is able to return to its earliest state and to its divine home. The ethical ideal consists in harmony between body and soul: more specifically it involves justice, wisdom, fortitude, and temperance.

In his last years Plato came increasingly under the influence of the mystical and numerical theories of the Pythagoreans, and established a reconciliation between them and his own Theory of Ideas, the result being pictured in mathematical figures and relationships. He also concerned himself, as we said above, with the constitution of the ideal state; and in an early design for it, set out in his *Republic*, he idealized and completed the constitution of the city which had at that time become famous through its victory and its hegemony, namely Sparta.[15] He propounded a state consisting of three parts: the philosophers, educated in mathematics and dialectic, represented Reason, and were therefore at the head of the government; the warriors defended the state and advanced its gymnastic and musical education; and finally there were the peasants and merchants, who had no part in politics. The main task of this state was to advance under discipline towards justice,[16] and as a consequence all particular interests, such as the family and private property, had to be eliminated. Later, when his attempts to give his Republic reality at Syracuse had failed and when the Spartan hegemony had fallen,[17] Plato in his *Laws* made a new constitutional design, taking more account of the actual political and social conditions of the Greek world.

Plato's literary output was immense. In the main he wrote short dialogues in which he applied the Socratic dialectic and set out to defend his master's theories and his own by confuting the Sophists and representatives of other schools. In these the characters are drawn with great artistry in their real features. They engage in lively discussion in a language of the purest Attic; the style is harmonious and controlled, capable of becoming stirring or tense, ironical or lyrical, as occasion demands. In some passages too one can feel the poet in Plato, and it is not surprising that some of his works, in the enthusiasm of his dialectical triumph, actually end with mythical sections.

Apart from the poetical fragments, the ancient corpus of Plato included forty-two dialogues, thirteen letters, and a certain number of 'definitions'. But the ancients already recognized that seven of the dialogues were spurious, and some modern scholars have shown good ground (in my view at least) for supposing the same for many letters and the definitions. The authorship of some of the remaining thirty-five dialogues is also in doubt.

The school founded by Plato had a long life and was directed by a long succession of heads. Its history, to which we shall return later, is normally divided into three periods, called the Older, Middle, and New Academies.

g. *Aristotle and the Peripatetics*

Yet Aristotle, the greatest of Plato's pupils (384–322), founded a school of his own. He was born at Stagirus in Chalcidice of a family of doctors, and his own early education,[18] which had an important influence on his philosophical studies, was concerned with medicine and natural science. In 367 he came to Athens and stayed there for twenty years: though a very faithful pupil of Plato he also came under the influence of Isocrates' teaching. When Plato died in 347, Aristotle went to Asia Minor and on to Mitylene; then in 343/2 he was made the tutor of the young Alexander of Macedon; then when Alexander took Athens in 335/4, Aristotle settled there with his friend Theophrastus, opened a school in the Lyceum, and taught there for twelve years. The scholars of the school were known as Peripatetics because their master used to teach while walking up and down the avenues. Finally Aristotle was attacked as a friend of Alexander and prosecuted for impiety. He gave charge of the school to Theophrastus and left Athens in 323. Shortly afterwards he died.

Aristotle's output was enormous; one should perhaps rather say the output of his school, since his pupils collaborated with him and the works which have come down to us are often drafts for his lectures or notes and versions made by pupils. Diogenes Laertius tells us that Aristotle wrote 146 works in 400 books (others speak of 1,000 books), a total of 445,270 lines. His scientific curiosity, sustained by a rich library, was universal and encyclopaedic. He concerned himself with everything that could be known, and had so vast an acquaintance with all philosophical schools that he can also, with reason, be called the first historian of Greek philosophy.

Many of his works are lost, for instance a few dialogues of the Platonic type and some popularizing writings. The collection which has come down to us was derived from a copy of the Aristotelian corpus brought to Rome in 84 BC after having been hidden away for a long period.

With his *Organon*, the collection of works on logic and the theory of knowledge, Aristotle was the founder of knowledge through syllogisms, that is to say the understanding of causes by means of reasoning. In this process one either passes from general premises to particular deductions or from particular premises to general inductions. Experience leads to knowledge, by means of the senses, of individual substances which have real existence; and from experience one proceeds, by means of thought, to intellectual understanding of being or intelligible form.

The work called 'First Philosophy' is devoted to metaphysics, and in it Aristotle rejects Plato's Theory of Ideas.[19] The live individual or organism is a union of two basic elements, one potential, the other actual. It consists, in other words, first of indeterminate matter, possessing no form but capable of assuming form, a potential element able to become something and be made perfect; and secondly of form, the actuality which determines its nature, the perfect 'idea' of the species it represents. Beings are arranged in a hierarchy with two heads, God and crude matter. Every intermediate being is matter or potentiality in relation to the being immediately above it. One being only is entirely pure actuality and unchanging form: that is God, who gave the first impulse to universal movement and life.

On the natural sciences or 'physics' Aristotle wrote his *Physics, De Caelo, Meteorologica, Historia Animalium, De Generatione et Corruptione, De Generatione Animalium,* and other works. Many lesser writings on kindred topics seem to be spurious. There are for him two opposing worlds: the heavens full of unalterable, unchanging ether, moving in circular motion; and the earth, on which everything is composed of the four elements, moving vertically and continually being transformed. The earth is fixed and spherical, surrounded by the moving planetary spheres, besides which there are the fixed stars and the ethereal sky. On the earth there exist inorganic beings, composed of elements but lacking soul, and also living organisms possessing soul. Plants have only a vegetative soul; animals have a sensitive soul as well; only in man is there a third soul, the intellectual. Aristotle's studies on the behaviour and psychology of animals, on anatomy, and on physiology are most remarkable, and his classifications of being in a scale of nature are still fundamental.

The treatises *De Anima* and the so-called *Parva Naturalia* are concerned with psychology, dealing with such subjects as perception, memory, length of life, sleep, and death. The soul, which is form and act, is the principle of life, being joined to the body, which is potentiality and matter. The philosopher also examines the various moments when human cognition becomes actual, when sense-perception (*anima sensitiva*) and intellectual (*anima intellectiva*) are acting together. He goes on to study the senses, the operation of the intellect, and other matters.

His works on morals are the *Nicomachean Ethics*, the *Eudemian Ethics*, and the *Magna Moralia*.[20] The supreme good of man is happiness, consisting not only in riches and pleasure, or in friendship and health, but essentially in reason or virtue. Moral virtue is to keep the just mean between too much and too little: and intellectual virtues include intelligence, science, and wisdom.

On political and allied questions he wrote the *Politics*, and there are fragments of some of 158 short works on constitutions, among which we possess on a papyrus the *Constitution of Athens*. The *Economicus* also exists, though with substantial re-editing and rearrangement. Man in these works is regarded as a social being by nature, and individual happiness can only be attained within social organization, which from the primitive bond of the family evolves towards its most perfect form in the state. Yet it is strange that Aristotle, who lived in the days of the great state organisms like that of Macedonia, still conceives his ideal state, with the exception of some remarks on kingship, in terms of the tiny size of the ancient Greek *poleis*. In order to write his work on politics he wanted to be acquainted with individual constitutions, and his school accordingly collected material on the history of 158 Greek constitutions, together with those of Carthage and Lycia, although some (the *Athenian Constitution* for example) were written after the *Politics* had been completed. In his view no constitution was wholly good or wholly bad, since much depended on the temper of the people concerned. He laid down three superior forms of government, monarchy, aristocracy, and republic; and three inferior forms, tyranny, oligarchy, and democracy. His preference was for a constitution in which all had equal rights in law but in which the rulers were the older members of the middle class, the best men, the aristocracy of intellect and virtue rather than the aristocracy of birth and wealth. He also devoted his inquiries to the method of apportioning the powers into which sovereignty of the state can be divided; the deliberative powers, the executive, and the judiciary.

The *Poetics*, an incomplete work, and the *Rhetoric* are concerned with literary theory. Art in Aristotle's view depended on the spirit of imitation and tries to purify the emotions. It allowed one to overcome the failings of

(a)

[von Matt

41   HELLENISTIC STATUARY

(a) *Head of Medusa, from Acrae, Sicily*

(b) *Fisherman, from the Esquiline. Rome, Palazzo dei Conservatori*

(b)   [Alinari

42   *The battle of Alexander and Cyrus; mosaic from Pompeii. Naples, National Museum*

a) [B.M.

43 MOSAICS

    (a) *from Utica depicting a hunting scene. London, British Museum*

    (b) *from Ostia depicting tritons and marine deities. Ostia, the Thermae*

b) [Alinari

[Alinari

44

(a) *Volterra, the 'arch gate', c. 300 BC*

(b) *Rome, the aqueduct of Claudius completed AD 52 and the Appian way*

[Alinari

nature by drawing one nearer to the universal. Beauty consisted in order, grandeur, and morality.

The breadth of his knowledge and scientific insight, the rigour of his researches, and the results he achieved made Aristotle the greatest among Greek philosophers and scientists. Philosophy with him was contemptuous of any stylistic dressing and literary artifices. It became a genuine science, and was expounded in a style which was precise and simple, although sometimes unduly monotonous and dry. We must not forget, however, that his works are often not books of his own, but 'notes' taken from scientific lectures.[21]

h. *The Stoics*

In the Hellenistic age it is generally true that philosophy mainly developed in the older Greek world, to which even people born in eastern parts migrated if they wanted to be philosophers; but that progress in science was chiefly the product of the new colonial lands in the East.

In Athens when Aristotle departed the direction of the Peripatetic school fell to Theophrastus of Eresus (*c.* 372–287), who had once been a pupil of Plato and was later Aristotle's most faithful follower. Although he never made great advances in ideas, he worked in every field where his master had sown, especially in natural scientific research; and he made a powerful contribution to the school's reputation. He wrote 240 works, and also organized the school in a manner which served as a model to the Museum of Alexandria. We have already spoken about his scientific works. There survives, in a very heavily edited and corrupt text, a short work on 'Characters', comprising a description of thirty defects common to all mankind. They are described and analysed with great liveliness and polish, his style being simple, clear, and reasonably elegant.

The culture and output of Aristotle and Theophrastus were so enormous that one is not surprised to find pupils of theirs in every branch of knowledge. But most of these ignore the scientific side, to which their masters had devoted so much attention, and concern themselves rather with ethics, metaphysics, and so on.

The new school of the Stoics was in its origins connected with that of the Cynics. Zeno of Kition on the island of Cyprus (*c.* 334–262) was an Easterner like the last group of Cynics; indeed he was actually of Semitic blood, the son of a merchant. About 313 he took up residence in Athens, and attended the schools of Crates the Cynic, Stilpo the Megarian, and Polemo of the Academy. Later he founded his own school, and this was given the name of the Stoa because it was located in the portico painted by Polygnotus (*stoa poikile*). It quickly acquired a throng of young men, including the later king of Macedonia, Antigonus Gonatas, the son of Demetrius Poliorcetes, but its master continued to live a life of poverty in the Cynic style. For his teaching he used an Attic which was terse and epigrammatic, though perhaps not of the purest; and gradually he evolved his whole system. At the age of 72 he died by his own hand, leaving a number of works of which we possess only the titles and a few fragments: they included a *Politicus*, written from the communistic standpoint.

His successor at the head of the school in 262 was Cleanthes of Assos in the Troad (331–232). He lived in extreme poverty, for a long time exercising himself as an athlete and in later days watering his garden, replying to the mockery of his companions with wit and good temper. He continued to develop Stoic theories in a number of works on logic, rhetoric, physics, and theology. His *Hymn to Zeus*, which has survived, lays down the essential pantheistic principle of Stoicism. Cleanthes finally starved himself to death.

The next head after Cleanthes, from 232 onwards, was Chrysippus of Soloi in Cilicia (280–206), who before becoming a Stoic had belonged to the Academy. A tireless worker, formidable dialectician, and possessing an astonishing capacity for absorbing knowledge, he left behind him an imposing collection of writings in 705 books, which, though their style is careless and hurried, constitute a complete summary of Stoic theory. Numerous fragments remain.

With these first three heads of the school Stoicism completed the evolution of its doctrine. For them philosophy was wisdom in matters human and divine, and this wisdom led to virtue of thought (logic), virtue of understanding (physics), and moral virtue (ethics). Logic was the science of thought and discourse (it therefore comprised grammar and rhetoric as well), and the Stoics took pains to establish every possible form of syllogism. Knowledge came from sensations imprinted on the virgin human soul; the soul remembered them, and then from the multitude of similar images attained, by means of reason, to general notions. True representations were distinguished from false ones (phantasms) by their clarity, which compels belief in them.

Physics was the true science of everything material, that is everything that was real, namely nature, man, the principles of the universe, and God. Bodies had two principles, the passive one given by matter, and the active one which gives life to matter. The human soul, which resided in the heart and regulated the senses, speech, reproduction, and the principle of direction, was itself matter and destructible. God was the immanent soul of the world; and the old mythology was interpreted allegorically and rationalistically, since the gods were simply the forces of nature. The cosmic fire was the essence which gave life to nature, and from which the soul was formed. This fire changed chaos into air; from air came water, and from water earth; and after a Great Year (12,945 natural years) all would return to chaos. The world was governed by cause; all was linked together in a chain of cause and effect.

There was Good and Evil, but even from Evil Good could come; and the free man was he who lived according to the rules of Fate, which moved in accordance with reason. The end of life was happiness, which consisted in the Stoic virtue of living according to nature; for man this meant living according to reason, human reason being a part of universal or cosmic reason. Man must be self-sufficient; but just because his reason was part of universal reason he must live in society according to law, and all men must be considered equal in relation to nature.

This is pre-eminently a dogmatic and theological system of philosophy. It sprang from the minds not of true Greeks, but from those of Semites and Hellenizing Easterners. After these founders of Stoicism the school expanded and prospered down to late imperial times. Mention may be made here of Panaetius and Posidonius, who were 'eclectics' rather than orthodox members of the school.

Panaetius of Rhodes (180–110) studied at Pergamum with the grammarian Crates of Mallus and then at Athens with the Stoics Diogenes and Antipater. Later he lived for a long time at Rome in the Scipionic circle, was a friend of Polybius, and became the founder of Roman Stoicism. From 129 he was head of the Athenian school and published a number of works, especially on ethics, including *Duty* (drawn on by Cicero in his *De Officiis*), *Providence*, and *Politics*. He did not believe in divination or astrology; and he modified Stoic doctrines by contaminating them with whatever he found to be good in the works of Plato, Aristotle, Xenocrates, Theophrastus, Demetrius of Phalerum, and others.

Among Panaetius' pupils was Posidonius of Apamea (135–51), a man of encyclopaedic culture, who came to Rome in the course of his travels and conceived much affection for it. He later founded a school at Rhodes, which was attended by Cicero. Though a Stoic, he had eclectic views, verging towards mysticism: he believed in divining and in the immortality of the soul. Like Panaetius he wrote a work *On Duty*.

i. *The Epicureans*

Epicurus (341–271) was born at Samos, the son of an Athenian cleruch who had become a teacher. He began his studies at Samos, did military service at Athens in 324/3, and after teaching for a while at Mitylene and Lampsacus opened a school in a garden at Athens in 306. Three hundred books of his writings, of which 37 were *On Nature*, were current in antiquity. But his doctrine was also published in summaries of varying length, of which the most concise edition is that which has come down to us from Diogenes Laertius. In addition we possess substantial fragments of the work *On Nature*, together with some letters and some sayings. Moreover the ideas of Epicurus inspired the work of Lucretius, Philodemus, and Seneca, and are also quoted by opponents like Cicero and Plutarch.

According to Epicurus the objective of philosophy is a happy life, and therefore any science which does not conduce to that end is futile. The sole purpose of getting to understand nature is to free man from fear and superstition. Our senses do not deceive us, but our hypotheses about the causes of facts can often be erroneous. There certainly exist bodies formed of matter, for the senses tell us this: and reason adds that void exists as well. Matter is composed of atoms, innumerable, tiny, indivisible bodies of a simple kind, which are constantly uniting and separating. They fall in the void with a slant: so they strike one another, combine, and form bodies, and the bodies then dissolve again into atoms. In the measureless infinite void of the *cosmos* there exist, separately from the void itself, a vast number of worlds, though we have acquaintance with only one of them. These worlds are born and move without any purpose. By dint of successive experiments nature has made the world we live in, and man as we know him.

The soul is composed of the lightest kind of atoms. It cannot live without the body nor the body without it: when the body dies, the soul dies too. So it is absurd to fear death. All bodies emit images of themselves, composed of very light atoms which make their way to our senses and leave an impression there. Sometimes these images combine, this being the source of errors of the senses and concepts of the unreal. Epicurus was opposed to religion and to accepted forms of worship, but he was not an atheist. He believed that there were gods, since we have the concept of gods. But in his view they were blessed and immortal beings who did not concern themselves with mankind, living in the spaces between the worlds, an area where there existed only ether and where there was no movement of atoms. Accepted religion was born of fear, and its practices were wholly useless. Providence did not exist.[22]

In ethics Epicurus came under the influence of Cyrenaic theories. By nature man seeks pleasure and avoids pain, but happiness consists not in isolated and desultory pleasure but in *eudaimonia*, pleasure which was moderate, lasting, and serene. It is then that the body is without pain and the spirit free from cares. So happiness consists in a life which follows moderation, reason, and virtue.

j. *The Sceptics and the New Academy*

The philosophers of the Megarian school, who were affected also by Cynic ideas, were inclined towards scepticism, both in religious questions and in their theories of knowledge. This scepticism was developed into a regular system by Pyrrhon (*c.* 360–270), who drew negative conclusions from the disagreement between the ideas of different philosophers. Pyrrhon was born in Elis, and always resided there. He was a pupil of the Democritean philosopher Anaxarchus, and was heavily influenced by the Megarians: it is not impossible that he drew something from the idea of *ataraxia* put forward by the Indian ascetics, with some of whom he was personally acquainted. His sceptic doctrine can be roughly summarized as follows. Nothing exists in real truth; good and evil are only conventions; reason cannot construct anything, nor can it attain knowledge of what is real; all hypothesis is futile; there can be no science; so the ideal of happiness is to remain indifferent to everything, and not to speak (*aphasia*) or to make a judgement. The life of this original philosopher became a tissue of legend. His theories, preached rather than written, quickly reached a ready public, and were then inherited by Timon of Phlius (320–230), another pupil of Stilpon and a wandering philosopher-sophist. Timon wrote tragedies, satyric dramas, iambics, and such-like; but there is special interest in three books of *Silloi*, of which fairly extensive fragments survive. In a parody of the Homeric Nekyia the poet pretended he was descending to the lower world among the philosophers and carrying on discussions with them, particularly with Xenophanes. In this way he was able to criticize and caricature all the characters he depicted.

The Sceptics did not create a regular school. After the earliest period of their preaching (the Early Scepticism) their theories were largely taken over by the Academicians, starting with Arcesilaus of Pitane in Aeolis (315–241), who was head of the Academy from 264 to his death. His philosophy was a compound of Academic, Megarian, and Sceptic doctrines, markedly opposed to Stoicism. He wrote little and what he did write was generally in verse; but he had a magnificent reputation as a dialectician and controversialist. He maintained that the human spirit could not grasp the truth, because what was false presented itself just as irresistibly as what was true; a wise man should remain doubtful or 'moderate' in relation to the truth, contenting himself with what was probable.

Arcesilaus brought about a revival in the Academy, which now became gradually more eclectic. Carneades of Cyrene (215–129), a great dialectician and orator, maintained that there were three degrees of probability, but that objective truth was unknowable and unattainable, since human beings could know only appearance. When, on an embassy to Rome in 156, he gave two discourses, the first to prove the existence of justice and the second to disprove it, he shocked the virtuous public of Rome profoundly by his sophistries.

6. ROME

a. *Forms of Religious Observance*

'Sua cuique civitati religio est.' This trite observation of Cicero (*pro Flacco*, 28) reflects the varied condition of religion among the diverse groups of people, in city and country, within the parts of the world which had been made Roman. To some extent at least, local cults were preserved in all regions, either in their original state or in forms resulting from syncretism with the Graeco-Roman pantheon. We can prove this from literary evidence, but still more from epigraphy and monuments derived from the various regions.

The phenomenon was most noticeable among the poorer members of the *populus* and among the countryfolk, who were shocked at what to them were incomprehensible and heretical deviations on the part of the upper classes. In all districts they attached themselves tenaciously to such primitive native cults as had survived, in other words to a small number of beloved and kindly deities whom they felt were always near them in their families and houses, in the streets or fields, or at their work, and to whom there was an age-long tradition of sacrifice on the domestic altars, or at the cross-roads and in little shrines. The most traditionally-minded people were of course the countrymen, the *pagani*. This situation was grounded in the original differences of race, culture, and religion between Rome and the conquered peoples which came into political unity with it. It was a situation perpetuated by the almost complete freedom of thought which Rome allowed to its subjects.

But meanwhile soldiers, traders, and other persons of moderate education were more and more apt to find themselves quartered in the provinces, especially the provinces of the East. There were also educated slaves and other immigrants from various parts of the East who were domiciled in Rome and the Western provinces. All these classes contributed to a rapid spread of particular Eastern cults in the West. The Magna Mater of Pessinus was identified with Cybele and her cult was installed on the Palatine in 204 BC. Isis and Serapis were introduced in Sulla's time, and four separate attempts to prohibit the cult between 58 and 48 came to nothing. Mithras was taken over by the pirates and then brought to Rome by Pompey and his veterans.

Finally, there was the attitude of the most highly educated classes. Not only were they quite blankly incredulous of the mythology of the Greek poets, which had been grafted on to the native Roman cults, but they showed no interest in the cults themselves and were eventually quite ignorant about them. Although certain cults survived, their observance was now a mechanical affair carried out by the priests without evoking feeling or even attendance on the part of devotees. Although in Rome itself the *pontifices* sometimes took radical steps to defend the ancient cults, Varro predicted that many of them would die through the *incuria* of Roman citizens.

In 249 BC P. Claudius Pulcher was put on trial for impiety when he cast the haruspical chickens into the sea because they refused to drink. But less than three-quarters of a century later Ennius could translate the atheistical Sacred History of Euhemerus for a Roman public; and Plautus in the *Amphitruo* (I, 126) and in the *Pseudolus* (III, 2, 50) was making telling parodies of sacred figures, in which he was followed by other writers of comedy and mime and by the poets in general. Pomponius caricatured the *haruspices* and the augurs, and a saying attributed to Cato the censor, to the effect that *haruspices* could hardly meet each other without laughing, showed a similar attitude. Lucilius (*Sat.* XV, 2) ridiculed the frightening religious devices ascribed to Numa Pompilius. Varro's laments have been mentioned above, 'the gods are dying, not at the hands of our enemies but because our citizens do not care'. It may be added that some of the priestly offices were for a long time left unfilled, that of *rex sacrorum* from the second century, and that of *flamen Dialis* from 87 to 11 BC.

The fact was that the old myths and ritual had often become incomprehensible, and could no longer be articles of faith with educated and cultured people. Sceptics had by now eaten their way into the old speculative proofs of 'being' and had made men tired of the constructions of Greek dialectic with its endless assertions and denials. Moreover the general development of moral and social ideas had led to a change and a sublimation in the outlook and purpose of religion: men now tended to put their faith and trust in the suggestions made, however obscurely, by the consciences within them. So it was not to atheism that they had recourse: one can prove this by the failure of the Epicurean doctrine so passionately upheld by Lucretius, which was designed to show that religion was born of fear of death and of the gods and was the cause of all ills. The movement was instead towards the triumph of 'religious sentiment'.

We reach the same conclusion if we remember the great interest in religious problems shown in the writings of Varro and Tarquitius Priscus. When Rome conquered the Mediterranean world it ordered it on new and more up-to-date principles, and so many social, moral, and legal ideas had been renovated that there was inevitably going to be an attempt to revolutionize religion too. Provision therefore had to be made for a religion of 'sentiment' by taking account of other movements of a spiritual kind. For a small group of men the yearning for a moral law was satisfied by the study of philosophy, but by now it was becoming obvious that Stoic teaching could not provide the means for a definite social reform of the population as a whole. The remainder of mankind, whose religious aspirations were stronger than those of this small group, embraced syncretistic cults of Eastern origin, even though they were not genuinely Eastern but a jumble of heterogeneous elements brought together quite arbitrarily.

b. *Diffusion of Religion and Philosophy*

These new syncretistic ideas were indeed spreading fast, especially those of a neo-Pythagorean and Hellenistico-Jewish variety. Juba II, the learned king of Numidia, made a collection of neo-Pythagorean writings. At Rome they found a ready audience, since Roman scholars much enjoyed spending time on religious problems. The first effects can be seen in the *Rudens* of Plautus;[23] the first reactions in the other direction came as early as 181 BC, in connection with the books ascribed to Numa Pompilius.

As was indicated earlier, the attention given to religious problems by Varro in his *Antiquitatum rerum humanarum et divinarum libri* is a characteristic example of Roman treatment of the subject. For instance he maintained that there were three different conceptions of divinity, the poetical, the political, and the philosophical (here he was drawing on the Stoics, and in particular on Posidonius). The work was pervaded throughout by philosophical speculation, popular belief, and a fondness for evolving syncretisms between various religions on very much the same principles as Caesar used. We are told that Varro was buried with neo-Pythagorean rites (Pliny, *N.H.*, XXXV, 160). The same tendencies are displayed in the study of various foreign religions, for instance in the *De Disciplina Etrusca* of Tarquitius Priscus; and they are the reason why Rome was invaded by Eastern syncretistic cults of an astral nature, exemplified in the apotheosis of Julius Caesar as a star. Eastern Messianic conceptions and neo-Pythagorean purificatory doctrines find an echo in Virgil's IVth *Eclogue* and in the descent of Aeneas to Elysium described in the *Aeneid*. Even Cicero is writing under the influence of some version of these new ideas in the passage called *Somnium Scipionis* which closes his *De Republica* and in which he asserts that good works open the road to heaven; and in another passage he writes that the prayers of the Vestals secure pardon from the gods. Sallust too declares that the gods watch over the good and evil acts of men. The movement found its greatest exponent in Nigidius Figulus (98–45), whom Rome regarded as a magician and astrologer. He was a neo-Pythagorean, and in his *Sphaera Graecanica* and *Sphaera Barbarica* gave explanations of the heavens and of the metamorphoses of men into stars.

All this new type of feeling towards religious atmosphere, this longing for mysticism, does something to explain Augustus' conception of a religious revival. It also accounts for some of the conditions which somewhat later favoured the spread of Christian ideas, despite all earlier Roman legislation and despite the new imperial cult.

c. *Foreign Cults*

In the fourth century BC Rome under Camillus' leadership resumed the advance to hegemony and at the same time instituted the system of making gradual concessions to the conquered peoples, enabling many of them to migrate to Rome. This threatened the ancestral religion with extinction, and it must have been at this time that Rome passed a law which was the basis of its religious policy in later times. It is recorded by Cicero in the *De Legibus* (II, 8, 1; 10, 25), and runs 'no citizen may worship special gods, either new or foreign, unless they have first been accepted publicly by the state; and in private only the gods of our fathers may be worshipped'. So in law gods not accepted by the state could not be worshipped by citizens even in private. On the other hand non-citizens, either in their own countries, or in private at Rome if they resided there, could worship their own ancestral gods—which might or might not be syncretized with those of Rome—once an appropriate decree of the senate had sanctioned them.

The law to which Cicero refers was never repealed, but in practice it was rigorously enforced only at periods of crisis. Generally it was employed leniently and then only at occasional moments; for instance in 242 when the *sortes Praenestinae*[24] were banned. So in the course of the fourth and third centuries almost all the major divinities of the peninsula found their way into the Roman pantheon for practical purposes, either directly or in syncretism with other gods; and the state did not seriously interfere.

The matter became more complex and worrying when the Roman empire began gradually to include territories outside the peninsula, with peoples to whom Rome had no intention of granting citizenship and cults which were obviously very different from its own. It was at this point that a more rigid line began to be taken, for instance when foreign cults were prohibited in 213. Later, however, partly as the result of the alternating dominance of phil-Hellenism and anti-Hellenism at Rome, the educated classes were first attracted by the fantasies of Greek mythology and then began to see how inconsistent it all was. A whole flood of mystery cults and of oriental doctrines about the after-life then proceeded to invade Italy by various paths, the state neither giving them an enthusiastic welcome nor being able or willing to offer any effective opposition. After a time, however, the *pontifices* and the anti-Hellenist members of the senate, who believed that in Greek cults and in Hellenic influence in general they could detect the main causes of the corruption of Roman *mores*, were successful in organizing a reactionary policy of intolerance and religious persecution. Their leader was M. Porcius Cato, and their policy was undoubtedly based on the illegality involved in introducing such cults and on the danger of moral and political decline they were supposed to bring. In this atmosphere there was held, over a period of five years, the famous inquiry into the *Bacchanalia*, in which 7,000 persons were implicated; and another manifestation of the reaction can be seen in 181, when the 'Pythagorean books' ascribed to King Numa were burnt by the public executioner. All this led naturally to suppression of any innovation which seemed to be a corrupting influence, one consequence being the expulsion of philosophers and rhetoricians in 161.

Certain general propositions were in this way reaffirmed. First, that a new cult might not be practised without the state's consent; secondly that cults which were tolerated for non-citizens and foreigners might not proselytize among Romans without incurring grave danger; and thirdly that all religious practices which could be shown to be morally objectionable must be uprooted. For this reason the Chaldean diviners were banished in 139, and the early Jewish conventicles, then engaged in promoting worship of their God (wrongly identified by contemporary Romans with the Phrygian Sabazios), were made illegal.

But no law, especially one applied spasmodically and within a society which was in part opposed to it and in part indifferent, could check the spontaneous growth of a new culture. It crept in through countless channels which were scarcely visible, and it brought with it new ideas in religion to meet men's hopes and longings.

So although there was still vigilant opposition, illustrated in the four
T*

decrees against the resurgent Isis cult which were mentioned earlier, none the less new cults and foreign rites, especially those reflecting the prevalent syncretism of the East, continued to make their way more or less secretly into Rome. They were still brought in by Easterners living in the West, by slaves of diverse origin, by Italians who had been initiated during their residence in the East, and by Chaldeans wandering round the world. The most difficult problem was to prevent such people proselytizing among the Italians, although it was a problem which worried only the conservative elements in politics.

d. *Religious and Political Difficulties with the Jews*

One reason for the dispersion of Jews about the Roman world had been the assistance given by Rome to the Hasmoneans (the Maccabees) against the Seleucid attempt to Hellenize Judaea. From 165 BC there was a pro-Roman party in Judaea, but this did not prevent a wholesale expulsion of Jews from Rome in 139 when the first Jewish communities there were indulging in organized efforts to make proselytes. Relations were again strained during the Mithradatic War, when one Jewish party, the Sadducees, still supported Parthia, and the other, the Pharisees, retained their philhellenic policy. The next decisive events were the victory of Pompey over Mithradates VI and the reduction of Judaea to a vassal state under the leadership of Hyrcanus II with Pharisaic support, though the anti-Roman and pro-Parthian party was still in opposition. The assistance offered by Hyrcanus to Caesar for his Egyptian campaign in 47 had beneficial results not only for him personally but for the Jewish settlements scattered throughout the Roman world. They were allowed to live in peace, still paying their 'didrachm' to the Temple at Jerusalem, and Rome allowed them to possess 'collegia'. But throughout the civil wars the anti-Roman factions could continue to hope for the ruin of their overlord. After Caesar's death they supported the Caesaricide C. Cassius Longinus, who had established himself in Syria and entered on an alliance with Parthia. When M. Antonius became master of Syria the pro-Roman party was restored to power. But stability was still threatened, first by the Parthian invasions of Syria, and secondly by Antonius' assignment of much of Palestine to the Pharaonic domain of Cleopatra.

The victory of Octavian over Antony and his accord with Herod, much resented by the anti-Roman party, made peaceful co-existence between Jews and Romans possible once more. Then, however, new difficulties appeared. In 4 BC Herod died, and his possessions were divided among his three sons, whose kingdoms were in a state of discord. There was increasing dependence on Roman procurators, who had little knowledge of local conditions. But the chief trouble was the compulsory imposition by Augustus of the cult of Dea Roma and of the deified emperors. The difficulties were in part surmounted by the able dispositions of Augustus, but they again became acute in the time of his successor.

e. *Augustan Religion*

In 27 BC, after assuming the title 'Augustus', the first emperor began his reconstruction of the Roman world. He at once showed himself markedly hostile to foreign cults, and he also created new factors which made it still more difficult for Rome to come to terms with the monotheists among its subjects. Once he had put Italy in a position of political and economic superiority to the provinces, he wanted Italy to show itself morally worthy of the mission he had entrusted to it. Cassius Dio (LIII, 36) asserts that Maecenas gave the young Octavian the following advice: 'do you yourself worship the divine power everywhere by every means, in accordance with the tradition of our fathers, and compel others to honour it too. Hate and punish all who try to introduce innovations in this regard, not only for the sake of the gods . . . but because those who introduce new divinities persuade many to change their thoughts and practices; and from this there spring up conspiracies, revolts, and factions. . . . Do not tolerate atheists or magicians . . . and keep your eye on philosophers too'. Augustus seems to have had a fair measure of superstition himself and to have been attracted by neo-Pythagorean doctrines, but he undoubtedly thought religion was indispensable both on account of his personal feelings and also for political reasons. Yet his general plan for the state demanded that his religion, for Italians, should still be the ancient Roman system. He wanted Italians to return to the cults of their fathers and be deflected from the supposedly subversive propaganda which accompanied foreign cults, though he inevitably deceived himself in thinking that this return, being forced and made in the face of history, could ever be an intimate affair rather than remaining purely external. So he restored eighty-two temples, had altars to the Lares erected at the cross-roads in every *vicus*, revived forgotten festivals such as the Lupercalia, celebrated the Secular Games with solemnity, and had the Sibylline Books put into order once more, at the same time consigning hundreds of false oracles and works on ritual to the flames.

Much more important for Rome's relations with religions of mono-theistic type was Augustus' new conception of a cult of Dea Roma and of emperors who were deified after their deaths, a cult which was to be obligatory throughout the empire. It was intended to be something above all national religions, cementing political and spiritual cohesion and ensuring the loyalty of the provinces. In actual fact the origins of this conception lay far in the past, and were not Roman but Italiote and Hellenistic. Since the third century BC the Greeks, who were fond of personifying abstract concepts, had imagined a Dea Roma, whom we find depicted on 'Romano-Campanian' coins and also given temples in Greece and Asia Minor from 196 and 195, although this goddess was not yet worshipped in Rome. Likewise the Hellenistic East, which was accustomed to worship living rulers, quickly paid divine honours to Roman personages of regal bearing. In this way

Caesar was a god as Alexander had been, and after him there was Antonius, the neo-Dionysus. Augustus himself after Actium was portrayed on statues as a god, his hair curled and bound with a fillet inlaid with jewels, or wearing a radiate crown. He too, even in his lifetime, was worshipped as a god, not at Rome, except by colleges of freedmen, but in Asia, Spain, Gaul, and eventually Germany. In Rome he did not yet dare to institute such a practice, but people already spoke of the Caesar's protecting genius.

Yet the compulsory adoption throughout the empire, including Italy, of the cult of Dea Roma and of the emperors deified after their deaths was definitely willed by Augustus, who was responsible for the deification of Caesar; and when Augustus died, he too was deified, and the first temple to him as *divus* was set up on the Palatine at Rome by his widow Livia. Later on Caligula was the first of a discontinuous series of emperors who, copying Antonius, desired to be worshipped as gods, in Rome and Italy, during their actual lifetimes.

This new imperial religion, like the previous enforcement of a return to the forgotten gods of Italy, did not move the minds of the masses by any poetical myths or philosophical theology. It therefore left a void in men's hearts, which they more than ever sought to fill with the new faiths imported from abroad. Yet it was regarded as essential for the life of the state, since, as Virgil and Horace maintained, the permanence of the empire depended on religion. In time, however, it came to be a formidable obstacle to the existence and growth of monotheistic religions, such as Judaism and later Christianity, among Roman citizens; and these two faiths in any case made things more difficult on their own account, owing to their uncompromising denial of all other gods. But for the moment Augustus attempted to overcome friction with the Jews by confirming and extending the measures taken by Pompey and Caesar. He allowed Jews of the Diaspora to meet for Sabbath observance and to send the traditional two drachmas to the Temple at Jerusalem. Their only obligation, seeing that they were not willing to sacrifice to the gods of Rome, was to make sacrifice to Yahweh for the emperor's good fortune and to send the emperor a donative.

f. *Eclecticism and Philosophy (Marcus Tullius Cicero)*

Amid the great flood of philosophical doctrines, all claiming to set forth the absolute truth, and with controversies sometimes raging no less fiercely in that they were directed to disinterested questions of the spirit, it was natural for the general tone of philosophical studies to be lowered, a consequence which would have in any case followed from the heresies and schisms within the various schools. Inevitably men tried to find agreement through contaminating different doctrines, in other words through 'eclecticism', one of the features of late Hellenistic philosophy. We find, from time to time, contamination between all kinds of doctrine, Cynic and Cyrenaic, Academic and Sceptic, Academic and Stoic, and so on. We should not forget that many schools were in agreement on basic points and were at variance mainly on particular questions. The tendency towards eclecticism grew stronger all the time and became the prevailing mood in the Roman period.

From the outset there had never been real philosophers at Rome. There were orators, historians, and jurists who came under the influence of Greek philosophers, the Stoics appealing mainly to the jurists and the Academicians to the orators. Cicero says that before his time Rome possessed practically no philosophical work except from the Epicurean school. From them he cites three Latin writers, Amafinius, Catius and Rabirius; and of course we must add the great Lucretius.

But Greek philosophers were finding Rome a suitable soil for their teaching and writing from Panaetius' time. This meant that when Roman philosophy made its appearance with Cicero it had the general features of the eclectic Stoicism professed by Panaetius and Posidonius, and the same interest as they had in moral and political, rather than in metaphysical, problems. Rome's additional contribution was an aversion from the endless inconclusive disputes of dialectic.

Cicero's first effort at philosophical writing was made in a letter to his brother Quintus in 60 BC and was concerned with provincial government, in other words with political philosophy. His earliest philosophical treatises, the *De Re Publica* of 54–51 and the *De Legibus*, have the same theme. Of these the former, of which we possess only a part, is a dialogue imagined to have taken place in 129 between persons of the circle of Scipio Aemilianus. It upholds the need for a mixed form of government, with a temporary 'princeps' at its head. The *De Legibus*, which has survived with a gap in Book III, is concerned to redraft the laws on the principles of natural right. Later Cicero sought consolation for his political and private troubles by writing a series of works of philosophical type, which succeeded one another rapidly in 45 and 44, so rapidly indeed that some have held the exaggerated view that they were simply translations or refurbishings of Greek texts. In 45 he published the following: a *consolatio* for the death of his daughter; the *Hortensius*, an exhortation to philosophy; the *Academica*, designed to expound the various Greek schools by setting one against another; the *De Finibus Bonorum et Malorum*, where he shows that Sceptic and Stoic views on the *summum bonum* and *summum malum* came to the same thing; a translation of Plato's *Timaeus*, now almost entirely lost; and his five books of *Tusculan Disputations*, in which he takes the Stoic view. In 44 he wrote a lifeless compilation entitled *De Divinatione*, and his *De Fato*; later on a number of works of genuine feeling, mainly derived from the Stoics, the *Cato Maior* (or *De Senectute*), the *Laelius* (or *De Amicitia*), and the *De Officiis*; and finally the *De Auguriis* and *De Gloria*, both of which have perished.

This hurried set of philosophical writings by Cicero has certainly no originality. It is a blend between Sceptic Academism where 'pure reason' is concerned and eclectic Stoicism where he is dealing with 'practical reason'. But Cicero can take credit for a number of things. He gave the Romans a clear picture of the opposing Greek theories, which are upheld by the various characters in his dialogues. To some extent he created a philosophical terminology in Latin. And finally he caused the treatment of philosophy to assume once more the graceful form it had practically lost in Greece since Plato's day.

g. *T. Lucretius Carus*: *Epicureanism*

Before Lucretius a number of didactic writers of Latin verse had addressed themselves to philosophical argument. T. Albucius, an Epicurean enthusiast for things Greek, had put the theory of Epicurus into verse; C. Sallustius had composed his *Empedoclea*, which Cicero considered unreadable; and Varro, among all his other works, had written a philosophic poem mentioned by Quintilian.

We have very little biographical information about T. Lucretius Carus (99/94–55/50 B C). His *cognomen* and certain allusions in the poem have made some scholars believe, without adequate foundation, that he was a Celt and the son of a freedman. Jerome states that he was driven mad by a love philtre, but had lucid intervals during which he composed 'aliquot libros', and later committed suicide. It has indeed been thought that evidence of his *insania* can be found in certain passages where with great liveliness he describes nightmares and the madness of love and the agitation of the soul. However all this may be, he left behind him a poem *De Rerum Natura* in six books, complete but not revised, and later published on Cicero's advice. The latter was unwilling to alter it. He left abrupt transitions and preliminary arrangements of the poet's material, especially in the last book.

Although Lucretius played no part in public life, he had suffered like others from the ills which tormented his generation and had witnessed riots and massacres. He wanted to offer his contemporaries a means of salvation, a word of truth in which he believed with all his heart. This was the theory of Epicurus.

In Lucretius' view nothing is born of nothing, and nothing returns to nothing. The universe is a matter from eternity, and consists in an infinity of immortal atoms, which are falling without any pause in infinite space. These atoms meet, and so create bodies: they separate, and so dissolve the bodies, all in accord with absolute laws. The soul too is formed of slender atoms composed of wind, heat, air, and a fourth very fine element. The soul is diffused throughout the body, and both the instincts of animals and the characters of men depend on the varying blends between the four components. When the body dissolves, the soul dissolves too. From the surface of objects there move off thin tissues, which stimulate our senses, even during sleep. In perception it is not the senses which err, but the reason in the process of interpreting them; for human judgement is misled by passions,

which it is our duty to avoid. The poet describes the origins of the world—
of the earth, and of plants, animals, and men, begotten and made fruitful
by the earth herself. Primitive men, through the work of heroes, gradually
made life less harsh. They created the family, the state, and language; they
made technical and artistic discoveries; and they were governed by monarchies. But there followed a general upheaval, and the thrones began to fall.
Then things returned to order with the institution of laws, magistrates, and
punishments; and religion was invented, because man was ignorant of the
true causes of cataclysms (which the poet digresses to describe) and attributed such things to the wrath of the gods.

It is not the power behind his reconstruction of Epicurean science which
makes Lucretius' poem so magnificent. The science is often *simpliste*, and the
system contains too many flaws and internal contradictions to be admired
for its coherence. Even the happiness which he so longs to achieve is not
depicted without some lack of clarity. The poet's greatness lies rather in the
granite faith with which he believes he can attain truth by reason. This gives
him the boldness and burning light of a prophet, and he shows an eager and
passionate longing to propound a new ideal and a new truth to a sceptical and
disorientated world. There is greatness too in the boundless admiration shown
for his master, Epicurus, and in the enthusiasm with which he attacks his
task, though it may be that here we can detect the influence of the pathos of
Empedocles or even a certain hypersensitiveness in the poet's make-up. But
it is certain that Lucretius' enthusiasm and tenacity, which contrast so
strongly with the litigious arguments of his Greek contemporaries, are no
isolated phenomenon in the Latin world, where conviction became an absolute
rule of life.

NOTES TO CHAPTER XI

1. The authors attribute the development and diffusion of Taoism in China, with its
   mysticism, gigantic pantheon, etc., to the fact that the local and state cults of heaven,
   earth and ancestors were insufficient to satisfy the people's religious needs, and that the
   people yearned for 'some emotional uplift of the soul'. In fact it was not the people who
   called into being a religion that could satisfy their 'religious needs' but, on the contrary,
   all the age-old popular beliefs in gods, holy spirits, werewolves, etc., as well as everyday
   superstitions, beliefs in mystical reincarnation, and so on—all of which in the course of
   time came to be embraced within the framework of a religious teaching, based on a
   particular religious treatment of the philosophical concept *tao*. (L. S. Vasilyev.)

2. It is questionable whether Indian philosophy has its origin in religion. It is never
   produced quite simply from changes in cults or religious ideas. More account should
   be taken of the efforts at rational cosmological explanations of the world and the human
   condition, the existence of which is particularly attested in the ancient Buddhist texts
   (*Dīghanikāya*) denouncing them as erroneous (an allusion is made to them on p. 829).

3. It would be interesting to recall here that among the religious policies of the Achaemenids
   was the installation of the *arta brazmaniya*, 'Brahmanic good order' (ancient Persian
   arta, or Vedic *ṛta*), which reveals another case of probable contact or an original relationship between Iranian and Indian doctrines.

4. The various philosophical schools that contended with one another in Greece during the fifth and fourth centuries BC were closely connected with the bitter social struggle going on at that time in the Greek city-states. The problems of the structure of society and the state, and their possible reconstruction, of the duties and tasks of the individual and the citizen, and his relationships with his native *polis* and the human race in general —all these questions were hotly debated by the broadest social circles, were discussed by orators at public debates, and were taken as the themes of comedies and tragedies staged before crowds of spectators. One might also say that there are few periods of history when one can see more clearly that the struggle between ideologies stemmed from the struggle between social classes. (E. M. Shtaerman.)

5. Most scholars have now abandoned this view of the *Bacchae*. Professor B. A. van Groningen, for example, writes 'All we can assert is that, at the end of his life, Euripides' artistic soul felt with great intensity the charm of the passionate Dionysiac cult. But his soul was the soul of an artist, and that is hardly the same thing as the soul of a believer.' See above all E. R. Dodds' edition of the play (Oxford, 1944).

6. See above, p. 469, although Professor A. Lesky maintains that Professor Pareti has exaggerated the oriental origins of Stoicism, and Professor B. A. van Groningen points out that Zeno was the only Easterner among the founders of the school.

7. See also Part I, pp. 248 ff. As has been emphasized by Dr P. Oliva and Professor C. Danov, the origins of Greek philosophy, which are discussed in the following paragraphs, are intimately linked with the all-important Greek work on physics and cosmogony, from Thales to Anaxagoras and Democritus; and one must remember the materialist strain in this thought, not least in the last-named thinker.

8. Yet the idea is found in two older contemporaries of Anaxagoras, of very different outlook from each other, namely the poets Aeschylus and Pindar.

9. Another famous Sophist was Gorgias of Leontini (*c.*483–376), who wrote a treatise to prove the impossibility of positive knowledge, and then devoted himself to showing his contemporaries the power of words and to the evolution of a prose style. He was said in antiquity to have influenced both Thucydides and Isocrates.

10. As Professor A. Lesky shows, Protagoras too must have made a notable contribution to political thought. The Platonic dialogue bearing his name shows him upholding that virtue, both social and political, is teachable, a doctrine which disturbed Socrates. For an attempt to reconcile the doctrine with Protagoras' alleged subjectivism (for which the evidence comes from Plato's *Theaetetus*) see A. Levi, *Mind*, 1940, pp. 284 ff.

11. The *daimon*, as Professor A. Lesky points out, was more a warning than a motive force.

12. *Translator's Note*. In the sections on Socratico-Platonic philosophy the Italian words 'concetto' and 'idea' have been directly transliterated since no other translation would be free from controversy. But the reader should be warned that the history of philosophy has dealt differently with these two words in Italian and English.

13. Still more responsible, perhaps, were his own anti-democratic convictions, formed in the latter part of the Peloponnesian War and strengthened by the fate of Socrates.

14. See Note 12 above. (*Translator.*)

15. Professor Pareti's view that the *Republic* was an idealization of the Spartan constitution needs qualification. No doubt he was extremely interested in Sparta, but there are revolutionary, and entirely un-Spartan, elements in his ideal state; and some of these are described in Professor Pareti's next sentences.

16. With the help of an elaborate system of education, which, as Professor F. M. Heichelheim notes, was not far removed from the modern division into 'primary, higher, and University' education.

17. Here too, as Professor B. A. van Groningen points out, it may be unwise to regard the contemporary history of Sparta as an important force in turning Plato towards the more rigorous system propounded in the *Laws*.

18. In particular Aristotle was greatly influenced by Democritus (see above, pp. 421).

19. For a brilliant short summary of Aristotle's relationship to Plato, both in epistemology and in ethics, see W. D. Ross, *Oxford Classical Dictionary* (1946), s.v. 'Aristotle'.

20. This work is often regarded as spurious.

21. Alternatively his own notes for his lectures, which notes he may have revised at various times during his life.

22. Dr P. Oliva, adding to Professor Pareti's analysis the fact that Epicurus denied life after death, considers that the materialistic strain in Epicureanism is under-emphasized.

23. This play is modelled on a Greek original by Diphilus (fourth century BC), and it is therefore not quite safe to assume that the neo-Pythagorean elements are due to Plautus.

24. One of the many Italian forms of divination, probably a simple drawing of inscribed lots (Polybius, VI, 11). It was later greatly in vogue among the higher classes, including the imperial family, during the first century AD.

CHAPTER XII

LITERATURE AND ART: 500 BC TO AD 1

I. THE DEVELOPMENT OF LITERATURE

a. *China*

Chinese literature in the Warring States period (fifth to third centuries B C.) is concerned on the one hand with the development of philosophical thought; this is mainly prose and has been dealt with in the preceding chapter. It should be remembered that the Discourses of Confucius (*Lun-yü*) seem to employ the spoken language of the time and are an outstanding example of fresh, unsophisticated prose, full of idioms and supple phrases. Poetry, on the other hand, is less connected with philosophy, although the style of the *Tao-te-ching* is very often near to poetry. The poetical production of the Western Chou had been a strictly official, court-sponsored, and impersonal body of writing. It was only much later that a quite novel note was struck. This happened about 300 BC in the Ch'u kingdom in the Yangtze-kiang valley. This new poetry was produced by an originally non-Chinese society, in which the common people was still 'barbarian' and only the cultural élite spoke and wrote Chinese. The 'elegies of Ch'u' (*Ch'u-tz'ŭ*) are thus something quite different from the tradition of the 'Book of Odes'. Their background is mainly magical, and this is true even for its longest composition, the *Li-sao* (meaning probably 'Sorrows of banishment'). Its author Ch'ü Yüan complains of his disgrace and his inability to serve his sovereign. He expresses himself in a rather stilted and unpoetic language full of allegories, invocations, and mystical allusions, not devoid of real eloquence. This luxuriant poetry is magical and religious in character, and not political like the Chou Odes with their sober and chaste style. The metre of the Ch'u poetry is based on a verse of six syllables (as against the Odes' four). From this, in the course of the Han period, there arose the *fu*, a sort of unfettered recitative, bound only to a strong rhythm, but also making use of rhyme. The contents of the *fu* were usually descriptions of cities, palaces, gardens, etc., in a highly strung language that tended often to fall into ornate but rather empty rhetoric. The chief representatives of this poetry were Chia I (201–169) and Ssŭ-ma Hsiang-ju (179–117).

Chinese history writing goes as far back as that venerable document, the 'Spring and Autumn' (*Ch'un-ch'iu*), i.e. the Annals, whose compilation, or at least revision, is traditionally attributed to Confucius. They cover the period 722–481 and are a dry-as-dust chronological register of events centring

* The passages within square brackets were contributed by Professor Pierre Grimal, to supplement the original text, after the death of Professor Pareti.

round the principality of Lu, Confucius' home country. Only slightly later (fourth century) is the *Tso-chuan*, a real attempt at writing history. It is highly impersonal, the author disappearing behind the events he relates; his opinion is reflected, at the most, in the choice of the event to be registered. In its impassive style it still succeeds in giving a quite lively and colourful picture of Chinese life at that time.

Afterwards the taste of the reading circles leaned rather toward the *bon mot*, the anecdote, the dramatic effect, as evidenced chiefly by true or supposed political speeches. These are the main contents of such works as the 'Discourses of the States' (*Kuo-yü*) and the 'Politics of the Warring States' (*Chan-kuo-ts'ê*). From these writings one reaches nearly fictional works, and historical novels such as the travelogue *Mu-t'ien-tzŭ-chuan* 'Biography of the Son of Heaven called Mu'). Much of this literature was destroyed on the occasion of the 'burning of the books' ordered by Ch'in Shih-huang-ti, and even more when the Imperial Library in Hsien-yang was ravaged by fire during the civil war following the fall of the Ch'in; but a not inconsiderable body has survived to this day.

All this is not yet true history. Yet it showed the path for the future, and set down once and for all two of the foremost characteristics of Chinese historiography—impersonality, and love for detail. The father of Chinese historical writing, the 'Herodotus of China', was Ssŭ-ma Ch'ien (*c.* 135-87). His work, the 'Historical Memoirs' (*Shih-chi*), a private undertaking, was finished about 90 BC, but was published only after the death of its author. Its terse and pithy style, and its well thought out structure, served as a model for all the later dynastic histories, which were written by imperial command, each dynasty as a rule undertaking to compile the history of the preceding one. This enormous collection contains today twenty-six dynastic histories and carries the history down to 1912. The normal pattern, as set down by Ssŭ-ma Ch'ien and by Pan Ku, the author of the second history, provides for four separate sections: (1) basic annals (*pên-chi*), a rather jejune chronological list of court events and of imperial mandates; (2) monographs (*chih*) on special subjects, such as astronomy and calendar, geography, economy, administration, rites, bibliography, music, etc.; (3) tables (*piao*) of imperial genealogies, lists of officials, etc.; (4) biographies (*lieh-chuan*) of the most outstanding personages of the period; this forms the bulk of the work, both for size and importance of the contents. This pattern lent itself to rigid and mechanical imitation, but Ssŭ-ma Ch'ien was a highly original and talented writer, whose personality shines through the apparently impassive and cold array of facts and information in his huge work.

We notice also that the need to recover, sort, and settle the classical texts after the storm of the Ch'in persecution gave rise, thanks to the labours of Liu Hsiang (79-8 BC) and of his son Liu Hsin (died AD 23) to a highly refined technique of philological criticism, which was far in advance of anything else in Asia and finds its counterpart only in the Alexandrian schools.

b. *India*

Indian (Sanskrit) secular literature may be said to begin with the stories and ballads of an epic character found in the later Vedic texts; such as the *Cycle of Suparṇa*. In the later and artificial classification of Sanskrit literature, epics (*itihāsa*) are placed after the *Atharvaveda*, to which they are said to be closely related. The authors, transmitters, and preservers of this heroic poetry were professional singers (*sūta*), who lived at court and recited their songs at great festivals in honour of their protectors. They also followed the king in battle, in order to be able to sing of his heroic deeds from their own observations. This form of poetry seems to have been widely diffused, but all the early poems are lost and only two great epic cycles have come down to us: that of the Bhārata war, and that of Rāma.

The *Mahābhārata* has been defined as not one poetic production, but rather a whole literature, a repertory of the whole of the old bardic poetry (Winternitz). This enormous poem of about 100,000 *śloka* in eighteen sections (*parvan*) plus a supplement (the *Harivaṃsa*, which is really a *purāṇa*) centres round the family feud of the two branches of the Bhārata family in northern India, the Kaurava and the Pāṇḍava. A long, bitter, and bloody war ensues, in which all the Indian heroes (including Kṛṣṇa) take sides for one or other family. The war ends with the complete destruction of the Kauravas, but also with the withdrawal from worldly life of the few Pāṇḍavas left. The poem, it appears, grew around an original nucleus that was favourable to the Kauravas, and was later modified in a pro-Pāṇḍava sense. It is not the work of one poet, although tradition attributes it to the mythical sage Vyāsa; it grew over the course of centuries, chiefly through a luxuriant efflorescence of side-themes, episodes, and digressions, until it reached its present unwieldy bulk. In the process its character as an essentially secular poetical work was modified, as the Brahmans, and chiefly the court priests (*purohita*), introduced into it more and more mythical and didactic matter, of a clearly Vishnuite character. Even philosophical and ascetic portions are not missing, and we need only recall in this connection the *Bhagavadgītā*. Prose-pieces, too, have found their way into the *Mahābhārata*, which, as we have it now, may be best defined as an encyclopaedia of ancient Indian lore. All this process was long drawn out and may be taken to have occupied seven or eight centuries, from about the fourth BC to fourth AD. By the Gupta period it was already settled in its final form, substantially the one we know today.

The other great poem is the *Rāmāyaṇa*. It is an account of the youth of Rāma, his feats, and of his winning Sītā as his wife. Sītā is carried away by the demon Rāvaṇa, who brings her to Laṅkā (Ceylon). Rāma collects an army, wins the help of the monkey-king Sugriva, overruns Laṅkā, slays Rāvaṇa, and liberates Sītā. The story of their further destinies is a later accretion. The poem is divided into seven *kāṇḍa* and consists of about 24,000 *ślokas*. It is preserved in three recensions, with fairly serious differences. It is, however, much more of a unit than the *Mahābhārata* and responds more closely to our ideas of what an epic poem should be. It is traditionally attributed to the sage and seer Valmiki, and it may indeed be probable that at least its nucleus (substantially *kāṇḍas* 2–6) is the work of one poet, or at least of one poetical school. Its style is more polished and more advanced, and it already contains the first beginnings of ornate art poetry (*kāvya*). As Winternitz said, 'while we found in the *Mahābhārata* a mixture of popular epic and theological didactic poetry (*purāṇa*), the *Rāmāyaṇa* appears to us as a work that is popular epic and ornate poetry at the same time'. The core of the *Rāmāyaṇa* is more archaic in appearance than the earliest portion of the *Mahābhārata*. Thus Rāma is only a hero and the Vedic Indra is the supreme god. We are still on Late Vedic ground, and only the later portions (first and seventh *kāṇḍas*), which are strikingly similar to the *Mahābhārata* in character, make Rāma a god and identify him with Viṣṇu. The chronology of the *Rāmāyaṇa* may be best defined as follows. In its present form it is older by about a couple of centuries than the *Mahābhārata* we have now. On the other hand the legend of Rāma appears to be of later origin than that of the Bhārata war; its atmosphere is more polished and gentle than the cruder one of the *Mahābhārata*, so full of passion and hatred. The period during which the *Rāmāyaṇa* grew appears, therefore, to lie encompassed within the longer period of the *Mahābhārata*: we may suggest about the third century BC to the second century AD.

Something can also be said about localization: the larger poem belongs to north-western India, mainly to the zone around Delhi, while the theatre of the *Rāmāyaṇa* is mainly northern India, in the western portions of Uttar Pradesh.

Both the great poems became very popular, in the sense that their core became part and parcel of Indian life of all ages. Over and above this the *Rāmāyaṇa*, chiefly as recast in modern Indian dialects (the most famous is the Hindi *Rām-carit-manas* of Tulsī Dās) became a true devotional book, which exerted a deep influence on the spiritual life of the masses in India.

c. *Hebrew Historiography*

Given the complexity of the problem of creation and chronology for each part of the Persian *Avesta*, with the exception of the *Gāthā* which is its earliest section and which was discussed in Part I, it is preferable to assemble the data in Part III.

We have also preferred to treat the books of the Hebrew Bible as a whole, though indicating which are the latest sections—the fifth century for *Chronicles* and *Job*, the fourth for *Ezra* and (conceivably) *Daniel*, third for *Ecclesiastes*, the second and first for the *Works of Wisdom*, etc. Here we would like to deal only with Hebrew historiography after 500.

After the end of the exile and in the succeeding centuries the historical genre was much in vogue among the Hebrews, but a fundamental distinction made itself felt within this branch of literature, since some writers of the period write genuine historical books and others edifying monographs. Among the latter it is possible to pick out the stories of Esther, Judith, Tobias, and Jonah—the stories themselves give very little information but they are important as literature; some parts of the *Book of Job* should be added to this catalogue; the dating of *Ruth*, however, remains difficult. The *Chronicles*, the *Book of Ezra*, the *Book of Nehemiah*, and the *Maccabees* excel among the historical works; names and brief fragments alone remain of the various other authors.

We need not modify the observations made earlier on the character of Hebrew historiography. It deals always with 'sacred history' in which religious purpose predominates in the most obvious way; and the preoccupation with drawing a moral and a lesson from the narrative facts is constant. Yet it should be explained that in the monographs listed above it is impossible to draw a precise line between the historical event from which it begins and the embellishments added for various reasons (sentiment, liturgy, reason, as well as legitimate artistic requirements, which imposed the need for effects, the use of parallelism, etc.). However, there is no need to talk about pure legend, nor to give an exclusively allegorical interpretation to their story. One must simply recognize that these compositions resulted from the elaboration of certain facts which really existed, although they are mostly unidentifiable now.

The historical books, like the others, are always supporting a thesis, and therefore the selection and presentation of facts do not respond to the needs of pure erudition; however these works are of considerable importance because they have made use of varied sources (often in a rather free way), and have adapted documents and oral traditions, of which we would have very little knowledge without these echoes. The first *Book of the Maccabees*, the most important of them all, tells the history of the Palestinian Hebrews from 175 to 135 BC, and shows the struggle they maintained in defence of their faith: the objectivity is absolute, though coupled with a genuine poetic sentiment, even in the bare description. The studied aim of the author is achieved better by the simple recollection of facts than by the pressure of personal considerations. The original Hebrew has been lost, but the text exists in a Greek translation: one can believe that it was composed in the last decade of the second century BC.

The first *Book of the Maccabees* mentions a chronicle on the life of the priest John Hyrcanus, but this has been lost; so also has been a vast work in five books, written by Jason of Cyrene, a learned Hebrew, who, shortly after 161, described the events of 175, having collected contemporary accounts of that year: however the second *Book of the Maccabees* is simply a recapitulation of Jason, as the author explicitly explains. Therefore the two *Books of the Maccabees* have a chronological period in common, but the tone of the two accounts is very different, and they use different evidence even where they deal with the same fact; from the historical point of view the first Book is in every case the respected authority; on the other hand the second Book is more theological, being based upon a profound conviction of the working of Providence in human historical events. From the end of the third century BC many Hellenistic Jews wrote several books to exalt the glory of their people, and to defend their co-religionists from the accusations current among the pagans. The names remain of Demetrius, Eupolemus, Artapanus, Aristeas, Cleodemus; Alexander Polistor made an important collection of their writings, and from there some fragments found their way into Christian works, and were inserted in their books.

d. *Greek and Roman Literature*

Epic Poetry. [Greek thinkers of every period regarded the Homeric epics as the source of all literature. Homer haunted the poet's imagination long after the end of what we call the *epic age* (once the Homeric poems had settled into their final form, at the end of the sixth century BC); but his lessons were applied in different ways, according to individual judgement.

Some poets tried to imitate the historical aspect of his compositions (for the *Iliad* was regarded as an account of historic events, substantially true in spite of its mythological 'embellishments').] The result was that instead of creative works of art inspired by specific great events, Epic gradually became history in verse. Examples include *The Foundation of Colophon* and *The Foundation of Elea* by Xenophanes of Colophon (see p. 250). [Other poets set themselves to amplify certain themes which they thought Homer had dealt with too cursorily.] This alternative was short episodic or biographical poems of a partly lyrical, partly epic form. The best-known poet of the latter type was the second of those known as Stesichorus (see p. 279): he was the son of Eucleides from Himera in Sicily, who had prevented Gelon from taking possession of his city; then he migrated to Greece in 485, and later returned to his own country after the defeat of the Carthaginians in 479 near Himera. One of his undoubted aims in his *Geryonis*, which deals with the adventures of Heracles in the West (including western Sicily), is to justify the recent enterprise of the 'Heraclid' Dorieus to appropriate the area of Mount Eryx. *Iliou Persis*, the *Orestiad*, the *Hunting of Wild Boars*, and the *Nostoi* must certainly all be attributed to him. [The *Iliou Persis* and the *Nostoi* claimed to supplement Homer's poems. The former gave an uninterrupted, consecutive account of the episodes that culminated in the fall of Troy,[1] while the latter described the heroes' adventures on their way back to their respective countries, and was thus an 'expansion' of the *Odyssey*.[2]]

[Again, some poets tried to transpose Homer's method to cycles of legend not included in the classical epics.] Thus, the ancient mythical material was further expanded in the *Thebaid* by Antimachus of Colophon (died in 404) which was variously evaluated in the ancient world. At the same time the events of the recent Persian Wars provided the argument of the *Perseid* by Choerilus of Samos, who was still alive in 404; he was also the author of *Samiaca*.

The poets of the Hellenistic age still considered that the epic represented the highest form of poetry, with the result that many epic poets of the Hellenistic era wrote poems of varying length, some on mythical stories, others on recent events. These were primarily philologists, filled with great love for Homer, but not always equipped with the capacity to write epics. The most famous of them was Callimachus of Cyrene (*c.* 310–235) an erudite and prolific poet [whose influence spread far beyond the Alexandrian court circle in which he lived, not only as a court poet, but as a highly reputed philologist; after his death, this influence became supreme in Rome from the middle of the first century BC. Catullus, writing about 55 BC, and shortly after him Propertius, strove to be 'the Roman Callimachus'. The chief concern of Callimachus himself was to arrive at poetic beauty through absolute perfection of style. He therefore sometimes rejected the Homeric model—not out of contempt, but from a feeling that times had changed since the heroic age and that 'modern' poetry should take a new turn.] Callimachus is the author of the *Coma Berenices*, in which a lock of Queen Berenice's hair, transformed into a newly discovered constellation, tells its own story; it is a slight plot overloaded with astronomical erudition and reflections on love and marriage. [The poem is written for a particular occasion, and is a delicate allegory drawing upon oriental beliefs which connected certain divinities with particular stars—beliefs which the Ptolemies, like other dynasties founded when the Alexandrian empire was dismembered, had taken over as mystical appendages of the royal house. Religious inspiration plays a leading part in the work of Callimachus, who lived in a profoundly religious, even mystical period. He treats the ancient classical Greek myths in the light of the new sentiments, so that they emerge as legends to be approached ironically, in the certitude that religion, the divine reality, is on quite a different plane.] His six surviving hymns were in part supposed, like the ancient *Nomoi*, to be the central theme of sacred celebrations: they sing the praises of the gods and relate legends about them. To the modern reader it may seem that the praise is made up of tepid enthusiasm, rhetorical flights, and learned pieces of fiction; the story is told not by a true believer, but by a scholar in search of romantic tales and marvellous transformations. [This is an opinion frequently expressed, but it by no means does justice to these pieces, many of them extremely subtle and packed with meanings which are difficult to interpret.]

Callimachus' great poem the *Aetia* ('On the Origins', i.e., 'on the reasons for things'—explaining certain rites, etc.)—considerable fragments of which have been recovered in papyrus—is in four books of the epico-mythological type: there are gathered together, in many episodes, what the Muses 'have told him' about the origins of a number of historical events, geographical facts, curious customs, and stories of love affairs. It is therefore a sort of erudite encyclopaedia of mythology, history, and folklore, in which he uses great precision in quoting sources and a wide range of learning. [In this part of his work Callimachus is inspired not so much by the Homeric spirit as by Hesiod, whom he takes up and modernizes.]

Callimachus was convinced that a literary work should be short to be appreciated. Stung by the challenge of his opponent Apollonius (the objective of his poem the *Ibis*, a ferocious invective of which we get some idea from the imitation written by Ovid) he composed a short poem of about 500 verses, *The Hecale*, which, in his view, was to be the model of a new epic. This short poem took its name from an old country-woman who entertained Theseus before his struggle with the bull of Marathon and passed the time by recounting old legends, all done in the most meticulous detail.3

Apollonius 'Rhodius' (295–215), the pupil and rival of Callimachus, was a devotee of Homer and set himself as a young man to compose the *Argonautica*, which appeared eventually as four books of about 6,000 verses. He wanted to reconcile the acceptable part of traditional mythology with what he thought was required by the tastes of his own time: in other words he had to include information about geography, etymology, and the customs of barbarians. He also wanted to introduce love, an important factor in poetry. The resulting poem was of very varied merit and appeal. The part which describes heroic deeds is smothered by oppressive erudition, and the epic practically becomes prose. On the other hand in the love passages, the figure of Medea is wonderfully outlined, with an analysis of passion and feeling which no other ancient author knew how to give. Apollonius indulged the taste of his own period by also composing brief poems concerning the beginning and the history of the two areas known to him. Alexandria, Naucratis, and Canopus were one; the other was Rhodes, with Cnidus and Caunus.

Among the historical epics of the Alexandrian period the *Messeniaca* by Rhianus of Bene in Crete should be mentioned: this describes the Messenian Wars in an anti-Spartan spirit.

In the Greek world, where life now seemed hardly heroic, Epic was dying. [In central Italy the spirit of the heroic era seems to have survived for some considerable time, thanks to the Etruscans, who drew extensively on Homer's tales in their art and (perhaps) in their literature. It is also possible that the Roman national traditions were embodied in literary form—passed on in some cases by word of mouth—and thus paved the way for Roman epic poetry.] But the great events during their rising hegemony gave the Romans inexhaustible subjects which, together with the material from their ancient folk-songs, were transformed into great artistic poems once the Homeric models were known. [The earliest surviving epic poem in the Latin tongue was composed by a Greek from Tarentum, Andronicus, a freedman of the *gens Livia*, who went by the name of L. Livius Andronicus.] It is thought that, taken to Rome as a slave in 272, he made these Homeric models known to the Romans; he wanted them to appreciate the superb beauty of the Homeric epic. Rome in 272 had already become the ruler of the Italiote area, and was becoming so in Siceliote territory. Before he died about 204, Andronicus in fact wrote in rough and uninteresting Latin an 'Odyssey', a free translation of the great poem of the same name, composed in Saturnian verses, after substituting Latin ideas for Greek ones; his work was successful enough to be used as a text in some schools even in Horace's day.[4]

[It may be wondered why Rome felt the need to develop a literature, and why it was so late in doing so. Incidentally, the first Latin writers were not Romans but southern Italians, either from Tarentum (like Livius Andronicus) or from Campania (like Naevius and Ennius); in other words from regions where the Greek influence of the former Hellenic colonies (Tarentum, Naples, etc.) had been grafted on the old Italic stock and brought it to fresh flowering. But it is remarkable, too, that these earliest works were written in Latin rather than in one of the southern tongues, such as Oscan, the national language of Campania. This shows that the influence of Rome had also been important, even, perhaps, decisive. The emergence of a Roman state, with a sense of community and national pride, was required before the need for a literature could be felt and the means develop; and that literature was 'Roman' from the outset. The forms with which it began, epic and drama, have a social function to fulfil—the former commemorating the glories of history, the latter connected with religious festivals. Roman literature came to birth in the Rome that had defeated Carthage, after the First Punic War; not until the beginning of the third century, after routing Pyrrhus and unifying almost the whole peninsula in confrontation with Grecian Sicily and the power of Carthage, did Rome begin to regard itself as a national community and therefore to feel the need of literary expression. But the Romans were already acquainted with Greek culture, to some extent at least; it was not a revelation opened up for them by their first writers. The more modest task of those early authors was to adapt Hellenism to the demands of a Rome just awakening to an interest in the Muses and in the kind of immortality— and spiritual development—they can bestow.]

Shortly after Andronicus, about 235, the Campanian Cn. Naevius, who had taken part in the First Punic War, started his prolific literary output in Rome; this was interrupted by his exile to Utica in 201, and he died about 194. Naevius too used Homer as his model and aimed at writing a form of Latin *Iliad* in which the legends linking Rome with Troy would be blended with those glories of the 'cives Romani' which had reached their greatest fulfilment in the victories over Carthage. But only the last five cantos of his poem refer to that war: the first two were devoted to the great mythological antecedents of these conflicts, in fact the origins of Rome and Carthage, tragically united by the adventures of Dido and Aeneas. With Naevius the anonymous Roman epic poetry became an artistic genre with new characteristics. It had a Roman subject and a Greek form; it glorified facts which were in part ancient and mythical but in part recent and historical. But even in the form of the poetry there was a survival of native Roman practice in the use of the ancient 'Saturnian' metre, though he made it more supple and stirring, a less unpolished instrument than that employed by Andronicus.⁵

Q. Ennius, almost a compatriot of Andronicus, had been born in Messapian Rudiae (239–c.169), and came to Rome in 204, where he displayed his knowledge of three languages (Greek, Latin, and Oscan). [Like his two predecessors, he was both a dramatic and an epic poet. He had begun his career as a centurion in an army corps in his own country. During the Second Punic War he served in Sardinia, where he attracted the attention of Cato (the Censor). Cato sent for him to Rome and gave him the semi-official post of *poeta*, in which he succeeded Naevius. Ennius began to write his epic in the atmosphere of fiery patriotism prevailing at that time, when Rome's whole strength was banded against Hannibal, shortly after it had seemed in danger of destruction.] Ennius named his poem the *Annales*: it was an epic containing the whole of Roman history, from the beginning to the recent events seen by the poet himself. [He is much more 'modern' than either of his predecessors, and reveals the influence of contemporary Hellenism much more strongly. He shows certain characteristics in common with the Alexandrian poets (a taste for virtuosity, a bold tendency towards verbal innovation, and a leaning towards didactic verse, in which he even included such an unexpected subject as gastronomy, dealt with in his *Hedyphagetica*). He is the least deeply Italic of the ancient Latin poets, full of disdain for the 'barbarous' style of Andronicus and Naevius.]

A great admirer of Homer, whose soul he proudly believed he had inherited by metamorphosis, he wanted to be the Roman Homer: he was the first to introduce to the Latin world the famous metre of the Greek Epic, the dactylic hexameter. This involved him in great linguistic difficulties but he braved them, not without some noticeable strain in scansion and in his use of the caesura, syncope, and the like. He was the true creator of the noble and lofty language of Roman Epic and Tragedy, a language which when compared with that of Andronicus and Naevius demonstrates the great cultural and aesthetic progress accomplished in Roman letters between the First Punic War and the end of the Second. The great poem to which he applied himself for many years was divided into books, which may have been published either in groups or one by one. The treatment grows in breadth as it descends in time: ancient myths are unfolded in the first books; in the others the epic tone is maintained by heroic stories in lofty style and pure language (although it is a little artificial because of the numerous alliterations). Everything betrays a great love for the Roman world and its heroes. He drew on every source for their adventures—the ancient epic folk poems, the *Annales Maximi*, Naevius, the Greek Timaeus, and the first Roman annalist Fabius Pictor. Only small fragments of this great work, about 600 badly mutilated lines, have survived.

[The Romans considered Ennius as the founder of their literature. This, though unfair to Andronicus and Naevius, is true inasmuch as he was the first to achieve the transposition of Greek writing and the Greek spirit which, generally speaking, constitutes Latin literature. They gave him the title of *Pater*, which he thus shared with Juppiter, Mars, Janus, and others of the greatest, most benevolent, and venerated gods; and both Virgil and Lucretius borrowed heavily from him. In that sense he is really the Father.]

P. Vergilius Maro (79–*c.* 19 BC) of Andes near Mantua, perhaps the school friend and later in his life protégé of Octavian, was already experimenting with a type of Hellenistic lyric and with his *Bucolica* and *Georgics* (see below p. 588, and also p. 572 on the *Catalepton*). Towards 30 BC he began the great epic poem, the *Aeneid*, which was to eclipse all the work preceding Roman epic writers, and in which he proposed to glorify the predestined rule of Rome and of its ruler Augustus. [In embarking upon his epic poem, Virgil was faithful to the Roman concept of the *epos* as a nationalistic poem expressing the requirements of patriotism and setting up a common ideal for the citizens. Maecenas, and the political leaders of the new régime, would have liked a poet to extol Octavian's military exploits and compare him, after his defeat of Antony, to the great heroes of ancient times. But Virgil had the happy idea of imitating Naevius and Ennius, rather than writing a rigidly historical poem. Better still, he gave his theme a legendary setting, thus conferring upon it an extra dimension, a depth in which it seems to be the channel of Destiny. In so doing he recaptured an essential feature of Homeric poetry; for the *Iliad*, too, is a poem that reverts to those 'origins' whose nobility, glory, etc., illuminate the present day. By going deliberately back to Homer, Virgil remains faithful to the spirit of the Greek *epos*, regarded as the touchstone of national culture. Thanks to him, Rome is seen more clearly than ever as the cultural heir of Hellenism (in the widest sense). This intention was in keeping with the policy of Augustus, who was anxious to 'reconcile' the two halves of the empire, the Hellenized East and the Romanized West, and to create a single, syncretic culture, shared by Rome and Greece.]

The wanderings of Aeneas and his conquest of Latium are like a compendium of a new *Odyssey* and a new *Iliad*; and in fact the Homeric poems were always present to the mind of Virgil, who draws inspiration from them in many episodes which rival the models he was imitating. The Roman poem differs widely from the *Iliad* in that it sets the stage for a duel between two peoples (Rome and Carthage) not for a woman but for the dominion of the world; and the work of Aeneas is not an end in itself, but the task of a man predestined by fate to pass through human events and sorrows and achieve something of superhuman importance for the history of the world. The *Aeneid* is the celebration of Italy, both its history and natural beauties, which pass before our eyes throughout the various books. But at the same time it is an acknowledgement of the beauty of the whole Mediterranean world, which Rome had united; it shows sympathy therefore towards the Asian peoples, from whom came the hero who put ashore in Latium, and similarly for the Africans of the afflicted Dido, where Augustus had revived the flourishing and powerful *Colonia Iunonia* of Carthage.

The *Aeneid* is also a poem of religious feeling, pious and profound, the feeling which Augustus counted on being able to revive in order to achieve his restoration of Italy. The Penates of Troy are the same as those of the empire. Aeneas is guided step by step by the divine will; sanctified by his superhuman knowledge of the mysteries of Elysium, he begins with his undertakings the foundation of Destiny's preordained history of Rome. In this poem Virgil, who had already moved from his early Epicureanism to Stoicism, climbed another rung and reached an almost Neoplatonic mysticism; this is at its most impressive in the episode of the descent into Hell in the sixth Book, which is connected with rediscovered Hellenistic epic fragments, and where we see the purification of souls liberated from bodies, with the reincarnation of those who were not yet sufficiently purified, and the final liberation of others into Elysium.

Originally a 'Poeta novus' (new poet) of the Alexandrian type, in his last two great poems Virgil left the school for ever; he maintained the technique he had acquired, but he gave his didactic and heroic works a loftier and nobler content. He combined passionate devotion to polished workmanship with the spontaneous lyrical power which springs from his deep sympathy with his themes. He thus achieved great dignity and restraint of style, with a remarkable facility for concise utterance. His diction is in general modern, [but he draws extensively upon the vocabulary of Ennius and Lucretius, who thus appear as his forerunners. Virgil established a definite 'poetic language' in Latin; it was used after his time, but of course to less effect, for while with him it was a creative process, his imitators were using it as an academic exercise. Virgil achieves a great and apparently effortless variety of tone; sometimes he is epic, in the Homeric style, at other times he writes simply, almost like a folk poet; and he is also capable of tremendously vivid description and tragic intensity. Some of his imagery has remained famous and even shapes our present-day imagination—such as the '*Ibant obscuri sola sub nocte, per umbram* . . .' by which he describes Aeneas' descent into Hell, accompanied by the Sybil, drawing a picture the subtlety of which is enhanced by its sober restraint. Virgil's style is that of a 'classic';] he preserves a healthy equilibrium between this modernity and the restrained use of archaisms and verses from early poets. The flow of his hexameters is well-nigh perfect, each line often corresponding to the complete expression of an idea.[6]

Elegy, Lyric, and Epigram. With the first decades of the fifth century BC we reach in Theognis the last of the great Greek elegists. He has been regarded as a native of Megara Nisaea in Greece, living about 540 BC; but in our opinion this is incorrect since there is evidence that he was a Siceliote Greek, born at Megara Hyblaea, and that he flourished in the early part of the fifth century.7 The manuscript tradition ascribes to him a collection of poems in two books, one of 1,230 the other of 159 lines. He came from a rich and noble family and with other nobles became involved in a struggle against the *demos*. Eventually he was overpowered in a riot, deprived of his property, and reduced to the most squalid poverty. When his city was taken by the tyrant Gelon in 482 (and shortly afterwards destroyed), he retired to Megara Nisaea in Greece, where in 480–479 he mourned the dangers which his new country was encountering from the Persians, though soon afterwards he was celebrating their liberation after the battle of Plataea. Theognis composed many detached elegies, but what has come down to us is only a collection or anthology, compiled about 400 BC, in which extracts from various poems, divorced from their contexts, are juxtaposed, contaminated, and subjected to interpolation by fragments of various other poets. Sometimes the non-Theognidean elements can be identified, and in this way distinguished from about eighty definitely authentic poems among the collection of 370. Theognis was sober, realistic, and restrained in his ideas: flights of lyric fancy were not his way. Unassuming in his constructions and prone to abstraction, he showed himself an experienced thinker, one who knew the human heart and was also passionate, bitter, and easily roused over matters of politics: in this last he was very far removed from Solon, despite the great resemblances between the two poets as dialecticians and moralists. As to morals, Theognis was clear and moderate: following the views of conservative thinkers of his day he believed that the foundations of virtue lay in right judgement, tranquillity, and balance. He also showed himself reverent towards his god, whom he regarded as a being free from human passions.

During the fifth and fourth centuries elegy and epigram were used occasionally by all the great writers of the time (Aeschylus, Sophocles, Euripides, Thucydides, Plato, etc.). They were the favourite genre for certain lesser poets, such as Euenus of Paros (460–390) who wrote elegant and pithy aphorisms, or Critias, or Antimachus, the author of an epic-elegiac poem on ancient heroes crossed in love.

In addition certain forms of iambic composition were still to be found. Cercidas of Megalopolis with his *Meliambi* anticipated the Horatian spirit; and the militant Cynic philosopher Crates of Thebes, who flourished about 325, wrote *Iambi* directed at improving men's behaviour. There was also an output of parodies of ancient myths.

The form of lyric which survived with greatest vitality was the choral poem. [In Greece in the late sixth and early fifth century, this was the dominant form of poetic expression, having succeeded the epic and not being yet ousted by the tragic form. Choral poetry at this time was already scenic, for it constituted a complete performance, comprising the movements of a chorus, with chanting, recitative and music. It is difficult for us today to imagine what such a performance can have been like, for the words alone have come down to us, without their accompanying melody. We even find it difficult to reconstruct the rhythm, with its complex pattern, its repetition of symmetrical triads (strophe, antistrophe, epode), and can only form an abstract idea of it. These choral poems were splendidly spectacular, for they were songs of praise, extolling the glorious deeds of past heroes and above all those of the chief heroes of Greece in their day, the victors in the great Games.]

The first and most important name in this period is that of Pindar the Boeotian (about 522–446), whose earliest datable ode is in 498 and the latest 446. His fame as a panhellenic poet was such that, although his praises were never servile, all the nobles in the Greek world sought to receive them and have him as their guest, so that his life was a peregrination from court to court. Of his seventeen books of choral songs of all types all that has survived —apart from various fragments—are the four sets of *Epinikia* for victories in the Olympian, Pythian, Nemean, and Isthmian games. His poems are in a stately metre, in a dialect derived from that of earlier lyricists, tending both towards Doric and towards Aeolic. The style is almost inimitable, imaginative and sensitive. The odes were sung to the accompaniment of a flute or lyre, or of both instruments together. They celebrate not so much the actual victors as their cities (Pindar preferred aristocratic or tyrannic régimes, provided that they were moderate). With them he celebrates the cities' gods, his conception of whom is based on profound religious feeling, influenced by Orphic and Pythagorean theories; he therefore corrects his legends to suit the dictates of morality.

Thirteen odes to victory, elegant and polished rather than gay, together with fragments, have survived from Bacchylides of Ceos (late-sixth to mid-fifth century). He too wrote many types of poems: they show analytical, narrative, colourful, and decorative talent, but have no overriding conception of a religious, political, or moral kind. They must have lost a good deal of their original attraction from the loss of the music which accompanied them.

During the Attic period there were great developments in the lyric field, in dithyramb and other forms,[8] which reached their highest point at the beginning of the fourth century.

The use of more complicated musical instruments, and the new polyphonic conceptions, both allowed and required that the lyrical and dramatic compositions to be set to music should be long, yet not monotonous. At the same time prose was being used for arguments of a moral or didactic nature; and the flowering and the fame of the dramatic style were concentrating the taste of the Greek public on 'pathetic' poetry (by which the Greeks meant sensuous forms or those which arouse passion). All this meant that from the fifth century onwards Greek lyric was normally limited to two forms, the dithyramb and the *nomos*.[9] Both forms were heavily dramatized, with choral sections, while other parts were sung and presented by actors. In this way the musical element became more important than the poetry and ideas, and the two forms were eventually very similar. Their poetical sections, which were often reduced to a mere 'libretto' of an affecting and imaginative kind, are known to us by the fragments which have survived. But they have lost the musical portions which were their very being, and it is therefore impossible to get an adequate idea of the artistic value and interest of this form of literature.

For these lyrical, dramatic, and musical compositions, many of which we know only from comments by playwrights, there were regular competitions at a number of annual festivals at Athens from the end of 508 BC; and about 440 Pericles constructed a covered theatre called the Odeion to be used for this purpose.

We also possess some fragments of the 'soft' dithyrambs of Melanippides of Melos (died before 413). We are told too of comic poets who were immoral, obscure, vacuous, and pretentious, such as the Athenian Cinesias; and of effeminate poets such as the Mytilenean Phrynis, the winner of a competition in 412. Philoxenus of Cythera (435–380) was the author of twenty-four dithyrambs, and in one of them, the *Cyclops*, a bucolic piece dramatizing the love-affair of Polyphemus with Galatea, he revenges himself by tart allusions to the Syracusan tyrant Dionysius I who had imprisoned him.

The ancient world possessed eighteen books of lyrics by Timotheus of Miletus (*c.*450–360); we can judge the value of the poetry, but not fully that of the rather revolutionary music, from various fragments and also from part of a *nomos* called *The Persians* (much admired by Hellenistic scholars for its music), which was discovered on an Egyptian papyrus. In this work he describes the victory of Salamis in an extravagant and bizarre style, rather like the libretto of a melodrama, and reduces historical truth to an absurd level. An opera by Timotheus sings of the pains of *Semele's Delivery*; others were dedicated to Scylla, Niobe, and Odysseus.

Greek lyric poetry in the Hellenistic period[10] was not addressed to the populace; it was poetry well stocked and heavy with erudition, which could be enjoyed only by a suitably restricted circle of connoisseurs. Refined in style, chiselled in its phrases, accomplished in the choice of its vocabulary, it did not gush from the heart but from the brain. The favourite subject was love, and its metre the hexameter. The mode was either elegy, normally of a sad and sentimental tone, or epigram, the brief vivacious composition designed to express wit and 'ideas'.

The first representative of this new artistic tendency was Philetas of Cos (*c.*340–280) a grammarian who lived surrounded by a circle of friends. His most famous work was a series of elegies of love praising his Bittis, all of which poems were certainly inspired by Antimachus' *Lydia*. We know too of his other poetic works on Telephus, Hermes, and Demeter. Theocritus recognized him as his master, and Propertius considered him as a poet of the highest order; it is clear that he must have provided them with new models for elegies on love and mythology, and for the well-chiselled epigram.

45   Etruscan sarcophagus so-called 'Del Magnate'. Tarquinia Museum

(a)

46 ETRUSCAN PAINTING

   (a) *Mastarna or Servius Tullius;*
        detail from the fresco of the
        so-called 'François tomb' at
        Vulci. Rome, Torlonia Museum

   (b) *Episode from the Roman-Samnite*
        wars, fresco on a tomb on the
        Esquiline

(b)

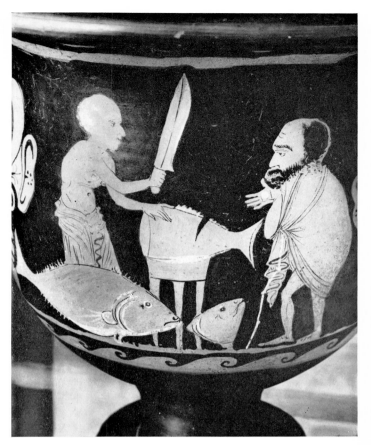

47   (a) *Hellenistic vase from Sicily depicting a fishmonger* (*detail*)
      (b) *Campanian plate depicting a war elephant*

(b)   S.A.E.M.

(a)

[Alinari

48 *The so-called 'Ficoroni' casket,*
fourth century BC. Rome, Museum
of the Villa Giuglia
(a) *Front view*
(b) *Detail of the lid*

(b)

[Alinari

At the same time the epigram, in the form that was common in the peninsula and in the western colonies, inspired by the contemplation of nature and by a longing for peace of soul, found talented expression in the work of two poetesses, Anyte of Tegea and Nossis of Locri. Another Asiatic form of the epigram, full of erotic passion, was launched at the same time by a great poet, Asclepiades of Samos: in his brief odes, written in new metres which have taken their name from him, he confesses his love-pangs, exalts the beauty of his beloved, and describes the impassioned life of the city with a fineness and vigour that are truly exquisite.

Leonidas of Tarentum (about 300–270), a poor wandering poet, lived by writing epigrams for tombs, offerings to the gods by humble people, inscriptions on statues, and the like. Only about a hundred have survived, but they show him to be a true poet, capable of moving us and of being moved, neither banal nor stuffed with erudition.

Later Meleager of Gadara (100 BC), the pupil of the Cynic Menippus, was a famous epigrammatist, whose love-poetry is veiled by a moving melancholy. He also helped to publish his predecessor's works, and collected them in an anthology which he called the *Garland* (*Corolla*).

While the Greek world was producing a rather decadent lyric form which was seldom of true worth, Latin lyric, at first based on the Hellenistic model but later following other paths, was gradually asserting its place. About most of the works written between 150 and 60 BC, when the school of 'new' poets became prominent, we have only poor and fragmentary information.

But it was approximately between 60 and 50 BC that the school of the 'new poets', whom Cicero in derision called the *cantores Euphorionis*, established themselves at Rome. Lovers of form above all, they preferred brief but polished poems, metrically rich in spondees and a vocabulary of neologisms. They were a closed circle far from the common world; some of them were even cut off from any public career. In this way they led frivolous and fastidious lives amid their pleasures and their loves. They adored the foreign women, the courtesans from the East, who were flocking into Rome: and with them they loved those Roman women who competed with the foreigners in fastidiousness of culture, in freedom of attire, and in political intrigues. Their natural tendencies were developed by their literary contacts with Greek poets of the same temperament who were then living at Rome, particularly Parthenius and Philodemus.

But though Greek in form and tastes, the best of them were none the less true lyricists, who based their poems on the sentimental episodes of their own lives. The passion which they describe is Roman, often violent, often generous. In general their poetic worth, precisely because they were more sincere and more inspired, was better than that of their Greek friends, among whom there was no Catullus.

The earliest among these new poets (or 'Neoterics') were quickly eclipsed by their greatest pupil (C.) Catullus, a Veronese of noble birth who came to

Rome and lived in its poetic circle among both many friends and many enemies. [Although we have lost almost all the short lyrical poems (epigrams and short pieces after the manner of Meleager of Gadara) written by Catullus' Roman contemporaries, everything he himself wrote has come down to us. It is a variegated collection. It includes 'occasional' verses, most of them satirical, alluding to leading citizens and events at Verona, and others which refer to Caesar and his friends, at a time when Catullus and his own friends were 'members of the opposition' and ranked with the conservatives. These pieces are cruel, sometimes coarse, and contrast sharply with those in the other two groups—the love-poems and the great 'Alexandrine' poems.

Catullus relates in some detail the story of his love for a certain Lesbia—a pseudonym for Clodia, a sister of the demagogue P. Clodius Pulcher, Cicero's enemy. The choice of pseudonym is not accidental, for Lesbia is intended as an allusion to Sappho, and Catullus is the disciple of the Aeolian lyrical poets. Like Sappho, he strives to express the joys and fears of the lover.] This part of his work consists of sincere poems, even though the form follows the school; they deal with true passion, now sweet and gentle, now violent and vulgar, and even repugnant in their crudity. At times the passion of love reaches the utmost limits of feeling and is expressed with indescribable freshness and spontaneity even in passages where the poet has paraphrased Sappho and other Greek lyricists. They are impressionist poems which reflect fleeting moments of the heart: love and happiness, unrestrained sensuality, anger, hate, sad resignation, hopelessness of a hypersensitive sentimental mind.

[The third section of his work, comprising the great Alexandrine poems, is of more difficult interpretation. Catullus is trying here to paint sweeping pictures in the style of Callimachus, combining a sense of composition with great perfection of detail. He has been attracted by religious sensibility in its most extreme forms of expression. His *Attis* (an evocation of the worship of the Phrygian Great Mother, with its orgiastic, bloodthirsty, and sensual rites)] represents a violent movement and feeling—turbulence, noise, murmuring, and despair—and therefore employs the characteristic 'Galliambic' metre. [Even in the quieter pieces (such as the *Epithalamium* of Thetis and Peleus which, with its 408 lines, is the longest of all the poems) the religious spirit is always present; the tale is always pervaded by moral considerations. They are written] in hexameters, or sometimes elegiac metre. We find an imitation (rather than a translation) of Callimachus' *Lock of Berenice*; a marvellous lament for the death of his brother and his own sorrow; the story of the marriage of Peleus and Thetis; and with this the episode of the pitiful weeping of Ariadne when Theseus abandoned her.

Virgil had composed his *Catalepton* when still a youth of hardly sixteen. These are short pieces of poetry, together with a narrative poem, the *Culex*, which imitates Alexandria in its subject and style. A mosquito stings a sleeping shepherd, saving him from a serpent's bite; squashed by him the mosquito reappears in a dream, describing the inhabitants of the underworld. The shepherd raises to the insect an altar bedecked with flowers.[11]

[The work of Horace stands out from the rest of Roman lyrical poetry, if only through its metric form. In his *Epodes*, and subsequently in his *Odes (Carmina)*, Horace set himself to imitate the Aeolian poets. For the *Epodes*, many of which are violently satirical, he usually takes Archilochus as his model, while in the *Odes* he chiefly follows Sappho. The first three books of *Odes* were published together, in the year 23 BC, and it is often very difficult, or even impossible, to ascribe a date to a particular poem. Thus, any attempt to trace the chronological development of Horace's ideas must be largely conjectural. It is rash to assert, for instance, that Horace's admiration for Augustus' achievements only began after the victory at Actium. For since the spring of the year 38 BC, at latest, Horace belonged to the group surrounding Maecenas, who was devoted to Augustus. He was not merely a fair-weather friend, but remained faithful through the dark days, and by the year 38 he was already convinced that Octavian's party alone could restore peace in Rome and in the outside world. It is quite plausible that he may have collaborated with Virgil in framing Augustus' future programme, though not always in complete agreement with the policy of the *Princeps*. For instance, he repeatedly calls for war in the East, against the Parthians, as a revenge for their routing of Crassus in 53; but Octavian always firmly refuses. It is also an error to ignore everything except the political aspect of Horace's lyrical writings, for that is only one side of the moral, gnomic character inseparable from the lyrical poetry of classical antiquity. The *Odes* reflect a philosophical attitude towards everyday life which at first is Epicurean (delight in the passing hour, as a protection against melancholy and the thought of death), but which gradually takes a more virile turn (praise of freedom in all its forms, outward and inward, liberation from wealth, from the passions, from pleasure itself). Horace's feeling for nature, one of his chief sources of inspiration, is inseparable from thoughts of death, and provides a starting-point for meditation on man's place in the creation. This concentration on thoughts, which are more important to Horace than perfection of style, sets him clearly apart from the Alexandrian spirit and that of the *Neoteroi* from whom, like Virgil, he originally set out. In this respect Horace is profoundly 'Roman'—even his most playful and charming poems are marked by an undeniable *gravitas*.]

The Latin poets seem to have invented the erotic personal elegy once more and carried it to the highest levels of artistic development, in their technique of couplets or groups of couplets covering a single theme. [In point of fact, the circumstances attending this 'invention' are by no means clear. The Roman elegists took as their model, to some extent, the series of poems in the elegiac metre composed by certain Alexandrian poets and dedicated to the woman they loved (see above). But the latter used another style as well, that of the love-epigram in the manner of Meleager of Gadara. The Roman love-elegy combines the narrative elegy and the erotic epigram, accentuating one or the other aspect as the mood suggests. This explains why the *Elegies* of Tibullus and Propertius include poems of very different character, some of them inspired by love, while others come much closer to the *Aetia* of Callimachus (see above). The Roman love-elegy developed slowly, during the generation from 60 to 20 BC.] The first examples had already been produced by Catullus, but the acknowledged master of the school was Cornelius Gallus, a poet, the friend of Virgil and another member of the 'Alexandrine' group then flourishing in Cisalpine Gaul; his highly praised *Lycoris* (about 40 BC) contained the four books of his love-elegies.

His greatest follower was Albius Tibullus (*c.* 59–19 BC) a Roman knight and a friend of Horace. Afflicted by ill-health, economic disasters, and unlucky love-affairs, he lived a mainly retired life in his villa at Pedum, dying while quite young. Tibullus' unhappy love for Delia and for Nemesis are given fanciful expression in his elegies. These have a deliberate plot in which memories and personal feelings are entangled, in a nimble and smooth flowing verse which fascinates the reader, with philosophical thoughts and moral hints, but above all with flights of fancy about bygone days of legend. [The most characteristic feature of Tibullus' poetry is his feeling for nature— his love of the countryside and of peace, his horror of war. He is torn between two sentiments which the Roman soul generally managed to bring into harmony—love of the soil, of peasant life, and admiration for military valour. Tibullus was intended for an active career; his patron, Valerius Messalla, summoned him to take part in Octavius' eastern campaigns; but he accepted reluctantly and was delighted, in his secret heart, when illness prevented him from following his comrades-in-arms and compelled him to return to Rome. There, at least, was Delia, the woman he loved. He longed to take her to live with him on his family estate, so that he could concentrate on farming. Unfortunately, Delia—a courtesan—was only happy in Rome, living in luxury amid male admiration. So Tibullus suffered deeply. No poet excels him in describing the charms of rustic paganism, with its family divinities and picturesque ceremonies. In this respect he comes very close to the Virgil of the *Georgics*. To the mythological evocations favoured by the Alexandrine poets, he preferred more measured phrases,] given us without any straining for erudition in a series of eposodic pictures; and the whole work is as though it were covered by a thin veil of gentle melancholy, of romantic sadness, which again and again brings the poet back to images of sorrow and of death.

Sextus Propertius of Asisium (*c.* 50–15 BC) possessed greater vigour, learning, and fancy. He had come to Rome to devote himself to politics, but was carried away by an unlucky love for a girl he called by the pseudonym Cynthia.[12] The first book of the *Elegies* takes us back to the period of this love-affair, [or rather to the beginning of this adventure, which filled Propertius' whole life and provided him with the essence of his poetical inspiration.

This first book is significantly entitled *Cynthia Monobiblos*; for Cynthia is to the poet an 'Iliad' in herself, a universe he never quite finished exploring. This is an important milestone in the history of human sentiments, the beginning of the 'worship of women' which is not always recognized as having originated in Rome. This book includes some 'epigrams' in the traditional style, and the love-poems are already more concerned with mythology than were the elegies of Tibullus. In this respect Propertius comes closer than Tibullus to their Alexandrian forerunners, especially Callimachus, whose influence is even more evident in his later work (Book IV). But he does not use mythology for purely ornamental purposes; with him it is a way of thought, an expression of sensibility, sometimes a channel for religious feeling. Propertius realizes the religious value of love—and here he is faithful to a certain Roman tradition. For him, love has mystical connotations, it opens the door of eternity to the soul. This Platonic strain in Propertius finds vent in his recourse to myths—the power of love makes Cynthia the equal of the heroines of ancient times, she becomes their companion in the other world.

Propertius is also the poet of unhappy love. Cynthia is not faithful to him —quite naturally, for she was not his wife, but a courtesan, free to lead her own life—and this makes him wretched. The contrast between what he had expected from love and what love brings him—between *Dichtung* and *Wahrheit*—which had torn cries of rage from Catullus, induces Propertius to study his own feelings and to realize the fatal character of a passion which is not amenable to reason. This analysis of unhappy love takes up most of the two following books (II and III), though into these he was already also incorporating mythological, social, and political themes.

Book IV, which was published after his death, deals almost entirely with a new source of inspiration—the Roman legends, treated in the manner of Callimachus. Propertius, the friend of Virgil and a member of the group which had Maecenas as its patron, plays an active part in extolling the Roman past and the religious and moral works of the new régime.]

Publius Ovidius Naso (Ovid) (43 BC–AD 17) who came from a well-to-do family of Sulmo, never wished to be anything but a poet, and lived until the age of fifty as an idle gentleman. But in AD 8 Augustus, in an unexpected decree, exiled him as a corrupter of morals to Tomi on the Black Sea, and he never succeeded in getting recalled. Ovid himself separates his work before the exile into light and serious writings. The *Heroides*, supposed letters written about their loves by women, both mythological and real, belong to the first category, so do *Amores* in which he speaks of his facile, frivolous, numerous, and passing relationships. There is also a group of pseudo-instructive works: *De medicamine faciei*, *Ars amatoria*, and *Remedia amoris*. To the second, 'serious', group belong the *Fasti*, descriptions of the calendar to extol Augustus' religious policy; and the *Metamorphoses*, mythical stories of the transformation of human beings into plants, animals, and inanimate bodies, for which he had collected 250 legends and bound them together into a lightly connected history. He was not interested in the myths apart from the romantic element, the story; and he was unconcerned when he produced doublets or even triplets of the same episode. They are a series of vignettes, of which the most eloquent illustration is given by Hellenistic reliefs and paintings, since poetry and visual art lived in a continuing alliance and were constantly borrowing from one another.

His exile provided the background for the last Ovidian writings. The *Tristia* and the *Epistulae ex Ponto* are lyrical letters from the poet to his friends, his songs of exile. They are no longer art for art's sake, but sincere personal poetry, full of truth and melancholy, human even though tiresomely circling the same ideas. They offer a defence for his poetry, regret for all that he has lost in his homeland, contempt for the country and conditions in which he lives, and hatred for his critics and the friends who have betrayed him.

A facile poet, spontaneous, but for the most part an improviser and a fertile rhetorician, Ovid as an 'impressionist' passed from image to image, picture to picture, and love to love, without pause. All too frequently his work lacks depth, restraint, and finish: at times it even lacks adequate learning. Too often he is satisfied, like an able Alexandrian versifier, with his fancy and a general feeling for beauty.[13]

Tragedy and Comedy. In the fifth century tragedy, particularly at Athens, assumed, aesthetically and didactically, very great religious and moral importance; religion, history, rhetoric, and ethics were focused and taught by its means. The tragic performances became a form of cult, prepared for solemn festivals. This happened at Athens during the various Dionysiac festivals; and also at Syracuse, Epidaurus, Argos, and gradually in all the cities which had developed real theatres out of the primitive open space on a slope or an area with a flight of steps. The characters (originally one but they finally grew to three and exceptionally to four), their faces covered by a mask, obtained their scenic effects by voice and mimicry alone; they had a choral retinue of twelve, later fifteen, with a leader supported by a flautist and, in monodies, by a lutanist. The themes were those of heroic history, and therefore in general the heroes of mythology; but they also included the most important and stirring deeds of contemporary history, such as the *Sack of Miletus* by Phrynichus, and the *Persae* by Aeschylus, as well as purely imaginary themes such as the *Anthos* by Agathon. Originally the choral sections, with their songs and lyrics, had predominated over the recited passages, but later the balance was the other way. Three great tragic poets stand out in fifth-century Greek literature, Aeschylus, Sophocles, and Euripides.

Aeschylus of Eleusis (*c.*525–456/5) was an actor and an author; twenty-eight times winner of tragic contests, he wrote about ninety tragedies and satyric dramas. Apart from many references in authors and especially extensive fragments on papyrus, we have seven of his tragedies, of which four are independent, and three form part of the same tetralogy.[14] Simple in plot, they are developed around a moving heroic or historic event, using characters with superhuman features hieratically drawn in the grand manner. But the sentiments are deeply analysed, and the tragedies are dominated by lofty religious and moral concepts in the mythological tradition. Certain guiding ideas are put forward throughout. There is the destiny which hangs over human life; the intervention of the gods on behalf of their adherents, and their jealousy of excessive human glory;[15] the hereditary taint which is derived from sin and from the curses to which it gives rise; the inferiority of brute force over spiritual strength; the superiority of the laws of civilized peoples; and there are the claims of love.

Sophocles (c. 500–406/5) was born at Athens, and lived almost all his life in that city where he was the idol of the mob. One hundred and twenty-three of his dramatic works are recorded, often repeating themes treated by Aeschylus and others; and seven tragedies have come down to us. Profoundly persuaded that the world is governed by a divinity of inscrutable wisdom, and an independent-minded critic of the theories of the philosophers and sophists, he presents characters who are still a little stylized, but yet are deeply human because of their will, their feelings, and their weaknesses. He captivates the audience with the lively struggles between these characters, with the nobility and drama of his dialogue, with the ease with which he unravels his plots, and with his analysis of character and feeling (particularly of women).

Euripides (c. 485–406) was not very popular with the people because of his religious and moral audacity, which stemmed from his passionate participation in the sophistic movement. We know of ninety-two tragedies of various types of which only seventeen authentic ones (apart from a spurious work) and extensive papyrus fragments have come down to us. As a rule they are indifferent to dramatic unity, and include a succession of episodes brought on by theatrical expedients, the connection between them lying outside the play. The main intention is to portray the development of feelings, even at the cost of having to explain the plot to the audience either by anticipating its outline in the prologue or by summarizing it in the final scenes. The whole artistic power of the tragedy appears in the monologues. The choral sections meanwhile have lost part of their importance and tend to become lyrico-melodic 'intermissions'. Their words were a vehicle for the accompanying music, of which we unfortunately know nothing.

Euripides was not really a true philosopher, though he had an open mind about the many moral, philosophical, and cosmogonic theories which excited learned men from Heraclitus to Socrates. Some of these are reflected here and there, often in a contradictory form, in his dialogues, and in the subtle and sometimes paradoxical discussions between his characters and the chorus.

He was inclined to scepticism, and did not scruple to bring forward his criticisms of established beliefs and opinions, both religious and moral. His characters are neither supermen, nor stylized humans, but real men and women, individuals whom the poet had observed in the world around him, whose instincts, passions, feelings, and intrigues he reproduced with maximum effect. From them he acquired material for satirizing the public and private habits of society, especially of women, and thus opened the way to the satires on behaviour which became the fundamental theme of New Comedy.

Chance has preserved part of the work of these three great tragedians, but they had competitors who were also writers of great power. We know the names of another 140 such plays, while it is calculated that in the fifth century at the Great Dionysia of Athens alone 1,200 tragedies and satyric dramas were presented, written by the most brilliant minds in Greece. As had already been the case with epic and philosophy, there were families and clans of dramatic authors, who handed down works and teachings to one another, as well as taking charge of recitations and bringing the old tragedies up to date.

Tragedy, however, slowly declined. The same overworked themes had been put too often into competitions by the artists; they had lost the original deeply religious purpose; too much attention had to be paid to public taste which was hostile to certain characters and took exaggerated account of the actors' ability. Moreover tragedy became saturated with rhetoric, philosophy, and dialectical virtuosity, and abused the employment of unlikely shifts of fortune and theatrical scenic effects (which gave rise to parodies such as those by Diogenes of Sinope and Crates of Thebes). At the same time it had to meet competition from lyrical compositions set to music. It is true that Ptolemy Philadelphus about 284–281 tried to imitate Athens by instituting tragic contests at Alexandria; eventually he selected from among the best competitors a list of the seven greatest and compared them with the seven stars of the 'Pleiades'. But these writers, like their competitors, were no longer genuine tragedians. They were learned philologists, who attempted in a curious fashion to restore drama to its original form (at least in theory). Thus Sositheus tried to reproduce the earliest dithyrambs, and Philiscus brought historical characters like Themistocles on to the stage. They were unsuccessful in producing anything vital, writing dramas which had to be read with learned commentaries, while real tragedy as a creative genre remained silent; and the dramas of Euripides continued to triumph even though they were abbreviated and deprived of their choral passages. From the authors of the *Pleias* there has survived a most peculiar work, the *Alexandra*, which made the reputation of its author Lycophron of Chalcis in the first half of the third century. Its 1,474 iambic trimeters describe how Cassandra, a prisoner in a tower, predicts the history of Greece up to the time of the author. In this composition, which lacks any breath of poetry, and is full of undigested learning, there is a continuous effort to enhance the

tragic style by obscurity, pedantic eccentricity, and the use of foolish metaphors. This hotch-potch of almost incomprehensible phrases is indeed far
from the flights of Pindar or the pathos of Aeschylus.

The nature of Roman tragedy was complex because it was a Greek plant
growing on Latin soil. Its earliest subjects, as well as the actual genre, were
derived from the Greek tragedians, above all the themes from the Trojan
cycle, which became Roman by adoption. But plots were altered, ideas
were Romanized, and subjects were contaminated. The Roman custom
(perhaps originally Etruscan) of giving the senators and magistrates places
in the orchestra limited the space and the action, and consequently the
importance of the chorus.[16] Tragedy came to Rome through the medium of
Etruria, the home of the *Histriones*; and this, as well as the adoption of
motifs and innovations on the Roman model, was probably responsible for
some of the differences from Greek plays. In fact probably from its first
appearance Latin tragedy presented plots concerned with national myth and
history. These are found in the *fabulae praetextatae*, which at least in their
content are entirely indigenous.

L. Livius Andronicus, the Tarentine who wrote an abridged *Odyssey*, is
known as the first tragedian, from about 240 BC onwards. He produced and
acted his plays and was the first organizer of recitations, which later were
regularly incorporated in both tragedy and comedy. His tragedies dealt with
Greek themes, but we know nothing of his sources or the extent of his debt
to them.

From Cn. Naevius, on the other hand, we are told not only of several
tragedies abridged from Greek, which sometimes amalgamate more than one
model, but also of two *praetextatae* with genuine Roman plots, the *Clastidium*
and the *Romulus*. The same can be said of Q. Ennius from whom we possess
twenty-two certain titles of tragedies with Greek subjects, and also the titles
of two *praetextatae*, *Sabinae* and *Ambracia*. The Ennian fragments show
that though he sometimes translated literally from his Greek source, yet he
would often revise both story and text, rearrange the chronology of events,
and use more than one model. Moreover we can see in his work great pathos
and sententiousness; his plays are full of moral maxims, philosophic motifs
and dialectical terms; there are dashing descriptions of wars, and songs of
high lyric quality. In fact we can appreciate all the virtues which, combined
with the variety of his metres, enabled his tragedies to dominate the Roman
stage for two centuries.

M. Pacuvius, from Brundisium, a nephew of Ennius, was a painter as well
as a poet (220–132). We know the titles of thirteen tragedies with Greek
themes, most of them corrupted by the insertion of material adapted to
Roman taste; and he also wrote the *Paulus*, a play with a native background.
He knew how to fascinate his public and his actors with emotional parts;
he had a wonderful power of description; he could utter serious maxims,
and was also bold in style and in the use of imagery. Cicero, though he

U*

criticized his language, thought him the greatest tragedian; and it is certain that his plays were still alive at the end of the Republic, when the recitation of his poem on Ajax dying (from the *Armorum Iudicium* in imitation of a play by Aeschylus) served to excite the people against the murderers of Caesar.

L. Accius of Pisaurum (179–90), succeeded Pacuvius, and for half a century dominated the Roman tragic stage. He wrote numerous tragedies on Greek subjects and inspired by Greek models, and also some *praetextatae*, of which the *Brutus* and *Aeneadae* (or *Decius*) are recorded. His works were accorded a very favourable judgement by later men of letters. The fragments show him as sceptical about religious questions, vivid in narrative, sententious, fond of moving oratory, and convincing in his dialectic.

This tendency to oratory and declamation in Roman tragedy was accentuated, and reached its height in Seneca. The reduction of the choral part, and the custom of reciting tragic monologues in halls of recitation, contributed to this trend.

The origin of comedy lay to some extent in the work of Epicharmus (*c.*540–457) in Syracuse. Of his thirty-five recorded comedies nineteen provide caricatures of the mythological traditions about gods and heroes; a dozen are of the descriptive type with very little plot, forerunners of the 'mimes' which put typical human beings on the stage, imitating and exploiting their gay and amusing angles; and three are 'controversies' (e.g. does Land or Sea give greater blessing to man?). His comedies did not set out to be didactic satire, nor to attack individual political characters; they are good-humoured and popular caricatures and parodies of human life. The dialect he uses is also a popular one (a hybrid Syracusan); the plot is schematic; there is frequent play on words and utterances which can be taken either seriously or in jest. They even formed the material for a 'book of maxims', to which spurious material was added. Epicharmus enjoyed such a reputation that Plato put him on a level with Homer.

In Sicily in the fifth century there were other comedians, such as Phormis, his son Deinolochus, and Meson of Megara. But comedy ended by setting off a new literary genre, the 'mime'; and this enjoyed wide popularity. It consisted at this period of a short scene drawn from life, with either a monologue or a dialogue between two people, composed in rhythmic prose and in Doric dialect with much use of native Siculan terminology. It was performed at banquets and at public contests as an interlude, and an essential part of it was the imitation of behaviour and typical characters.

Sophron of Syracuse, who lived 'at the time of Xerxes and Euripides', wrote many mimes full of jokes, sometimes decorous, sometimes vulgar. Some were called 'masculine' (*The Fishermen in the Country*, *The Fisher of Tunny*, *Prometheus*, etc.); others were 'feminine' (*The Woman Doctor*, *The Sorceresses making the Goddess Appear*, *The Spectators at the Isthmian Games*, *The Lady's Maid*, *The Mother-in-law*, etc.). Plato read these mimes for pleasure; and their vivid realism and supple dialogue technique seem to have influenced the composition of his own dialogues.

Sophron's son Xenarchus, on orders from Dionysius I, is known to have composed a mime in which he burlesqued the cowardice of the people of Rhegium, comparing them to fleeing hares.

Rhinthon, who was famous for 'phlyacic' comedies, was a native of Syracuse, but later moved to Tarentum, where he was living at the end of the fourth century. It is not clear whether 'phlyax' means 'chatterbox', 'buffoon', or specifically 'demon, imp of fertility'. It is certain that these 'phlyacic' comedies, which were widespread throughout Magna Graecia as far as Campania (where they were called *Atellanae*), and which were recited by actors, clumsily and indecently disguised, were fairly coarse parodies and farces. Often they parodied divine figures and the myths depicted in tragedies, being also called *Hilarotragodiae*. We know something of the contents of the *phlyakes* not only from fragments but from scenes represented in pictures and reliefs.

At the same time as Sicilian and in part under its influence, Attic 'Old Comedy' established itself on similar lines to tragedy in the half-century before the Peloponnesian War. At first it was performed in the 'demes' and city suburbs; but at least from 488 the Athenian government created a contest for it, which was inserted in the plan of the Dionysiac competitions. The comedian was not governed by the limits of time or space; for the more improbable the situation, the more it made the audience laugh. The characters of comedy were shameless and rascally buffoons; the chorus sang, danced, did mimicry and acrobatics, chattered, interrupted one another, and passed judgement. Even the gods were not spared; and clouds, wasps, birds, frogs, Attic demes, and islands were put on the stage. Born of the iambics composed by men in their cups, and developed in a free democratic atmosphere, Attic Old Comedy remained a comic fable, an irreverent satire, an extravagant carnival revelry. It was illogical and disorganized, but ready to pierce like a steel knife, and to fight for its own basic ideals. Being handled by skilful fencers it was a potent weapon; the state had to take account of it, and in 440 and 416 passed laws which prohibited comedians from making personal allusions. But the genre pleased the Athenians and was greatly cultivated: it is enough to say that we possess the names of 170 comic writers and the titles of almost 1,500 comedies.

The Athenian Aristophanes (*c.*446–385) is the only author of Old Comedy whom we know well and directly; and with Eupolis and Cratinus (of whom we have extensive fragments on papyrus) he was also the most famous. There have survived eleven out of his forty comedies, the earliest of which were presented under pseudonyms. He had inexhaustible invention, dazzling, malicious, and impudent, with an unsurpassed repertoire of jokes and contrivances. He was skilful in devising lively plots to support his allegory and satire, for the most part grouping his scenes into two parts, the intrigue and then its consequences. For his attacks on people he was content with the slenderest factual basis and some remote resemblance to the person to be shot at: to these he added features to make the whole thing absurd, including slander, gossip, and invention. In this fashion he assailed and caricatured with incredible audacity all the powerful and eminent figures, and also institutions; no literary, artistic, musical, moral, religious, political, or social innovation escaped his lash. He has the mentality of the critic and caricaturist which sees the comic side of everything; but also of the sceptic who scorns to seem to have been taken in.

It is not surprising therefore that, though a defender of the old religion, he frequently burlesques the gods in front of a people who rigorously observed the national religion; though a supporter of morals, he is shameless in his allusions; though the enemy of rhetoricians, he relies on logic and frequently on sophistry; though a detractor of Euripides, he shows signs of his influence. His imaginative, comical songs, full of double meanings, were the delight of the people, who learnt them by heart; his works dominated the Athenian comic theatre for forty years.

The latest Aristophanic comedies, sometimes without a chorus or *parabasis* (the verses in which the poet, through the chorus, had addressed his audience on topical themes), and directed to social themes or parodies, already take comedy into its second phase, which then underwent a great development and is called the Middle Comedy (*c*.400–338). Many changes in environment and in taste combined to modify the literary genre. Athens had been defeated and subjected by Sparta; then, after its internal quarrels had been ended with an amnesty, it with great difficulty managed to make some headway towards redeeming its independence. It was no longer possible to want a satirical comedy full of incidental allusions, which would wound individuals and rekindle the old hatreds. By this time refined taste had turned away from the obscene language of earlier times, and the spread of reflective thought had killed enjoyment of illogical flights of fancy. Finally the exhaustion of public finances and the reduction of individual fortunes had compelled the cutting-down of expense on stage representations.

For all these reasons, and for others as well, comedy had to do without the traditional use of a *parabasis* and regular chorus,[17] and also to change its tone. Personal attacks were excluded, speech became more refined, plots were made less illogical, and the obscene costumes of actors were abolished. As to subjects, there was still a fondness for parody of the myths which were dramatized in tragedy; but the trend was towards bringing everyday life, with all its natural humour, upon the stage, and to substitute the representation of types for that of individuals.

We therefore find comedies which display such features of particular trades as could be made the subject of satire. We have the cook, the peasant, the painter, the slave-dealer, the braggart soldier, or the gardener. There are people from various countries and various social levels (the parasite, the philosopher, the doctor, the poet). Plots were now based on human impulses (depicting, say, an enemy of villains, or a crime), or on casual combinations (such as twins, or homonyms).

Middle Comedy was therefore more reflective, less popular, less vivacious, and profoundly influenced by the Sophists and rhetoricians. Tradition preserves the names of no less than fifty-seven poets and 607 titles of Middle Comedy: but our knowledge of them is entirely from fragments. We can get a better idea of works of this type from the Latin comedies which probably derived from them, such as Plautus' *Amphitruo* and *Persa*.

What we call New Comedy flourished at Athens in the period between Alexander and the city's loss of its liberty. It never took root outside Athens, although many tried to make it do so. It is no longer a mirror of political life, of parties in the *polis*, but of universal humanity. It is no longer a parody of exceptional and ridiculous types. For although it still makes use of stock figures (parasite, braggart soldier, intriguing slave, pimp, etc.), it represents the life and normal habits of ordinary people excited by common human passions; and the commonest passion is love, into which fathers, young men, women, harlots are drawn across a thousand intrigues, contretemps, surprises, and catastrophes. For each category of person comedy created a particular type, which the public soon recognized from the special masks used by the actors; for each hitch in the plot it had an artificial device ready to untie it; each character is given a form of speech suited to his state of mind; in every discourse reflections of common experience are inserted. Although not banal these last are sometimes ridiculous, but they made people think. New Comedy, now so different from Old, perfectly reflects Greek Hellenistic civilization with its taste, its eloquence, its spiritual Epicureanism, and its vivacity.

The most famous of these comedians was the Athenian Menander (343/2–292/1), who so loved his city that he would not leave it for Alexandria, and had a superb understanding of the society he put on the stage. His finesse in presenting types, the perfection of his language and its adaptation to his characters and their feelings, the nobility of his moral maxims and his ability to give fresh life to trite themes and traditional forces, all these were qualities not always appreciated by the Athenian public. Many of them preferred Philemon, but Menander has gained the admiration of posterity. He was the author of 108 comedies, of which very extensive fragments have been rediscovered on papyrus.[18]

In the meantime mime had spread from Sicily. Syracuse had had a new practitioner in Boeotus; and now Phoenix of Colophon and Herodas, perhaps of Cos, who lived about 250, distinguished themselves; seven mimes by the latter have been found on papyri, and also one fragment. He presented, with great fidelity, probably earlier than Theocritus, scenes from daily life in temples, law-courts, schools, shops, and so on. They are rapid dialogues between two or three people, sometimes monologues, in which persons of all sorts of quality and moral talent are presented. They are sketches cleverly drawn; the characters spring to life without disguise, and we are given insight into their souls. The metre is choliambic (i.e. iambic with a final long foot); the language is Ionic with Attic and Doric infiltrations.

Much later, though it still engaged authors of worth such as Philistion, Greek mime declined, reducing itself to mime 'hypotheses' (situations or plots suitable to mimes) with a stage setting. These are a set of canvases to be developed under the direction of an 'archimimus'.

Latin comedy was more natural and indigenous in its origins than tragedy, because of the bantering tendency (the 'Italum acetum' of Horace) of the Italian people. In the rural festivals of grain, wine, etc., and at marriages, this mockery was made the occasion for piquant poetic contexts, which in one small Faliscan town named Fescennium developed into regular farces improvised by masked peasants (*Fescennina carmina*). In this form they were transplanted to Rome. But the licentiousness of these Fescennines was such, and the attacks which men made on their neighbours were so unrestrained, that a curb was put on them in a law of the XII Tables.

Livy, noting that in 364 the first 'ludi scaenici' were registered, says that in that year some Etruscan jugglers (*histri*) came to Rome and danced to the music of the flute. The young Romans, who were already producing improvised Fescennines, now added music and dance to them; and from this was derived the *Satura*, an elaborate dramatic text presented by comic actors. Since, however, a more likely etymology for the name 'satura' would be from satyrs, it is more probable that it was derived, via the Etruscans (or Etruscanized Campania), from the Greek satyr drama and from its Italiote form the phlyax-plays and 'Rhinthonic' farces. It also corresponds to them in its content.

To the two types of Fescennines, the native type and the Graeco-Etruscan *Satura*, can be added the Oscan *Atellana* (from Atella in Campania, influenced by the *phlyakes*) which continued to be used by some of those who spoke the Oscan dialect. These *Atellanae* were transferred to Rome; and though at first they were produced in a popular manner with amateur actors they eventually reached the dignity of an art, and were recited by professional actors. Like the satyr dramas in Greece, they were used as an *exodium* after the performance of tragedies. They were short farces about some form of entanglement; the themes were drawn from the life of the people and countryside, full of obscenity and crude jokes, and founded on a few fixed types. There was Maccus, the young peasant, greedy, and boorish; Pappus, the miserly and stupid old man; Bucco, the young glutton and braggart; and Dossennus, the hunchback and astute swindler.

Finally there was added the translation or the re-fashioning of Greek comedies and the Siceliote *Hilarotragodiai*; and these were called *palliatae* because the actors wore Greek dress. Some of them used subjects from Old Comedy which lent themselves to personal satire; but most subjects were drawn from Middle and above all from New Comedy, and therefore revolved round an almost standard series of stock types. After Naevius' period Greek comedies were often contaminated; in fact the plots of one or more authors were amalgamated. But the Greek plots were only the form into which Roman writers placed what, for them and for their audience, were in fact the essentials: the comedy of the situations, gay fantasy, the continuous cracking jests, the implications, the double meanings, the parody of noble style, the medley of ideas in newly composed words, and mock scenes of stateliness; in fact the whole of typical Roman comedy which we know from Plautus' inexhaustible vein. The themes of indigenous characters soon attracted the attention of the writers of *palliatae*, and it developed in the following fashion: through the strong influence of the *palliatae*, 'togata' comedy, which placed the Roman world and characters on the stage, drew from them as much value as from the Greeks, and divided them into appropriate social types representative of their class.

As a writer of comedy we know little of L. Livius Andronicus other than that he wrote three comedies entitled *Gladiolus*, *Ludius*, and *Virgus* or *Verpus*. In contrast there are titles and fragments of thirty-three comedies by Cn. Naevius, some of which seem to be *togatae* of the 'taverna' type, and others of the Atellane farces.

The greatest Latin comedy-writer, T. Maccius Plautus, who was born at Sarsina in Umbria (*c.*254–180), was a little younger than Naevius. A businessman, he lost all his property, and so he went to Rome where he earned his living, so it is said, turning the grinding-stone in a flour-mill. He put together three comedies, slowly recovered his financial position, and from then on wrote comedies in the years that followed (130 pieces according to Varro, 100 according to Gellius: many of them are spurious). The stage direcions show that there was an early corpus of twenty-one authentic comedies, and they have survived completely except that the *Vidularia* is fragmentary.[19]

The prologues and allusions in the text in a good many of these comedies inform us that in ten cases Plautus availed himself of one or more Greek comedies. But what of the other eleven? Though he may have used Greek sources and often takes us to Greek cities and the life of Hellenistic people, Plautus knew how to give his comedies the sharp stamp of originality as well as Romanization.[20] And this is not only a matter of form, in which there is evidence of many innovations, but even more so one of substance. There are whole comedies for which it is not possible to indicate either the Greek source or plausibly to show its existence; in them all, and even in those in which the original Greek is certainly employed, we find new Roman types inserted, and representations of surroundings and habits which are frankly contemporary and Roman; there is clear Romanization of Greek myths, and new uses for old comic expedients. But where Plautus' comedy is most Roman and original is in all his expression, line after line: he uses the genuine language of daily life, and varies the mode of speech according to the mentality and class of his characters, who are contrasted in the dialogues with wonderful spontaneity. There is continual brilliance in the humour of his witticisms and double meanings: there is turbulent vivacity in his discussions and altercations; and the fluency of his verse is obtained in so wonderful and skilful a fashion that the ancient grammarians eventually claimed that it was not verse but prose.

Between Plautus and Terence there was a whole series of *palliatae* and *togatae* which have been lost, one reason probably being that they were unable to stand up to the two great authors.

It is not possible to give precise dates for P. Terentius Afer's short life, but in any event it was between 200 and 160. Born at Carthage and probably a Libyan by origin, he was taken as a slave to Rome, but was later manumitted, and became the friend of distinguished people. In each of his six surviving comedies half the play is entirely based on a Greek model, and the other half is influenced by one or more authors. Recitation and dialogue in these comedies are less than are to be found in Plautus. Their originality is revealed particularly in the characteristics of the people, who seem particularly to conform to Roman types and tastes; there is a tendency to idealize (virtuous, reasonable, and submissive matrons, courtesans capable of generosity, modest and loving fathers, polite children, servants who are fond of their masters). In addition a wonderful effect is produced by the original style. Living at a time when Roman comedy was very advanced, and when many of his contemporaries had great knowledge and respect for Greek models, Terence was a target for severe criticism, against which he defended himself more or less openly in the prologues to the comedies. Like his predecessors he was accused of contaminating the Greek comedies which were much admired, and of having secret collaborators, a charge for which evidence was brought. His fame was in every sense greater and more lasting after his death.[21]

The Greek-inspired *palliatae* comedies had no more famous authors after Terence, though the *togatae* with their Roman themes took new forms. L. Afranius, who was writing about 94 BC, produced about forty-four, which deal with familiar themes, individual characters, and types from the professions and trades; they resemble fairly closely the plots and developments of the *palliatae*, putting forward Greek comic models as well as Roman. A clever psychologist, he gave great importance to both feminine and regional types, and as a moralist he drew close to Terence. Of T. Quinctius Atta, who died in 78 BC, we know the titles of twelve *togatae* and a few fragments; the scenes of the latter take place during feasts, or are reproductions of daily life and familiar happenings. He too seems to have given great importance to women.

At the same time, in Sulla's period, we find a new form of art, the popular Atellanes; these gradually came to resemble the 'fabula togata tabernaria', a more humble type of art, and were ultimately merged with them. Atellanes by Novius, and those by Pomponius (who was born at Bononia and flourished about 89), present various innovations on the earlier versions: they were written by educated men, presented by professional actors, and written in Latin, with the Oscan dialect reserved for particular characters. Both these two authors were prolific writers. They brought on to the stage not only the four fundamental characters of the Atellane, but country-people, personifications of vice and misery, important or mythical people in parody, fantastic beings, and talking animals, all in a continuous passage from comedy to farce, parody, and fable.

Meanwhile the mime, a genre very similar to comedy and Atellane, had been transferred to Rome, and developed an even stronger resemblance to the other genres because of the poetical form in which it was clothed (cf. the *mimiambi*). At times it took on the characteristics of satire. The best-known Latin writer of mimes was Decimus Laberius, a knight, who was forced by Caesar in 46 to go on the stage, as a mimic, in a contest in which he was defeated by Publilius Syrus. The latter was an ex-slave of Syrian origin who was famous for his witty maxims which were gathered into collections. A place apart belongs to the *mimiambi* or comic iambics, with their life-like scenes and wit. The fragments which were written by Cn. Matius provide excellent justification for Gellius' great praise for him as a writer.

Bucolic and Didactic Poetry. Theocritus was considered the last of the great creators of Greek literary genres, his invention being bucolic poetry. A Syracusan (about 300–250), he lived for a long time on the island of Cos, then for some years at Alexandria; then he returned to Cos, and in the end went back to Sicily. The surviving collection of 'small compositions' (*Idylls*) or of 'selected compositions' (*Eclogues*) have certainly been altered. They contain poems of varied moods and of different types. The bucolic poems are the most characteristic type, in which the poet made the traditional poetic duels between the shepherds of his land into a form of art. They sing against a joyful background of rustic life, in the middle of gentle, smiling nature, among the animals who love them: they are ingenuous creatures, superstitious and true to life, although greatly idealized. There are other, related poems which record mythical legends about shepherds: but in the collection there have also been included real mimes, some short poems which are half-lyric and half-epic, two elegies for great lords, and twenty-six beautiful epigrams.

Theocritus is a lyric poet of exquisite sensibility, whose senses always respond to the stimulus of nature, as well as a vigorous dramatist who knows how to create and animate living characters. He is a realist who depicts the most delicate shades of feeling, but an idealist too who enhances the more poetical and idyllic sides of his characters. He is finally a scholar of good taste who knows how to conceal his erudition. A poetic innovator, he uses the dactylic hexameter in all types of poems, is musical in his style, and writes in a lively though moderate language without pedantic affectation. His shepherds speak a Syracusan dialect which is a little unrefined; speech in the mimes has some Ionic influence. Other dialects are used in other forms of poems.

In the Greek world Theocritus had annotators and imitators such as Bion and Moschus, but his only worthy rival and successor was a Roman, Virgil.

Virgil's *Bucolica* (which he too called 'Eclogae', probably because the ten published poems were a selection) mainly differ from the Theocritean poems in that their material is drawn from literary sources rather than from contact with the rustic world: they thus have an artificial aspect for which the model was the genre of poetry called 'Arcadian'. From this literary inspiration stem in part the most outstanding characteristics: the imprecise contours of the unreal landscapes; the ill-defined characters who preserve their names, but change appearances and types; the continuous contradictions in the plot. But the fact that the poet, generalizing a system sometimes used by Theocritus, has given an allegorical significance to some of his Eclogues, hinting at episodes from his own life, and identifying himself time and again with his characters, so that they seem to have double lives, contributes to all this confusion. Nor are some of these allegories easy to understand, and attempts to interpret them, both in ancient and in modern times, have been sometimes grotesque[22].

Didactic poetry too, in the period in question, had more able devotees in the Latin world than in the Greek. The names of Aratus and Nicander stand out in the Greek world. Aratus of Soloi (about 315–240 BC) was a philosopher, a mathematician, and a poet. In his work, called *Phainomena*, he popularized the astronomical and meteorological teachings of Eudoxus of Cnidus, in very competent verse, but in a somewhat heavy style. Nicander is credited with poems on poisons, on antidotes, on bees, and on *Georgics*. *The Wonders of Italy* of Heliodorus, the *Chronology* of Apollodorus, and the *periegesis* of the pseudo-Scymnus are compositions with a purely mnemonic purpose.

In Latin the heights of poetry were reached by Lucretius with his *De rerum natura*, of which we spoke earlier on, by Virgil with his *Georgics*, by Horace with his *Ars poetica*, and by some works of Ovid.

Virgil was inspired to write the *Georgics* by one of the canons of the great programme of restoration of Augustus by which Italy would regain its prosperity through the rebirth of agriculture and love for the land.[23] Virgil devoted seven years to this work (37 to 30 BC) although it consisted of little more than 2,000 verses. The *Georgics* consist of four books which deal in turn with agriculture (the working of the land, seeds, and the periods and signs of the zodiac); with arboriculture; with the breeding of animals; and with bee-keeping. Although Virgil was the son of a peasant family and had early on shown himself in the *Bucolica* to be a lover of nature and of the land, he devoted a long time to studying the specialists beginning with Hesiod's *Works and Days*, in order to become a specialist too. The writings of these two poets agree in the conception that work is a duty imposed upon men and that sweat cannot be avoided on the path to virtue. It must not be forgotten, however, that Virgil held the view that work was the essence of the successful history of Rome (let us remember the motto of Aeneas to his son: 'my son, learn from me virtue and true work; others will teach you happiness') and in any event the *Georgics* dealt with Italy and not with Greece. This poem also demonstrates the stage in Virgil's philosophical thought when he was absorbed by the Stoic theory of immanence which led him to perceive divinity in every small particle of the universe. Yet he did not succeed in freeing himself entirely from Epicurean deterministic conceptions: they come out in the *Georgics* here and there. The main characteristics of the work are first a deep awareness and love of nature and of animals and plants, which are described by the poet with sincere and vibrating lyricism; secondly its novel ideas on the blending of tradition with a direct sensation of reality. A love of nature is combined with the glorification of the anonymous work of millions of workers who collaborated with Augustus in the rebirth of Italy.

Horace's *Ars Poetica* is the last of the *Epistulae* of the second book, and was soon published as a short poem on its own. It consists of 476 verses which the poet based upon a work by Neoptolemus of Parium. Contrary to the episodic production of the Alexandrines, Horace requires unity of conception in a work of art. He then speaks of expression, by which he means language; of metre and literary form; and finally of characters and plot. He dwells upon the theatre, insisting upon the rule of five acts and four actors, and he criticizes the abuse of choral and musical parts. He maintains that poetry does not depend only upon inspiration, but also upon technique, and that, as it must 'delight' and 'profit', it cannot be either pure art or amoral.

There are also several works of Ovid which can be described as didactic. The *Ars Amatoria* consists of three books which teach men how to conquer and dominate women; but in the last book Ovid suggests to women the means to defend themselves against men. All this work is pervaded by a subtle sense of humour and is full of salacious anecdotes. The *Medicamina Faciei* deals with the ways of keeping the skin white, smooth, and without blemish. The *Remedia Amoris* teaches desperate lovers how to avoid suicide. The *Fasti* was conceived to glorify the religious policies of Augustus: it was designed as a description of the calendar in twelve books, one for each month, which illustrated with episodes and suitable scenes those days which were auspicious or ill-omened, and days when the *comitia* were permitted or forbidden. Ovid's description is enlivened by a series of vivacious and graceful pictures, where the gods are made to have an outlook very similar to that of the capricious mortals of the Hellenistic age. The *Fasti*, however, lacks any sense of religion and any harmony with Augustus' strict and pious work of reform.[24]

There were at least four different types of Roman satire, although all of them had more or less fundamental characteristics in common. We have already spoken of the first type, which is the dramatic theatrical satire. The second type was also burlesque and moralizing, but consisted of books on all kinds of subjects written partly in prose and partly in verse of various metres. The works of Ennius were of this type. They comprised general 'saturae' and also other satires with their own titles which were probably part of the major general work. There was a *Dialogue between Life and Death*, an *Epicharmus*, and an *Euhemerus* with a translation of the *Historia Sacra* by that author.

The work of Lucilius of Suessa Aurunca (about 180–103 BC) belongs to the third type of satire. He wrote thirty books from which 1,375 verses are still in existence. His satire was influenced by Iambic writers and Old Comedy, by philosophical and burlesque polemics, and by the *silloi* of Timon and his imitators, including Clitomachus who was a friend of Lucilius. In his first composition Lucilius used a most colourful variety of metres, but later on he preferred a monometric verse of the kind used by his great successors, namely the hexameter.

His satires describe every kind of person around him, portraying their different types, recording anecdotes and dialogues, drawing caricatures and making hints. His accent varies from the clearest epic tone to the completely vulgar and scurrilous. He lashes the new rich, the people who were mad about anything Greek, and also women. He hits at political opponents, and on occasion the whole Roman people, tribe by tribe.

He wrote gentle satire against writers and literary works, tragedies in particular, and against the taste of Romans (whom he put last after the people of Tarentum, of Cosa, and of Sicily); he wrote philosophical satire, against the doctrine of perfection of the Stoics in particular, although he preferred philosophy to inventive poetry, even that of Homer.

A fourth type of satire found its origins in the works of Menippus of Gadara, and because of this Varro called it 'Saturae Menippeae'.

We are told that M. Terentius Varro of Reate (116–26 BC) produced 74 works in 620 books. The works which concern us in the field of satire are: four books of *Saturae* which were probably of the same type as those of Lucilius; six books of *Pseudotragoediae* or *Hilarotragoediae*, which consisted of humorous criticism of tragic characters set out in dialogue form; and, of particular interest, the *Saturae Menippeae*, from which we know 96 titles and 600 fragments. Varro in these satires uses a variety of metres and also follows Menippus in that he joins parts written in prose to those in verse and interposes Greek in the Latin. The content of his satires was extremely diversified. There were attacks on personal enemies; criticism of Epicureans and Stoics in defence of an eclectic philosophy; criticisms of the customs of the time; literary, grammatical, and historical criticism; spirited anecdotes; humorous explanations of mottoes and proverbs; a sort of 'code of table manners'; and a burlesque treatment of myths. The style of Varro was imaginative and descriptive, as in his other works. Yet it lacked conciseness and agility; it was fond of classifications, archaisms, and obscure hints; and often it was artificial, with a long series of adjectives and diminutives.

The satirical works of Q. Horatius Flaccus (65–8 BC) can be divided into two groups with largely different characteristics. The first group was written between the years 45 and 30 BC and the second from 23 to about 13 BC.

The first group belongs to the period before the imperial domination of Augustus and consists of Horace's aggressive and personal writings in iambics. To this period belong the seventeen *Epodes*, which remind us of Archilochus; and also eighteen satires, which recall Aristophanes and Lucilius, in the first two books of the *Saturae*. The poet had an irritable temper and was embittered by life, and although wanting to find 'the happy mean' he preferred to give vent to bitter invective and personal criticism of the Stoics and their hypocritical followers, literary men of various schools, 'neoteric' poets, Lucilius, and politicians.

After the victory of Actium, however, and during the rule of Augustus, Roman society changed deeply. So when Horace, then a mature man, went back to writing satire his mordacity gave way to humour, and the *iambus* to a calm criticism of customs and tendencies. He rightly said that he was, at that time, nearer to Terence than to Aristophanes. The satires of this new type which are contained in the first book of the *Epistles* tend to be philo-sophical. Horace was an Epicurean, who took life in a happy way, but his eclecticism made it possible for him to accept the precepts on moderation and on the 'aurea mediocritas' proclaimed by the Cyrenaics and by Aristip-pus.

The contents of the second book of the *Epistles* are mostly literary. In the *Epistles* the poet turns to Augustus and makes a subtle criticism of the archaic tendency of a new taste which had begun to prevail; he criticizes ancient poetry and hopes for the rebirth of the theatre and of epic; he apologizes for doing so little work, for, he says, the torment of artistic production tires him. He puts forward his *Ars Poetica* (of which we have already spoken).[25]

Prose: The Greek Historians. Perhaps in no other field, except in tragedy, is the strong influence of the Sophists felt so much as in historical literature. The same difference which divides Euripides and Sophocles can also be seen between Thucydides and Herodotus, although there are barely twenty years between the two. Only a few fragments are left to tell us anything of the works of the later *logographoi* such as Hellanicus of Mitylene, the author of works on local history, on mythical stories, and on chronology. Fragments remain of the work of Damastes of Sigeum and Antiochus of Syracuse, author of a history of Sicily up to the year 424 BC and of a history of Italy. The works of Herodotus have survived complete.

Herodotus (about 484–425 BC) was born in Halicarnassus. He took part in the colonization of Thurii, but both before and after this time he travelled to Athens and in the Greek peninsula, and to Asia Minor, Persia, Egypt, Cyrene, Magna Graecia, and Sicily. His history was written in Ionic and was later divided into nine books. The purpose of the writings of Herodotus was to recount the long fighting between the Greeks and the barbarians of Asia, a struggle which started in mythical times. The part which deals with more recent times describes the wars between the Lydians and the Greek settlers, and between the Greeks and Persians. It seems that he wrote each single section of his work separately and then fitted them together into a pre-established framework. Characteristics of his work are the long geographical and ethnographical digressions inspired by his travels; it is not very clear, however, how much information Herodotus drew from traditional stories which he heard locally and how much from the Greek writers of before his time.

The mind of Herodotus wavers where mythology and religion are concerned, for he does not know how to choose between or reconcile the various tendencies. Sometimes he rationalizes like Hecataeus, at other times, he refers to myths and oracles with respect. There are moments in which he seems to echo the criticism against the pantheon and the traditional gods; but for the most part he repeats the common ideas of his time, such as the belief that envy moves the gods to oppose human actions. He thinks that, apart from occasional divine interventions, historical events depend as a rule on the actions and the free will of men. But when it comes to great historical figures he does not succeed in co-ordinating the conflicting traditions; and there are many apparent contradictions in his work, for example in his portrayal of Miltiades and Themistocles. Herodotus is faithful to a Homeric model and does not try to get to know the concrete causes of events, or to teach politically, or to improve morally. He wants to please with his artistic narrative, the events of which are well chosen and well arranged; he writes in a form which is simple, ingenuous, fascinating, and suitable for public readings. He transformed history into a work of art and because of this he became the 'father of history'.[26]

Time had already greatly altered the contents of tradition, and Herodotus, while usually omitting the precise sources of it, elaborated upon it artistically and not critically. (He said that he recounted what he believed without always being fully convinced of it.) When speaking of tradition he resorted to fantasy: he invented dialogues, conversations, and anecdotes. There are many errors in his narrative because of the scant knowledge he had of military and political matters, and because he was uncritical of his sources of information. He is a decided partisan of Athens and of the democratic cities against the others. He is partisan against Themistocles and in favour of the family of the Alcmaeonids: for the latter were related to a man he esteemed very greatly, namely Pericles.

Thucydides (about 465/460–395 BC) was the son of Olorus, a name associated with Thrace.[27] He was a friend of the Sophists, and was general at Athens in 424. Luck was not on his side, however, and in that year he was banished from Athens for twenty years. He wrote an incomplete history later divided into eight books, which dealt with the contemporary events

of the Peloponnesian War, and had a preface on the preceding period of
fifty years. He obtained his information from the stories of eye-witnesses
which he weighed in the light of his own experience. For chronological
precision he divided the events into years and seasons and according to areas
of activity.

There is a gulf between the poetic and religious sense of Herodotus and
the natural interpretation of Thucydides. Thucydides never speaks of
divine intervention, though on some occasions he speaks of *Tyche* (luck).
When mentioning the oracles he does not hide his scepticism; and he is sometimes sarcastic. All phenomena are brought back to natural causes; and
according to him historical events depend upon a conflict of forces and upon
the ability of men. For this reason, he says that the death of Pericles influenced
the course of the war, for it was entrusted to successors, demagogues, who
were far inferior. Thucydides was very skilled in outlining military events.
He did not deal directly with the internal struggles of political parties,[28]
though he gave some information about them in the form of conversations
which he invented and put into the mouth of his characters. This method he
used for the purpose of clarifying different points of view which were in
contrast. It was ideas more than men which counted with Thucydides, but
his characters became alive and real from their magnificent and learned
Antiphontean speeches and their dramatic debates, in a way which was far
better and could not have been achieved by any description. He also made
indirect use of speeches to insert his opinions, for his greatest aim was that
of remaining impartial. Thucydides never had a great interest in economic,
commercial, or financial problems; and he was not infallible, for there
are a few errors and gaps due both to erroneous information and to lack
of revision of his work. He did not like digressions, but he had to use them
when he wanted to rectify the stories of his predecessors or to teach. When
he speaks of ancient history his critical sense is occasionally faulty, but he is
capable of acute deductions from the archaeological evidence at his disposal.

The writings of Thucydides are a typical example of the works of prose
and science which were produced in Attica at the time of the Sophists. The
language is sometimes too affected, as in Gorgias, with a large number of
new terms and new meanings; the style is forceful although at times it is labor-
ious and mannered. All this, however, is proof of a gigantic struggle between
thought and form, and it does not prevent us from considering Thucydides
as the founder of scientific history, in which he has left us a masterpiece
never surpassed in ancient times.[29]

The works of Herodotus had rivals in the *History of the Medes* written
by Ctesias of Cnidus, physician to Artaxerxes, and the *Persica* by Deinon
of Colophon which finishes with the year 340 BC. Thucydides too had
various imitators, as for example Philistus of Syracuse, author of *Sicelica*;
and Cratippus, Xenophon, and Theopompus wrote sequels to his work. The
scant information we had of the Athenian Cratippus has now been completed

by the discovery of large fragments, which almost certainly are his work, and from which it is apparent that he dealt with the events of the period between the years 415 and 393 BC and perhaps until the year 386 BC. In politics he appears to be moderate, averse from the demagogues, anxious for agreement between the Greeks and for a war against Persia. As a historian he carefully ascertained facts: he searched for their causes and thought that the actions of individuals were important. He kept psychological analysis within moderate limits, and preferred to deal with military events. As a stylist, although in part he followed Isocrates, he wrote in a manner which was clear but unpolished, avoiding any tendency towards fancy and romance, or towards rhetorical declamation, or even towards moralizing. It is due to the lack of rhetoric that his works were supplanted by those of later rhetorical historians, who made great use of his work as a source. Polybius is the great Greek historian who resembles him most.

Xenophon (about 430–354 BC) was an Athenian aristocrat. He started as an opponent of the democrats in his own city; then he enlisted as a mercenary together with the 10,000 who supported Cyrus the Younger against his brother. In the *Anabasis*, which he published under a false name, he described the events of that expedition, and the difficulties met by the Greek survivors who elected him their leader during their return to their homeland; in all this he was not averse from exaggerating his own merits. The *Anabasis* is not a true historical work outlining the grave consequences which fell upon Greece for having taken part in Cyrus' attempt; it is a diary with clear descriptions of feats of arms and the life of a mercenary army. It is written in pure Attic language and is a literary masterpiece of the new type of post-Sophist prose.

In the year 400 BC war broke out between Sparta and Persia, and Xenophon enrolled in the Spartan army. Later, in the year 394 BC, he fought on the side of Agesilaus of Sparta against the Athenians, and after having been banished from his country spent the rest of his life in places which were under the sway of Sparta. His major historical work is the *Hellenica*, which consists of seven books covering the period between the years 411 and 362 BC. The nucleus of this work is the hegemony of Sparta; and whereas in the first part he follows the outline of Thucydides and is under his influence, in the other parts he does not write a complete 'Greek History' but a narrative of the things which he has seen personally without regard to the rest. His partisanship is great even if achieved by silence and not by direct distortion. In other respects Xenophon is an honest narrator, well informed, and an expert on military and political facts. He never poses general problems to himself, and it is therefore useless to seek from him the explanation of the establishment and dissolution of the Greek hegemonies of which he writes.

Of historical character also is the praise of Agesilaus, written in the years 361–360 BC, to be found in the manuscript of the *Hellenica*. The *Constitution of Sparta*, *Hieron*, and *Cyropaedia* are different, being semi-historical and political; and the last of these is stylistically the most perfect work that Xenophon ever wrote. It is a kind of imaginary constitution for a monarchy according to his ideals. The famous semi-legendary king of Persia, Cyrus I, is the main character; and the place in which he was brought up is not the real Persian capital but an ideal city in which the system of education is partly Spartan and partly a Xenophontine version of Socratic teaching.

There is another group of works by Xenophon which deals with Socratic subjects. This group includes the *Memorabilia* (*Apomnemoneumata*) of Socrates, which is a dialogue; the *Symposium*; the *Apology of Socrates*, a defence of that philosopher; and the *Oeconomicus*, which also deals with agriculture. These works show how the teaching of Socrates had been understood and transformed in the mind of Xenophon.

In matters of religion, this pupil of the enemy of the Sophists does not go back to the Herodotean conception of divinity. His opinion is that the gods do not take sides but punish those who violate the moral law.

The work of Xenophon must be judged as a whole. He was an honest and prolific writer, a lover of justice, and an enthusiast.[30] He was rather superficial in matters of history, philosophy, and politics, but an expert in military matters. Finally he was an excellent stylist with great literary talent, and he wrote the purest and most charming Attic prose of the post-Sophist epoch.

Up to this time Greek historical literature was of monographic character, for even the historical works of Herodotus were not really universal. However, when a great part of the Hellenic nation was united into a political system by Philip II, and when Alexander enlarged this system into an almost universal empire, there was need for comprehensive general history. It was then that the pupils of the two rival schools of Isocrates and Polycrates competed to satisfy this need, the first school represented by Ephorus and Theopompus and the second by Zoilus and Anaximenes.[31] Here we shall only mention that Zoilus of Amphipolis (about 400–330 BC) wrote a *History from the Theogonia to the death of Philip*, and Anaximenes of Lampsacus (380–320 BC) the *Hellenica*, the *Philippica*, and the *Deeds of Alexander*.

Ephorus was born in Kyme of Aeolis probably between the years 408 and 405 BC. He was a pupil of Isocrates and did not busy himself with politics: indeed he was perhaps the first Greek historian who lived only amongst his books. This was a great advantage to his impartiality of judgement, but it became a disadvantage to his understanding of the facts. His historical work was simply called *Historiae*, and was divided by him into twenty-seven books. It dealt with the period from the return of the Heracleidae to the years 367–366 BC and it was continued by his son Damophilus with a further three books dealing with the period down to the years 341–340 BC. The subject of his writings was Greek and Western history, but it excluded the history of the barbarians. When Ephorus dealt with the history of ancient times he followed the system of Hecataeus in that he rationalized myths. Further he maintained that summarized sources of information were enough for this kind of history, whereas more detailed sources were necessary for writing the history of recent times. He liked rhetorical embellishments and was very fond of moralizing judgements. He praised and regretted the passing of the hegemony of Thebes; he was a friend of Athens, and an enemy of Sparta.

Theopompus of Chios (about 377–300) was born of an aristocratic family and suffered many political vicissitudes because of repeated banishments. His first work was a summary in two books of the works of Herodotus. He then wrote twelve books of *Hellenica*, in which he continued the work of Thucydides and dealt with the years between 411 and 394 BC. Lastly he compiled the lengthy *Philippica* in fifty-eight books which came out about the year 320 BC. He was a fierce enemy of Athens, but a great friend of Macedonia, of Sparta, and of Agesilaus; severe and impetuous in his judgements, a fanatical oligarch, ignorant of military matters, inclined to moralizing, and capable of psychological analysis. A profound rhetorician, he filled his works with orations, dialogues, endless digressions, and mythical tales.

The deeds of Alexander were the subject of a work by Callisthenes of Olynthus, author of other historical writings; of fabulous tales by Onesicritus of Astypalaea; of a bombastic and fanciful *History of Alexander* by Cleit-archus of Colophon; and of serious memoirs by Ptolemy, son of Lagus, Aristobulus, and Nearchus. In the fourth century BC there was a series of flattering works devoted to the hegemonies which in turn followed one another, those of Athens, Sparta, Thebes, and Macedonia.

After the conquest of the Eastern world the Hellenes were anxious to learn the histories of the peoples they had vanquished. It would have been natural for them therefore to have collected, with the help of the natives, genuine historical documents. Yet for the most part they did nothing of the kind; and after the death of Alexander they continued to talk about the history of the East with much the same imperfect foundations of knowledge as had Herodotus and Ctesias.

Works of greater historical value were written in Greek by Eastern authors. Berosus, for example, who was a priest of Bel in Babylon and later an astrologer in Cos, wrote his work between the years 281 and 261 BC. This was less a history than a chronology of kings (*Babyloniaca*) in three books. He dealt also with astronomy and astrology. There are only a few fragments of his work extant and his works did not influence the Alexandrian chrono-graphers. Another Eastern author was Manetho (first half of the third century). He was a priest in Heliopolis and wrote three books on the thirty-one Egyptian dynasties, from their origin to the time of Alexander. This work was written with the aim of acquainting the conquerors with the history of Egypt; and although it was based on authentic documents it was not free from serious errors because of the author's lack of criticism. There remain, however, some very useful fragments.

We shall omit a number of authors of the fourth and third centuries BC, who tried their skill on general and regional history and on biography; here we shall speak only of Duris and of other major authors who dealt also with the West, such as Timaeus, Polybius, and Poseidonius. Duris of Samos (340–270 BC) was the prototype of the new rhetorical and learned tendencies, and was a pupil of both Theophrastus and the rhetoricians. He wrote at least twenty-three books of history divided into two parts—*Hellenica* and *Macedonica*—which covered the period from the beginning of the Theban hegemony up to the final constitution of the Hellenic states. His work was very learned but deeply rhetorical, and it aimed at gaining the interest of the reader by vivid descriptions of events, presented with picturesque details and in anecdotal form (*mimesis*). Duris, however, found some difficulty in recounting his anecdotes without lingering on descriptions of the dresses of his characters or on the sound of the trumpets in battle. It was said of him by some of the ancients that he lied even when there was no occasion to do so. Yet his work, which we can know from many fragments, was learned: it was much appreciated, and had a great effect on later writers.

The historical work on the West which supplanted all its predecessors was written by Timaeus of Tauromenium (about 345–250 BC) who was exiled by Agathocles and for half a century lived in Athens, where he was engaged solely on rhetorical studies. He was exclusively a man of science, and during his long exile he gathered much information on the history of Greece and of the barbarians of the West. He wrote a great historical work which told the history of the Italiotes and Siceliotes from their origins until 264 BC—the year which marked the beginning of the First Punic War. He made use of the writings of all the authors who had gone before him and added the findings of his own very careful research into the field of chronology and constitutional history. When he recounted recent events he was uncommonly tendentious in favour of friends such as Timoleon to the prejudice of enemies such as Agathocles and the tyrants in general. He was so bitter against his predecessors that he earned the nickname of *Epitimaeus* (the slanderer). He was rhetorical in style, superstitious in thought, and everywhere saw the work of divine providence revealed through miracles. His work became the acknowledged classic on the history of the West.

The historical works of Timaeus were continued by Polybius (210/8–128/6 BC) of Megalopolis in Arcadia. After Pydna he was one of the thousand Achaeans deported to various Italian towns, where he remained for seventeen years, although he was given permission to visit Magna Graecia, Sicily, and Spain.[32] Meanwhile he had an eye-witness view of how things stood in Rome, became a friend of the younger Scipio Africanus, gradually convinced himself that Rome's hegemony was unavoidable and that it would be wise for the Greeks to submit to it. He was therefore sent home to settle conditions for the Greek towns, and achieved his mission with great satisfaction to both sides.

The work of Polybius deserved the fame it received,[33] for it reveals an author who is learned, diligent, and clear, hostile to rhetorical and romantic writers of history, competent in military and political matters and worthy of standing at the side of Thucydides although inferior to him. It is evident that, so far as his religious opinions are concerned, this historian does not believe in the popular gods and that he follows the line of thought of the Stoic philosophers. He tries, however, to explain human events by human causes if he can do so; and if he cannot do this, as in the case of epidemics, he falls back upon *Tyche*. His work also contains some errors: he was not infallible. Information is sometimes incorrect (especially in respect of more ancient events for which he had to depend upon previous sources of varying worth, such as Fabius Pictor, Philinus, Aratus, Silenus, Sosilus, etc.). There is bias in favour of the Romans,[34] pedantry in his criticism, and a utilitarian conception which excludes any tendency towards idealism.

The work of Polybius was carried on by Poseidonius of Apamea (135–51 BC), whom we already know as a Stoic philosopher. His fifty-two books of *Historiae* were a continuation of the history of Polybius dealing with events beginning in the year 146 BC and ending with the dictatorship of Sulla (82 BC). Only fragments remain of his work, but it is certain that they were the main source for all ancient authors who later dealt with that period of history. Poseidonius was a man of science; he had good literary taste and was an able psychologist who had a deep interest in social questions. But he was no expert in military matters and believed in miracles.

Leaving out the Chroniclers we will pause to consider the Biographers. When Hellenistic scholars were confronted by literary masterpieces of the past they felt they wanted to know their authors; therefore, everything which was known or believed to be known, or which could be deduced from the works themselves, was collected and set out embellished with anecdotes and invented stories. This form of literature can be related to some extent to the *elogeion* used in Greece in the fourth century BC, because the eulogies necessarily contained many biographical facts. It was enough to fit the known facts into a predetermined pattern to achieve a 'bios'. The Hellenistic philological schools, descendants of the Athenian Peripatetic school, gave great impulse to this new form of literature.

Diodorus of Agyrium in Sicily (about 90–30 BC) settled in Rome and lived there for a long time after wide travels which he described with great enthusiasm. He states that he worked for thirty years on his *Library of History*, which consisted of forty books and which covers the period from the beginning of history to the consulate of Caesar. Only part of his work remains, and it is a universal history in that it deals with different peoples, one after the other. It is, however, no pragmatic synthesis, but a juxtaposition of extracts from the works of other authors which were different in value, character, and style, and which Diodorus summarized in such pedestrian form that they still contained allusions which had become absurd or anachronistic in the new work. Yet the practical value of the work from our point of view does lie in the fact that it preserves for us the writings of many authors which might otherwise have been lost. Diodorus followed the chronological pattern provided by the *Chronicle* of Castor of Rhodes. Over long periods of time he normally takes information on all subjects from a single source, without making additions of his own or drawing upon other authors. His work contains obvious contradictions, false emphases in the summings-up, and chronological errors.

Dionysius of Halicarnassus (about 60–5 BC), rhetorician and critic of historians, went to Rome in the year 30 BC. He wanted to write not merely a simple account of wars or of constitutions, but a work rich in political thought and practical philosophy. The period he selected was Roman history before the year 264 BC—an earlier epoch than had been dealt with by either Polybius or Poseidonius. After twenty-two years of research, twenty books of the *Ancient History of Rome* came out in the year 7 BC, but they have come down to us only in part. Dionysius made use of many Roman sources, particularly the more recent and less truthful annalists; he used few Greek sources; and he embodied the whole in a heavy miscellaneous work, which had the pretence of being pragmatic history but which showed no clear understanding of how real history differed from false history or legend. He had no clear notions of the law, though he dealt continuously with constitutions; he was frequently anachronistic, and made use of ornate orations which were tedious and spun out; he had a pedestrian and scholastic style, monotonous and heavy; and he wrote in the full conviction that the writing of history meant the piecing together of miscellaneous evidence to achieve a rhetorical piece of literature.

Strabo of Amasia (about 60 BC–AD 25) was rich and studious; he sat at the feet of many teachers; he made long journeys (in Asia Minor, Armenia, Syria, Egypt, Greece, and Italy); he read widely, and remained faithful to the models of Polybius and Poseidonius. His forty-seven books called *Historical Studies* started with a preface on the conquests of Rome and then dealt with the history of the period beginning in 146 BC. They did not deal with detailed history, for the work was directed at the Greeks and the Romans and tried to extract the experiences of the past from its facts. Strabo dwelt only on the major historical figures and events, enlarging on the more recent ones not dealt with by Poseidonius. He was, in fact, very like Polybius and superior to Poseidonius.

Nicolaus of Damascus, born in 64 BC of a Greek family, was secretary and confidant to Herod the Great, King of Judaea: in that capacity he often went to Rome. His most important work was the *Historiae*, written between the years 16 BC and AD 4 for the purpose of entertaining Herod, and consisting of 144 books. This was a hurried work, similar to that of Diodorus. It included a universal history, which spanned the period from the earliest times to the time of Augustus. The larger part of it dealt with more recent periods, for as much as sixty books were devoted to the last century. Of this work we know the first seven books on primitive Greece fairly well. This hasty piece of writing paraphrased the works of other authors with narrative and moralistic purpose. The average output was five to six books a year, which were to be read as they were published. They lacked originality, particularly in the first part as there had been no research into Eastern history. The value of the account of more recent events must have been greater, as the author had the benefit of his own observation and knowledge although he showed himself to be tendentious.

Timagenes of Alexandria went to Rome as a prisoner in 55 BC; later he became a freedman under the protection of Asinius Pollio. He wrote some books called *About Kings*, which were a history of Mediterranean peoples with frequent descriptions of geographical and ethnographical character, and were written with deep personal anti-Roman feeling. If we note the common aversion from Rome, the similarity of pattern, and the almost literal dependence of Timagenes' fragments and Justin's summary of them upon the *Philippic Stories* of Trogus Pompeius, it seems possible that Timagenes was translated into Latin by Trogus and this author summarized by Justin.[35]

Early Roman Prose Writing. Roman literature seems to have been acquainted with poetry (in the widest sense) before prose. At all events, poetic expression was the first to rise to literary value and to have a social function, for it is essentially the vehicle of sacred matters. The requirements of religion and of political and judicial life led to the use of a language different from that of every day. Thus it is that, going back to the sources, we find *Carmina* before any prose writing existed. The surviving fragments of the law of the Twelve Tables and of the hymns used in the liturgy have a rhythmic form, if they are not metrical in the strict sense. Prose may be assumed to have originated when the laws began to be put into writing and reports issued on the proceedings in the senate; another early example may well have been the *Annales* of the pontiffs, which recorded any daily events deemed to be noteworthy. Early Latin prose is preoccupied not with art but with clarity; there must not be the slightest ambiguity in the text. This accounts for certain fundamental features of this Latin prose, which were to be retained for a long time—a taste for tautology, for the *copia verborum* (verbal prolixity) to which Cicero resorted systematically; the care with which statements were differentiated (to make a clear distinction between an objective statement and one influenced by the opinion of the speaker or of some other person); the insistence on establishing absolutely definite connexions by repeating the theme, etc. Prose of this nature, governed by such requirements, could not rapidly produce literary works. But when political changes made it necessary to throw open certain subjects for public debate, the great leaders were compelled to invent eloquence and discover the art of persuasion.

The earliest Roman orator whose name has come down to posterity was the old censor, Appius Claudius the Blind. Cicero records some of the arguments he put forward in the senate against the party which was inclined to favour Pyrrhus. But it was not until the period of the Punic Wars that eloquence began to develop into an art in Rome. Parallel with it was another 'style', that of the funeral orations, which Cicero tells us had some influence on the earliest Roman historical writings. (He adds that the influence was disastrous, because the orations were so biased.) These speeches of praise were delivered at funerals by some close relative of the defunct (usually his eldest son) and no doubt described his past achievements. We may suppose them to have been fairly short, but we do not know exactly when they came into general fashion.

Such were the circumstances in which the earliest Latin prose developed. It had not yet reached maturity at the time of the Second Punic War, for the first annals, dating from that period, were written in Greek.]

The Roman Annalists and Historians. The reason why the first Roman annalists, from Q. Fabius Pictor to C. Acilius and A. Postumius Albinus, wrote in Greek is controversial. Was it because there was not yet a true Roman prose form? Was it because of a love of the Hellenes? Or was it done in order to spread the glories of Rome outside the Latin world?[36] It is possible that all these reasons played their part. The very number of the first annalists and the Latin translations of at least two of their works (of Fabius Pictor and C. Acilius) proves that this new form of literature had success with the public. The contents of these *Annales*, which took as a model the ancient *Annales Maximi* of the pontiffs, must have been for the greater part as arid and disconnected as the pontifical entries. (Every year they carried the names of the supreme magistrates, of victories, of triumphs, of portents, and so on.) Parts of the new *Annales*, however, must have had a very different character, in that some of them either directly, or through oral tradition, or through the *Annales Maximi*, went back to the old epic poems and, in the case of the work of less ancient annalists, also to the new great poems of Naevius and Ennius. Other parts were derived from historians of other nations such as the Greeks (from Greece itself and from the Western colonies), the Oscans, and the Etruscans. These parts must have had different characteristics from the others because of their length, their sentimentality, and the frequent learned hypotheses they contained. Between the various groups of stories, therefore, there must have been a great difference in tone; they must also have been disconnected and of different lengths. On the other hand there was the common feature of a desire to give prominent space to early history, which was rich in myths and legends already well known in the Roman world and also to the period of the authors themselves (because they had at their disposal wider sources of information, whether oral, personal, or documentary). All this was at the expense of the middle period between the fall of the monarchy and the first years of the third century, a period which was dealt with quickly and drily. The typical defect of the annalists, which increased with time, was that of magnifying the real or fictitious glories of their own families. Ancient opinions and fragments show that the form of these works was crude and naïve and that their authors loved brevity without purposeless ornament. Historical criticism was still in its infancy, and it was seldom that attempts were made to choose between contradictory stories, or to pragmatize by inferring from various traditions, or to classify facts on the basis of relations between cause and effect.

The first and most remarkable of the annalists who wrote in Greek was Q. Fabius Pictor, who was born about the middle of the third century and took part in the war against the Gauls in 225 BC. There is also a Latin version of his *Annales*, but it is not known whether it was written by him. His work dealt with the period from the earliest days up to his time. In narrating ancient events he drew his information from every kind of source, but for recent events he drew on his own personal memories and those of his contemporaries. The annalists who followed him, as well as Polybius, Livy, and Dionysius, made use of his text. His work was full of exaggerations, omissions, and errors, but it must have been a very important source of information, even though, like Polybius, he separated his evidence from his judgements.

Fabius Pictor was followed by other annalists who wrote in Greek. They were L. Cincius Alimentus, C. Acilius, A. Postumius Albinus, and others. As a reaction against the foreign language and the system of these authors, M. Porcius Cato (234?–149 BC) wrote his *Origines* and can be considered the father of the art of Latin prose. His life and his multifarious activities made him one of the most outstanding people of the Rome of his time and of the great debates which took place in it. Cato's historical works are two: one, written in 185 BC, was a compendium which had the purpose of teaching his son; the other, the *Origines*, consists of seven books at which he worked for a quarter of a century until his death. The title recalls that of the Greek *Ktiseis* and perhaps also Etruscan and Oscan annalistic literature.

This title is perhaps better suited to the first three books, of which Book One dealt with the origins of Rome, and the two others with the origins of those Italian towns which were gradually coming into contact with Rome. The following four books dealt with the period of the Punic Wars from 264 until 149 BC, the year of his death. He made use of Roman, Greek, Etruscan, and Oscan sources; and he made great changes from the pattern and nature of narration used by the annalists. His interests lay only in the most important events in the life of the Roman people and not in the life of the real or fictitious heroes of the *gentes*. For this reason he omitted almost any mention of specific characters.[37]

National pride in Roman conquests, a religious feeling for the past, a love for learning, the example of the great Latin work by Cato, and a new mine of information to be found in the *Annales Maximi* (published in full in 148 BC

[Ward Perkins (b) [Ward Perkins

49 *Roman building techniques:*

  (a) opus incertum, *with quoins of dressed stone. Temple of Juppiter Anxur, Terracina*

  (b) *opus reticulatum, used with brick courses and relieving arches, Villa of Hadrian, near Tivoli*

  (c) opus latericium, *showing that the brick is only a facing to the core of rubble concrete. Villa of the Gordians beside Via Praenestina, Rome*

[Ward Perkins

[Alinari

(a)

50

(a)

    Susa, Piedmont, the
    of Augustus, 8 BC

(b)

    Aosta (Augusta Praet
    Piedmont: the praet
    gate and the propu
    culum

[Alinari (b)

(a)   [Alinari

51   *Roman tombs:*
     (a) *of Caecilia Metalla, c. 20 BC, on the Appian way*
     (b) *of Marcus Virgilius Eurisaces (the Baker), in Rome*

(b)   [Alinari

(a)   [Alinari

52 *Roman sculpture*
    (a) *after Arcesilaus, 'Venus Genetrix'.
        Rome, Terme Museum*

    (b) *Augustus as* Pontifex. *Rome, Vatican
        Museum*

(b)   [Alinari

by P. Mucius Scaevola), all gave impulse to a great new output of annalistic history by Roman patricians. It will be sufficient to mention the names of C. Calpurnius Frugi, Cassius Hemina, Q. Fabius Maximus Servilianus, C. Fannius, Cn. Gellius, and C. Sempronius Tuditanus.

Meanwhile a new type of historical writings was born. These were inspired by the model set by the great Greek Polybius and perhaps by some indigenous efforts as well. A large number of annalistic works had already been published, and these showed a natural inclination to deal with recent history. Added to which there was the magnitude of pressing events happening all around and the wish to recount things which had been seen by the authors. These new works were in the nature of monographs of pragmatic reconstruction, memorials of witnessed events, autobiographies, and *Commentarii* recording the author's own deeds. There were also some epistolary writings.

L. Coelius Antipater (140–91 BC) was younger than Polybius and wrote at least seven books of *Annales* (or *Bellum Punicum*) which dealt with the war against Hannibal. Besides Polybius, his sources were the Greek writer Silenus[38] and certain Roman annalists; and in his turn he was largely used, along with Polybius, as a source by Livy. Antipater's work was an attempt to produce a pragmatic historical monograph; and, interspersed as it was with long harangues, it was a monument of oratorical style in accordance with the new prevailing taste. It earned him praise from Cicero and Fronto.

Sempronius Asellio (born about 160) wrote the *Historiae* or *Rerum gestarum libri*, and was still working at this when a very old man in the year 91 BC. His style was dull and unpolished, and was a narrative of things he had seen. But it contained attempts at pragmatic explanations in the Polybian manner, of which there is evidence in the fine statements on method preserved in some of the fragments. He argued against annalistic works which were like diaries, and said 'to tell what has happened does not suffice me; I must show the reason which caused the event to happen and the means which were used'; and he criticized savagely the old system: 'id fabulas pueri est narrare, non historias scribere'. Like Polybius he was an expert on military matters.

In the age of Sulla there was yet another group of annalists who retold the whole history of Rome according to the canons of the new rhetorical and artistic methods of historical writing. Sometimes they were content to forget the truth, and none of them shrank from the most blatant falsifications if they would bring glory to their ancestors. It is enough to mention here the names of Q. Claudius Quadrigarius, Valerius Antias, and Licinius Macer. The *Historiae* of L. Cornelius Sisenna, however, were somewhat more austere and truthful.

With M. Terentius Varro (116–26 BC), work on the ancient history of Rome was linked again to the *Origines* of Cato. He also gave play to the new antiquarian tendencies, and spread his studies, with a great love for learning and for Rome, to a whole series of side researches into the public and private life of past centuries. Varro wrote historical investigations into the period of

Roman origins, the primitive conditions of life in the Eternal City, the tribes, topographical matters, and the explanation of customs. He wrote some essays on contemporary history, and also two great works, one on the philosophy of history (*Logistorici*) consisting of seventy-six books, the other on ancient matters, divine and human (*Antiquitatum rerum divinarum et humanarum* in forty-one books). Lastly there was a very complicated biographical work, the *Imagines sive hebdomades* in fifteen books, which related to 700 people who had been famous in different fields. These were divided by him into seven groups of 100 weeks. Each group (kings and generals, orators, prose-writers, scientists, and others) was dealt with in two books, one devoted to seven weeks of Roman figures and the other to seven weeks of non-Romans. The work had a preface on fourteen 'inventores' of different sciences and arts. Some Ciceronian works of similar type have been lost. They consisted of memoirs on his consulate in the year 63 BC written in Greek, and the *De consiliis suis*, edited in 43 BC and containing serious accusations against Caesar, who was recently dead. They must have had little regard for real truth.

The *Commentarii* of C. Iulius Caesar (102–44 BC) have survived entire. Caesar made use of his reports to the senate, of official acts, and of war diaries; and in the winter of 52/51 BC he very rapidly completed the commentaries *De bello Gallico*, which included all events to the end of 52 BC. Later on, after having vanquished the followers of Pompeius, he wrote in the last months of his life, equally quickly and making use of similar sources, the story of the first two years (49 and 48 BC) of the civil war in his *De bello civili*.

Both works are brisk, extraordinarily simple and clear in their naked purity; they bear no traces of outside influence or theories, and they reveal the spontaneous genius of a great author. Some of the ancients, however, for example Asinius Pollio, complained that they were tendentious and inaccurate. It is true that it is easy to point to errors which were intended, to prudent silences, and to a partisan version of the facts; but the faults of this apologetic polemic work must not be exaggerated. They could not have been very great, for they referred to events known to everybody of those days. Indeed Caesar's writings must be greatly valued for the contribution they make to the knowledge we have of great events, of the habits and customs of the barbarians, and of the ingenious military tactics which Caesar employed in his wars.

The *Commentarii* remained incomplete because of the death of Caesar, with gaps covering the years 51–50 and 48–45 BC. Aulus Hirtius, one of Caesar's generals, started to fill those gaps with an eighth book of the *De bello Gallico* and with the *De bello Alexandrino* for the year 47 BC; but he too died, and two other authors carried on his work. One, who must have been an educated person, wrote the *Bellum Africum* on the year 46 BC; and the other, a rough man of arms, wrote the *Bellum Hispaniense* dealing with the year 45.

C. Sallustius Crispus (86–35 BC) was a wealthy plebeian from Amiternum who fought on the side of Caesar and the democrats. He was expelled from the senate in 50 BC, was elected to the office of quaestor in 48 BC, and again became a senator with the help of Caesar and supported his action in the civil war. After his appointment as governor of Africa Nova he was accused of corrupt administration and therefore retired and devoted the last ten years of his life to literary work. In his *De Catilinae coniuratione* he tried to defend Caesar after his death from the accusations of Cicero according to whom Caesar had been in league with Catiline. To achieve his purpose he even went to the length of showing the Catilinarian movement to be of less deep social significance than it was, and of distorting chronology. The work of the senate is shown as centring around Cato, and Sallust belittles Cicero, reducing him to the role of a secondary character (while seldom missing an occasion to mock him). There is no attempt at historical criticism in this short work and Sallust only states his theses to glorify Caesar. The *Bellum Iugurthinum* gave him the opportunity to show the corrupt and venal behaviour of the Roman aristocracy, which is blamed for the never-ending war. Their conduct is contrasted with the quick and decisive action of C. Marius (who in fact only had to complete the work of the patrician Metellus).

Sallust began to write his *Historiae* as a continuation of those written by Sisenna. They began with the death of Sulla, and there were five books covering the years from 78 to 67 BC. But the work was never finished, and all that survives are some scattered sheets of an otherwise lost manuscript. Sallust tells history in his own way and in the light of his outlook as a democrat opposed to the aristocracy. He believes that history is motivated by the action of a few men who follow their 'ingenium'. This belief is the reason why he dwells so greatly upon some characters, and on the description of their nature shown in his biographical and psychological pictures, which from a literary viewpoint are magnificent.

His style is oratorical and he applies it in his work, which is full of orations and deeply moving documents. He believed that in this way he followed the model of Thucydides. But much more successful is the way in which he imitated the style of that great author by launching a beautiful new anti-Ciceronian style, of neo-Attic type. The main characteristics of this style are a nervous conciseness, a truncated and asymmetrical building of sentences, and a refined use of archaic forms.

As the new generations required yet more up-to-date treatments of general history, there appeared two new types of this kind of literature. There were the works of Hyginus and Cornelius Nepos which were very much a collection of biographies, and those of Livy and Trogus Pompeius, greatly different from one another but with a tendency to systematic treatment. Hyginus was a librarian of Spanish origin who lived first in Alexandria and then in Rome. He wrote *De vita rebusque illustrium virorum, Exempla, De familiis Troianis, De origine et situ urbium Italicarum.*

Cornelius Nepos (99–30 BC) was born in the Po valley in Cisalpine Gaul, the land of the Insubrians. He did not take part in political life but concentrated upon works of an historical nature. He wrote a summary of universal history which determined Graeco-Roman synchronisms, including typical Euhemeristic interpretations of myths and a number of fables and literary notes. His *Exemplorum libri* were a collection of anecdotes and of historical, geographical, and ethnographical curiosities. He also wrote a *Life of Cicero* which was full of praise, and a *Life of Cato the Censor*.

The most famous work of Nepos, however, was the *De illustribus viris*, consisting of sixteen books which in couples (one book for the Romans and one for the foreigners) dealt with kings, generals, poets, orators, historians, philosophers, jurists, grammarians, and scientists. This work had a moral purpose in that it set out to tell the 'virtutes' of the characters, who were all equally great and heroic men. The book on foreign generals has survived, together with separate biographies of Cato and of Pomponius Atticus; this provides us with twenty-three fairly short biographies with many errors and confusions, devoid of criticism of facts or sources, but drawn in clear and simple form. Nepos did not produce a work of science, but he did much to spread a taste for biographical literature at Rome.

Titus Livius (59 BC–AD 17) has given us a great annalistic history of Rome, of a type which had gradually developed from the time of Fabius Pictor to the age of Sulla. Livy's was the artistic masterpiece which closed that series at the time in which the greatness of Rome was at its peak. He was born in Patavium and went to Rome before the year 30 BC. He wrote *Ab urbe condita libri CXXXXII*, which covered the time from the origins to the year 9 BC; when he had reached that point death cut short his work. He did not follow the oldest and purest historical works such as the *Annales Maximi*, Fabius Pictor, and Cato, although he was acquainted with them. He based his work on later and less reliable sources such as those of the Sullan age, because they were longer and more rhetorical. It was seldom that Livy intended to draw from tradition a pragmatic reconstruction; for he was satisfied to deduce facts here and there and mostly only to juxtapose contrasting traditions. He never bothered to check or to make use of such ancient documents as still existed in Rome, though they had attracted the attention of foreign authors such as Polybius and Dionysius. It must be added that when he used Greek sources he often misunderstood them or translated them very approximately; that he did not try to have a clear idea of geographical or topographical matters even if they were of basic importance; that he had inadequate knowledge of military art; that his attempts at psychological interpretation were often empty and superficial; and lastly that he did not make sufficient efforts to understand the great social and economic struggles nor the evolution of institutions although he continually spoke about them. Despite all these obvious faults, Livy had several outstanding qualities, which caused his historical work to gain immediate and far-reaching fame in

Rome. It became a classic book, and put all previous *Annales* into the shade, at the same time making it impossible for posterity to try to rival it. His work had the qualities of honesty, of patriotism, of artistic perfection, of moral greatness, and of balanced political tendencies. Livy's history, if not a great work of science, is a great work of art; the poetry of its narrative, the eloquence achieved by the construction of its sentences of Ciceronian type, and the gracefulness of its descriptions are truly great. The language, often poetic and tending towards the archaic, has a fascination that never fails.

Livy, together with Cicero and Plutarch, was an exquisite representative of ancient humanity. In politics he was a moderate, in that he accepted for his world the order of ideas common to his times. There was latent in him, however, a lively passion for the greatness of the old Republic and for oligarchic republican theories. He was, therefore, an aristocrat by inclination, but a moderate in practice. Augustus rightly called him 'Pompeianus', for he loved the Republic without hating the monarchy too much, and he found the realization of his state of mind in the Augustan régime in which the monarchy had come to an agreement with the senate. He was, therefore, in perfect unison with the Restorer of Rome, for he admired the work of the emperor and he praised at the same time the ancient glories of the Republic.

Roughly coeval with the work of Livy, but deeply different in its plan and tendencies, was the historical work of Pompeius Trogus, a Gaul from Narbo. His forty-four books of *Historiae Philippicae*, which were finished about the year AD 9, have survived through a badly proportioned and disorderly epitome by one Justinus who lived in the second or third century. We have already noticed the anti-Roman character of the work of Timagenes. The Augustan era also produced the *Historiae* (from 62 to 42 BC) of Asinius Pollio; the commentaries and the memoirs of M. Valerius Messala Corvinus; and the histories of the civil wars by the Elder Seneca (50 BC–AD 37). Then there were the historical works of Augustus himself: the *rescripta Bruto de Catone* which were a defence of the monarchy; thirteen books *de vita sua*; a *vita Drusi*; and the *Index rerum gestarum* which survives in epigraphic form and consists of thirty-five chapters. This last work tells with extreme simplicity but great efficiency of all the honours and offices which were bestowed upon him, of all the deeds accomplished to improve the Roman world, and of all the works carried out to increase its power and its welfare.

Oratory and Rhetoric. We have spoken already of scientific and philosophical literary production (Chapters IX and X); it remains to speak of oratory. The Greek people was always fond of eloquence; and the epic of Homer is evidence of how important it was for the kings and the 'shepherds of people' to be able to speak 'like gods', often giving examples of speeches and debates. Primitive Greek eloquence had definite characteristics. It dwelt on subjects which were intimate and moving; it relied upon religious principles; and it

made use of demonstrative argument. It was an ingenuous and spontaneous
way of speaking which can still be found in the speeches of the histories of
Herodotus. There were two regions, however, which because of their democratic life made people more alive to oratorical skill than the others. These
were Athens and Syracuse. The Athenian citizen had constant occasion to
try his skill as an orator in front of an intelligent audience which was hard to
please. The assembly of the people, where everyone was free to speak,
became the teaching place of deliberative and political eloquence. The trials
before popular juries trained contenders and logographers (who prepared
speeches and learned them by heart) to act with adroitness in judicial oratory.

Patriotic ceremonies and public days gave opportunities to eminent
people to deliver 'epideictic' speeches (speeches on a set theme). Our sources
give us constant proof of the oratorical ability of the great Athenians of
the fourth century. In Sicily, and particularly in Syracuse, countless trials
followed the fall of the tyrants. It was this that gave rise to an early desire
to theorize and to write books on practical oratorical art (*techne*) which would
teach the people concerned the way to prevail in their cause by being convincing in its formulation. We know of two Syracusans, Korax and his pupil
Teisias, born about 480 BC, who published two books, or two versions of the
same book, on practical rhetoric, and who for payment would teach that art.
In these first schools of rhetoric, which moved from town to town, the
teacher would give some examples, and the pupils would practise by debating
with him. The new teaching had no moral object: its sole purpose was that
the thesis of the orator should prevail. This teaching was connected with
culture, however, because it enlarged literary and legal knowledge. It was
not teaching of a philosophical or artistic nature; but it became so when
oratorical *techne* was combined by Gorgias with sophistry, and when, with
him, these schools went from Syracuse to Athens. With the fusion of rhetoric
and sophistic, Attic oratorical prose reached a perfection, a strength, and a
pathos which can be compared with that attained by historical prose between
Herodotus and Thucydides and by dramatic language between Sophocles
and Euripides.

Antiphon (480–411 BC) of the deme of Rhamnus, can be considered as a
typical representative of this first phase. After the fall of the new régime he
was condemned to death for being one of the promoters of the oligarchic
revolution of 411 BC. Thucydides states that the speech he made in his own
defence at his trial was one of the best ever spoken; and a fragment which
has come down to us shows that it was both scornful and noble. During his
life, Antiphon was essentially a logographer: the ancients knew of rhetorical
treatises published in his name, as well as thirty-five genuine orations,
of which three surviving tetralogies are models of judicial debate.39 They
contain the speeches of the prosecution and those of the defence, the reply
of the prosecution and the counter-reply of the defence; and they concern
capital trials. Antiphon proved to be very able both in dialectic and in the

art of influencing and moving the judges. A further three judicial orations by him have come down to us. They are: *On the murder of Herodes*, *On the choral dancer*, and *On the poisoning charge against a stepmother*. The Athenian Sophist Antiphon, of whom we have recovered in papyrus considerable fragments of his work *On Truth*, and who debated with Socrates, is probably the same person.

Even oratorical prose felt the effect of the anti-sophist reaction, which called for a style which was both strong and graceful. The new rhetoric met with great success and moulded the taste of the whole nation. Although its aim was to achieve pathos, it had to give up many antitheses and symmetries; it had to be graceful and harmonious, moderate, and exquisitely Attic.

Andocides, Lysias, and Isaeus were the three great orators of that time who dealt mainly with judicial oratory. Andocides (born in Athens about the year 440 BC) was the least of the three and his judicial orations concerned him personally; for he led a very eventful life and was continually involved in law cases.[40] His earliest known oration is dated to 408 BC and is entitled *On his return*: this still reflected the style of Gorgias. We have, however, two further orations which are clear and attractive. Their titles are: *On the mysteries* (the best and more convincing) and *On the peace*; both follow in style the new tendency.

Lysias (about 440–380) was the son of a rich Syracusan who had settled in Athens. He studied art in Thurii at the school of Teisias and went back to Athens in the year 413 BC where he looked after his business with his brother Polemarchus. In 404 BC, however, his property was confiscated and his brother killed by the oligarchs. He returned to the city in 403 filled with a desire to avenge his brother, and accused Eratosthenes, whom he considered to be the guilty person, despite the fact that he was protected by an amnesty. The speech he made was a brilliant masterpiece vibrating with passion and sarcasm. He had, however, the bad idea of attacking the memory of Theramenes who was considered a saint by the people, and as a result he not only lost the cause he had pleaded, but his decree of citizenship was annulled. He became a metic again and was reduced to poverty, so he started on the profitable but delicate and difficult profession of logographer. He died in 380 BC. Lysias wrote many things and the ancients knew at least 233 of his speeches. Only thirty-four have come down to us, and not all of these are genuine; some are written for the courts, others are 'epideictic' (rhetorical pieces on a set theme). As an orator he knew how to embody in a speech the style and language suited to his clients and he succeeded admirably in disguising this skill. The dialectic part, however, was disconnected and not always faultless, and the pattern used over and over again led to monotony. His style was very graceful, simple, moderate, and elegant. He used the purest Attic language and was indeed a great artist.

Isaeus was born in Chalcis and later became Athenian. He wrote his orations between the years 390 and 353 BC. It seems that he was a pupil of Lysias and the teacher of Demosthenes. We have his judicial orations on questions of inheritance. The language and style he used were similar to those of Lysias, but his dialectic was much better, his reasoning more compact, his explanations more convincing; and his thought was imparted in a manner which was more authoritative, vigorous, and profound.

At the beginning of the fourth century BC there were several rival and contrasting tendencies both in decorative oratory and in the theory of oratory. Exponents of these theories were Polycrates, Alcidamas and Isocrates.

The main work of Polycrates consisted of examples for teaching; he gave paradoxical theses to his young pupils to make them practise in difficult subjects. Alcidamas, on the other hand, argued the merits of improvised oratory, which he thought should contain poetical forms and rhetorical figures, and be natural, clear, and pleasant.

Isocrates (436–338 BC) was an Athenian and the son of an industrialist. When he was young, he followed Prodicus, Socrates, and Gorgias. After the fall of Athens, however, he was left poor and so he started to work as a logographer. Yet the weakness of his voice, his slow composition, a shyness which he could not overcome, and the competition of Lysias, soon forced him to give it up. Therefore, in the year 388 BC he opened a school of rhetoric and made his fortune: he succeeded in attracting a constant stream of able students from all parts of Greece. He did not influence his pupils, but encouraged them to follow their own tendencies; and he introduced them to all the different fields of literature. Meanwhile he prepared his epideictic orations, which he did not proclaim in front of the general public but published as small pamphlets.[41] In this way cultivated people in all parts of Greece could read them, re-read them, and meditate upon them, especially when he spoke of a Greek federation against Persia. His physical defects prevented him from taking part in political life, but he was nevertheless very keen to talk about politics. By writing his orations he succeeded in making his views known to everybody, whether near or far away, to contemporaries and to posterity. Isocrates used pure Attic language; it was carefully selected like that of Lysias; it had no poetic terms and made careful use of rhetorical figures; but it was constantly rhythmical and scrupulously excluded the hiatus.

He was skilful in the choice of his form, was smooth and polished, and expressed himself in lengthily constructed phrases. Nevertheless this admirable prose leaves us cold, as it merely dazzles without either enrapturing or stimulating.

Political eloquence had its outstanding representatives in Athens during the last decades in which the city fought its final struggles for independence. The greatest men of different political parties fought each other in the assemblies and in court with fiery speeches in which patriotism rose high above personal interests. The tragedy of events and strong party feelings explain the tone, which was aggressive yet full of pathos, of their wonderful oratorical efforts. The greatest of the patriotic speakers was undoubtedly Demosthenes (384–322 BC). He was the son of a rich industrialist and a pupil of Isaeus. While he was a minor his fortune was squandered by his guardians, and he therefore decided to become a logographer and to improve his historical and legal culture; it is said that he also had some pupils. Sixty-five orations are ascribed to him, sixty-one of which have come down to us: many of the latter, however, are of doubtful authenticity, particularly some of the court speeches. These court speeches are less interesting from a literary point of view, for he had to adapt them to the mentality and class of his clients and because the subject was less congenial to his tendency to pathos. But the true Demosthenes is the man who delivered political orations, such as those he started in 351 BC and directed for ten years against Philip of Macedon. They were attacking speeches so long as Demosthenes was a member of the anti-Macedonian opposition. But in the year 346 BC he became the leader of the party which dominated Athens and from then on his orations were delivered in his own defence. The same thing can be said about the speech *On the Crown*, which was aimed against Aeschines, orator for the opposing party. The first political orations of Demosthenes were delivered in a style which was still hard and Thucydidean, though they show evidence of the orator's passion. Later orations, which were deliberative, are unsurpassable masterpieces. Demosthenes was a skilful improviser if the situation required it, but he liked to prepare his speeches very carefully, and he edited them with equal care before he published them as pamphlets which could be read and meditated upon. From Isocrates he learned the art of polishing but he did not abuse it; he wanted not only to achieve literary fame, to please the ear, but still more to defeat the enemy, to win his cause, and to carry away the public with his passion. The art is there, but it is hidden; it can be perceived in the harmony of the rhythm, in the planned absence of the hiatus, and in the placing together of short syllables. It is an art which has no monotony, and which does not impair either spontaneity or enthusiasm. The passion of the orator reveals itself in the style, rich in metaphors and images, in the lively syntax, in transparent feelings of passion. The way of reasoning is superb; the descriptions are concise and wonderful; the language is very simple and pure choice Attic with few poetic terms. It was mostly during the twenty years between 350 and 330 BC that all the great Attic orators fought for their political ideals. Some of them, such as Lycurgus and Hyperides, were for the most part in agreement with Demosthenes; some of them, Aeschines for example, were in the opposite camp.

Lycurgus (about 390–324 BC) was an Athenian of the famous family of the Eteobutadae; he was a pupil of Plato and Isocrates, and a political friend of Demosthenes. When the power of Athens was broken at Chaeronea he became for twelve years the leader of his town and the supporter of its

x*

finances. His speeches were mostly accusations made to defend the state from guilty citizens; they were implacable and dominated by an overwhelming passion for his country, but they were full of legal sophistries.

Hyperides (389–322 BC) was an Athenian, a pupil of Isocrates and perhaps of Plato. When young he worked as a logographer (professional writer of speeches for others to deliver); he became rich and he liked to spend his riches. He started to take part in public life from the year 362 BC, and became the accuser of many people. For a long time he collaborated with Demosthenes against the Macedonians, but later he disagreed with him about the affair of Harpalus. The two became reconciled for the Lamian War against Antipater in 323; but they disagreed again later. Antipater ordered Hyperides to be executed. The ancients knew fifty-two of his orations; but only some parts of six of them have come down to us. Four of them are on judicial matters; one is political (*Against Demosthenes*); and one is written to commemorate the dead of the Lamian War (*Epitaphius*). His style was simple and clear like that of Lysias and almost as vigorous as that of Demosthenes.

The greatest opponent of Demosthenes was Aeschines (about 390–320 BC). He came from a simple family and entered political life in 357 BC after having been a clerk and an actor. At the beginning he opposed Philip; later on, after a mission to Macedonia, he went over to the party of peace. This was the starting-point of his relentless battle with Demosthenes, which ended when he was banished from Athens in 323 BC to Rhodes where he started a school. Whatever judgement may be pronounced on Aeschines as a party man, it cannot be denied that artistically he was a great stylist. His style was strong and simple, musical and elegant. He had dialectical ability and emotive power. His language was pure and precise.

After the time of Alexander Greek oratory differed according to the different places from which it came. Whereas in Greece itself there was public oratory in some towns at various periods, in other regions with a monarchic régime oratory had to follow new ways. It had to become more refined and learned for teaching purposes, or it had to be the bombastic substance of a panegyric or gala lecture. After the conquests of Alexander and the end of the works of Lycurgus, Demosthenes, and Hyperides, political and forensic debates went on in Athens for quite a while. Deinarchus, for example, was thirty years later, and other orators later still.

Deinarchus of Corinth took up residence in Athens and was a pupil of Theophrastus. He started his career as a logographer in 336 BC and was very active between the years 322 and 307 BC. He was then banished; but went back to Athens in 292 BC when he was employed in a trial. He wrote about a hundred orations, but only three of them are left, and they concerned the affair of Harpalus. He followed the style of his predecessors and this earned him the nickname of 'The country Demosthenes'.

Meanwhile, in addition to the style of the great orators of the fourth century BC, there was a simpler, though elegant, style which became common in Athens. It was mostly the work of the Peripatetic school of Aristotle and Theophrastus. This was called the 'middle style' and was later transplanted to several Hellenistic cultural centres such as Alexandria and Pergamum, partly through the activity of Demetrius of Phalerum. The ancients considered Demetrius' eloquence elegant but lacking in power. The oratorical art taught in Pergamum by Crates of Mallus had similar qualities but it tended to philosophical speculation. Crates had a deep knowledge of dialectic and encouraged imitation of the old Athenian models.

The oratory favoured at Rhodes was not very different, for here the school of Aeschines had developed a moderate style. The school was directed by Molon when Caesar and Cicero attended it.

All these arts of oratory were more or less similar. Greatly different, on the other hand, was the oratory taught by Hegesias of Magnesia (about 250 BC) in the Greek towns of the Asiatic coast. This was a prolific writer, with a style which was pompous, solemn, affected, metaphorical, tortuous, sententious, and with a broken rhythm. The new system was conceived in the luxurious towns of Asia Minor; but it had some popularity even in the Greek peninsula.

The main tendencies developed by Hellenistic oratory in the third and second centuries BC lasted through the following century as well. There were two types of tendency which were in strong contrast with each other. The 'Asianist' type was pompous, affected, richer in fanciful Eastern images than in logic or dialectic, declamatory, full of mimicry, and sensational. The 'Attic' style was terse, severe and tending to archaism, and was based on Thucydides and on orators of the fourth century BC. Aeschylus of Cnidus and Aeschylus of Miletus were the representatives of the 'Asianist' type; whereas Gorgias was the chief exponent of the 'Attic'. The latter was the teacher of Cicero's son and the author of a work on *The figures of rhetoric* of which a Latin summary was later made by Rutilius Lupus.

The most flourishing schools, however, followed a path between these two contrasting types of oratory. The Rhodian school had great similarity with the Asianists, while the school of Pergamum was nearer to the Atticists. The orators of the Rhodian school wanted to keep the flamboyance of the Asianistic style under control and to approach the style of Hyperides, the richest among Attic orators. As a rule, however, they avoided pre-established patterns and left room for inventive freedom or 'anomaly' (irregularity). The orators of the school of Pergamum required a philosophical culture from their speakers; they modelled themselves on Demosthenes, and from their insistence that the declension of nouns and verbs was capable of regular classification were called 'analogists' (believers in similarity of forms).

Two ardent and active Atticists carried on their profession in Rome at the time of Augustus. They were Dionysius of Halicarnassus and Caecilius of Calacte. They opposed contemporary authors with some success by reacting against the eclecticism of the *koiné*; but they did not demand a pure Atticism as happened later in the second century AD.

Dionysius of Halicarnassus (see above p. 599) had a learned and bookish culture. He dogmatically divided literary men into two groups—those who were infallible and to be idolized, and the reprobates who were to be routed —not because of their passions and their purpose, but because of the style and forms they used. Many of his rhetorical works have come down to us. Archagathus was a Jew of servile origin from Calacte in Sicily. He took the name of Caecilius from his liberator and went to Rome about the year 2 BC where he opened a school. He was an ardent admirer of Demosthenes and of Lysias, but had a low opinion of Plato and of the Asianists. He wrote a significant treatise on oratorical technique, and various critical and historical works.

Oratory had great importance in the formation and establishment of the art of Latin prose.[42] In Rome, with the development of public and judicial life, and because of practical needs, it very soon achieved a high degree of excellence. We have little information, however, of orators who lived before the second half of the second century BC until we come to Cato.[43] Cato and his followers in vain opposed the establishment of Greek oratorical theories in Rome; despite their efforts Greek schools of rhetoric were opened.[44] In Rome these schools found a larger field of expression than they did in Hellenistic capitals, for the orators did not speak only in the schools and before an initiated audience, but in the presence of the general public in the forum and the senate. They did not deal with dead scholastic themes, but with great and vital problems which stirred the city and the world. The theories of the rhetoricians had, therefore, to be adapted to the hard realities of life. (The expulsion of rascally and ignorant orators by the censors in 92 BC should be remembered.) Asian artificiality had to give way to clarity of dialectic, which was indispensable in political debates. Roman orators were men who both led a practical life, and were politicians and thinkers. They welcomed, therefore, the thesis of those Greeks who wanted to end the age-long disagreement between sophistic and philosophy, and between rhetoric and historical experience. They created an oratorical art in which beauty of form was completed by a profound philosophical doctrine about history and law.

Cicero, in his rhetorical works, the *Brutus* particularly, gave long lists of Roman orators with short appraisals of their activity which we can no longer check. All the great public men of Rome are recalled to us.

Fragments show that Roman eloquence started to show the influence of Greece and particularly of the Asian schools with Tiberius Sempronius Gracchus, who was tribune in the year 133 BC and a pupil of Greek rhetoricians and philosophers. The same thing can be said about his brother Gaius Gracchus, who according to Cicero excelled all other orators in oratorical vehemence. He was incapable of speaking without getting excited; and he started his speech by tuning his voice to the sound played by a flute-player.

The group of the Asianists can be completed with the names of Q. Hortensius Hortalus (114–50 BC), who was its greatest champion, and by Marcus Antonius who was one of his successors.

The *Rhetorica ad Herennium*, which most certainly was not written by Cicero, but was very probably used by him, reflects the debates which took place about rhetoric between the years 86 and 82 BC. This work was published in four books (about the orator, his themes, and his elocution) by a Marian democrat who wanted to reduce the mania for things Greek, together with the excessive rules and erudition which were current in oratory. He used Greek ideas and classifications, but his technical terminology is both Latin and precise.

M. Tullius Cicero (106–43 BC) was born in Arpinum, and as a very young man accepted the Asianist theories, which he supported in his *De inventione*, written when he was only twenty. He made use of these theories in his first orations, but after he returned from his travels in the East he became a supporter of the 'middle style' which he had learned at the school of Molon at Rhodes. Cicero was a politician, an orator, a theorist on the subject of eloquence, a philosopher, a geographer, an historian, a letter-writer, and a poet. He was a complex many-sided figure and he embodied the splendour and the weakness of his troubled age. Although he was a literary man and a great master of style his great ambition was to become a politician, and, through his oratory, to be an outstanding figure in a world which was then dominated by the sword.

But he lacked courage and a firm line of conduct, for he was eclectic both in politics and philosophy and he never had a directive 'credo' of life.45

There were at least 106 orations, but only 58 of them have come down to us together with 17 fragments and 31 titles. We have no means of judging his speeches as they were delivered, for he often improvised and we know them only in the form in which he published them. Speaking of the *Pro Milone*, Asconius states very clearly that there were great differences between the two drafts of it, both in style and in the facts presented. We can be sure that the same was true of many other Ciceronian orations. All of them, whether judicial, deliberative, or epideictic, have certain common characteristics. They are full of pleading pathos designed to carry away the public; their style shows supreme virtuosity; and there is rhythm in the endings of paragraphs and sentences, which transforms the orations almost into poetry.

But there are faults too. The dialectic was questionable; the violence of the accusations was too great, since it was a habit of the age to make charges which could not be fully proved. Rhetorical tricks often overshadowed and displaced sound oratory, and the style was frequently overloaded.

Cicero also set out to be a theorist on oratorical art. We have already mentioned his *De inventione*, written in the year 86 BC, in which he supported rhetorical eclecticism. In 55 BC he published the *De oratore*, written in the form of dialogue on the Platonic model, in which he imagined a discussion between several orators taking place in the year 91 BC. In this work, some of the orators were shown as maintaining that an orator had to have a wide culture; whereas others contended that he had to rely on inspiration. In 46 BC Cicero wrote another dialogue, entitled *Brutus*, in which he argued against the Atticists and recounted a long history of Roman eloquence. His *Orator ad M. Brutum* written in the same year contains yet another polemic against the Atticists; in it he states that a real orator is a man who knows how to make use of every tone and style, and he dwells on the theory of rhythm. Lastly, in his *De optimo genere oratorum*, which is a preface to a translation of Aeschines and Demosthenes, Cicero attempts to show that they are more like him than like the Atticists. The long and repeated polemics of Cicero prove that the school of the so-called Atticists was very strong and ready to argue for itself. This school made almost the same criticism of him, namely that of pomposity and exaggeration, as he had made of the Asianists. It consisted of a group of young people who desired to achieve a form of spontaneous oratory. They wanted to see Art emerging from an idea, instead of being an embellishment to the idea; and they considered that the fundamentals of an oration should lie in a sincere exposition of the facts and in dialectic. This school had two teachers, the orators C. Licinius Calvus and M. Iunius Brutus (the murderer of Caesar). Both died young. The popularity achieved by anti-Ciceronian styles was due to this school, although such was not the intention of its adherents. It was a popularity already established by C. Iulius Caesar, whose style was very similar to that of Lysias, and by C. Sallustius Crispus who recalled Thucydides.

C. Iulius Caesar had been active all his life as a political and military orator and his orations must have had the same qualities of style as are shown in the *Commentarii*. He also wrote a work, *De analogia*, in which he maintained that the fundamental task of an orator is the choice of words, and that the orator must avoid using irrational terms which are not appropriate to his methods of argument. We know he wrote three collections of witty sayings (*Dicta collectanea*); but their publication was forbidden by Augustus. Sallust's orations are illustrated in his historical works; we also possess his *Invective* against Cicero, which was mentioned by Quintilian.[46]

Ciceronians like Messala, and Atticists like Asinius Pollio and Augustus himself, were still opposed to one another. But it was not long before all polemics quietened down, and the style of oratory became enfeebled. This was because, with the coming of the empire, political debates were restricted and the art of eloquence died. It was once again confined to the courts of law, where it was exhibited in the presence of bureaucrats, or to schools, where it became once again merely an exercise upon banal themes, or to formal performances before specialist audiences. It should be added that very soon the professional teachers of this new rhetoric were generally not Italians but Spaniards; it is easy, therefore, to understand its history down to the Elder Seneca's time.

It became fashionable to declaim—sometimes in a sing-song voice—speeches which consisted of witticisms, of far-fetched ideas, of extravagant metaphors, and of play of words around fictitious themes. This was done following either the form of 'suasoriae' (to persuade some ancient personage to take a certain decision) or the form of 'controversiae' (to support, on the basis of imaginary laws, the two opposite view-points upon a legal controversy). Both were rightly criticized by Petronius, by Quintilian, and by the Elder Seneca. The last-named recounts the plots of these orations, and we therefore know the names of their authors. He himself was L. Annaeus Seneca (50 BC–AD 39), born at Corduba in Spain; and he wrote for his sons (who studied rhetoric about the year AD 37) at least ten books on *Oratorum et rhetorum sententiae, divisiones, colores controversiarum*, and seven on *Sententiae et divisiones Suasoriarum*. He had an exceptional memory and his information came from declamations he had heard in the past. These he could not refrain from criticizing very sharply.

2. ART

a. *China*

The crumbling away of the old feudal state into a feudal confederacy and hence into anarchy pure and simple, coupled with the rise of a few strong regional states, exercised a markedly decentralizing influence on Chinese art. The single centre of attraction represented by the court of the Chou was replaced by half a dozen regional centres, which rivalled one another not only in politics, but also in the display of pomp and splendour, and therefore in art. Hence the Late Chou period shows a courtly and luxurious art with a lavish use of gold, silver, jade, and turquoise. Jade carving now reaches its zenith; but even more important is the fact that, after the decay during the Middle Chou period, bronze-casting improves rapidly and soon once more becomes supreme, its rich variety being due to the blending of several regional styles. Among these the 'Huai style' (a name introduced by the Swedish archaeologists) is dominant. It marks a reawakening of Chinese creative genius after a long period of semi-barrenness. Geometric elements are full of movement and fantasy; the ancient *t'ao-t'ieh* mask fades into a purely ornamental assemblage of curves and lines. A favourite subject is animals, treated with a levity and exuberance of details that contrast deeply with the austerity of Middle Chou. The best products are perhaps those from the tombs of the princes of Han (fifth to third centuries BC)(Pl. 25, a) at Chin-ts'un near Lo-yang. Here for the first time we also meet the bronze mirrors that were to become so characteristic of Han art. They are exquisite objects, ornamented with geometrical designs (T and L patterns); it is noteworthy that the spirit of this decorative style is quite opposite to the animal naturalism of the vases.

Among the latter, those of Li-yü on the northern frontier present a rather close analogy with the Ordos bronzes; Hsiung-nu and Chinese did not merely clash on the battlefield, but exchanged, at least to a certain extent, artistic motifs and ideas. In this particular case it appears that the 'barbarians' were the givers and the Chinese the receivers.

Quite another school, indeed another art, is that of the wooden sculptures and of the lacquer boxes of Ch'ang-sha, in the territory of the ancient state of Ch'u. They include also peculiar funeral figurines, made as substitutes of real people for funeral purposes: the *ming-ch'i*. Their sly archaic smile characterizes them as belonging to another world, to a psychology different from the austere milieu of the north Chinese courts.

Architecture and painting of this period are known only from literary texts and from imitations on vases and (for painting) on lacquer boxes.

Ch'in art was only an appendix to that of the Warring States (or Late Chou). At that time the background of Chinese art changed once more, its main features being the centralized bureaucratic empire and the contacts with the West. This meant that art production under the Han centred again around the imperial capital Ch'ang-an and was exposed to various aesthetic influences introduced from central Asia. The foreign motifs, however, were incorporated into, but did not dominate, the aesthetic rules of Early Han times (202 BC to AD 23).

Little has survived of the sculpture of this period, and this little is mostly associated with burial and tomb construction. The most imposing monument of this period is the tomb of General Ho Ch'ü-ping (d. 117 BC) in Shansi; a stone figure of a horse standing over a fallen warrior (probably a Hsiung-nu) is a quite remarkable piece and a fitting epitaph for the young hero of the Hsiung-nu wars.

Painting of the Early Han is little known. The lacquer finds and the highly interesting painting on silk from Ch'ang-sha have been believed to have originated in the Ch'u territory. As known from the literary texts, this was above all an age of wall-painting, and the Ch'ang-an palaces contained large amounts of it; but nothing has come down to us.

b. *The Art of the Steppes*

In southern Siberia, around the metallurgical centre of the Minusinsk, the culture of Tagar II (c.400 to 100 BC) perfected the animal style of the steppe art. The most characteristic motif of this period are the galloping stag and the hunting tiger crushing down a stag. Farther south, the *kurgans* (funeral mounds) of Pazyryk in the Altai, frozen from top to bottom, have miraculously preserved corpses of men and horses, with clothing and accoutrements, in fact the whole funeral furnishing of rich local princes. The art of Pazyryk (c. fourth to first centuries BC) is quite clearly influenced by Achaemenid art,—a posthumous influence, being later than the overthrow of the Persian empire by Alexander (Pl. 25, b).

In a more eastern region, the Ordos bronzes (Pl. 21, b), plaques, agrafes, buttons etc. (c. fourth to first centuries BC) derive partly from the art of Tagar, but represent an original development, which in its turn made its impact felt on the Chinese bronzes of the Warring States period. The bearers of this art were, at least in its later phase, the Hsiung-nu. We have direct evidence in the tomb of a Hsiung-nu chief found by Kozlov at Nain Ola near Ulan Bator Khoto, containing beautiful bronzes and strips of woollen cloth woven with motifs of fighting animals. It is datable to the beginning of our era.

c. *India*

Apart from descriptions of buildings in the epics and in the Buddhist *Jātakas*, no specimen of Indian art after the end of the Harappā civilization and before the fourth century BC has come down to us, with the possible exception of the funeral mounds at Lauriya Nandangarh, already mentioned above. The sculptural remains are so scarce and of so crude a quality, that we have to assume a very substantial hiatus in artistic development from Harappā to the Mauryas.

Indian art of the Maurya period (c. 321–185 BC) is characterized by a strong foreign influence, that of the Achaemenid court, exerting itself after the latter had been wiped out of existence by the conquest of Alexander the Great.[47] Chandragupta's palace at Pāṭaliputra, as known from Megasthenes' descriptions and (to a very small extent) by excavations, consisted mainly of a central audience hall (*apadāna*) supported by eighty huge monolithic columns of sandstone, on the pattern of the royal palaces of Iran. We know nothing of the buildings of Aśoka, except for some of his religious foundations, such as the façade of the Lomasa Rishi cave. It ushers in a long series of Buddhist assembly halls (*caitya*) and monasteries (*sanghārāma*, *vihāra*) hewn into the rock or adapted from already-existing caves, in painstaking imitation of wooden buildings.

Maurya sculpture too is in the main a local development of Achaemenid themes. This is the case above all for the lotus-shaped bell capitals that topped the pillars on which Aśoka inscribed his edicts; they are imitated from the capitals of Persepolis, although their beautiful finish and careful execution make up for their lack of originality. The capital in its turn was usually surmounted by one or more heraldic lions and sometimes also by one or more wheels, symbolizing the 'turning the wheel of the Law', i.e. the preaching of the Buddhist religion. We are thus confronted for the first time with a fact that was to be characteristic of most of the art of north-western India for the next five centuries: the expression of purely local (Buddhist) ideas through foreign stylistic modes. We have at least one statue of the Maurya period (if not earlier): the Yakṣa (semi-god) of Parkham, a squat completely frontal figure of no real aesthetic value. For once it is completely Indian in character and seems to be directly descended from the art of

Harappā. But already the late Mauryan Yakṣa from Patna shows unmistakable reminiscences of Persepolitan art.

Although the fall of the Mauryan empire was accompanied by an anti-Buddhist reaction, and although the Śuṅgas in northern India (c.185–72) and later also the Andhras in the Deccan were both Hindu dynasties, Buddhism continued to dominate the inspiration and content of Indian art.[48] The Śuṅga period is chiefly represented by the decoration of the railings and gateways that surrounded the *stūpas* of Sanchi and of Bharhut. The *stūpa* was at first a funeral mound covering the relics of the Buddha or of some holy man. Later it became a dome-shaped structure of masonry surmounted by a cube (*harmikā*) from which a mast (*yaṣṭi*) emerged; the whole was meant to symbolize the world with the Heaven of the Thirty-Three Gods above, and the *axis mundi* transversing both. The *stūpas* were usually enclosed by elaborately carved railings. The typical examples of such sculptures from the Śuṅga period (c.100 BC), representing subjects drawn from the *Jātakas* and from the life of the Buddha, are those of Bharhut, now dispersed in several museums. (Pl. 26.) Achaemenid influence is still present, but now only in faint reminiscences; the reliefs are somewhat archaic in aspect and strictly functional in character, the aim of telling a story or conveying a religious idea predominating over the aesthetic features. The ornamentation of the *stūpa* n. 2 at Sanchi may be slightly earlier (end of the second century BC), (Pl. 27, a) while the railings of the Mahābodhi temple at Bodh Gaya belong to the end of this period.

Śuṅga art is continued by and culminates in (during the so-called 'Early Andhra' period, c.72–25 BC; a misnomer) the magnificent sculptural decoration of the *stūpa* n. 1 at Sanchi. It is characterized by four huge gateways (*toraṇa*) literally covered with reliefs which are the finest in early Indian art. Nothing can match the sensuous vitality and the fulness of form of the female figures of Sanchi, or the rhythmic and choral effect of some of the great scenes from the life of the Buddha. In all these sculptures the Buddha, however, is never portrayed, but his presence is hinted at by a symbol (the sandals, a parasol, etc.).

As a parallel with Sanchi we find also the first extant relics of Indian painting, those in Cave X at Ajanta (Bombay State), representing the *Saddanta Jātaka*, with their free-moving and naturalistic figures of elephants and other animals in an entirely formalized setting.

The architecture of the last two centuries BC is characterized by several rock-cut cave *caityas*, which developed yet farther the pattern set at Lomasa Rishi. The elaborate imitation of wooden vaults with their rafters led to ever more imposing structures, such as can be seen e.g. at Bhaja (c.50 BC), where the sculptural decor seems to be connected with the Bharhut school. (Pl. 27, b.)

d. *Greek Art*

Architecture. During the fifth century and the first half of the fourth, a singular phenomenon is to be observed both in art and in literature. Architecture, sculpture, painting, and ceramics had originally progressed faster in several regions of the Greek world than in Athens. The same thing happened in the literary field. After Athens had felt and assimilated this progress, however, it took the lead in the aesthetic movement and produced the most magnificent examples of different artistic styles such as those conceived by Myron, Pheidias, Alcamenes, Polygnotus, Micon, Nicias, Euphronius, Duris, and Meidias.

If we observe the whole Hellenic production of this period in both art and thought, it appears that the arts evolved at different speeds which depended upon the technical progress made in the various fields. The same new tendency, therefore, developed spontaneously at different times in different kinds of artistic and literary productions. It is not therefore anachronistic, from a conceptual point of view, to discover a close link between Pindar, Aeschylus, Polygnotus, and Myron—or between Pheidias, Sophocles, Zeuxis and Parrhasius—even if they were not completely contemporaneous.

That same study of the individual which brings into existence psychology in the philosophical field, and the writing of 'Lives' in literature, is the force which creates the portrait in art. The ideal beauty which inspired Plato and later Epicurus is to be found during the intermediate period, in the pure and serene sculptural creations of Praxiteles; the search of Isocrates for a delicate style finds a counterpart in the supreme delicacy of Lysippus; the study of nature by Aristotle and his first pupils is a fore-runner of the deep and meticulous anatomical studies and the representation of landscape and animals of the Hellenistic age; the idyllic subjects of Theocritus are to be found again in the sculpture and paintings of the age after Alexander; and finally, the frightening realism of tragedy finds, through the statuary of Scopas, its last terrific echo in the *Laocoön*.

Greece enjoyed about half a century of relative calm which lasted from the expulsion of the Persians to the Peloponnesian War, and was particularly peaceful just after the treaties of 449 and 446. For the Greek world of the West, peace followed for a few decades after the victories over the Carthaginians in 479 and over the Etruscans in 473. The improvement in financial resources and the gratitude towards the gods, dispensers of victories, stimulated an understandable desire to have new temples worthy of all the gods. At first, almost all the new temples were built in the Doric style, which had different characteristics according to the period of time and to the places where the temples were built. This style tended to a refinement of the relative proportions of the width and the length of a building, and of the height and diameter of its columns. In later years there developed a taste for hybridism between different styles, so that the elements of one, two, or even three styles were to be found in the same building. Most temples of the period were vast and were very precisely designed, at the cost of great financial outlay. It must be remembered that Pericles spent around 2,000 talents for public buildings in a few years.

The first task of the citizens of Athens was to provide their town with powerful defensive walls and with adequate harbour installations. After the treasure of the League had been taken to the city, both means and leisure were available for a magnificent restoration of the Acropolis, which was still full of the ruins caused by Persian devastation. Between the years 449 and 432 BC Athens built the Parthenon. (Pl. 28, a.) It was the most magnificent temple of its period in all the Greek peninsula, the abode of the protecting goddess to whom the treasure of the League was entrusted. About 70 metres by 31 metres, it was a peripteral (i.e., one completely surrounded by columns) Doric temple with some elements of Ionic style, and was built by the architect Ictinus, who worked under the supervision of Pheidias. It glittered with Pentelic marble, and was decorated with carved pediments, metopes, and friezes; in it was the gold-and-ivory statue carved by Pheidias. Inscriptions give us a day-to-day story of how this great artistic work came to be achieved.

Where the monumental entrance erected by Peisistratus stood at the door of the Acropolis, Mnesicles built (437–432 BC) his magnificent and harmonious *Propylaea*. (Pl. 28, b.) The plan of this construction was complex but well suited to the lay-out of the ground, and it was decorated with pictures and statues.

At the same time as the Parthenon, the Athenians built the so-called Theseum in the lower part of the town near the market. (Pl. 29, a.) It was a peripteral Doric temple (probably the temple of Hephaestus), and was resplendent with white marble. It is well preserved to this day. A few years later, after the peace of 421, many new buildings were erected in Athens. There was a small elegant Ionic temple, surrounded by a balustrade in honour of Athena Nikē; and the Erechtheum, Philocles' reconstruction of the temple of Athena Polias (built again in the fourth century after the fire of 405 BC), which consisted of a fusion of many buildings into one of 23·50 metres by 13 metres. It had two graceful balconies, one of which forms a porch supported by the wonderful statues of six Korai, young maidens of exquisite designs. (Pl. 29, b.)

Of the same period as the Parthenon and the Theseum were the peripteral Doric temples built on the headland of Sunium (Pl. 30, a); the temple of Nemesis in Rhamnus, built in the place of one which had been destroyed by the Persians; and the Telesterion for the celebration of Mysteries, also replacing a sanctuary destroyed by the barbarians. This last temple was the work of the architects Coroebus, Metagenes, and Xenocles, and the general plans were drawn by Ictinus. It was a large building of Doric style, almost square, on two floors. Inside the temple were rich colonnades of seven rows of columns, with forty-two columns in all, to receive the faithful worshippers of the goddesses.

In the Peloponnese, at the *Altis* of Olympia, Lybon erected a great temple
(64·10 metres by 27·60 metres) of Doric style, in honour of Zeus. It was
built of stuccoed and polychromatic limestone and of marble. The basic
structure of the building was finished in 456 BC; it had two large pediments
and sculpted metopes and was ready to receive the gigantic chryselephantine

FIG. 5. The Corinthian Order.

statue of the god later executed by Pheidias. The temple of Apollon Epicurius
on the slopes of Bassae, near Phigaleia in Arcadia, was a new work by Ictinus
(about 430–420). Its style was hybrid in the extreme, for it was Doric but
has Ionic columns and Corinthian capitals (the first example of the new
Corinthian style). (Fig. 5.) At Mycenae in the Argolid, Eupolemus of Argos
built in the year 423 BC a new great temple of Hera in place of an earlier
temple which had been destroyed by fire.

In Sicily, some temples were built even earlier. There was the temple of

Demeter and Korē in Syracuse, which was started by Gelon and finished by
his successors, and the Athenaeum with its tall columns (today a cathedral).
A series of new temples were built at Acragas in the fifth century: they
justified the opinion of Pindar, according to whom Acragas was 'the most
beautiful city of mortal men'. (Pl. 30, b.) The temples of Heracles and of the
Dioscuri were built to celebrate the victory over the Carthaginians in the
year 479 BC. After they had been completed Theron started to build a vast
temple in honour of Olympian Zeus (121 metres by 55 metres), which had
not yet been finished when the town was destroyed in 405 BC. It had the
characteristic colonnade closed by huge half-columns and tall 'telamons'
(gigantic male figures supporting the roof over 7 metres high) which were
probably to support the flat ceilings from the inside. The so-called temples
of Athens, of Concord, of Vulcan, of Asclepius, and others were also built
at Acragas during the course of that century (Pl. 30, b.); at the same time the
so-called temples A., O., and E. were built at Selinus, and E. (the peripteral
Doric temple of Hera) contains a wonderful series of metopes. At Himera
there was a temple in memory of the victory over the Carthaginians. Because
of Greek influence an ancient sanctuary in Segesta was surrounded by a
temple-like construction; the lack of grooves in its columns shows that
subsequent events in the town and in the island prevented the temple's
completion. (Pl. 31, a.)

At Poseidonia (Paestum) in Magna Graecia a peripteral Doric temple,
the Poseidonium (Pl. 31, b) (60 metres by 24 metres) was finished about the
middle of the century. This is perhaps the most beautiful and harmonious
temple of that time built in western Greece. In it archaic styles are blended
with a general softening of architectural lines.

As well as the temples, the walls of the great panhellenic sanctuaries
enclosed several small buildings erected for the purpose of keeping in safe
custody the ex-voto offerings of each town, the so-called treasures which were
of a variety of types. There was, for example, the extremely beautiful
treasure of the Athenians which was kept at Delphi and which was consecrated after the battle of Marathon.

The inhabitants of the Greek peninsula did not build many temples
during the fourth century BC. Their finances were not sufficient and even
Athens did not build any temple of importance. Building, in those days,
sometimes merely consisted of a reconstruction of ancient and ruined buildings, normally with an amalgamation of different styles. It is interesting to
notice, however, that temples and votive monuments were sometimes
constructed on a circular plan: this revived the old Mycenaean dome (tholos)
style, which had never fallen wholly into disuse and may have been employed
for roofing parts of open-air meeting-places (skiades) in sixth-century Sparta.
For musical auditions, therefore, temples and votive monuments were
sometimes built on a circular plan. The following buildings are the most
worthy of notice: a new large temple to Apollo built at Delphi and finished

in the year 394 BC; the temple to Athena Alea erected at Tegea in Arcadia after the battle of Leuctra (371 BC) under the supervision of Scopas; and the Asclepieum at Epidaurus, of the first decades of the century, which was the work of Theodorus and had columns in all three orders. Polycletus the Younger built a *tholos* (diameter 21·82 metres) next to it, with a circular colonnade. This type of building was repeated at Olympia in the Philippeion, which was erected by Alexander in memory of his father and endowed with many statues of people of his family. It was copied in Athens as a graceful monument to the choregic victories of Lysicrates (335–334), and the Athenian building has remained almost intact.

In this period the wealth of Ionia revived, and with it came a revival of building activity: the temples were still in ruins after their destruction by the Persians. The new buildings, however, were still in the old local Ionic style. The Branchidae built the Didymeion near Miletus in honour of Apollo. It was started in the year 333 BC by Paeonius and Daphnis and was still not finished in the year 150 BC. It was the largest temple of the Greek world (132 metres by 73 metres) and as it was built very slowly with a double colonnade it clearly reveals all the variations of style of a couple of centuries. Pythius built a peripteral temple to Athena Polias in Priene, which was dedicated to the goddess by Alexander in 334 BC. Vitruvius tells us that about 340 BC Paeonius reconstructed the Artemisium of Ephesus, which had been spared by Xerxes but in 356 was burned by one Herostratus,[49] who wanted to make himself famous. It had very tall columns (18 metres) with reliefs sculpted by Scopas and Praxiteles, and it was immediately regarded as one of the wonders of the world.

Other great buildings were erected during the fifth and fourth centuries. There were covered theatres, such as the semicircular Odeum at Athens, built about 440 BC by Pericles for musical performances. Then there was the open-air stone theatre at Athens, reconstructed in the fourth century by Lycurgus; and similar theatres at the Piraeus, at Thoricus, at Corinth and at Syracuse. This last originally had a trapezoidal arena, constructed by Damocopus at the time of Hiero I, but it was made circular in Dionysius' day. There were many others, such as the exceedingly fine theatre of Epidaurus built in the enclosure of Asclepius by Polycletus II about the middle of the fourth century (Pl. 32, a) (Fig. 6), and the Thersileion of Megalopolis. The latter is named after its architect, who built it in 371 BC: it recaptured the style of the Telesteion of Eleusis, and could seat 6,000 people (66 metres by 52 metres). Its colonnades were situated in such a way that an orator in its centre could be seen by the whole audience.[50]

The *Stadium* for athletic contest and races was built in Athens at the time of Lycurgus. The oldest parts of the stadium of Delphi are of the fifth century.

Harbour installations often had architectural importance, as for example those of the Piraeus and of Syracuse. Also important were the walls of towns, such as those of the linked fortification Athens-Piraeus-Munychia, and those built by Dionysius for the defence of Syracuse, with its vast circle and strong castle. The first doors with a real arch appeared in Acarnania in the fifth century; and architecturally important also are the urban plans of Piraeus, of Selinus, of Rhodes, and of Thurii, all of which are attributed to Hippodamus of Miletus.

When monarchy revived in the Greek East, and in the West imperialistic

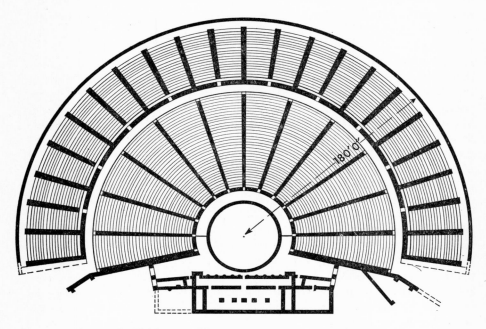

FIG. 6. Epidaurus: Plan of the theatre (after B. Fletcher).

tyrannies obtained repeated successes, there was a rebirth of court architecture appropriate to buildings of a type which had fallen out of use, just as there was a rebirth of a court epic. Royal palaces were built, such as those of Pella in Macedonia, famous for its frescoes by Zeuxis; of Alexandria; of Antioch; of Pergamum; of Syracuse; that of Rhegium built for Dionysius I; and many others. There were tombs for princes such as the Charmylion of Cos: and the Mausoleum which Mausolus, king of Caria (who died in 353 BC), ordered the architect Pythius (with the help of the sculptors Scopas, Timotheus, Bryaxis, and Leochares) to build in Halicarnassus for himself and his wife Artemisia. This Mausoleum was one of the most remarkable buildings of the fourth century. It had a high paved base (66 metres by 77·50 metres) surmounted by a temple-type building of Ionic type. It was crowned by a pyramid of steps with a large four-horsed chariot on top. It was about 46 metres high altogether, and was beautifully decorated with reliefs.

Painting. Our knowledge of Greek painting in the fifth and fourth centuries BC is very incomplete. Classical writers tell us of a large number of artists and works; but their references are too vague and can be interpreted in more than one way, and we have no original paintings which could explain them. Luckily we can deduce some information on paintings of great art, however small and formal, from paintings on ceramics, which were more 'industrialized' and technically simplified, and of which we have many beautiful examples.

During the first half of the fifth century, monumental painting for decoration of interiors established itself first of all in Ionia. Mandrocles of Samos, for example, painted in the Samian temple of Hera a scene depicting the passage of the Persian army into Europe. Later on Ionians like Micon and islanders like Polygnotus of Thasos brought this kind of art to Athens. Micon and Polygnotus, sometimes by themselves, sometimes together, and sometimes with Panaenus, brother of Pheidias (who at first had been a painter), decorated many Athenian buildings with their works. They painted, for example, the decorated porch (*stoa poikilē*) near the market with scenes representing episodes of ancient history (wars of the Amazons, the war of Troy) and of recent history (the battles of Marathon, of Oenophyta, and others). Several other works by Polygnotus were to be seen in temples and buildings in Athens, in Plataea, and in particular in the porch of the Cnidians at Delphi. We know of the existence of many other artists who were either fellow-workers of his (as his brother Aristophon) or pupils (Onasias for example). Although his perspective was faulty and the colours at his disposal very few, his art appears to have been as powerful and great as the tragic art of Aeschylus, who was his contemporary. He painted scenes which were complex and full of groups of people. Each person was represented in a different attitude and movement, and his name was painted at his side. The paintings of Polygnotus depicted mythical and historical episodes, which were pervaded by a deep religious feeling; and the people were shown as superhuman heroes.

The style of the art of Polygnotus and of the painters of his school influenced the art of ceramics. Potters of that time often copied the style of composition of Polygnotus; and like him they chose noble and great subjects and gave 'instantaneous' glimpses of bodies in rapid movement.

During the second half of the fifth century, people discovered the third dimension, perspective, and shadows. (This discovery was probably helped by the art of theatrical painting.) Artists, therefore, were able to produce paintings which were perfect in their conception and with a strong suggestion of suppleness. The masters of this new style were Agatharchus of Samos; Apollodorus of Athens; and, above all, Zeuxis of Heraclea in Italy, and

Parrhasius of Ephesus. These two last painters lived in Athens for a long time and were the masters of what may be called 'flowered' painting. The works of Zeuxis were both monochromes (depicting subjects in chiaroscuro) and polychromes. The picture of Eros crowned with roses is famous for its beauty, and it is said that when he painted his Helen, he did good business by charging money to allow people to see his picture. The most famous work of Parrhasius was a picture of Theseus in brilliant colours. Timanthes of Sicyon, the younger Aglaophon, and Pauson, the caricaturist, worked in a similar style. Some echo of this new technique can be found in a painted *stele* in Thebes and in some paintings of much later date at Herculaneum, Pompeii, and Rome. There are also fourth-century ceramics in which the painting has some 'flowered' characteristics: the graceful, but sometimes affected, work of Meidias is one example. Their imitation of the style of painters brought wide technical changes in the potter's art. This was due to the fact that the simple lines of red colour on a black background were not sufficient: potters, therefore, started to touch up the designs with added colours as in a real picture. This method was applied in many of the loveliest Athenian *lekythoi*.

The most important progress made by Greek painting during the fourth century consisted of the representation of the pathos and spirituality of the figures and of a masterful use of light and shade.

The most famous painters of that time were the following: Aristeides of Thebes of the Attico-Boeotian school, who lived in the age of the hegemony of his town, and who is said to have made fabulous earnings: his son Nicomachus; the Athenian (?) Euphranor who was also well known as a sculptor; his pupil Nicias, famous for his female figures (Io, Andromeda, Calypso and others), and for the skilful use of light and shade.

The school of Sicyon had a similar tendency and took great care to achieve purity of design and beauty of colour. It specialized in the technique of encaustic painting (painting by burning in heated wax), which was very suitable for small paintings and which gave brilliant results. The most famous artists of this school were Eupompus of Sicyon, Pamphilus of Amphipolis, Melanthius, and Pausias of Sicyon, who was a famous painter of flowers, fruit, and scenes of battles in encaustic technique. Apelles of Colophon, who afterwards settled in Pella, and later, at the time of Alexander, in Miletus, attended the school of Sicyon to perfect his work. His best-known painting is the Aphrodite Anadyomene (rising out of the sea), commissioned for the Asclepieum of Cos. He was so renowned as a portrait painter that the town of Ephesus paid him twenty talents to paint the portrait of Alexander. Protogenes of Caunus is also worthy of mention as the famous author of the picture of Ialysus, the eponymous hero of Rhodes, at which it seems that he worked for seven years.

We can get a better idea of Greek painting of that time from works of art painted in far-away lands, such as Etruria and Magna Graecia (Capua and

Poseidonia); or from those painted in later generations (at Pompeii for example), which show Greek influence. Knowledge can also be obtained from the art of painted ceramics which tended more and more to a technique of superimposing one colour on another. The simple technique of a red design on a black background was now used only for the production of commercialized wares which were exported to distant lands, to the north Euxine in particular.

Italiote pottery had a place of its own. It was probably started by potters who had left the Greek peninsula and moved to Italy, and particularly to Tarentum; it spread throughout Magna Graecia, developed its own individual style, and became Italiote. The Italiote potters wanted to achieve a pictorial effect more than a fine design, and they liked to depict scenes drawn from tragedies (including historical tragedies as Aeschylus' *Persae*), from comedies which were parodies of epics, and from the *phlyakes* (see above, p. 581). (Pl. 32, b.) Asteas of Poseidonia was the most famous master of this school, which was later subdivided into at least three schools, in Campania, in Lucania, and in Apulia, each with its own regional tendencies.

Sculpture. By about the time of the Persian Wars, it is already possible to perceive the characteristics of individual masters and of each school of sculpture, for we have copies of works which can be identified with complete certainty (as, for example, the *Tyrannicides* sculpted by the Athenians Critias and Nesiotes). We also have some works which are original, even if we cannot attribute them to any particular sculptors. Finally information about many artists is to be found in the works of ancient authors. We know that Calamis (of Argos?) sculpted the famous statue of Aphrodite Sosandra, which was once kept in the Propylaea on the Acropolis of Athens. We have information of Onatas of Aegina; of Aigias, teacher of Pheidias; of Pythagoras of Rhegium, who worked between 476 and 452 BC, and who was famous for his Philoctetes and for his sculptures of athletes. To try to attribute the works which have come down to us to the individual artists we have mentioned above would be too subjective a piece of research and would lie outside our scope. We shall simply try to define the characteristics of three well-defined schools, all of which developed from foundations laid in an earlier age. The 'Ionic' school continued its preference for gracefulness and has given us some delicate masterpieces, such as the *Birth of Aphrodite*, and the so-called 'Ludovisi throne'. (Pl. 33.) The school of Argos, Aegina, and perhaps Rhegium, has a stronger style tending towards the archaic, and reveals a careful study of anatomy and of the movements of naked bodies. The works of this school, however, show little interest in facial expression; the features are toneless with formalized smiles (see the *Charioteer* of Delphi (Pl. 34, a), and the scenes on the pediments of the temple of Aphaia on Aegina). The Attico-Boeotian school strives to reproduce a perfect anatomy and eurhythmic movements of human bodies, for example in the *Tyrannicides* mentioned above. At the outset this school was incapable of reproducing facial expressions: in later years, however, it made use of simple technical means and succeeded in giving the features of its sculptures a uniformly severe sadness. This school also began to understand the importance of drapery, although in this department its sculptures continued to show a certain archaic rigidity.

The first great artist of the Attico-Boeotian school who gives a glimpse of the tendency of his style and of his personal innovations is Myron of Eleutherae (about 500–450 BC), The ancients praised the naturalness and the boldness of movement of two of his works, which were the statue of an athlete called Ladas, and the statue of a cow. We can still see these characteristics in the copies of his *Discobolus* and of his statuary group of Athena and Marsyas. Myron likes to portray movement which is sudden, violent, and unstable (even if a little hard and contorted), for it allows him to show all his skill in the field of anatomy. He likes the contrast between violent movement and solemn stability. But even this artist did not give much attention to spiritual expression, and he sculpted head-dresses with archaic artificiality. (Pl. 34, b.)

This, then, was an art which had archaic tendencies of style but liked to portray movement and anatomical skilfulness. A reaction against it is seen in the sculptures by an anonymous artist on the temple of Zeus at Olympia (those on the eastern pediment in particular, which portrayed the struggle between Pelops and Oenomaus) (Pl. 35, a). This artist disdained excessive anatomical analysis, and preferred to put into his work only the important elements, even at the cost of producing bodies which were of great solidity. (Pl. 35, b.) He did not like stylized and expressionless faces; they must be alive even if somewhat vulgar. His drapery was natural but stiff; and through the contrast between his figures he searched for unity in the scenes of his groups. He became aware, however, that his reaction had been too strong; and he modified his style in the western pediment of the temple which portrayed a battle of Centaurs.

It seems possible that the author of the impressionistic reaction was an Athenian. He was certainly followed and surpassed by Attic artists who also wanted to improve on archaic methods, but who did it with a noble idealism and not with a rustic realism.

The consummate master of this style was the Athenian Pheidias, son of Charmides (about 500–432 BC), who was the brother of the painter Panaenus. Pheidias began as a painter but later became a sculptor, and he used all kinds of materials (wood, marble, bronze, ivory, and gold). He sculpted in bronze two famous statues of Athena (Promachus and Lemnia) (Pl. 34, c), and about the year 460 he made the statuary group which was sent to Delphi by the Athenians in memory of the battle of Marathon. The huge 'chryselephantine' statue of Zeus (447–440 BC) for the temple of Olympia was his work. He became the adviser of Pericles on all works for the Acropolis; he directed the execution of the Parthenon sculptures (the ninety-eight metopes and the frieze, 160 metres long, which portrayed the Panathenaic procession) (Pl. 36);

and he made the chryselephantine statue of Athena Parthenos (439–434 BC). In the years 433–432 BC he was brought to trial by the Athenians, who during those years tried to strike at all the friends of Pericles; he was condemned for a supposed theft of ivory, and ended his life miserably either in prison or in exile some fifteen years later.

Regrettably we have no means to form a direct and precise opinion of this great sculptor of ancient times, because all that survives from his masterpieces are some bad copies reduced in size. We can get a fair idea of him, however, from the work of his pupils, which is to be found in the sculptures of the pediments, metopes, and friezes of the Parthenon. If we observe the individual statues which make up these sculptures, we can see in them the varying styles and ability of the pupils. The whole work, however, reveals the organic conception of Pheidias' mind. He wanted to portray gods, or superhuman beings who embodied divine beauty and the high ideals of ethics. Their bodies, therefore, so he considered, should be conceived as a synthesis of many individual beauties and not as a copy of just one human model. Their attitude must always be dignified, and their faces a reflection of solemn majesty, of sublime benevolence, of noble grace, of great power, and of Olympian calm. The scenes in which they take part must be worthy of the life of the gods. Given the beauty of these monochrome and rather hurried works of Pheidias' pupils, we can easily imagine the devastating charm and striking greatness of his chryselephantine works (the 'Parthenos' was about 12 metres high). The ancients have described the sensation of wonder, of awe, of mysticism felt in front of those giants of gold and ivory, resplendent in the faint light and reflecting in the surrounding marble—miracles of thought, of shape, and of colour.

The art of Pheidias was unsurpassed throughout all later ages, even if it appeared a bit monotonous because his figures were too perfect and therefore too much alike, and even if his idealization seemed sometimes unreal (for instance in his drapery). We know the names of many pupils of his: Alcamenes, still alive in 403/2, and very skilful with gold and ivory; Cresilas, the author of an idealized portrait of Pericles; Agoracritus; and Pyrrhus. We also know of many late fifth-century sculptures which definitely show the influence of Pheidias. They included reliefs on temples, funeral *stelae*, idealized portraits, and statues of gods and *victories*. Amongst these there was the beautiful work of Paeonius of Mende which the Messenians placed in front of the sanctuary of Olympia in about 425 BC or slightly later. Naturally these pupils and 'epigoni' never succeeded in achieving the virtuosity of their master. They exaggerated his methods, particularly in the drapery which steadily became more broken and transparent; they also came under other influences including that of painting.

Outside Athens, and at the same time as the school of Pheidias, the Argive school had a stamp of its own. (The school of Aegina was absorbed by that of Athens.) The teacher of the Argive school was Polycletus, born between

470 and 460 BC. After 423 BC he created a new chryselephantine statue for the temple of Hera in Argos, and in 405 he placed at Amyclae a memorial monument of the battle of Aegospotami. Like his contemporary artists, Polycletus reacted both against archaism and against an excessively dynamic impressionism; and he idealized human beings. In contrast to Pheidias, who wanted to portray the spirituality of the gods, Polycletus was satisfied if he could portray his ideal in human form, and show athletic beauty or a virile nude without overmuch attention to psychological expression. Polycletus' statues of athletes showed that his anatomical studies had concentrated upon the essential elements of muscular action, and that he had attempted to discover the law of eurhythmic relations and the proportions between different parts of the body. Polycletus wrote about these laws in a treatise or *Canon*. Time and again this master and his pupils reproduced beautiful human bodies in positions of repose and with a serene expression; and they rigorously applied to their work the rule of the *Canon*, even at the cost of being monotonous. Polycletus' statues were generally made of bronze, and the ones which the ancients liked most, as we can tell from the number of copies, were the *Doryphorus* (or lancebearer–Pl. 38, a), and the *Diadumenus* (or athlete wearing his crown of victory). There were many in antiquity who compared Polycletus with Pheidias, and some who held him in greater esteem.

We have already said that the economic conditions of the Greek peninsula in the fourth century were not favourable to the development of its artistic heritage. Schools of sculpture, however, continued to exist in Attica and in the Argolid, although they worked only for the towns and wealthy people of the Greek East. Attic art continued to favour the portrayal of gods and heroes, and Argive art the representation of athletes. But both schools tended to give more importance to the spirit than to the body, and this was in line with ideas developing at the time.

The new artists, therefore, abandoned the beautiful and impassive expressions of Pheidias and Polycletus and tried to put 'pathos' into the faces they created. They knew about the controversies on divinity which were taking place in a world divided into superstitious persons and sceptics. So in portraying the gods they chose deities who seemed to be relatively near to human nature (Aphrodite, Apollo, Dionysus, Asclepius . . .), or demons, or gods who personified human passions. (Pl. 38, b.) When, following this new fashion, these artists created statues of famous men, they idealized their subjects with moderation.

In Attica, the sculptor who broke the tradition set by Pheidias was Scopas. He was born in Paros, and he lived first in the Peloponnese, then in Attica, and later in Caria. Whereas we have ancient descriptions of many of his statues (for example that of a frenzied Maenad) we have only a few works by him or by his pupils and these have come down to us in fragments (for example the temple at Tegea and the Mausoleum). (Pl. 37.) These fragments have made it possible for us to attribute to Scopas and to his school other works which have survived only as late copies (the famous group of the *Niobids* is an instance). His reaction against previous tendencies was strong. He was not content to copy the true expression of feeling on human faces; he distorted his faces and turned them into masks showing pain and sadness. The heads of his statues were big and hanging; the faces were square; the mouths half-open and panting; the eyes tired and sunken; and the foreheads full and powerful.

To Praxiteles this reaction must have seemed to have gone too far. His father Cephisodotus had retained the style of Pheidias, for example in his beautiful group of Eirene and Plutus; yet the son accepted part of Scopas' technique. After 370 BC Praxiteles worked in Mantinea, then at Cnidus and Cos, then at Ephesus on the temple of Artemis, and finally at Athens. Two original works of his survive, the *Apollo and Marsyas* and the *Apollo Sauroctonus*. There are also several probable attributes, together with ancient descriptions of some of his statues and Roman copies of certain masterpieces (in particular the *Apollo Sauroctonus* and the *Aphrodite of Cnidus*). His statues were eurhythmically arranged in a system of inclined planes. Male deities were presented in graceful postures with effeminate bearing, and female deities were sculpted in the nude. Praxiteles mainly used marble, because its qualities of light and softness, shading and smooth planes, provided the best means of reproducing the skin. The colour of skin was in fact imitated, with the aid of the painter Nicias, by painting a thin layer of amber-coloured paint over the statue. The heads were large and had soft hair; and with their smile they gave an indefinable feeling of dreamy softness. (Pl. 38, c.)

There are some minor artists of the Attic school who seem to have kept their own individuality, such as the three artists who assisted Scopas in the building of the Mausoleum and the sculpture of the battle of the Amazons. One of these was Timotheus, who is known to us for his sculpture of the temple of Asclepius at Epidaurus. Leochares is the second, famous for his group representing the *Rape of Ganymede*, which is characterized by the effort of reproducing a complex movement of ascent. The third was Bryaxis, who made the statue of Sarapis at Alexandria. We cannot trace the activity of other individual artists, but there is anonymous work on many reliefs on *stelae* of varying artistic value: these were placed in front of the graves on the side of the roads which radiated from Athens.

The Peloponnesian school of Lysippus of Sicyon reacted against the representation of these frail, tired, dreamy gods of Praxiteles. Lysippus was a self-taught coppersmith, but he acknowledged two masters, Polycletus and nature. He was born probably about 370 BC and was already very famous when he did a bust of Alexander. In 314 BC he was at the court of Cassander; in 306 BC he was working at the statue of King Seleucus; and he died probably at the end of the century. The ancients attributed to him 1,500 statues, chiefly of bronze; we have none of his original work, but there are copies of works certainly attributable to him, such as the *Apollo Apoxyomenus* and the statue of Agias for Delphi, and these have made it possible to ascribe to him other unattributed pieces. Lysippus did not like to portray female figures; for his portrayal of the gods he chose those who had the most virile characteristics (Pl. 39, a), and if his subjects were human he chose athletes. He also created large statuary groups, for example the twenty-five *Companions* of Alexander who died at the battle of Granicus. He represented men 'as they should have been', according to a new rule which required them to be tall and slim, with a small head and soft hair, and with much emphasis given to the muscles and bone structure. They had to be in attitudes of restless repose, in the attitude of a single moment, alert and ready to spring, supple, but of thoughtful appearance. Lysippus liked to reproduce the realities of nature and was a great portraitist, the leader of all who followed him. He was so skilful in his portrayal of *Alexander leaning on a lance*, that the great Macedonian decided that no one else should represent him in sculpture. His skill is also apparent in the statue of Agias.

Lysippus had many pupils at his industrious workshop, such as his sons Boëdas and Euthycrates, and Euthychides of Sicyon, who sculpted a *Tyche* for the town of Antioch (300 BC). It can be rightly said that Alexandrian realism in the art of portraiture derives for the most part from his productive example.

e. *The Hellenistic World and Art*

Architecture. A new area well suited to artistic production was to be found in the Greek world outside the Greek peninsula. In the first place, the conquests of Alexander had led to the formation of rich Hellenistic states, and to the birth of new capital cities and many Graeco-Macedonian colonies scattered around the East. Secondly, Alexander and the Successors, followed in this by all the princes of small states, had shown great love of the arts. Thirdly, powerful federations had come into being in the older Greek world, and they were matched by Agathocles' empire in Sicily. Lastly, commerce had brought great wealth to certain Greek towns and states of the Aegean islands and of the Asiatic coast. This general state of magnificence and well-being in the outer Greek world contrasted sharply with the low economic and political condition of that part of the Greek peninsula which for long had been the mainspring of Hellenic civilization. All this was reflected in artistic production. A brake was put on its evolution in places where art merely confined itself to repeating the ideas of the past with slight variations. At the same time, the inherent sense of balance and moderation, which up to this time had characterized even the most audacious innovations of Greek art, disappeared completely. Architects had a vast field for their activity in the construction of new towns. From the time of Alexander's architect Deinocrates they generally applied the system of Hippodamus, which consisted of great roads dividing the flat areas into rectangles, and the hilly areas into

(a)

53 (a) *Arretine Vase in* terra sigillata. *London, British Museum*
 (b) *Detail of stucco work from the Thermae Stabianae, Pompeii*

54 (a) *The 'Ara Pacis'*, Saturnia Tellus, *first century BC*
   (b) *Tiberius conqueror of the Pannonians, cameo attributed to Dioscurides.
   Vienna, National Museum*

(b)

trapezoidal shapes rather like amphitheatres. Public buildings, as well as private houses, were built in these well-planned towns. No innovations were brought to the building of temples, but the Ionic style, with some elements of the Corinthian, was preferred to the Doric order, which was thought to be faulty in its proportions. The new temple of Zeus Olympius in Athens is an example.

More than anything else architects wanted magnificence. Famous amongst them was Hermogenes who built the temple of Artemis Leucophryene at Magnesia on the Maeander. Capitals of Egyptian style are to be seen in some places; at Alexandria and elsewhere there were ornamental obelisks, the tallest of which was in front of the temple of Arsinoe. New types of sacred buildings were erected and the lay-out was dictated by the needs of mystery cults. Samothrace had its temple for the celebration of the mysteries of the Cabiri, built probably in 260 BC; it had a double front porch with Doric columns, a tripartite *cella*, and at the back an apse on a raised plane over a crypt used for sacrifices. Magnificent sacrificial altars were built in many places. That built by Hieron II in Syracuse was 198 metres by 22 metres; there was another, even larger, in Paros; and at Pergamum a square altar (the sides of which were more than 30 metres long) was built by Eumenes II to celebrate his victory over Antiochus the Great.

The magnificent royal palaces with gardens and annexes were small towns in themselves; and vast numbers of architects were engaged on the construction of the rich houses of wealthy people. About these we have no archaeological information, but there are many traces of private houses, for example at Priene and on Delos.

The following architectural details of public buildings are worthy of mention: (1) the large porches—for example the porch of the sanctuary at Delos with bull's-head capitals, and that of the sanctuary of Athena at Pergamum supported by two tiers of colonnades (one Doric and the other Ionic) and by balustrades decorated with war trophies. (2) The *agorā* squares embellished by porticoes. (3) Buildings for meetings of the *boulè*, with internal flights of steps made of marble (at Priene and Miletus for example). (4) Gymnasia, sometimes regarded as *heroa* for benefactors. (5) The octagonal 'Towers of the Winds', which were also used for sundials and water-clocks (one of these still exists in Athens).

Sculpture. Sculpture is the form of Hellenistic art we know best, for we still have many original works. We have no records, however, which make it possible to know the output of each artist. During those centuries, indeed, there appear to have been no great masters (as there had been in earlier times) who made a personal impression upon artistic production as a whole. Instead, there was a general uniformity of types and tendencies which dominated the field of sculpture.

In Athens, the style of Praxiteles was continued until the beginning of the

third century by his sons Cephisodotus and Timarchus. So most work of
Athenian origin retained the main features of the style of that master. This
can be seen in the *Aphrodite of Melos*; in the portrait of Demosthenes made by
Polyeuctus in 284/3; and in the *Nikē of Samothrace* with its wonderful
movement of drapery blown by the wind, which was commissioned after
306 by Demetrius Poliorcetes. (Pl. 40.)

The style of the school of Sicyon, that is of Lysippus, survived for a long
time through his sons and pupils. Chares of Lindus is famous amongst these
pupils for his gigantic statue of the sun, made in Rhodes about 290, which
was to be a rival of the colossal statue of Zeus made by Lysippus for the
people of Tarentum.

These schools of the peninsula, the school of Lysippus in particular,
probably have some general connection with the Hellenistic statues of
athletes which portrayed professional boxers. These statues depicted brutal
faces and exaggerated muscular structure; the athletes were portrayed
bleeding; their features were bruised and stupefied by the fight. (Pl. 39, b.)

A peculiar feature of this period was its scant production of statues of
important gods: it preferred to portray minor deities and demi-gods (such
as Muses, Centaurs, and Satyrs). The few examples of deities which survive
come mostly from the mainland-Greek schools, for instance the Sarapis of
Bryaxis similar to the Zeus of tradition, which we have already mentioned.
The schools of Pergamum and Rhodes preferred great groups of statuary
on mythological subjects. (Pl. 41, a.)

The groups of statuary in the Acropolis of Pergamum, both those commemorating the victories of Attalus over the Galatians and the Seleucids,
and those on the altar erected by Eumenes II to Zeus, are violent expressions
of an overwhelming struggle, and of the terrifying anguish of impending
death. The movements displayed in these groups are daring in the extreme,
and the features become masks of pain. The mythological sculpture of Rhodes
shows similar violent and powerful representations of human pain in its
death agony. It is enough to remember famous groups like the *Laocoön*
(by Hagesander, Polydorus, and Athenodorus); or the *Menelaus and Patroclus*
and the *Execution of Dirce* (by the brothers Apollonius and Tauriscus). Love
of artistic realism developed the type of portrait conceived by Lysippus,
which made it possible to catch the character of its subjects by depicting
flashes of personal expression displayed on its features. Typical portraits
of this kind include a sad and old Demosthenes, a contemplative Epicurus, a
miserable and deformed Diogenes, a mocking Aesop, a Homer who can see
despite his blindness, and a vulgar and violent Euthydemus (I of Bactria).

The Hellenistic age also liked statuary which represented people as types,
for example those portraying simple scenes like that of the *Boy strangling a
goose*, or the thin and decrepit figure of an old fisherman (Pl. 41, b), or that of
a disgusting and drunken old woman.

Reliefs depict the same passion for realism. They often show obvious derivations from painting in their portrayal of excited groups of fighters and complex scenes of hunting. The same derivation can be seen in stuccoed murals (as in the *Terme Stabiane* in Pompeii) and in carving (as in the famous onyx known as *The Farnese Cup*).

Painting and Mosaic. Literary tradition has given us much information about the painters of the Hellenistic age and the subjects they preferred.

From this information we know of Protogenes of Caunus who was a rival of Apelles: of Theon of Samos who liked to depict mythological scenes; of Pausias of Sicyon who liked genre-painting of unimportant subjects; of Peiraicus who reproduced intimate scenes which recalled the Mimes. We can achieve a more adequate knowledge of Greek painting, however, by studying the few original Hellenistic paintings which are still extant, and by considering paintings of a later age which were based on Greek originals. There are mosaics too, both Greek and Roman, which recall earlier models.

Original paintings of the Hellenistic period can be found on the funeral *stelae* discovered at Pagasae, datable between the years 300 and 50 BC. They depict moving scenes which remind one of reliefs on the *stelae* of Attica.

In respect of later paintings, it is not unreasonable to associate the information we have about the historical picture by Aëtion (painted for the marriage of Alexander to Roxane) with the fresco found in Rome which is known as *The Aldobrandini marriage* (Pl. 55.) In the same way we can connect the references to mythical scenes painted in the third century by Athenion of Maronea, and in the second century by Timomachus of Byzantium, with the Pompeian painting called *Achilles discovered among the daughters of Lycomedes* and the painting at Herculaneum entitled *Medea in thought*.

The pretty still-lifes (*rhopographia*), in which the famous Egyptian Antiphilus excelled, and the genre-painting of Alexandria, find their echo in the beautiful series of Pompeian *amoretti* in the House of the Vettii, in the animal parody of *Aeneas and Anchises*, and in the scenes depicting *Fights of cockerels*. The model of these paintings was undoubtedly Alexandrian, for the flora and the fauna on them are those of the Nile.

The same observations can be made about mosaics, a new Hellenistic art originating from Alexandria and Pergamum. Here too the mosaic in the *House of the Faun* at Pompeii (depicting a *Battle of Alexander the Great* with wonderful movement and pathos–Pl. 42) recalls a famous picture which Philoxenus of Eretria painted for Cassander. The scenes which depict animals, or the picture of masked acrobats signed by Dioscurides of Samos, in the villa of Cicero, or the *Cat and the Quail* in another house at Pompeii, recall Hellenistic subjects of the East, as can be seen from the repeated reproduction of details characteristic of Nile scenery.

In this art, which is both pictorial and tessellated, we find the echo of a new artistic taste, which should be connected with naturalistic researches, with bucolic poetry, and with the natural tendencies of Eastern peoples.

It is a taste for plant and animal nature (Pl. 43, a), which recurs continually as the main subject and as ornament in all forms of art. Artists of the Hellenistic age were widely employed by kings and rich men to embellish public and private buildings; but there are clear signs that the new impressionist art, so violently pathetic, made people tired in the long run and turned their thoughts to the past. Scholars started to write the history of ancient artists, and scattered works of art began to be collected. In Pergamum, for example, the rulers started a gallery of sculptures which contained original works and copies of all the most famous artists, from the earliest times until Praxiteles.

Even the houses of rich private citizens tended to become museums of art, and this explains the vast number of surviving copies of statues made in the Hellenistic age.

f. *Art in Italy and in Rome to the Second Century* BC

Architecture. When we dealt with the previous period, we spoke of the huge constructions of city walls (built in some places of polygonal blocks, in others of small rows of rectangular blocks), which had been erected throughout the Etruscan, Italic, and Latin regions. We also mentioned the erection of the Servian walls in Rome, which had been destroyed in the Gallic fire, and which were replaced during our present period.

Meanwhile, first of all in Etruria, and later in Rome, architecture developed a new system of building by introducing the true arch and the true vault. An example of the employment of this new system can be seen and dated in several places. The 'Arch Gate' at Volterra in Etruria belongs to the fourth or third century (Pl. 44, a); the 'Door of Zeus' at Falerii near Rome was reconstructed in a new position by the Romans in 241. The first examples of arches and vaults in Etruscan tombs are to be found in the so-called *Temple of San Manno* at Perugia, in the *Tomb of Pythagoras* at Cortona, and in the *Tomb of the Grand Duke* at Chiusi.

Probably at the same time two other techniques of assistance to architecture were discovered. These were learned and employed to advantage by the Latins; and together with the arch and the vault they became decisive elements of Roman architecture, giving it effective supremacy and a style of its own. These techniques were: (1) The *opus latericium*, which consisted of bricks burned in an oven and joined by mortar: this was much superior to the technique of unburned bricks used in Sicily for the restoration of the walls of Gela and Heraclea Minoa. The Etruscan origin of this technique used in Rome is noted by Vitruvius, and is exemplified in the great brick walls of Arretium. (2) The *opus caementicium*, which consisted in the making of a form of concrete from stone and cement. The place of origin of this technique is not very clear; it is certain, however, that it was to be found in Rome at the end of the second century BC. By using both these techniques of construction, Roman architects were able to solve the problems of roofing large buildings (a problem which the Greeks were never able to overcome); for with these two techniques every stone or brick was tightly joined to the next, like the cells of an organism. It was therefore possible to attempt the construction of wide arches and spacious dome-shaped or vaulted rooms, suitable to magnificent buildings where crowds could gather (like basilicas, temples, baths, or covered theatres). Roman architects became so skilled that their services were asked for, even in Hellenistic regions. Vitruvius relates that as early as 175 BC Antiochus Epiphanes entrusted the erection of the Olympieum at Athens to M. Cossutius who came from Rome.

Links between Latium and Etruria in the designing of temples lasted down to the third century BC, for it was at that time that the type of temple described by Vitruvius became popular. This type of construction was square; the *cella* and columns were made of stone; and there was projecting guttering. The temple had terracotta decorations, consisting especially of free-standing groups of statues, or reliefs, in the pediments. Examples are to be found in the Etruscan zone at Orvieto and Marzabotto and in the Faliscan region (temple of Celle at Falerii).

In Etruria tombs were still constructed as more or less complex underground chambers hollowed out of the tufa with flat or vaulted ceilings. But side by side with these we now find new styles of vaulting, and a further innovation resulting from the use of painted decoration. The tombs of Praeneste in Latium show very clearly the successive influences of Etruscan styles, but they present a difference arising from an increased concern with the destiny of the dead person in the next world. Etruscan influence, both in architecture and in the decorative arts, can be found also farther south: in Campania (Nola, Capua, Cumae), in Lucania (Poseidonia = Paestum), in Samnium (Allifae), and in Iapygia (Ruve and Gnathia). Everywhere we find it combined with local styles.

Athens had had an aqueduct since the end of the sixth century. Others were later built in Samos, in many towns of Asia Minor, in Sicily (particularly at Syracuse, Acragas, and Selinus), and in the dry land of Apulia. No city, however, had such important water-carrying installations as Rome. From 312 the *Aqua Appia* brought water to Rome from 16 kilometres away, by a course which lay largely underground. This aqueduct was followed by the *Anio Vetus* in 272 BC and by the *Aqua Marcia* built between 144 and 140 BC, the latter 92 kilometres long and including 11 kilometres carried on arches. The habit of building aqueducts high above ground increased steadily, and this type of construction achieved real architectural merit. (Pl. 44, b.)

Sculpture. Etruscan sculpture of the period in question shows some outstanding peculiarities. The decoration of temples with terracotta friezes and plaques is enriched by a new range of flowers and plants which are extremely realistic. The *acroteria* and antefixes depict new types of gods, in place of the old groups of Sileni and Maenads. The lovely groups of the 'Temple of the

Scasato' at Falerii are a good example; but originality is shown most of all in isolated statues and sculpted groups placed inside the pediments. These sometimes depict mythical episodes and sometimes historical happenings (such as the battles with Gauls to be found in a pediment at Civitalba). The technique of such works at first shows the Greek influence of Praxiteles, Scopas, and Lysippus (the two heads and the figure of Apollo at the temple of the Scasato, for example). Later, however, it became exaggeratedly full of movement, as can be seen in a pediment at Telamone (*War at Thebes*), in one in Luna (*The massacre of the Niobids*), and even more in the pediment at Civitalba (*Bacchus rediscovering Ariadne*).

Another series of Etruscan sculptures is to be found in several sarcophagi and in a vast number of urns made of terracotta, travertine, alabaster, and peperino. They displayed for the most part mythical scenes with battles and brutal killings, which are based on Greek models but are given an Etruscan interpretation. They are interspersed with local historical and mythical figures. They sometimes constitute real masterpieces as, for example, two sculptured and many-coloured sarcophagi, one at Torre San Severo near Orvieto and the other (*Del Magnate*) at Tarquinia. (Pl. 45.) The covers of sarcophagi generally depicted the features of the dead person or of a dead couple with a sense of realism which was more expressive and faithful and less mannered than the style of Alexandrian portraits.

The most genuine impression of the ability of Etruscan sculptors in portraiture can be gained from statues made of bronze. There are graceful and realistic statues of children; and the statue of the so-called *Haranguer*, which was found near Lake Trasimeno, depicts a certain Aulus Metilius, whose face clearly shows the spiritual effort required to deliver a speech. There were other indigenous schools in central Italy, which reproduced Greek models in their own way. In Umbria for example, a bronze statue of Mars found at Todi reflects the posture of a Greek model, although it was made to look clumsy by the unskilful artist who added a breast-plate which was too rigid. Roman sculpture, and that of Latium also, shows a general Greek influence and a specific Graeco-Etruscan influence. This was due to the presence of Greek and Etruscan artists in Rome and to the vast number of monuments brought back from the regions which had been conquered (Veii, Volsinii, Syracuse, and the towns of Greece).

The following sculptures full of moving pathos show Greek influence: (1) The fragments of a male head found at Antemnae. (2) The statues on the pediment of a temple at the foot of the Capitol. There is, on the other hand, a similarity between the terracotta reliefs of Etruscan temples and the marble relief with a Typhon ending with snakes or the *Campana* plaques of marble about which we shall speak later. Roman sculpture achieved perfection and originality in portraiture much sooner than in other aspects; for besides external influence there was also the stimulus of the native practice of constructing funeral masks of ancestors. Not only the state, but private citizens and sometimes even foreigners, commissioned a large number of sculptured portraits to be made in Rome. These were exhibited either in public places or in private houses. At first they portrayed only people who had deserved well of their country, but in later years poets (beginning from L. Accius) and artists were depicted as well. The works of the age we are dealing with, however, are almost all lost. Moreover it is only for the ensuing period that we have any considerable remains of those commercialized works which are so typical of Rome and Italy. These consisted of marble or bronze copies of ancient Greek statues, and were intended as decoration for houses and villas.

Wall-painting and Ceramics. During the fourth and third centuries the paintings of artistic value in Etruria were to be found in the decorations of tombs. They depicted either scenes from daily life, or scenes of myth and the underworld with horrible and excited figures of demons, or famous historical scenes like those of the *François Tomb* at Vulci. (Pl. 46, a.) Greek influence, with its recent discoveries of foreshortening and chiaroscuro, shows itself very clearly in the technique; it can be seen in the paintings on tombs and on the sarcophagi (as, for example, the famous two at Tarquinia with their scenes of the wars of the Amazons).

As we have already said, these tomb paintings, and the shape of the undergound chambers which contained them, are very like those of Campania, Lucania, and Apulia. In these regions we sometimes find reproductions of battle scenes; and there are figures of soldiers (as at Capua) with their typical gaudy local costumes and with many-coloured trophies taken from the enemy.

Also in Rome, great wall-paintings were made portraying human figures and historical episodes of local character, despite the fact that houses were usually decorated by pictorial masterpieces brought from the conquered regions, or by copies of them. Historical tradition records a picture shown by Manius Valerius Messala on the wall of the Curia Hostilia in memory of his actions against the Carthaginians in 263/2 BC, another shown by the family of the Scipios in memory of victories in Asia, and a third shown to the people by L. Hostilius Mancinus to exalt his successful coup against Carthage in 147. A similar fragment was discovered in a house on the Esquiline, which can be dated to the end of the fourth century or the beginning of the third; it shows the surrender of a fortress by a Samnite called M. Fannius to the Roman Q. Fabius. (Pl. 46, b.) Tradition has also preserved the names of some famous Roman painters of that age, such as C. Fabius Pictor who in 304 decorated the temple of Salus on the Quirinal, and Pacuvius, the tragedian, who after 168 BC painted the temple of Hercules in the Forum Boarium.

For painted ceramics there was at this time a series of factories in southern Italy and in Etruria. They imitated Greek vases, Attic red-figured in particular, the importation of which into Italy was beginning to fall away. (Pl. 47, a.) Yet they used shapes, subjects, and techniques which for the most part had local characteristics; and they made a vast number of copies which were scattered all over the peninsula. The vases which were made in southern Italy generally go under the name of 'Apuli'. It is possible, however, to distinguish between them fairly well, for some were made in Apulia, some in Lucania, some in Campania. Some probably based their style directly on Greek models, whereas others derived it in a roundabout way through the Etruscans.

Amongst other things, the Apulian factories of Ruve and Canosa made huge vases of unusual shapes in an exuberant mass of colours, with a dark-red background and a greenish-black glaze. They were decorated with flowers, with mythical or historical scenes of great verisimilitude and tragic inspiration, or with funeral scenes.

Lucanian vases had a lighter background. The decoration was less exuberant and on a more modest scale, with a coarse design of scenes of comedy and parody (derived from the *phlyakes*).

Campanian pottery seems to have been derived most directly from Greek models. The shape is clumsy and the subjects disconnected: there are single figures, bits of still life, and heads of Sileni and Maenads.

There was another kind of pottery, typical of southern Italy and widely used throughout the Mediterranean world. It was covered by black glaze with ornamental drawings and scenes in superimposed colours (white, yellow, purple-red, and gold). By means of outline drawings and graffito it tried to imitate vases made out of metal. It is usually called 'Etrusco-Campanian' and was probably the product of factories in Campania and Apulia. (Pl. 47, b.)

There were, of course, also factories of purely Etruscan pottery, as for example at Chiusi and Volterra (where they imitated Attic pots), and perhaps also at Volsinii, which made many-coloured vases with decoration in relief (to imitate vases made of metal). Sometimes these vases were even silvered or gilded.

The most famous pottery factory of central Italy, however, was probably that at Falerii before the year 241 BC, when the town was transplanted elsewhere. This factory produced vases which were normally for daily use rather than for burial ornaments; they were simple in shape, decoration, and design; and they imitated Attic vases though they could be distinguished from them by a different form of background and by the use of black varnish of lesser depth. For the most part they depicted mythical scenes (Dionysiac in particular) and naked figures: the latter, in accordance with Hellenistic tendency, were mainly women.

Minor Arts. Even in the previous age, the Etruscans had been renowned engravers; and their works (statuettes, tripods, candelabra, censers, washbasins, arms, and decoration-pieces for furniture or triumphal cars) were widely known. From the sixth century onwards they had specialized in making bronze mirrors; they decorated them with engravings and reliefs, which at the beginning were more faithful to Greek models and mythical subjects, but which later became increasingly commercialized and conformed more to local taste.

During the fifth century and the centuries which followed the factories of Praeneste in Latium became famous for their artistic caskets of bronze. These had a cylindrical shape; they were covered with graffito drawings and surmounted by free-standing circular figures. The technique and subjects of their mythical graffiti recall works not only by Greek sculptors, painters, and potters, but by those of Apulia, the Faliscan territory, and Etruria— showing the large number of artistic currents which met and blended in Latian art of the fourth and third centuries BC. Generally the earliest caskets are the most beautiful, as for example the so-called 'Barberini' casket. It appears that an artist from Campania domiciled in Rome was commissioned to make the so-called 'Ficoroni' casket by someone from Praeneste. (Pl. 48.) This work portrayed admirably the scene of the landing of Jason and his companions in the country of the Bebryci; the artist derived his subject via Magna Graecia from a famous painting of Polygnotus.

From ancient times the Etruscans were also able goldsmiths; their work generally consisted of gold foil which was worked in relief or engraved. This art lasted until the end of the third century and was also carried on at Praeneste and Satricum.

The art of carving precious stones, which the Etruscans imitated and developed from Egyptian scarabs, also survived for some time in Etruria. But it gradually died, and its place was taken by the work of Roman cutters, who worked on small slabs of precious stone or glass paste.

Something should also be said about coins. The second half of the fourth century BC saw the appearance, both in Rome and in the towns of Etruria, of regular money made of a bronze alloy. The coin called *aes* had a fixed weight and was minted by the state. The earliest shape was a large disk, the *aes grave* (in Rome it weighed a pound), which was divided into twelve parts called 'unciae': later the weight was reduced and it became a fiduciary coinage. Meanwhile from the fifth century BC Etruria, following the example of the Italiotes and of the Siceliotes, started to coin silver money, and in rare cases even gold coins. The early minting was poor, but in the fourth century some coins have the imprint of genuine art.

At the end of the fourth century BC, the Romans started to commission the coining of their silver money from Capua; later, from 269 BC according to tradition, they coined their own silver *denarii* themselves.[51]

g. *The Celtic Civilization*

The Po Valley. The Gauls began to enter the Po valley in the sixth century:[52] from the second half of the third century they were gradually conquered by

Y*

the military exploits of Rome. About the year 150 therefore their cultural stamp must have been largely pre-Roman. Archaeological evidence proves that the Celtic peoples at first only entered the north-western part of the Po valley; it was only in later years that they succeeded in reaching the regions lying to the east and south of the Po, and in occupying part of the Adriatic coast which lay between the two arms of the delta of that river. (cf. Pseudo-Scylax 16–18.) They penetrated, and mixed with, the Ligurians, Etruscans, and related tribes. Later they carried out frequent expeditions over the Apennines to plunder Italian lands as far as Iapygia; these raids ended, however, with the defeat at Telamo in 225 BC, the year which marks the beginning of the Roman conquest. Polybius, as a contemporary historian, tells about their civilization as it was about 150 BC, and his narrative (II, 17) is confirmed by Diodorus (V, 26–31), who based his information on Poseidon-ius. Polybius says: 'They lived in villages without walls, and did not know of or use furniture; for they led a primitive life and slept on stacks of grass or straw. For the most part they fed on meat; they devoted their attention solely to wars or agriculture, and had no knowledge of art or science. The wealth of each person consisted of cattle and gold which could be used as currency on all occasions and taken about at will. They valued friendships most of all, because for them the greatest fame and power belonged to the man who was surrounded by many people dependent on his good-will.'

It is obvious, however, that the Gauls achieved an earlier degree of civilization (due partly to a knowledge of writing) in the regions where they kept in closest contact with the Etruscan survivors, and where they became ethnically mixed with them.

[*The Iberians and Celts.** Under Greek influence, one of the most remarkable bodies of art in barbarian Europe developed among the Tartesso-Iberian tribes of Spain and southern France.

The Celts of central Spain, Galicia, and Portugal prolonged the Hallstatt traditions (post-Hallstatt civilization). They built fortified villages similar to the European 'Ringwälle', and in Old Castile they had great burial-grounds in which Antennae swords and daggers, belt-buckles, fibulae, and other objects have been found. They used geometrical patterns for niello work and to decorate their gold and silver torques (Galicia). In the first Iron Age the Celts already had stone *stelae* carved with very primitive designs (war chariots) and groups of small bronze votive figures resembling those found in central Europe (Hallstatt). At the entrance to their fortified villages they set up stone figures of animals ('berracos'), and in Portugal stone figures of warriors have also been found. Finds in central Spain include great numbers of bronze fibulae engraved with figures of horsemen; these were influenced by Iberian art as, probably, was the stone sculpture.

The Tartesso-Iberian civilization established itself in a number of regional

* By Pedro Bosch-Gimpera.

centres in Spain, and in south-east France the Iberian influence was carried as far as the Marseilles area, before the invasion of the Volcae—a Celtic people—about the third century BC.

In south and south-east Spain there were towns, many of them fortified (e.g., Meca, in the province of Albacete), with monuments such as the temple at Cerro de los Santos, containing numerous ex-votos which bear witness to great skill in stone-carving (statues of warriors, and of women whose dress shows Greek influence and who are adorned with jewels). (Pl. 57, a.) At Galera (province of Granada) there were stone-built mortuary chambers with wall paintings. In other towns, shrines were set up in humbler buildings (e.g., La Serreta de Alcoy) and had ex-votos in terracotta, of the same types as the stone statues, while in the caverns of Andalusia there were rural shrines (Castellar de Santisteban and Despeñaperros, in the province of Jaen) where the votive objects included bronze figurines, articles of adornment, and even the reproduction of sets of false teeth. Here, too, the figurines are of the same types as the large sculpture and show the influence of Greek models, particularly of the early epoch. It is difficult to classify them in chronological order, as the same types were repeated until a very late period.

The influence of archaic Greek sculpture is also seen in some stone statues of animals in a deliberately archaic style, including the human-headed bull known as 'la bicha de Balazote', which Heuzeuy considered to be reminiscent of Mesopotamia, lions which recall the Phocaean lion, sphinxes, etc.

Iberian sculpture was influenced by classical models, as may be seen from the stone warrior at Elche and the bronze warriors and ladies in the sanctuary of La Luz (provinces of Murcia). Greek influence continued down to the Hellenistic period.

The theory has been advanced that some of the sculpture may be the work of provincial Greek artists—including, for instance, certain sphinxes and the statue of a woman seated on a throne at Verdolay, which may date from the early fifth century. One outstandingly fine work is a polychrome bust of a richly dressed lady with a veil on her head, held in place by a comb in the manner of the present-day Spanish 'mantilla'; this is the 'Lady of Elche', a unique piece generally believed to be the work of a Greek artist of about 400 BC. (Pl. 57, b.)

At Osuna (province of Seville) there are stone slabs carved with reliefs representing warriors or personages celebrating religious rites, musicians, and acrobats, in a style resembling that of archaic Greek art, but thought to date from the third century BC; the warriors carry bucklers of the La Tène B type.

Painted pottery had made its appearance, in all probability, by the end of the sixth century. The earliest decorative patterns were geometrical, imitated from the simplest Ionian ceramic work (coloured lines, concentric circles, parallel wavy lines, swastikas). (Pl. 58, a.) In Andalusia, these geometrical decorations—the only ones used in the pottery of that region—also show the influence of Phoenician ceramics. In south-eastern Spain the development of geometrical decoration went hand in hand with that of floral and animal designs, soon followed by human figures and scenes from life—as illustrated by urns found in the burial-grounds at Verdolay, Archena, and Oliva, and at the towns of La Serreta de Alcoy and Liria in the province of Valencia. The floral and animal decorations recall those of the latest Greek vases influenced by oriental models, with combinations of spirals ending in stylized flowers, or series of animals (carnivores and birds). This style presumably originated during the sixth century BC, for the oriental-type pottery could not reach Spain at a later date; but it survived for a long time, and its finest period was in the fifth and fourth centuries. During the fifth century the influence of the red-figured pottery produced in Attica resulted in the warrior vase discovered at Archena—the style of which is still somewhat rough—while the fourth-century urns found at Oliva are decorated with friezes of quite realistic horsemen and with a scene showing a fortress under siege. The same lavish decoration, in which floral motives are combined with scenes of warfare or ritual dances showing musicians and richly-dressed women, is to be found in the pottery produced at Liria which flourished for a long time, down to the second century. Here the latest urns, the style of which had notably deteriorated, show fishing scenes or sea-fights.

In the north of the kingdom of Valencia, Lower Aragon, and Catalonia, art included little or no sculpture. This was a peasant civilization, with fortified villages which, as the fourth century proceeded, grew into towns, some of them with strongholds (e.g. San Antonio de Calaceite, in the province of Teruel, and Los Foyos at Lucena del Cid in the province of Castellón). The pottery here repeats the floral and geometrical patterns found in the south-east, and sometimes reveals a strong decorative sense (e.g. Tossal de las Tenalles, at Sidamunt, in the province of Lerida). Ceramics from the kiln at Fontscaldes (province of Tarragona), or from potteries working in the same style, were exported to other villages in Iberian Catalonia, to the south of France (Ensérune, near Béziers) and even to Italy (Ischia). In the Ebro valley in Aragon there was a school of ceramists who used the geometrical motives in an original manner, more especially in some very baroque combinations of spiral lines; this survived down to the first century BC.

Near Tivissa, in Catalonia (province of Tarragona), a shrine in the Iberian village of Le Castellet de Banyoles contained silver-gilt ritual vases decorated with scenes of religious ceremonial by local goldsmiths, together with imported Hellenistic silver vases.

Treasure-hoards found in south-east Spain include some remarkable examples of goldsmiths' work, such as the diadem discovered at Javea, in the province of Alicante; and Andalusia abounds in silver vases (treasures of Perotitos and Mogón, in the province of Jaen). The Greek influence generalized the use of coins, which were minted in several native towns, and of writing, evidenced by letters scratched on vases and by inscriptions engraved on lead, such as the small plaque found at La Serreta de Alcoy and those at La Bastida de Mogente (province of Valencia), the latter constituting something very like a collection of records.

Iberian pottery spread into south-east France (Montlaurés, near Narbonne, Ensérune, near Béziers) and reached the vicinity of Marseilles. In course of time, and more especially after this region was conquered by the Volcae, it made way for Celtic pottery of the La Tène style. Catalonia was influenced by south-east Spain, or imported work from that region, as may be seen from the vase with a battle or hunting scene found at Emporion and from vases decorated with birds in the style of Archena and Elche, also found at Emporion and at L'Aigueta, near Figueras.

Provence developed Celtic sculpture, influenced by Greek art, which has remarkable parallels with Iberian sculpture. There is the same influence of the archaic, shown in the statues of warriors found at Sainte Anastasie and Grézan. This was followed, in the third–second centuries BC, by the Hellenistic influences traceable in the statues of the shrines at Entremont and Roquepertuse. Stone carvings of animals, similar to the 'berracos' of Celtic Spain, have been found in France as well.

The influence of Iberian pottery penetrated into Old Castile, and Iberian geometrical decoration appears on Celtic urns found in burial-grounds in the Jalón Valley (provinces of Soria and Guadalajara), which date from the post-Hallstatt period. At Numantia, where the lowest levels of the town have yielded painted Celtic pottery with scenes of battle and horse-breaking, a school of ceramists developed about the third–second centuries under the influence of Iberian techniques and styles of decoration; this produced curious and extremely original work. During the period preceding its destruction in 133 BC, Numantia grew into a populous city; its circumference still followed the line of the 'Ringwall', but inside this the streets intersected in a chessboard pattern apparently derived from the plan of Emporion, which also influenced the lay-out of the Iberian towns in the Ebro valley. The same combination of the Celtic 'Ringwall' with a symmetrical street-pattern is found in the Celtic towns of northern Portugal (the 'Citania' of Sabroso) and Galicia (Santa Tecla), in this case with stone-built houses erected on a circular ground-plan. A feature of Sabroso is its mortuary chambers which have façades crowned by a pediment adorned with geometrical designs apparently stemming from the Celtic goldsmiths' work which had spread to the north-west of the peninsula (gold torques found in treasure hoards).

In eastern Spain and Andalusia the Iberian traditions survived during the Roman republican period (painted ceramics, heads of warriors and horsemen on Iberian coins, decoration on silver vases). The school of ceramists at Azaila, in the Ebro valley, continued into the first century BC.

(Pl. 58, b.) The Iberian tradition in pottery was still fostered at Numantia, too, after it was rebuilt under the Romans. The Celtic towns clung to their existence in Galicia and Portugal as well, and it took a long time for the indigenous civilizations to be replaced by that of Rome.]

h. *Art in the Roman World from the Second Century* BC

Architecture. One of the fundamental characteristics of classical Roman architecture is the importance of the interiors in comparison with the exteriors of buildings. This was due to an inbred tendency towards the practical. So towns built on the Roman model, though they adhered to a geometrical plan whenever possible, did not offer a vision of monumental unity, with flights of façades and squares at road-crossings, such as the style of Hippodamus of Miletus demanded for new Greek towns. The different aspect of Roman towns was also due to the new technique of masonry which replaced the technique of building with rectangular blocks of stone. (These stone blocks, however, were still used, particularly for the exteriors of monumental buildings, such as the theatre of Marcellus, and later for amphitheatres.) The new techniques were as follows (cf. Pl. 49):

(1) The *opus incertum* which consisted of stones of irregular shape but flat on the outside and tightly cemented together. (It was used particularly from the second century BC to the first century AD.)

(2) The *opus reticulatum* which consisted of small pyramidal stones set in diagonal rows. (Used from the first century BC to the second AD.)

(3) The *opus latericium* which consisted of baked bricks of varying sizes and layers of cement of varying thicknesses. (Used from the age of Augustus on.) Buildings of major importance were lined with marble on the outside and covered with stuccoes on the inside.

Roman constructions were very compactly built because of the conglomerates used; they could be of great heights and contained rooms which were large and bright and covered by vaults or domes. They did not need intermediate lines of support from columns or architraves. The columns, which were tall and slender, were therefore used purely as a decorative element, and the entablatures were just ornamental strips.

The houses became bigger; the atrium was enlarged to take in a peristyle; the rooms increased in number; and buildings tended to become higher. But every effort was directed to beautify the interiors of houses in the great towns and even more so of houses in smaller towns and country villas. Yet exterior walls were normally plain and unadorned except for those which overlooked main roads.

The number of temples increased in both Rome and Latium. In the time of Sulla were built the temples of Fortune at Praeneste, Gabii, and Tibur. Pompey built the temple of Venus Victrix, Caesar that of Venus Genetrix, and others were constructed by Augustus. When these temples were not sited on high ground, they were placed on artificially raised stylobates and dominated surrounding buildings with their size. Tuscan columns were preferred to Greek in temples built on a rectangular plan; *cellae* were enlarged even at the cost of removing lateral colonnades or of encasing the columns in the outside walls. In the building of temples with a circular plan, care was taken to create either a straight approach (of Greek type in the case of grandiose buildings like the Pantheon of Agrippa), or to develop the rooms radially. The types of Roman temples, later listed in the works of Vitruvius, started to spread all over the world beginning at the age of Augustus. It was then that the following temples were erected: the temples of Augustus at Nemausus (Nîmes: the *Maison Carrée*) and at Vienne in Gaul; the octastyle temple at Tarragona in Spain; the temple at Ancyra in Galatia; and so on. Very often these temples had to be built by Italian architects. It was thus that Rome started to dominate and spread its influence even in the field of practical aesthetics.

Roman basilicas, although the word *basilica* is Greek, were very different from the usual porticoed promenades of Hellenistic regions. They were designed to be closed buildings with inside colonnades, and originally they had only one outlook, on one of the shorter sides. The first imperial *Fora*, those of Caesar and Augustus, consisted of wide spaces fenced in by walls with colonnades and shops on the inside. The Romans started to build permanent theatres, both in Rome and outside, at the time of Pompey. (Fig. 7.) If these were not roofed they were built with a deeper *cavea*,[53] and were enclosed by a stage of more than one floor. Roman architects specialized in the construction of theatres as well, and were invited to build them in the East. For example M. and C. Stallius rebuilt the Odeum in Athens after its destruction during the Mithradatic war.

There was a new type of monument which was purely Roman, the triumphal or memorial arch. The first known examples of arches erected by victorious generals, paid for by the booty of war, were built in 196 and in 190 BC. In 121 BC Rome built the first arch under which a victorious army could parade: this was inspired by the *Porta triumphalis* of the so-called Servian walls.

We have much information about the first type and there are many examples: the arch of the Sergii at Pola (31 BC); that of the Gavii at Verona; and that of Marcus Antonius at Aquinum, which is probably older (about 50 BC). Tradition recalls examples of triumphal arches on the Caelian and the Aventine. From the time of Augustus on, however, they were only built for emperors. There were arches erected in honour of Augustus in the Forum at Rome (20 BC), at Ariminum (27 BC), at Augusta Praetoria (25 BC) and at Segusio (Susa, 2 BC). (Pl. 50, a.) Other arches built outside Italy and worthy of mention are those of Glanum (Saint Rémy), Nîmes, Vaison, Orange, Thessalonica (the *Gate of Vardar*, 42 BC), and Ephesus (4/3 BC).

Pompey and Caesar built several monuments to commemorate their deeds in Spain; and there was a monument to Augustus at La Turbie in honour of his Alpine conquests.

Caesar's plan for improving the monumental architecture of the city of Rome was, for the most part, carried out by Augustus. He erected new public buildings; he restored temples, roads, and pavements; and he drew up a town plan in which middle-class districts and villas were moved beyond

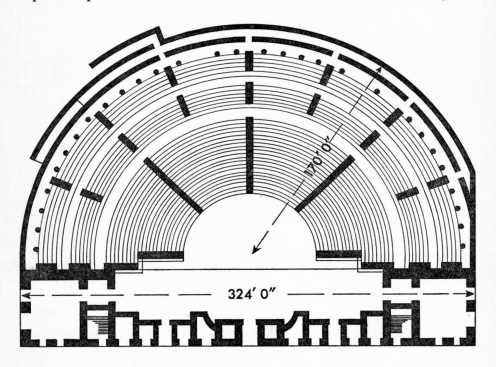

FIG. 7.   Orange: plan of the theatre, restored (after B. Fletcher).

the destroyed Servian walls. Similar great constructions were erected outside Rome for the housing of new colonies.

Both in Italy and throughout the provinces the great ways of communication were increased in number and their actual routes modified and improved (as in the case of the Flaminia). Outside Italy towns started to need a system of aqueducts which often required great and daring works of engineering. Examples can be seen in the imposing ruins of the aqueduct with a triple order of arches, which crosses the river Gard near Nîmes, and in the Augustan aqueducts of Tarraco and Ephesus. Amazing works of excavation were done by the architects of Augustus, by Cocceius in particular. They transformed the Lucrine lake into a gulf; they built underwater tunnels to improve

55
ROMAN PAINTING I
Detail from 'The
Aldobrandini
Marriage'. Rome,
Vatican Museum

[Alinari

[Alinari

56 ROMAN PAINTING II

(a) *Rome, the Palatine, Villa of Livia, detail of the frescoes showing the main characteristics of the second style of Roman painting*

(b) *Pompeii, House of Amandus, the Fall of Icarus, wall painting*

[Alinari

(a) *Cerro de los Santos, votive statue.*
     Madrid, Archaeological Museum
(b) *The Lady of Elche,* c. 400 BC.
     Madrid, Prado Museum

(a)   [*photo Mas*

(b)

(a)

58 IBERIAN POTTERY

(a) *Galera, Province of Granada, vase from the necropolis. Madrid, Archaeological Museum*

(b) *Azaila, Aragon, vase. Madrid, Archaeological Museum*

(b)

communications; and they constructed water reservoirs, such as the *Piscina mirabilis* of Bacoli, and arsenals such as the so-called *Cento Camerelle* of Misenum.

The baths at Rome became more and more magnificent. Those of Agrippa near the Pantheon (19 BC), besides the usual rooms, had large halls for swimming-pools, changing-rooms, assembly-rooms, and reading-rooms; and their model was copied in the provinces. Several town walls and their doors can be dated to the time of Augustus, such as those at Augusta Praetoria, Augusta Taurinorum, Fanum, Hispellum, Tergeste, and Iader. (Pl. 50, b.) City gates were often complex works of fortification; they had two ways of access, with a courtyard between them (*propugnaculum*), which was guarded by overlooking galleries. The *Porta Palatina* at Turin, in brick, has four arches, of which two are small but the other two have upper storeys with projecting or contained windows; and there are two battlemented towers with sixteen faces.

A simpler type is to be found in the following *Porta Augusta* of Fanum, the construction of which was attributed to Vitruvius and built in 9/10 AD; it had three arches of which the middle one was the highest. That in the walls of Aosta is similar; so is the *Arch of Riccardo* at Tergeste, low and wide, with one arch only, which is flanked by half-pillars with Corinthian capitals.

Roman tombs were of different sizes, and sometimes they had curious architectural shapes. The following are worthy of mention: (1) The tomb of a baker, of the first century BC, adjoining the Porta Maggiore in Rome (Pl. 51, b); this is shaped like an oven with doors, and has a frieze depicting the baking of bread, the cinerary urn for the baker's wife being shaped like a bread-bin. (2) The tomb of the Julii at Glanum (Saint Rémy) built for a family of freedmen of Caesar; it consists of a square platform, decorated with reliefs, which rests on two steps, and is surmounted by a *tetrapylon* with arched windows supporting a domed colonnade of circular shape. (It reminds one of the choregic monument to Lysicrates at Athens.) (3) The tomb of Sestius near the Porta Ostiensis in Rome, built shortly before the year 12 BC; this was an imitation of the Egyptian pyramids and its *cella* was decorated with painted stuccoes. Sometimes architects built tombs with a cylindrical platform surmounted by a dome, by a pinnacle or by a balcony. The Mausoleum of Augustus had a diameter of 95 metres, a front porch, and a pinnacle planted with cypresses which carried the statue of the emperor. The tomb of Caecilia Metella, built for the daughter-in-law of Crassus the triumvir, had a diameter of 28 metres, a square base decorated with a frieze, and a pinnacle on top. (Pl. 51, a.) Whereas the great and the wealthy people had monumental tombs, the middle and poorer classes adopted the custom, from the time of Augustus on, of joining together in brotherhoods to own a *columbarium* of the type found in Egypt in the Ptolemaic era. The *columbarium* consisted of large rooms, mostly underground, which had several recesses (*loculi*) with inscribed tablets, to contain the cinerary urns of the members of the brotherhood. Sometimes they were bare and plain, like that of the *Vigna Codini* on the Appian way; sometimes they were decorated with paintings like that of the Augustan Villa Pamphili.

Sculpture. At first native Roman tendencies of style in the field of sculpture risked being lost because authentic Greek works reached Rome very easily or were copied there by Hellenistic artists and their pupils who had settled in the capital. Even the statue of Caesar in the Forum Iulium derived from the model of a statue of Alexander made by Lysippus, in every detail except the head. Meanwhile, Greek and Italiote artists working in Rome turned to the new trends of the creative activity of Greece, of Athens most of all. This new trend started as a reaction against Alexandrian decadence and reverted to the models and shapes of the sculpture of the fifth and fourth centuries. The style of Praxiteles, therefore, was adopted for the statues of the gods; the style of Polycletus for the statues of athletes; and the Alexandrian style for figures of minor importance. At the same time, the people of Latium and the Italiotes, who commissioned the works, insisted that their tastes should be followed, at least in part; for they were still attracted by the old Etruscan and Italiote production. The result was an eclectic tendency which was typically Roman, though the schools of art were otherwise fairly different.

Arcesilaus, for instance (with the collaboration of a certain Coponius) preferred to draw his inspiration from Hellenistic masterpieces for a group of *amoretti* playing with a lioness. It is probable that his statue of Venus Genetrix, made for the temple which Caesar erected in honour of that goddess, was the prototype for many other works depicting the goddess in a languid lying position with Cupid on her shoulders. (Pl. 52, a.) On the other hand an Italiote called Pasiteles, with his pupil Stephanus and Menelaus the pupil of Stephanus (who as a freedman took the name of M. Cossutius Cerdo), liked to draw their inspiration from the great Greek models of the fifth and fourth centuries, and from the terracotta masterpieces which derived from them (Pliny notes this when speaking of the terracottas made by Pasiteles). Some of the works by Stephanus appear to be inspired by sculptors earlier than Pheidias (as for example the *Ephebe of the Villa Albani* and the *Pan* in the British Museum). The bronze head of the *Doryphorus* by the Athenian Apollonius at Herculaneum recalls the style of Polycletus. A third group of artists was very eclectic, including Salpion, Sosibius, Pontius, and others, to whom are ascribed the Artemis and the *Tyrannicides* in the Museum of Naples, some decorated stone curbs for mouths of wells, and some funerary altars. They used to combine faces of archaic type with draperies of Hellenistic design.

It is certain that these Greek and Italiote artists had local pupils and native workmen to whom they communicated their neo-Atticism, in its essential features at any rate. The pupils in their turn displayed it in every kind of decoration. The following are the better-known types of work: (1) Plaques of polychrome terracotta (the so-called *Lastre Campane*), series of which were used as friezes to decorate halls. Sometimes they depicted simple floral subjects, either realistic or stylized; sometimes they portrayed Bacchic scenes and dancing Corybants, or Satyrs, Maenads, Victories, or winged Genii; sometimes again they showed imaginary landscapes, mostly recalling the Nile. (2) Vases of precious metal, mostly silver, which were to be found in great quantity both in Italy (at Pompeii and particularly at Boscoreale) and outside the peninsula. These were decorated with floral scrolls either stylized in 'arabesque', or realistic; they depicted figures of animals, mythical scenes and allegorical figures. (3) The 'Arretine' pottery made of *terra sigillata* and produced from engraved moulds. These pots have a shiny glaze and slender shapes; the reliefs on them are Muses, Genii, nymphs, love scenes, and sometimes even Roman soldiers. (Pl. 53, a.) They were made by many factories (of Tigranes, of Bardates, of Cerdo). (4) Stuccoes to cover walls and vaults, designed to hide the rough surface of *caementicium* or *latericium*. (Pl. 53, b.) The recurrent types of ornament and figurines which these stuccoes contain were produced by casting; but the central scenes were laid on by individual plasterers with quick but often masterly strokes. Delicate examples of stuccoes of the Augustan era are those of the Villa Farnesina; these decorate three rooms. (5) The reliefs on altars, on the circular stones for wells, on fountains, on monumental vases, and on sarcophagi.

Native taste prevailed in the old Italic and Western centres still more than at Rome. Even at Rome, however, indigenous taste did not forget the Etrusco-Latin tradition, and was markedly felt in two departments of sculpture, namely portraiture and historical reliefs.

There was a first period in which portraiture shows traces either of an excessive native realism (as for example in the funerary relief portraying the family of L. Vibius) or of an excessive idealization attributable to Greek influence (as with the bust of Octavian in the Vatican Museum). But a rational balance between the two tendencies was soon achieved, as can be seen in three statues of Augustus, two showing the *princeps* in armour (Prima Porta and Cherchell), the third (in the Vatican) depicting him as *pontifex* in his toga. (Pl. 52, b.) The heads of these statues portray faithfully the lean but noble features of the emperor, and the proportions of the body are natural. Realism must have been even greater when the original colours survived. Despite this realism, in the statues where he is armed he becomes a hero, whereas when he is *pontifex* we can clearly perceive his spiritual nobility. The reliefs on the breast-plate of the statue at Prima Porta appear to be completely Roman: they glorify the victories of Rome and its emperor over conquered peoples, and portray the scene in which its Parthian enemies hand back the standards they had captured from Crassus. The same magnificent balance of tendencies is to be found in the surviving portraits of Livia, Octavia, Tiberius, Marcellus, Drusus, Antonius, Brutus, and many others. The same characteristics can be seen in coins, on which a few brief lines succeed in giving a wonderful outline of the characters.

Of historical reliefs the earliest example which draws our attention is a monument to Cn. Domitius Ahenobarbus made not much later than 42 BC. It supported a statuary group made by Scopas, which had been brought to Rome; but all that survives is the base, with reliefs depicting a procession of creatures of the sea, and a sacrifice offered by Domitius for the *lustratio* of the army. The *Ara Pacis* (consecrated by the senate in the Campus Martius in 9 BC) has several reliefs, four of which are of great interest as they depict mythical and allegorical subjects (Aeneas, Romulus and Remus, the Dea Roma, and Tellus). (Pl. 54, a.) Its frieze represents the ceremony of a libation to the gods to obtain peace in the world; this portrays the emperor and his family, the priests, magistrates, and senators, and the people with their women and children. The execution is so realistic that every person can be easily distinguished. The same is true of the reliefs on the Basilica Aemilia, of the scenes of the battle of Actium (now in Budapest and in the Vatican), of the reliefs now in San Vitale at Ravenna, and of the decorations on the earliest triumphal arches such as the Arch of Susa.

The same quality is to be found on certain exquisite products of toreutic art, for instance on two silver cups of Boscoreale. One of these depicts homage offered to Augustus by defeated provinces and peoples; the other shows the return of Tiberius from Pannonia, perhaps in AD 11. Glyptic art was also similar, particularly in the making of large and precious cameos. Fine examples include the cameo attributed to Dioscurides which again portrays Tiberius in front of Augustus, probably on his return from Pannonia (Pl. 54, b); or the cameo (now in Boston) representing Augustus as Neptunus after the battle of Actium.

There are some features common to all these reliefs. The mythical element of Greek type has declined, and is often represented only by a single god or hero; in contrast there is great emphasis on the indigenous element, particularly in symbolic personifications such as those of Rome, Italy, or the provinces. Roman manners are reproduced in the dresses; people of all ages, including children, are portrayed; background spaces are filled with crowds, landscapes, or architectural views; and finally there is clear rendering of individual feeling.

Painting and Mosaic. From at least the beginning of the second century BC Italians liked to decorate the interior of their houses with paintings. We have some examples of those in Rome, but many more from Herculaneum and Pompeii. The wealth of specimens makes it possible to perceive the existence of four pictorial styles current between the second century BC and AD 79, the year of the destruction of Pompeii. These can be identified fairly easily, and two of them come within the chronological limits of this chapter.

The first was the 'incrustation' style, which was used between about the years 150 and 50 BC. The walls were decorated with stucco frames containing rectangular painted panels, which at first imitated marble linings and later were painted in colours freely arranged.

The second style depended upon the use of perspective, and dated from about 50 BC to about AD 14. Examples are the *Villa of Fannius* at Boscoreale, the *House of Augustus* on the Palatine, and the *Villa of Livia* ('ad gallinas albas') near Prima Porta. This style was characterized by smooth walls without stucco, painted in brilliant colours, with false skirtings, false columns and slender pillars, and sometimes with porticoes and cornices. All this was painted in perspective and contained landscapes and mythical scenes. (Pl. 56, a.) In the *Villa of Livia* the paintings on the walls of a room convey the idea of being in a garden. The paintings within the frames on the walls, therefore, appear as real pictures which sometimes clearly derive from Greek models: this we noticed earlier in connection with the paintings representing Medea, Achilles amongst the daughters of Lycomedes, and the *Aldobrandini marriage*. (Pl. 55.) Italic technique and taste, however, can also be found in the carelessness of the design of the colouring and in some typical tendencies such as the theatricality of the poses. (Pl. 56, b.) Sometimes these paintings have an Italic subject, Aeneas and Dido, for example, or Aeneas wounded. Sometimes the subject reflects typical local beliefs (as in the wonderful pictures on epic and clearly Orphic subjects in the *triclinium* of the *Villa of Mysteries*).

In painting, too, the Romans were fond of portraiture. This is shown in the anecdote of a certain Arellius who lived in the last years of the republic, and who created a great scandal by portraying the goddesses with the features of his mistresses.

In those days, mosaic was the rival of painting, because of the delicacy achieved by using minute cubes of uniform size and many colours (*tessellae*). Sometimes they reproduced famous pictures of the Hellenistic age, such as *Alexander's battle* in the *House of the Faun* at Pompeii; at other times the subjects were genre or still life, both also to be found in the same Pompeian house. Sometimes they were undoubtedly the work of Greek artists, for example the scene depicting acrobats and signed by Dioscurides of Samos which was found in the *House of Cicero*. In those days wealthy Italians generally liked mosaics which depicted mythical subjects, genre-subjects, scenes of fishing, and borders of floral scrolls—with a certain amount of stylization. (Pl. 43, b.) They used to line columns and niches with minute pieces of either gold or deep-blue colour; and this type of decoration later developed into the admirable art of wall mosaic.

3. MUSIC

Music held an important place in Chinese society, especially after the final victory of Confucianism. The school of Confucius built up a system correlating the musical sounds with the order of the Universe; music was conceived as a transcendent or even magical power, of primary importance for the harmony and proper government of the state. As such, it was a primary concern of the ruler, and under Han Wu-ti (141–87 BC) an Imperial Bureau of Music (*yüeh-fu*) was set up. All this concerned the ritual music, of unitary character throughout the empire, and as such quite different from the tunes and happy songs of the common people with their unending local varieties.

Sonorous stones (*ch'ing*) and globular flutes (*hsün*) were known already in Shang times. The advent of the Chou had brought a great increase in the number and use of musical instruments. Among them, the seven-stringed zither (*ch'in*) soon stood out and became the classical instrument of the cultured classes. Another zither was the *cheng*, with thirteen brass strings.

The original scale was pentatonic (*do, re, mi, soh, la*). But already the first text on musical theory, found in the *Lü-shih Ch'un-ch'iu* of 239 BC, recognized two scales, male and female of six notes each. The *Huai-nan-tzu* (end of second century BC) seems to know a scale of seven notes. In 40 BC Ching Fang increased the 'male' to sixty notes, with which it ceased to be a scale and became a tablature.

As to actual remnants of notated music, no specimen earlier than the T'ang dynasty (618–907) has come down to us. We have only literary descriptions of orchestras and names of songs.

Indian music never had a unitary character like the Chinese ritual music, but embraced a wide field of different phenomena. The classical theory, along with that of acting and dancing, was settled in the *Nāṭyaśāstra* of Bhārata, attributed to the first century BC. It is divided into thirty-six chapters, of which chapters 28–33 deal with music proper. It seems to be a compilation of fragments of different origins. But the fully developed classic theory of music is found only in the much later *Sangītiratnakara* (thirteenth century AD) and cannot be dealt with here.

A position by itself is occupied by Bharata's *Gītalamkara*, probably of the first or even second century BC, which gives a different classification of the musical elements (male, female, and derivated modes). It remains outside the main current of classical theory, but it represents a popular tradition which dominated the field in the times of the Moghul empire (sixteenth–eighteenth centuries) and survives to this day.

The instruments were percussion (*ghana*), drums (*avanaddha*), wind instruments (*susira*) and above all stringed instruments (*tata*). Of the latter, the most venerated was the *vīna*, to which mythical origins were attributed. It was originally a fretted plucked instrument, with one gourd attached to each extremity, and with seven strings, of which four served for the melody.

Philo and Heron tell us of a noteworthy advance in the musical instruments of the Greek world, in that the mathematician Ctesibius (third century BC) produced, among his other inventions, a keyboard organ worked by hydraulic power.

Ordinary accompaniment to the recital of poetry, that is to say to epic or the like, gradually fell into disuse and was regarded as superfluous. But music as an accompaniment to choral song gradually gained in quality and variety. We are speaking now of the time of Pindar, the score for whose *First Pythian* is actually known. His victory songs, and those of Bacchylides, were sung, to the accompaniment of the flute or the lyre or of both, by a choir consisting of the companions of the victorious hero as he returned home. A choir-master conducted the performance, which was of great religious solemnity; and the construction of the verses, with their strophes and antistrophes, was highly diversified.

In later times Greek lyric tended to be confined to dithyramb and *nomos*, some portions being choral, others solos which were either sung or recited. The music tended to gain ground markedly at the expense of the poetry and ideas; a good example is the *nomos* called *The Persians*, by Timotheus of Miletus (450–360 BC). in which the *citharoedus* plays a predominant part.

But meanwhile drama (from Phrynichus onwards) established a new and fruitful opportunity for union between music and poetry. The solo parts, themselves accompanied by the zither, were interposed by choruses, intoned by anything from twelve to fifteen singers with a flautist in the background. At the outset the choral passages predominated, but from Sophocles' time the recitative lines were more numerous than the lyric; and in Euripides the lyric sections became just intermezzi, in which the words were nothing more than the occasion for the accompanying music. We see this from a fragment of Euripides' *Orestes* which has survived with musical scoring.

Certain 'Delphic hymns' of the second century have also come down to us with scores. These show that an archaizing tendency was combined with innovations, in that the maximum interval in the melody was extended from an octave to an eleventh and that modulation became more frequent.

Allusions to the theory of music, and some outline of musical history, are to be found among Plato's references to aesthetics, especially in the *Republic*; also in the enquiries into tone made by Eudoxus of Cnidus (390–337), and in some passages of Aristotle (the 'Aristotelian' *Problemata*, a spurious work, will be mentioned in Part III). Then there are the fundamental theories of Aristoxenus of Tarentum, known as the 'Musician' (*floruit* 320–300), who used Pythagorean teaching to good effect, and was followed in this by Euclides about 300. Finally there are the *Pneumatica* of Heron of Alexandria and the *De Musica* of Philodemus of Gadara.

In the Roman world Greek influence may be seen at work twice over. It first reached Rome through the Etruscans; and here we may note that the shapes of Roman musical instruments are Greek, but the words *subulus* and *lituus* are Etruscan. Then later there was direct contact between Rome and the Greeks and the gradual Roman conquest of Greek lands. So the techniques of Greek music passed wholesale to Rome, where musicians were generally Greek slaves or freedmen.

NOTES TO CHAPTER XII

1. Many attempts have been made to reconstruct the principal episodes in this poem with the help of the *Tabula Iliaca*, dating from Nero's period and now in the Capitol Museum in Rome; but the results are very inconclusive. (Pierre Grimal.)

2. In point of fact, Stesichorus was merely following a much more ancient tradition. There was an *Iliou Persis* by Arctinus of Miletus and *Nostoi* (in five cantos) by Hagias of Troezen. There were also *Nostoi* by Eumelus of Corinth, who lived in the eighth century. Useful information on all these problems is given in Jean Bérard's *La colonisation grecque de l'Italie méridionale et de la Sicile dans l'Antiquité* (second edition, Paris 1957), pp. 323 ff. (Pierre Grimal.)

3. Professor Pareti is much less appreciative of this poet than most recent scholars have been, and especially (as Professor Lesky protests) of his lively style and delicate irony. Erudite *par excellence*, Callimachus was none the less a writer of marked versatility and originality; and though much criticized by his contemporaries, he had important influence on several Roman poets, notably Catullus, Propertius, and Ovid.

4. There is a chronological objection to the theory advanced here by Professor Pareti. Livius Andronicus, who was still alive in 204, must have been a mere child when Tarentum was captured in 272. It is difficult to see where he could have obtained a thorough knowledge of Greek culture except at Rome, which suggests that Hellenism was already flourishing in that city before his arrival. His choice of the Odyssey as his theme may well have been due to political considerations, for at that time (about 220) Rome was taking an active interest in the Adriatic. (See my book *Siècle des Scipions*, Paris 1953.) Andronicus' *Odissia* has come down to us only in some scraps which it would be rash to take as the basis of an aesthetic judgement. The fact that this 'translation' was written in a national verse-form (known as 'Saturnian' because Saturn was the outstanding Italic god) implies the existence of an oral epic tradition, if not a written one, in which that metre was familiar. Andronicus was also Rome's earliest tragic poet (see below, p. 579) and must be considered under both these aspects if we are to appreciate his importance in Roman literary history. (Pierre Grimal.)

5. The epic writings of Naevius have been studied and annotated, on the strength of the few surviving fragments, by Marino Barchiesi in his *Nevio Epico*, Padua, 1962 (with the previous bibliography). (Pierre Grimal.)

6. Yet, as Professor A. Lesky points out, Virgil also showed consummate artistry by means of 'enjambement' (the carrying on of sense and sentences over the ends of lines).

7. This opinion which originated with K. J. Beloch, is now almost unanimously rejected. His *floruit* is placed between 548 and 540, and his birthplace at Megara in Greece, not in Sicily (despite Plato, *Laws*, 630a, who is taken up, for saying that Theognis was a Sicilian, by Didymus, *ap. schol. ad loc.*). Theognis was born at Megara in Greece, but may later have become a citizen of the Sicilian town of that name. As to the present state of opinion about Theognis, see R. Burn, *The Lyric Age of Greece* (London, 1960), pp. 247–58. (Pierre Grimal.)

8. For dithyramb see Part I, p. 278.

9. For *nomos* see Part I, p. 277.

10. With this section, and especially with what is said about Philetas, should be read the paragraphs on contemporary Alexandrian epic and *epyllion* (pp. 570 ff. above).

11. These pieces—the epigrams which make up the *Catalepton* (i.e., 'Light Pieces') and the parody-epic of the Gnat (*Culex*)—are included in the manuscripts among the works attributed to Virgil. But it is not certain whether he actually wrote them all—the *Culex* for instance, may be an imitation, written later. Some of the epigrams in the *Catalepton* are almost certainly by Virgil; they allude to incidents in his life which are confirmed by what may be regarded as independent sources. But this whole problem is still obscure. In any case, if Virgil did write some of the epigrams in the *Catalepton*, it must have been in his youth (before 44). (Pierre Grimal.)

12. This name, like those of Delia and Lesbia, was chosen with an intention we can easily divine. Lesbia was intended to recall the memory of Sappho (see above, p. 277); Delia and Cynthia belong to the sphere of Apollo, for they are two of the names of the goddess Artemis (born, as we know, on the island of Delos, at the foot of the Cynthe). Tradition has it that Delia's real name was Plania—and 'Delia' might be regarded as a Greek translation of that name (the Greek word *delos* means clear, evident, as does *planus* in Latin). So Tibullus was amusing himself with a play upon words. Cynthia's real name was Hostia, and in this case there is no connection between the two. It is therefore justifiable to assume that Tibullus was the first to choose the name Delia, and that Propertius, imitating him in spirit of courteous rivalry, decided to link his own mistress in name with the youngest and most beautiful of the goddesses. (Pierre Grimal.)

13. Ovid belongs to the second generation of poets of the Augustan Age. He has learnt from the experience of his immediate predecessors and we see a Roman tradition developing in his work, building up an output that includes all the principal aspects of poetry in that era. The epos is represented by the *Metamorphoses*, a tremendous cosmogony inspired by Pythagoras, the love-elegy by the *Amores* and the *Heroides*, Callimachus' elegiac style by the *Fasti*. Ovid also wrote a tragedy, *Medea*, which was famous in its day, but has now vanished.

Ovid is a prolific and skilful poet, adept at handling the verse-forms (hexameter and elegiac distich) already perfected by his forerunners; but many modern critics have censured him for this virtuosity, which enables him to produce a flow of banalities with no depth of feeling. His influence on mediaeval Europe was considerable. (Pierre Grimal.)

14. These three, the *Agamemnon*, the *Choephoroi*, and the *Eumenides* form the *Oresteia* (which the English poet Swinburne called 'the greatest achievement of the human spirit').

15. This doctrine was firmly rejected by Aeschylus (*Agamemnon*, pp. 757 ff.) in favour of the view that it was sin which brought suffering, and so further sin. See E. Fraenkel's *Commentary* (Oxford, 1950) on the passage, against the suggestion that there is any inconsistency with what Aeschylus says elsewhere.

16. This development had already started in the Hellenistic world. There, for instance, the actors had begun to be separated from the *orchestra*, where the chorus went through its part, and the chorus was contributing less and less to the action. There was in fact no break in continuity between the Hellenistic and the Roman theatre. When the audience was allowed to occupy what had formerly been the *orchestra*, it was because the latter was no longer needed; the *pulpitum* (the *proscenion* of the Greek theatre) had expanded, and now allowed for a greater number of performers, among whom were the *choreutes*—singers and musicians. (Pierre Grimal.)

17. The chorus was now limited to the singing of lyrics, almost wholly unconnected with the play.

18. Until recently we knew nothing of the work of Menander except a few fragments and the imitations made by Plautus and Terence. Now, however, it is being restored to us in part, thanks to certain papyri. The most celebrated and complete of these is the Papyrus Bodmer, containing an entire play, the *Dyscolus* (the *Man of Moods*), which was found in 1957 and has since been printed in many editions. This is a comedy, centred on Cnemon, an irascible old man, who has gone to live in the depths of the country, because his wife has left him owing to his bad temper. Cnemon has a daughter, and a young townsman falls in love with her—at the instigation of Pan, who wishes to reward the girl for her piety to the nymphs. Sostrates, the young man, is eager to marry the girl, but her surly father will let no one come near her. As a pretext for coming to the lonely spot where Cnemon lives, Sostrates disguises himself as a peasant and tills the soil. After various ups and downs, in the course of which the misanthropist falls into a well, undergoes a spectacular change of heart and is reconciled to his family, Sostrates is allowed to marry his love, and the whole thing concludes with a banquet, amid noisy festivities. (Pierre Grimal.)

19. Among them the *Menaechmi*, source for Shakespeare's *Comedy of Errors*, and the *Aulularia*, source for Molière's *L'Avare*.

20. For a more conservative view of Plautus' originality over plots and backgrounds, though not, of course, over outlook and style, see E. Fraenkel, *Plautinisches in Plautus* (Berlin, 1922).

21. Although Plautus and Terence both drew upon the same sources—the Greek poets of the New Comedy—there is a great difference between their works. The plots are similar, based on the same situations (the love of a young man for a young girl or a courtesan, the wiles of a slave who manages to get money from the youth's father, with which to buy the girl's favours or win her hand, etc.) and the same stock characters are introduced (the old father, the bright young spark, the astute slave, the grasping courtesan, etc.); but the spirit in which they are used is completely different. Between the generations of the two authors the spirit of Rome had altered, and with it the demands made upon comedy. Plautus is faithful to the old Roman moral standards; he regards love as a dangerous passion, not to be indulged in by a man who intends to remain a good citizen, to hold on to his property, etc., whereas Terence does not entirely blame young people for giving way to their feelings. Terence is the champion of human values—affection, freedom, indulgence, charity almost—as against the harsh, austere moral code of earlier times. Obsessed with the problem of children's upbringing (with which he deals in one of his comedies, *Adelphi*), he maintains that a father should not be too stern, but should make allowance for the feelings natural to youth, and be indulgent to them. This was a problem that Roman educationalists were continually discussing about 160 BC, when the influence of the Greek philosophers was rapidly increasing. The common talk was that Terence was merely the spokesman of the 'philhellene' group, led by his friends Scipio Aemilianus and Laelius, who were accused of helping him to write his plays. Generally speaking Terence's comedies were less popular than those of Plautus—the latter, though far less subtle, being more 'amusing' and closer to the common taste. (Pierre Grimal.)

22. Virgil composed his *Bucolics* approximately between 44 and 39 BC, when still under the influence of his Alexandrine models. He seems to have chosen this form because the others were already in use (the elegy by Cornelius Gallus, etc.), and in his desire to be original, he had to make the best of a style not yet adopted by any other Roman poet. But though Theocritus was his model, he at once began to make innovations. Having grown up in northern Italy amid the peaceful countryside of Cisalpine Gaul, he could not describe nature in the same terms as Theocritus, the Sicilian. So a first touch of originality comes with his choice of scene. Moreover the life he describes, the characters depicted in his little sketches, are those of the Roman countryside, not the Sicilian goatherds and shepherds. They have their own interests and adventures—those of the period, perhaps even, in some instances, those of the poet himself; for it is suggested that under the name of Meliboeus, Virgil was relating the tragedy he had experienced himself, when the Italian peasants were driven from their land in the year 42, to make way for the veterans of the triumvirs. It very soon becomes evident that these little poems are only Greek in the most superficial sense, that they are entirely Roman in content. Virgil is not a writer who can long remain absent from the contemporary scene, and his verses hold many echoes of current events. For example—though this interpretation is sometimes challenged—the *Fifth Eclogue*, which tells of the death and apotheosis of a mysterious Daphnis, is probably an allegorical account of the death and apotheosis of Caesar. And there is no doubt that the *Fourth Eclogue*, dedicated to Pollio, consul for the year 40, is a celebration of the treaty concluded at Brindisi between Octavian and Antony, and expresses the deep satisfaction of all Romans at the idea that peace was at last to be restored. This aspect of Virgil's bucolic poetry, which is quite alien to that style of writing in its original form, led him into increasingly close collaboration with Maecenas and the circle around Octavian. (Pierre Grimal.)

23. This long-standing interpretation must now be given up. For it has been pointed out that when Virgil embarked on his poem—certainly not later than the year 37, and more probably in 38—Octavian could not possibly have had an agricultural policy. Moreover, it is hard to look on the *Georgics* as a practical handbook of agriculture. Nor does Octavian seem to have adopted the agricultural policy thus attributed to him, even at a later date. In the reign of Augustus, the system of land tenure remained as it had been during the

republic, with *latifundia* worked chiefly by slave labour, etc. It was in response to his own feelings on the subject that Virgil began the *Georgics*. Just as he had formerly 'annexed' bucolic poetry, he now proceeded to take over Hesiod's form, that of *Works and Days*, which no one in Rome had imitated until then. At the beginning of Book III he boasts of this, comparing himself to a victorious general, laden with the spoils of a conquered country. In writing his *Bucolics*, he had been led to take an interest in the rustic 'plebs', and had even identified himself with them, in the two characters of the first *Bucolic*, Tityrus and Meliboeus. From this standpoint, the *Georgics* form a sequel to the previous work. Moreover, in its didactical aspect this poem is a successor to Lucretius, and contains many imitations of *De Rerum Natura*. Virgil helped to draw up the imperial ideology and to revive the old rustic traditions of Roman life; but he did it not to order, but merely in response to his own deep-seated urge. (Pierre Grimal.)

24. The *Fasti* are among the most valuable source-material for our knowledge of Roman religion; in this work, Ovid has recorded many details which would otherwise have been forgotten. He was, of course, a man of his own day, and reveals a certain scepticism with regard to the ancient beliefs. Besides, his attitude is that of the poet and artist, eager for picturesque features and fond of descriptions based on Alexandrine models. This may have led to accusations of irreverence, or at least have suggested that he was out of sympathy with the old Roman religion. But in point of fact that religion was no longer accepted in his day; it had already come to be regarded as a venerable but outworn survival from times gone by. Ovid is deeply religious, all the same, but after a more modern fashion. In Book I of the *Fasti*, for example, he gives the reasons why a particular victim was chosen for sacrifice to a particular divinity; but he lets it be clearly understood that his own conscience is revolted by these bloodthirsty ceremonies. Here his Pythagorean beliefs (see above p. 659, note 13) rise to the surface; holding them, he cannot approve of 'murder', not even the slaughter of animals. His own religious feeling has a spirituality which was absent from the ancient national rites. Hence his lack of sympathy for them—something not peculiar to him, but common to all progressive thinkers of his generation. (Pierre Grimal.)

25. No poem in Horace's 'satirical' compositions is actually entitled a 'satire'. The *Epodes* are called *Iambics* and, as already mentioned (see above, p. 573) were imitated from Archilochus. These are the only works by Horace which could be described as satires in the modern sense of the word—that is, as poems attacking a particular person and ridiculing his defects or his manners. These 'iambics', written by Horace from the beginning of his career as a poet (probably originating in 39 BC, with *Epode* XVI) and continuing until about the year 30, are essentially lyrical pieces. In the manuscript tradition, what are usually known as the *Satires* go by the title of *Sermones* (Conversations), which is reminiscent of the *Diatribai* (Discourses) published by the Greek philosophers. The two books of *Sermones* are, in fact, collections of moral discourses, true 'sermons' in which the poet exhorts men to wisdom and urges them to shake off their most serious vices, such as avarice, love of money, the taste for debauchery, etc. He is not mocking his contemporaries, but trying to teach them. The characters he brings in are either dead or fictitious and are only mentioned as illustrations of moral attitudes, for the purpose of edification.

Horace's other works include two books of *Epistles* which follow the same lines as the *Sermones* but differ from them in being addressed to an individual instead of to the general public. These *Epistles* also deal with moral problems (particularly those of Book I) or literary questions (those of Book II). 'Satire' in the modern sense did not yet exist—it was to be originated by Juvenal. (Pierre Grimal.)

26. Herodotus' claim to be the father of history perhaps rests most on his honest (if ingenuous) search for truth and his determined investigations into the causes of men's actions.

27. The Athenian statesman Cimon (see above, p. 334) had a Thracian grandfather of this name.

28. But Thucydides was keenly conscious of the conflict between oligarchy and democracy: besides his account in Book VIII of the Athenian oligarchic revolution of 411 BC, see his classic analysis of the civil war at Corcyra (III, 82 ff.), which he claimed was typical of conditions in Greek cities during the Peloponnesian War. He himself, though an

ardent admirer of the democrat Pericles and of many of the ideals of Athenian democracy (see the 'Funeral Speech' in Book II), expresses approval of the moderate oligarchy established after the fall of the Four Hundred in 411 (VIII, 97), and was violently hostile to Cleon and other 'demagogues'.

29. Despite this final judgement, Professor Pareti's account of Thucydides must strike many as unsympathetic. Thucydides' chief hope (I, 22) was that his work would be useful for the understanding of future events similar to those in the war he describes, and countless readers have found that he achieved his end. His great virtues are candour, determination, and insight into political life; his methods of research were like those of the medical scientists of his day (and this not only in his careful account of the Athenian plague, II, 48 ff.); and although he was frank about his likes and dislikes (what he most admired was the energy and far-sightedness of a Themistocles, a Pericles, or at times an Alcibiades), he is tireless in his impartial debates on the great problems of politics.

30. For instance in his uncritical admiration for Sparta and its constitution.

31. Until we come to Polybius, none of the works mentioned in this or the following section has survived except for small fragments.

32. Unlike the other Achaean hostages, Polybius obtained permission to settle in Rome, where he lived in the household of Aemilius Paulus who had defeated Perseus. He was the guide and counsellor of the youthful Scipio Aemilianus, and has left us a lively picture of philhellene circles in Rome about the year 160 BC. (Pierre Grimal.)

33. Polybius was the first writer of a 'Universal History', i.e. one of all the Mediterranean lands. His work covered the period 220–145 BC and was in forty books, of which the first five (to 216 BC) survive entire, the rest in fragments.

34. Polybius, as Dr N. I. Golubtsova points out, was a well-to-do Greek. He admired those Roman politicians who were thought to be philhellene, and was intensely interested in those features of Rome's constitution and military organization which had brought it dominion over the whole Mediterranean within a few decades. But he fiercely attacked such earlier historians as he considered to be uncritically biased in Rome's favour, and late in his life he was suspicious of certain democratic forces at Rome.

35. For criticism of this view see O. Seel, *Die Praefatio des Trogus Pompeius* (Erlangen, 1955).

36. The first and last of these factors seem to have been the deciding ones, for the phil-hellenism of a section of Roman society did not take definite shape until two generations later, at the time of Rome's Eastern conquests. The two reasons reinforce each other: during the Second Punic War, when Hannibal, having concluded an alliance with Philip of Macedon, was trying to stir up Greek opinion against Rome and turn the armies of the Eastern kingdoms against his own enemies, it was very important for the Romans to make a counter-attack. That was no doubt why the senate decided to send an embassy to Delphi, a lively diplomatic centre where the sacred deputations met together and anything said would be carried far and wide. It was hoped that a history of Rome written in Greek would convince the Greek peoples that the Romans were sincere, calling attention to their *fides* and their liberal policy, which had so often supported the Greek cause during the struggle between the Samnites and the Greek colonies in southern Italy. This history, written by Fabius Pictor, was primarily a diplomatic instrument. It would have been pointless to write it in Latin, where the prose style was still immature—and the Romans, long accustomed to use the Greek language, were perfectly aware of its superiority. The earliest Roman historians were thus trained in the Greek school, and it was the example of Greek prose that first impelled them to devise a more artistic vehicle of expression. (Pierre Grimal.)

37. Cato also deserves to be called 'the father of Latin prose' because of another book, likewise of great importance—his treatise *On Agriculture*, which has come down to us and draws a very interesting picture of the Roman rural economy at the beginning of the second century BC. Cato wrote it in imitation of the treatise written in Punic by Mago, of Carthage, because he wanted to give the Romans the benefit of foreign experience. He hoped thus to consolidate the rural, agricultural aspect of Roman society and economic life; for this he regarded as urgent in view of the increase in personal riches and the

expansion of trade resulting from Rome's defeat of Carthage, which brought it into direct contact with the great trading network of the Hellenistic world. Cato was seeking to prove that agriculture could be a source of wealth, that the good *pater familias* who wished to maintain a proper train of life had no need to launch into trade with far-off places (senators were prohibited by law from doing so). *De Agricultura* is written in a language already well established, but with no literary flourishes; in addition to observations concerning crops, and the prayers which should be offered to the gods in order to ensure good harvests, it contains culinary recipes and even old wives' remedies. In the reign of Augustus, Varro was to write three books of *Res Rusticae*, with the same intention as Cato; and a comparison of the two works shows that in the intervening century and a half, Roman agriculture had made considerable progress. (Pierre Grimal.)

38. This was a writer who saw things from the Carthaginian angle.

39. Although the authenticity of these works of Antiphon has been much disputed.

40. Andocides was exiled as a member of, and informer about, the aristocratic gang around Alcibiades who were supposed to have mutilated the Hermae in 415 BC.

41. These political tracts are the most important of Isocrates' surviving works. Already in 380 he wrote the *Panegyricus*, urging Athens and Sparta to compose their quarrels and jointly lead a crusade against Persia; in 368 he appealed similarly to Dionysius I (Letter I), and in 356 to the king of Sparta; finally in 346, with the *Philippus*, he turned to Philip of Macedon, to whom he wrote a congratulatory letter on the victory of Chaeronea, in the last year of his life. Significant in a different way are the *Areopagiticus* (c. 355), glorifying the times of Solon and Cleisthenes in contrast with the Athenian democracy of his own days, and the *Panathenaicus* (c. 340), also a survey of Athens' past greatness. But though Isocrates has received praise for a panhellenism which looked beyond the horizons of the single city-state, it is perhaps not surprising that his somewhat academic rhetoric failed to inspire his contemporaries: for pungent criticism see W. Jaeger, *Demosthenes* (Cambridge, 1938), pp. 17–18. His ideas, as well as his style, owed much to the sophist Gorgias (above, p. 554, note 9): his systematic rhetorical instruction was pregnant with influence on the future.

42. See above, pp. 600 ff.

43. Many characteristic fragments of Cato's speeches have been preserved.

44. The problem of the teaching of rhetoric in Rome, and of the attempts made by conservative Romans to prevent professors of eloquence from setting up as teachers, is a somewhat complex one. Put briefly, the situation was that while no one dreamt of forbidding the Greek rhetoricians to teach young Romans the Greek style of eloquence, many senators thought it dangerous to apply this teaching to the Latin language. Hence, though schools of Greek rhetoric could be opened in Rome, Latin rhetoricians were expelled from the city. The objections raised by the conservatives were the same that had induced Plato to pronounce against rhetoric, on the grounds that it might make the worse appear the better cause, and that those who could make use of it gained dangerous power over men's minds. Cicero, at the beginning of the first century BC, had to fight against prejudice, and that was no doubt one of his reasons for declaring that orators must go through a moral and intellectual training before beginning to practise rhetoric. (Pierre Grimal.)

45. This opinion of Cicero, though backed by tradition, has no foundation in fact. To contrast Cicero's political behaviour with that of Caesar and Pompey is really to compare two completely different things. Caesar, Pompey, and Crassus were trying to deflect the Roman political machinery for their own benefit, whereas Cicero wished to improve the system, for the benefit of a whole social class, that of the knights, an order which was not confined to Rome itself, but spread all over Italy. The former were ambitious men, straining every nerve to consolidate their personal authority, the latter a genuine reformer trying to apply new principles—those for which he pleaded towards the end of his life in his treatise *De Re Publica* (of which fairly ample portions have survived).

Cicero tried to combine action with reflection. Before his time, ideological speculation had been left to the Greek thinkers, more especially to the philosophers, while the Romans concentrated their ambition on military and political activities. Cicero pursued the habitual career in the magistracy (*cursus honorum*) and used his natural eloquence to win him a very prominent position in the state; but at the same time he made no secret of his intention to take that position as a starting-point for practising the theories he had formulated during his philosophical studies.

Cicero had been interested in philosophy ever since he visited Athens as a young man, and declared repeatedly that he would have devoted himself exclusively to the subject had he not been prevented by a life of action. Whenever he had leisure to do so—for instance, when Caesar's *coup d'état* and the defeat of the Republicans reduced him to enforced idleness—he wrote a philosophical treatise. Cicero refused to join any one school. This independence of mind had been inculcated in him by his masters when he was studying at the New Academy at Athens. Most important of all, he realized sooner than anyone else that the discussions of the Greek philosophers, who led a life of study, could not meet the needs of the Romans, who had the practical task of governing the world they had conquered. He did not feel himself called upon to acquaint the Romans with Greek philosophy (they all read Greek and spoke it fluently), so much as to compare Greek ideas, patiently, point by point, with Roman practice. This is what he proceeded to do, not only in treatises such as *De Natura Deorum* and *De Divinatione* but also in his *Tusculans* and *De Finibus*, dialogues in which Roman patricians frankly discuss the traditional views propounded by the different schools. These discussions tend towards a compromise between the Greek and Roman worlds, and instead of speaking of Cicero's 'eclecticism' it would be more accurate to describe this as the birth of a new philosophy, thanks to a revision of the accepted views.

As a writer on the theory of eloquence, and as an orator, Cicero was equally scrupulous in the defence of philosophy, holding virtuosity in speech to be of less importance than the search for truth and the proclamation of it, in all its forms. As a disciple of the Academicians he knew that the concept of truth is multiple, that there is a form of truth in action which can often be equated with probability; and this seems to be the doctrine he strove to put into practice. (See A. Michel, *Rhétorique et Philosophie chez Cicéron*, Paris, 1960.) (Pierre Grimal.)

46. Despite Quintilian's authority the authenticity of this *Invective* is much disputed.

47. The dependence of Maurya art on Achaemenid art appears here to be exaggerated: Persian influence, strong as it was, did not exclude all originality in the little that is known to us and, shortly after the Maurya period, Buddhist Sūṅga art developed a vigorous originality.

48. Professor Ch. Th. Saricakis calls attention to the influence exercised by Greek art on India, citing the fundamental work of W. W. Tarn, *The Greeks in Bactria and in India* (Cambridge, 1938), pp. 393 ff.

49. Allegedly a man who aspired to a place in history, even at the cost of doing an infamous act.

50. The normal construction of a Greek theatre allowed for a more than semicircular auditorium (Fig. 6), with a circular space (*orchestra*) inside this for the chorus, side passages (*parodoi*) at each end of the auditorium, and on the other side of these the line of the stage (*scenē*, originally of wood). See D. S. Robertson, *Greek and Roman Architecture* (second edition, 1943), p. 164.

51. But see above, p. 508, note 13. The writers there cited would date the earliest Roman *aes* to the early third rather than to the fourth century.

52. Professor Pareti's views on the Celtic invasion are more fully set out in Part I, Chapters I and II.

53. The Roman theatre, in contrast to the Greek (see above, note 51), had a semicircular auditorium (*cavea*) (Fig. 7). The stage was a wide raised platform, with a wall behind it as the *cavea*: this wall was normally an elaborate structure with columns, niches, and statues.